JUNG`S RED BOOK FOR OUR TIME

Searching for Soul under Postmodern Conditions

**Murray Stein
and
Thomas Arzt**
Editors

Volume 1

CHIRON PUBLICATIONS • ASHEVILLE, NORTH CAROLINA

www.ChironPublications.com

Interior and cover design by Danijela Mijailovic
Printed primarily in the United States of America.

ISBN 978-1-63051-480-8

Library of Congress Cataloging-in-Publication Data

Names: Stein, Murray, 1943- editor. | Arzt, Thomas, 1955- editor. | Jung, C.G. (Carl Gustav), 1875-1961. Liber novus.
Title: Jung's Red Book for our time : searching for soul under postmodern conditions / Murray Stein & Thomas Arzt, co-editors.
Description: Asheville : Chiron Publications, [2018-] | Includes bibliographical references and index. Contents: Introduction / by Murray Stein -- "The way of what is to come" : searching for soul under postmodern conditions / by Thomas Arzt -- "The way of what is to come" : jung's vision of the aquarian age / by Liz Greene -- Abraxas : Jung's gnostic demiurge in liber novus / by Stephan A. Hoeller -- C.G. Jung and the prophet puzzle / by Lance S. Owens -- In a world that has gone mad, is what we really need : a red book? Plato, Goethe, Schelling, Nietzsche and Jung / by Paul Bishop -- Confronting Jung : the Red Book speaks to our time / by John Hill -- On the impact of Jung and his Red Book : a personal story / by J. Marvin Spiegelman -- Encountering the spirit of the depths and the divine child / by Andreas Schweizer -- Imagination for evil / by Liliana Liviano Wahba -- Movements of soul in the Red Book / by Dariane Pictet -- Encounters with the animal soul : a voice of hope for our precarious world / by Nancy Swift Furlotti -- The Red Book for dionysus : a literary and transdisciplinary interpretation / by Susan Rowland -- Appassionato for the imagination / by Russell A. Lockhart -- "The incandescent matter" : shudder, shimmer, stammer, solitude / by Josephine Evetts-Secker -- "O tempora! o mores!" / by Ann Casement -- Jung's Red Book : a compensatory image for our contemporary culture : a hindu perspective / by Ashok Bedi -- Why is the Red Book "red"? : a Chinese reader's reflections / by Heyong Shen -- The Red Book and the posthuman / by John C. Woodcock -- Bibliography -- About the contributors.
Identifiers: LCCN 2017050411| ISBN 9781630514778 (pbk. : alk. paper) | ISBN 9781630514785 (hardcover : alk. paper)
Subjects: LCSH: Jung, C. G. (Carl Gustav), 1875-1961. | Jungian psychology.
Classification: LCC BF109.J8 J869 2018 | DDC 150.19/54--dc23
LC record available at https://lccn.loc.gov/2017050411

TABLE OF CONTENTS

Introduction

Murray Stein

When Thomas Arzt first spoke to me about putting together a collection of original essays on Jung's *Red Book* for our time, I was not certain that it was a good idea or even possible. Hasn't enough been written about *The Red Book* already? It seemed redundant to add yet more to what has already been said and published. What more is there to say? And weren't Jungian analysts and scholars by now rather tired of discussing *The Red Book* and ready to move on? But as we delved further into the concept, I came to understand what he was driving at. Most of the articles and books written to date about *The Red Book* have focused on considerations on what it meant for Jung himself or what it means for the history of Analytical Psychology as a field. On the one hand, it is a kind of fabulous diary or journal, a record of Jung's inner experiences during a critical time in his life as he broke away from Freud and psychoanalysis and looked for a way to make a new and different kind of future for himself. In many ways, *The Red Book* is a summary of how Jung became a Jungian, as distinct from a Freudian. It is an account of his midlife crisis and his transition into being the independent thinker he would become for the rest of his life. It is a personal story. As well, it can be seen to form the foundation for the theories that were to come in Jung's later psychological writings and seminars. But is there more to it? Is there something in it for us today, something to consider as we face the challenges of living "under the conditions of postmodernity"? Is *The Red Book* for today and not only for yesterday, for history? Is it still a *Liber Novus*?

One of the surprising things that Jung discovered about his very personal inner journey, which began in 1913 with shattering visions of devastation, was that it was not about him alone. This realization came as a shock, but also as a relief. For it meant that while he was going through a tremendous transformation process in his midlife and facing the risk of becoming insane, the whole culture that he was a part of—

Europe—was going through the same sort of profound crisis. This dawned on him when the Great War broke out in 1914. He recalled the visions he had while riding on a train from Schaffhausen to Zurich one day and seeing a map of Europe flooded and overwhelmed with blood and gore. A later similar vision of Europe covered in ice, frozen solid, also came to his mind as he saw what was happening on the continent in the early years of the war that was to change Europe decisively. In fact, the European world was going mad and descending into a vortex of unstoppable brutality and meaningless slaughter of its young, its future. As Jung proceeded with his own inner process, finding a way forward and emancipating himself from the past in order to build a new future, it must have occurred to him that what he was doing might serve the culture as a whole and not only himself. In fact, it was this conviction that led him to put his back to a massive effort to convert his insights into a language that would speak to the public. It was the language of depth psychology, a further extension of what Freud had begun in Vienna a generation earlier.

The question that I asked myself and discussed with Thomas Arzt was this: Can *The Red Book*, now published after more than a hundred years since its inception for all to read, offer a resource for orientation in our troubled and disrupted world today? As we see it, this is a world of enormous challenges, of geostrategic realignments, of severe climate changes and the urgent need for a fundamental energy transition, of threats of global pandemics, of resource scarcity and threats of a financial meltdown. Jung's world was similarly troubled in 1913, but there are also great differences between his inherited cultural and social conditions and ours. His period in Western cultural history is designated as "modern," ours as "postmodern." Are the problems he wrestled with in his day similar enough to ours today to make his solutions still viable and relevant? Thomas Arzt and I decided to ask a global group of Jungian analysts and scholars to reflect on this question. We invited them to consider writing an essay on the topic: "Jung's *Red Book* for Our Time: Searching for Soul under Postmodern Conditions." The response we received from this invitation was overwhelmingly positive and enthusiastic. The results will be published in a multivolume series, the first of which is now in the reader's hands.

Here is the proposal we sent to the authors, to guide their reflections in composing the essays for this collection:

> Many people today share the impression that we live in a historical phase of global volatility combined with deep uncertainty about the future. Most probably, this uneasy feeling will linger on for years to come. The problem is that we do not understand sufficiently the global transformation process we have entered into beginning many years ago, as already registered and reflected by Jung in the early 20th century in his *Red Book*.
>
> Some people have speculated that the publication of *The Red Book* in 2009 was a synchronistic event. The timing was extraordinary. When Jung embarked on his inner journey of soul searching, he found himself in similarly volatile times. Turning inward, he created a work that gave his work and his life a sense of meaning and direction with broad cultural significance. We are convinced that this work offers us guidance in our present turbulent and uncertain times. Today, we could speculate, *The Red Book* has enormous potential for becoming an epochal opus for a world living in the postmodern condition of the 21st century. Thus, its publication at this time was unexpectedly meaningful.
>
> The focus of our book project, *Jung's Red Book for Our Time,* lies not primarily in looking backward into the personal biographical issues that Jung faced in his own life as he composed the work, but rather in considering how *The Red Book* may be of use to the present and future generations of people who are disoriented and in need of psychological guidance for themselves, individually and culturally. To this end we would like the essays in the book to reflect on questions like the following (among others): Can Jung's *Red Book* help us to navigate meaningfully through the rough waters we find ourselves in today

individually, professionally, politically, and culturally? What are the "spirits of this time" today, and how can the "spirit of the depths" be found in a way that is meaningful in our contemporary world? Does *The Red Book* help us possibly to formulate a new worldview and god-image in order to sustain people in the present crisis the world finds itself in? With your help, we want to evaluate the importance of *The Red Book* for our times and its potential value as a resource in our postmodern world. Essays may range in perspective from the clinical and therapeutic to the cultural to the literary to the religious and spiritual to the political to the economic and beyond. Whatever domain *The Red Book* touches with useful and transformative impact may be included in these reflections.

To this challenge some 50 Jungian scholars responded positively to our invitation, and we are now pleased to offer the first fruits of their efforts.

The essays included in this first volume of the series vary quite widely in perspective and approach. We begin with an essay by co-editor Thomas Arzt that lays out the general assumptions operative in the project as a whole. As Jungians, we share the conviction that human beings have what Jung called a "religious instinct," which is a strong propensity to search for meaning beyond the immediate challenges of everyday life. This leads inevitably to a quest for transcendence. Traditionally, religious institutions and collective mythologies have provided this sense of ultimate meaning and orientation for people, but today in postmodernity, myth is considered to be metaphor at best and superstitious fiction at worst, and institutions of religion are unconvincing and ineffective for modern and postmodern individuals who have grown up in secular cultures with prevailing scientific and anti-spiritualistic attitudes and values. This has led to the worldwide phenomenon today of the "homeless mind," to use the memorable phrase of theologian and sociologist Peter Berger. Jung, as we know, felt this keenly in himself and wrote about this problem of modern spirituality much earlier, famously in essays such as "Modern Man in Search of a Soul." The alternatives for conducting this search for meaning are few and far between in our postmodern world. Where and how is one to look for "a soul" when culture denies the reality of such a "thing" at its very roots?

Of course, Jung was not searching for a "thing" when he set out on his inner journey. He did not know what he was looking for, in fact. But he did find his imagination powerfully awakened, and this impelled him to open himself to psychic experiences that were convincing. The net result was that at the end of his life, when asked in the famous interview "Face to Face" if he believed in God, he could affirm that he "did not believe" but rather that he "knew" about such transcendent matters. It was a quest that ended in knowledge, *gnosis*. In addition to embedding his discussion of modernity, post-modernity, and "*post-histoire*" within the broader context of Jung's speculation of an epochal turn, Thomas Arzt offers a reflection on *The Red Book* that can assist individuals today to do something similar for themselves, also to find psychic ground under their feet and a roof over their heads. It is a way for the mind to overcome the homelessness of postmodernity.

In the essay following on his, the highly regarded psychological astrologer and Jungian analyst, Liz Greene, presents us with a detailed scholarly essay on the planetary setup for what is generally referred to as "the new age" or the "age of Aquarius." In *The Red Book*, Jung shows his astute awareness of the implications of the waning of the Piscean Age and the dawning of the Aquarian, and he associates the turbulence and disruption of the times to this major transition in human history. Liz Greene fills out this picture in brilliant scholarly detail. The essays that follow build on this perception—namely, that we are entering a new chapter in human culture. The noted scholars of Gnosticism, Stephan Hoeller and Lance Owens, point to a new direction of spirituality as it is emerging from ancient roots. This is a position absolutely in line with Jung's intuitions and observed in many passages of *The Red Book*. Following on their essays, Paul Bishop invites us to sin boldly and follow our "madness" in a tradition that reaches all the way back to Plato and is vividly extended in the works of Goethe, Schelling, Nietzsche, and, of course, Jung. It should be noted that Jung did indeed fear madness during his descent into the netherworld of the collective unconscious and yet was richly rewarded for taking the risk.

In a more personal vein, John Hill speaks of "confronting Jung" as a result of playing the roles of several characters from *The Red Book* who did likewise in a theatrical performance staged with colleagues at ISAP Zurich. In this, he also discovers how *Liber Novus* speaks to our times in a meaningful fashion. Marvin Spiegelman, whose essay follows, discusses his own long and committed engagement with active imagination and how the sheer existence of *The Red Book*, even many years before its publication in 2009, guided him in his personal psychological and spiritual journey into old age. His story is a model for how *Liber Novus* can be used as a guide for personal psychological and spiritual development in our time or in any time. The method is timeless, even as the contents change according to personal and collective circumstances. "It was a pleasure to do and helps me avoid having to write an autobiography," Spiegelman wrote to me after he had completed his essay. In a sense it is a summary of his life and work.

Andreas Schweizer echoes some of the themes presented in the preceding essays and focuses on the birth of a new god-image in *Liber Novus*. In a passionate display of erudition, he speaks personally and movingly of what is required for the rebirth of spirituality in postmodern times, which involves nothing short of the death of the "hero" in each of us, a sacrifice of enormous magnitude particularly in our titanic times. Liliana Wahba reflects on the dark potentials within the psyche if the sacrifice proposed by Andreas Schweizer is not followed. From her reading of *The Red Book*, she concludes that Jung was fully aware of the reality of evil that extends beyond the personal into the collective and archetypal layers of the psyche.

Dariane Pictet and Nancy Furlotti turn their eyes to the feminine and to nature as this theme emerges in the course of Jung's journey through the inner world. These essays take us into the territory of the anima and the somatic levels of the psyche as Jung experienced them and as they are still urgently in need of attention in our times. Jung's *Red Book* experiences and developments offer a clue, in the minds of these authors, to how we might proceed today with raising consciousness in ways that our emergent global culture and our very survival as a species demand.

Susan Rowland takes up the themes posed by the previous two authors in a literary mode, looking at *The Red Book* through the lens of literary criticism and theory. She also picks up, in another key, the topic proposed by Paul Bishop, for Dionysos and madness, poetry and inspiration, are deeply related. A burning question raised in postmodernity concerns creativity itself. Is creativity possible under postmodern conditions? Has the deconstruction frenzy spelled the end of creative possibilities? Or is this a necessary precursor for a new world? Has everything worthwhile been said and done already? What is left for us? Russell Lockhart speaks to this in his essay, which follows upon Susan Rowland's. The way forward is inward, downward, to a radical engagement with the powers of imagination. This is the way Jung took as he followed the "spirit of the depths" in his day. This way is still available today for the courageous individual, despite postmodern conditions. The feeling tone of this path is vividly sounded in Josephine Evetts-Secker's poetic essay. It is the feeling described classically by the theologian Rudolf Otto in his discussion of numinous experience. As Josephine Evetts-Secker discovers and shares, the theme of the numinous threads vividly through *The Red Book,* and it finds strong expression in these essays as well.

Ann Casement makes a bold leap into classical culture with her reference to the last days of the Roman Republic. The comparisons between those long ago times when a cultural consensus was slipping out of human grasp and being replaced by new disruptive energies and powers are trenchant and sobering. Then reaching out to an even more ancient cultural tradition, Ashok Bedi brings *The Red Book* into contact with Hindu tradition and its deep wisdom, so highly prized by Jung. He finds *The Red Book* to be a guide to contemporary people, similar to the guidance offered by Hindu classics. Chinese culture was similarly valued by Jung, and Heyong Shen shines a bright spotlight on the symbolic meaning of the color red, so highly prized as a signal of ultimate value in traditional Chinese culture. These three essays tie together a number of threads deeply embedded in *Liber Novus* and lift them into our consciousness for further guidance in using *The Red*

Book in postmodern times. Ancient cultures and postmodern conditions find a common ground in these fascinating essays.

Finally, John Woodcock takes a look at a future development that he refers to as "posthuman." We found it fitting to conclude this first volume on this note of possibilities, echoing Jung's last word in the entry he made in *The Red Book* in 1959: *Möglichkeit.* John Woodcock's essay opens an intuitive window into a development that follows on the postmodern and links this with intimations from *The Red Book*, a creative leap of imagination.

I would like to acknowledge our debt of gratitude to a number of people for making this ambitious work possible. First and foremost, I thank profoundly the authors of the essays in this volume for their diligent and thoughtful efforts in writing on this challenging topic of the relevance of Jung's *Red Book* for our time. It has been a pleasure to work with them, and without exception they have delivered on their promised work in a timely fashion. As well, I wish to express gratitude to the editor at Chiron Publications, Jennifer Fitzgerald, for her scrupulous care with a multiplicity of texts from so many very different authors, each with a unique style and voice. And to Steve Buser and Len Cruz, the publishers at Chiron, I would like to speak my heartfelt thanks for their immediate and spontaneous positive reactions to our proposal for what will be a large investment of time and finances on their part. Finally, I want to thank Thomas Arzt, my co-editor for this series, and say that this series would not have been undertaken without his inspirational and constant enthusiasm for a project that at first sight looked improbably ambitious and has gradually become a reality.

"The Way of What Is to Come":
Searching for Soul under Postmodern Conditions

Thomas Arzt

> Our age is seeking a new spring of life. I found one and
> drank of it and the water tasted good.[1]
>
> C.G. Jung

A specter haunts our world today; its name is *Angst*. Small wonder. As former German Secretary of State Frank-Walter Steinmeier recently remarked: "The world is out of joint."[2] At the same time, German diplomats such as Wolfgang Ischinger have noted that the disintegration of international security structures has accelerated and that decision makers in politics and business are overrun by unexpected events on a daily basis. Diagnosticians of our times like German philosopher Peter Sloterdijk see the world "plunging forward."[3] The World Economic Forum's *Global Risks Report 2017* identifies a hazardous planetary risk landscape that does not invite for much cheerfulness and serenity. Our present age, which we may call "postmodernity," is characterized by an overwhelming amount of fluidity and volatility on a global scale as well as on the level of the everyday lives of individuals. Cynical contemporaries even speak of a "racing standstill"—although nothing remains the same, nothing substantial does in fact change.[4] Even if we cannot yet see the direction in which this unbridled fast train engine called globalization will take us, today's world is obviously undergoing historical transformations that are probably unique in size and scale. "*Pourvu que cela dure*" ("if only this will work out well in the long run"), as Napoleon's mother remarked while witnessing the coronation of her son.[5]

In fact, there have always been turbulent thrusts, cracks, faults, and "societal feverish states"—contemporary historians usually attribute these too exclusively to technological change and innovation. For example, if we consider the decade prior to the year 1914, as Philipp Blom's work, *The Vertigo Years: Change and Culture in the West 1900-1914*, impressively shows, we find that the first 14 years of the 20th century saw rapid socio-economic developments that put the individuals as well as many European societies into a highly agitated state.[6] The "spirit of this time," as C.G. Jung referred to it in his *Red Book*, then led Europeans, as though sleepwalking, to exhausting trench warfare and technological mobilization, giving rise to geopolitical realignments. What is disconcerting is Blom's observation:

> Then as now, rapid changes in technology, globalization, communication technologies and changes in the social fabric dominated conversations and newspaper articles; then as now, cultures of mass consumption stamped their mark on the time; then as now, the feeling of living in an accelerating world, of speeding into the unknown, was overwhelming.[7]

The tremors of World War I consequently led to World War II. In our time, "Total Mobilization"[8] has reached the planetary level—just one spiral turn higher. Once more, we are disoriented in an "epoch of angst,"[9] and now one hundred years after *the Age of Anxiety* we find ourselves again restless in *the age of burnout*.[10]

Artists and sensitive contemporaries who lived between the years 1880 and 1914, such as the German philosopher Friedrich Nietzsche, intuited the seismographic shift that was about to come. Bewildered by societal developments and generational world-weariness, trapped in the "prison of reason" and yearning for an absent meaning, the best minds looked for new ways out of the spiritual malaise of their time. Dadaist Hugo Ball described the collective condition of his generation as follows:

> The world and society in 1913 looked like this: life is completely confined and shackled. A kind of economic

fatalism prevails; each individual, whether he resists it or not, is assigned a specific role and with it his interests and his character. The church is regarded as a 'redemption factory' of little importance, literature as a safety valve ... The most burning question day and night is: is there anywhere a force that is strong enough to put an end to this state of affairs? And if not, how can one escape it?[11]

"God is dead," as Nietzsche announced, and the "iron cage" of modernity was (in the meantime having turned into an omnipresent digitalized "Gestell"[12]) rigidly established. Contemporaries sensed the severe implications of the erosion of the Christian myth: not to be at home in one's own time anymore. Then as now, the collective situation forced the search for transcendence and meaning in order to withstand the undertow of the postmodern chaos that has undoubtedly revealed a nihilistic signature.

The Swiss psychologist C.G. Jung undertook perhaps the most challenging "deep dive" to seek answers to the questions posed by the epoch. Alarmed by visions and dreams, which reflected the tensions of his era and presaged the coming World War, Jung daringly searched for his soul in an "experiment" to learn his "personal myth." After the descent, Jung not only formulated his own myth but was also able to suggest the framework for a new collective myth. As will be illustrated later, Jung's *Red Book: Liber Novus* is both a highly intimate testimonial and a reference to the framework of this new collective myth.

Even though the term "postmodernity" is difficult to define and contains a high degree of ambiguity due to its notorious lack of conceptual clarity, attempts at diagnostic analysis have shown several general characteristics, such as deconstructionism, radical plurality, arbitrariness, liquidity, fragmentation, decanonization, acceleration, "muddling through," increase in complexity, ambiguity, and "slippery slopes." In a few sentences, German writer Hans Magnus Enzensberger masterfully portrays our contemporary postmodern condition, in which the increase of entropy can even be witnessed right in our own backyards:

Lower Bavarian market towns, rural villages in the Eifel, small towns in Holstein are populating themselves with figures that nobody would have considered imaginable just thirty years ago. Golf playing butchers, wives imported from Thailand, undercover intelligence officers in allotment gardens, Turkish mullahs, female pharmacists in Nicaragua-committees, Mercedes Benz-driving vagabonds, anti-authoritarians with organic gardens, gun collecting tax officers, farmers breeding peacocks, militant lesbians, Tamil ice-cream vendors, classical philologists trading commodity futures, mercenaries on home leave, extremist animal rights activists, cocaine dealers with tanning salons, dominatrices with customers from top management, computer-freaks commuting between Californian databases and Hessian wildlife reserve parks, carpenters delivering doors made of gold to Saudi Arabia, art forgers, Karl May scholars, body-guards, jazz experts, palliative care physicians, and porn producers. The loners and village idiots, weirdos and misfits all have been replaced by the mediocre deviant, who does not even stick out anymore among the millions of his ilk.[13]

In one important aspect—and this is the essential point with regard to Jung's *Red Book*—the diagnoses of our time appear to converge: There is, according to French philosopher and sociologist Jean-François Lyotard, himself a disappointed Marxist by his own admission, no major, meaningful and integrative metanarrative anymore, no "grand narrative" that is able to impart an all-encompassing conception of humankind's role in the world.[14] For any "grand narrative" such as is offered for example by the Epic of Gilgamesh, the Bible, the Odyssey, the Enlightenment, the belief in science, or Marxism, the following postmodern analysis applies:

Simplifying to the extreme, I define postmodern as incredulity toward metanarratives. This incredulity is undoubtedly a product of progress in the sciences: but that progress in turn presupposes it. To the obsolescence of the metanarrative apparatus of legitimation corresponds, most notably,

the crisis of metaphysical philosophy and of the university
institution which in the past relied on it. The narrative function is losing its functors, its great hero, its great dangers, its
great voyages, its great goal. It is being dispersed in clouds
of narrative language—narrative, but also denotative, pre-
scriptive, descriptive, and so on. Conveyed within each
cloud are pragmatic valencies specific to its kind. Each of us
lives at the intersection of many of these.[15]

From a spiritual point of view, the horizon of meaning offered by a
divine order—the "great order of Being"—is seemingly lost, while
from the perspective of the postmodern subject, the world as well as
life itself is not readable, understandable, or shapable anymore.[16]
Whereas prior epochs had a meaningful "grand narrative"—here
Dante's *Divine Comedy*, Johann Wolfgang von Goethe's *Faust,* and
Nietzsche's *Thus Spoke Zarathustra* come to mind—the modern or
postmodern man is left without a timely, central, and vivid myth. In
Edward Edinger's estimation, this condition of spiritual and metaphysical homelessness, a state of being perhaps best captured by
Nietzsche's "Last Man" or Martin Heidegger's "They," has only
deepened in later times:

> It is evident to thoughtful people that Western society no
> longer has a viable, functioning myth. Indeed, all major
> world cultures are approaching, to a greater or lesser
> extent, the state of mythlessness. The breakdown of a
> central myth is like the shattering of a vessel containing a
> precious essence; ... Meaning is lost.[17]

Referring back to Jung's work, Edinger continues: "... as Jung's
discovery of his own mythlessness paralleled the mythless condition
of modern society, so Jung's discovery of his own individual myth
will prove to be the first emergence of our new collective myth."[18]

Edinger's statement is only understandable if one puts aside the
discourse of academic sociologists, cultural theorists and professional
philosophers. Opening up to the sphere of individual *core experience*
[*Kern-Erfahrung*] in the sense of Karlfried Graf Dürckheim or Jung's

experience of the self, one approaches the psychological, religious-spiritual, and metaphysical realms of life that are generally thought to be off-limits by today's postmodern academic establishment. Nothing causes greater tedium and disregards the central questions of our time more than the ignorance and prevailing bustle witnessed within the self-referential and detail-obsessed chairs of our university institutions. In all likelihood, nothing revelatory will come from their discourse.

It might be this near-universal bypassing of the central questions of our present age that is globally driving an increasing interest in Jung. The 21st century could be "Jung's century,"[19] a century in which a postmodern state of mind and the demise of the secular conception of the human stimulates the intense search for sustainable alternatives to an epoch dominated by positivism, materialism, reductionism, and atheism.[20] After all, in a spell of "pneumaphobia" modernity's enthronement of *Déesse Raison* led to an oppression of all phenomena of the "spirit" or the "sacred." Subsequently, the spirit (as well as the *anima mundi*, according to Nobel Prize-winning physicist Wolfgang Pauli) has disappeared into the unconscious.[21] Jung described this process in *The Spiritual Problem of Modern Man* as follows:

> Whenever there exists some external form, be it an ideal or a ritual, by which all the yearnings and hopes of the soul are adequately expressed—as for instance in a living religion—then we may say that the psyche is outside and that there is no psychic problem, just as there is then no unconscious in our sense of the word. In consonance with this truth, the discovery of psychology falls entirely within the last decades, although long before that man was introspective and intelligent enough to recognize the facts that are the subject-matter of psychology. ... So also a spiritual need has produced in our time the 'discovery' of psychology. The psychic facts still existed earlier, of course, but they did not attract attention—no one noticed them. People got along without them. But today we can no longer get along unless we pay attention to the psyche.[22]

Dieu se retire—nonetheless, one has to follow God, according to the view of German writer Ernst Jünger. Hence, the engagement with the unconscious becomes a vital necessity not only for the individual but for the social collective since it has become a matter of survival. Ironically, the historic moment of the proclamation of the "iron cage" by sociologist and philosopher Max Weber coincided with the beginning of depth psychology—perhaps an unexpected "Cunning of Reason." From the perspective of Jung's understanding of the evolution of human consciousness, the project of modernity could only lead to the "darkening of the world" (*die Verdüsterung der Welt*, as Heidegger said[23]):

> ... for all ages before us have believed in gods in some form or other. Only an unparalleled impoverishment of symbolism could enable us to rediscover the gods as psychic factors, that is, as archetypes of the unconscious. ... Since the stars have fallen from heaven and our highest symbols have paled, a secret life holds sway in the unconscious. That is why we have a psychology today, and why we speak of the unconscious. All this would be quite superfluous in an age or culture that possessed symbols. Symbols are spirit from above, and under those conditions the spirit is above too. Therefore it would be a foolish and senseless undertaking for such people to wish to experience or investigate an unconscious that contains nothing but the silent, undisturbed sway of nature. Our unconscious, on the other hand, hides living water, spirit that has become nature, and that is why it is disturbed. Heaven has become for us the cosmic space of the physicists, and the divine empyrean a fair memory of things that once were. But 'the heart glows,' and a secret unrest gnaws at the roots of our being.[24]

The "spirit" is waiting in the collective unconscious for recognition, for integration into the collective consciousness of our postmodern times. Today, the spirit is "knocking at our door" or, as Jünger put it, the "primordial essence is alive."[25] Many pathologies of our age emerge from the lack of having an "alchemistic vessel" to integrate these archetypal-spiritual energies into the sociocultural context. If the individual or society denies these energies the chance for expression, they will turn to confusion, destruction, and violence. *Mercurius duplex*: It was alchemy that found the adequate expression for this—good with the good and bad with the bad. For the time being, though, it remains a mystery how the oversaturated, overaged, and overregulated societies of the West, run by disoriented and unimaginative guardians of the *status quo* in politics, media, and business, should approach this monumental challenge. We are devoid of any vision for the future. "The best lack all conviction, while the worst are full of passionate intensity," lamented William Butler Yeats during Jung's day. Meanwhile, much would be gained if the planetary turbulences of postmodernity could be interpreted as a pregnant phase of initiation, as a *rite de passage*.

In this sense, future generations would be inclined retrospectively to understand our postmodern era as a phase of *nigredo*, as a time of collective disorientation and confusion, with its attitude toward the world manically oscillating between a baroque lust for life and an apocalyptic foreboding of death. From Jung's perspective, it is important, though, to face the insecurity and abyss of postmodern life and to accept our "spiritual nakedness" as well as the obvious dissolution of traditional belief systems. An openness to the psyche, so that its intimidations can be consciously realized, is crucial too. Further, we have to learn how to deal with existential insecurity, uncertainty, and ambivalence, because at the center of anxiety something may want to speak to us. If we are in a state of "darkness," it is "divine darkness." If we feel ourselves to be stuck in a state of "void," it is a "divine void." In a similar point of view, German philosopher Leopold Ziegler considers the state of Western "Seinsvergessenheit" (forgetting of Being) a *Gestalt* of a divine being *in absconditus*. Within the metaphysical loneliness of modern consciousness Jung detects a "divine providence," or rather an occasion for a renewed experience of spirituality, especially as the living spirit attempts to resurrect from the ruins of the Christian edifice of beliefs.[26] In this sense, the "deconstruction frenzy" of the 20th century would be understandable, as

Richard Tarnas has pointed out: "… the twentieth century's massive and radical breakdown of so many structures—cultural, philosophical, scientific, religious, moral, artistic, social, economic, political, atomic, ecological—all this suggests a necessary deconstruction prior to a new birth."[27] If Tarnas has it right, coming generations, hopefully, might perhaps look back one day also on a phase of *rubedo*, the emergence of a new post-Christian spirituality.

How to continue now? We are currently living in a historic moment in which all aspects of human existence have to be reconceived and radically put to the test with respect to the secret life of the living spirit. Support may be offered by Jung's "psychological law of energy conservation," stating that "if anything of importance is devalued in our conscious life, and perishes—so runs the law— there arises a compensation in the unconscious."[28] What Jung is saying is that if the archetypal world of spirit gets ignored by a purely materialistic worldview for too long, the former will be subsequently activated with a proportionally high energetic value in the collective unconscious. Even for the simple-minded, this should be plausible insofar as the "religious impulses" of the soul—*anima naturaliter religiosa*—cannot merely vanish into thin air; rather it will be forced to change locations due to the overdose of modern rationality. "It may be possible to suppress them, but it cannot alter their nature, and what is suppressed comes up again in another place in altered form, this time loaded with a resentment that makes the otherwise harmless natural impulse our enemy."[29] Since the archetypal world cannot be suppressed without substantial consequences, and since contemporary society and culture are not able to tackle the actual problems, let alone draw up feasible solutions, it is the individual that ultimately has to face this conflict. Sensible, sensitive, even "deranged" contemporaries once again have to restore the spiritual anchorage that has been undercut by postmodern categories of interpretation leading to the ensuing psychological crisis.

The challenge today, therefore, is on the one hand not to discard our Christian tradition and heritage, and on the other hand to face up to the state of *nigredo* into which we have descended. In Jung's view, we are standing at the beginning of a new psychological culture and era, one still however without collective guiding images, symbols, rituals, or myths. Entering unchartered territory within this new culture goes hand-in-hand with the following prerequisite developments already underway: new integration efforts concerning the inclusion of "evil" within the understanding of wholeness, as well as the unsightly and banal; integration of the feminine and nature as significant dimensions repressed and neglected by Christianity; reinterpretation of religious scriptures as poetic and symbolic rather than as purely historical and literal; reinterpretation of the figure of Christ as a symbolic expression of the inner dynamics of the soul.[30] At this point, it seems clear that under postmodern conditions only one path forward remains passable: if we have interpreted the signs of our time correctly, the "metamorphosis of the gods" will require the individual's utmost commitment to an ongoing process for which Jung proposed the term "individuation." The narrative for this is contained in *The Red Book,* and with it begins Jung's new myth showing *"The Way of What Is to Come."*

****

"My soul, where are you? Do you hear me? I speak, I call you—are you there?"[31] On November 12, 1913 Jung began his inner work on what would eventually become his *Red Book.* This dramatic passage occurs in the chapter titled "Refinding the Soul." In a preliminary remark, Jung had noted that he had been able to attain "honor, power, wealth, knowledge, and every human happiness," while distress in his inner and the outer worlds had overcome him with "horror."[32] Given his break with Sigmund Freud and the resulting state of questioning his previous understanding of the psyche, Jung's distress becomes understandable. Weighing heavily also was a series of remarkable dreams, visions, and waking fantasies that left him bewildered to the point of suspecting an impending psychosis. Slowly, however, Jung began to realize that, for instance, his waking fantasies in October 1913 in which Europe was flood-ravaged described in precognitive form events that were about to happen not uniquely to him but to Europe collectively with the outbreak of World War I.[33] Within this personal, highly disturbed state of mind and within the catastrophic

world situation, something else that had already bothered Jung after
putting the finishing touches on *Wandlungen und Symbole der Libido*
again became painfully evident to him, namely that a "man who thinks
he can live without myth, or outside it, is an exception. He is like one
uprooted, having no true link either with the past, or with the ancestral
life which continues within him, or yet with contemporary human
society." Then, stating his own personal dilemma, he continues:

> I was driven to ask myself in all seriousness: 'What is the
> myth you are living?' I found no answer to this question,
> and had to admit that I was not living with a myth, or even
> in a myth, but rather in an uncertain cloud of theoretical
> possibilities which I was beginning to regard with
> increasing distrust. I did not know that I was living a myth,
> and even if I had known it, I would not have known what
> sort of myth was ordering my life without my knowledge.
> So in the most natural way, I took it upon myself to get to
> know 'my' myth, and I regarded this as the task of tasks,
> for—so I told myself—how could I, when treating my
> patients, make due allowance for the personal factor, for
> my personal equation, which is yet so necessary for a
> knowledge of the other person, if I was unconscious of it?
> I simply had to know what unconscious or preconscious
> myth was forming me, from what rhizome I sprang.[34]

And so, in November 1913, during an experiment of self-discovery,
"my most difficult experiment," Jung embarked on a search for his
own myth. This search would lead him to "a new spring of life,"[35]
about which he would later write to Victor White: "I wanted the proof
of a living Spirit and I got it. Don't ask me at what a price."[36]

Initially, Jung wrote down his fantasies and active imaginations
in the so-called *Black Books*, which are regarded as a personal
protocol of his self-experiment. From there they found their way into
a red leather-bound folio volume for which he revised the material
while also enhancing it with commentary and carefully drawn and
meticulously arranged pictures.[37] In Sonu Shamdasani's summary
view, *The Red Book* presents

... a series of active imaginations together with Jung's attempt to understand their significance. This work of understanding encompasses a number of interlinked threads: an attempt to understand himself and to integrate and develop the various components of his personality; an attempt to understand the structure of the human personality in general; an attempt to understand the relation of the individual to present-day society and to the community of the dead; an attempt to understand the psychological and historical effects of Christianity; and an attempt to grasp the future religious development of the West. Jung discusses many other themes in the work, including the nature of self-knowledge; the nature of the soul; the relations of thinking and feeling and the psychological types; the relation of inner and outer masculinity and femininity; the uniting of opposites; solitude; the value of scholarship and learning; the status of science; the significance of symbols and how they are to be understood; the meaning of the war; madness, divine madness, and psychiatry; how the Imitation of Christ is to be understood today; the death of God; the historical significance of Nietzsche; and the relation of magic and reason.[38]

Wolfgang Giegerich argues that *The Red Book* is to be read as Jung's answer to Nietzsche.[39] Like many of his generation, Jung tried to confront the implications of modernity head-on—here, by the way, one may be reminded of Heidegger's and Jünger's disputation, *Over the Line*, in which both with respect to the question of nihilism navigate in Nietzsche's wake. But Jung did not see his solution represented in Nietzsche's *Übermensch*. It was rather in the formulation of a new spirituality. The title of this solution is the process of individuation:

The overall theme of the book is how Jung regains his soul and overcomes the contemporary malaise of spiritual alienation. This is ultimately achieved through enabling the rebirth of a new image of God in his soul and developing a new worldview in the form of a psychological and theological cosmology. *Liber Novus* presents the prototype of Jung's conception of the individuation process, which he held to be the universal form of individual psychological development. *Liber Novus* itself can be understood on one hand as depicting Jung's individuation process, and on the other hand as his elaboration of this concept as a general psychological schema.[40]

Along with Jung's narrative of individuation, many philosophical, theological and psychological questions concerning topics such as God, knowledge, language, logic, meaning, chaos, death, and evil are raised in *The Red Book*. Several distinct themes and concepts circumscribe Jung's attempt at conceiving a new cosmology.[41] Among others, these are:

Finding the Soul: At the beginning of his self-experiment, Jung is instructed by the "spirit of the depths" to turn away from the "spirit of this time," which represents the scientific-materialistic worldview, and follow the "spirit of the depths," which as the ruler of the depths of world affairs "from time immemorial and for all the futures possesses a greater power than the spirit of this time, who changes with the generations."[42] The soul should not be considered as an object of science, an object of a "dead system" or a "dead formula," but rather as "a living and self-existing being."[43] The path to the soul is difficult and fraught with danger, for "the signposts have fallen, unblazed trails lie before us. ... May each go his own way."[44] Further: "My friends, it is wise to nourish the soul, otherwise you will breed dragons and devils in your heart."[45] *The Red Book* documents Jung's journey to the rediscovery of his lost soul as well as his method of active imagination used to enter into dialogue with what he discovers.

Soul and the Experience of God: The view that the soul is a "place" for the experience of God permeates the entire *Red Book*. "I am ignorant of your mystery. Forgive me if I speak as in a dream, like a drunkard—are you God?"[46] In Jung's encounter with Soul, "God" does not reveal himself as the "God of theologians," who is "dead" and in need of renewal, but in overwhelming experiences of paradoxical dichotomies found within. For example, the "God yet to come" is the "melting together of sense and nonsense"[47] in the "supreme meaning," and "as day requires night and night requires day, so meaning requires absurdity and absurdity requires meaning."[48] Thus, the divine encompasses meaning and absurdity, the greatest and smallest, and "the supreme meaning is great and small, it is as wide as the space of the starry Heaven and as narrow as the cell of the living body."[49] The "new God" is a *coincidentia oppositorum*, and God's birth takes place in the inner world: "I saw a new God, a child ... The God holds the separate principles in his power, he unites them. The God develops through the union of the principles in me. He is their union."[50] Viewed in a broader context of Western intellectual history, Nietzsche at the end of the 19th century proclaims the death of God while Jung in *Liber Novus* presents the rebirth of God at the beginning of the 20th century.[51]

Renewal of the God-image: A key to Jung's oeuvre can be found in the encounter with the wounded mythical figure Izdubar, whom Jung would like to heal. Like modern man, Izdubar becomes paralyzed by the poison that is science because this "awful magic" only leaves words in place of gods. Science has destroyed the capacity for belief:

> Iz: "But this science is the awful magic that has lamed me. How can it be that you are still alive even though you drink from this poison every day?"

> I: "We've grown accustomed to this over time, because men get used to everything. But we're still somewhat lamed. On the other hand, this science also has great advantages, as you've seen. What we've lost in terms of force, we've rediscovered many times through mastering the force of nature." ...

> I: "Now you perhaps see that we had no choice. We had to swallow the poison of science. Otherwise we would have met the same fate as you have: we'd be completely lamed, if we encountered it unsuspecting and unprepared. This

poison is so insurmountably strong that everyone, even the strongest, and even the eternal Gods, perish because of it. If our life is dear to us, we prefer to sacrifice a piece of our life force rather than abandon ourselves to certain death."[52]

Jung knows that he has to stand by the side of the lame and ill Izdubar, who is his brother, to cure him.[53] After squeezing Izdubar into the size of an egg and putting him in his pocket, Jung succeeds in healing and transforming him, thus leading to a rebirth of mythic sensibility. In the teaching of *The Red Book*, man embodies the "… gateway through which crowds the train of the gods and the coming and passing of all times."[54] With Izdubar's rebirth, an understanding of soul, self, and God becomes visible, which Jung would much later formulate in *Answer to Job* as the desire of God to continuously incarnate, but already in *his Red Book* this finds expression as follows:

> Just as the disciples of Christ recognized that God had become flesh and lived among them as a man, we now recognize that the anointed of this time is a God who does not appear in the flesh; he is no man and yet is a son of man, but in spirit and not in flesh; hence he can be born only through the spirit of men as the conceiving womb of the God.[55]

Jung's "new God" therefore is a "pneumatic God," as Jung elaborates in a letter to Joan Corrie on February 29, 1919:

> The primordial creator of the world, the blind creative libido, becomes transformed in man through individuation & out of this process, which is like pregnancy, arises a divine child, a reborn God, no more (longer) dispersed into the millions of creatures, but being one & this individual, and at the same time all individuals, the same in you as in me. Dr. L[ong] has a little book: VII sermones ad mortuous. There you find the description of the Creator dispersed into his creatures, & in the last sermon you find the beginning of individuation, out of which, the divine

child arises ... The child is a new God, actually born in many individuals, but they don't know it. He is a spiritual God. A spirit in many people, yet one and the same everywhere. Keep to your time and you will experience His qualities.[56]

Imitatio Christi: With the *Red Book* identifying the individuation process as the royal road to rediscovering soul and "God," Jung revises the traditional Christian teaching of *imitatio Christi*. Simply being a devout Christian does not suffice anymore. Instead, the new form of spirituality requires searching for the *inner Christ*, who stands for the sacrifice and willingness needed to take one's *own life* into one's *own hands* while staying faithful to one's essence and one's love.[57] As opposed to remaining in an infantile attitude of imitation, the individual is asked to find a place for Christ in his heart and then follow his independent path during a process of personal growth, living his own life just as Christ lived his.[58] "The new God laughs at imitation and discipleship. He needs no imitators and no pupils."[59] In addition to the individual dimension, an eschatological one is of relevance as well, when Jung writes:

> ... I believe you have completed your work, since the one who has given his life, his entire truth, all his love, his entire soul, has completed his work. ... The time has come when each must do his own work of redemption. Mankind has grown older and a new month has begun.[60]

In Jung's later writings, such as *Mysterium Coniunctionis* and *Aion*, the symbol of Christ as a symbol of the self will play a significant role.

The Union of Opposites: The theme of the unification of opposites is a central motif of *The Red Book* and, like the symbol of Christ, is further elaborated in Jung's later works. This theme deals with the recognition of the neglected and ignored aspects of the psyche as well as with the consideration of the opposite as the missing half of wholeness. "You begin to have a presentiment of the whole when you embrace your opposite principle, since the whole belongs to both principles, which grow from one root."[61] The psychological formulation of the problem of opposites is regarded by Jung himself as a "renewal." In *The Red Book*, numerous pairs of opposites are found: sense and nonsense; fullness and void; creation and destruction; love and hate; spirit and matter; insanity and sanity; above and below; order and chaos. Phases of psychic order are succeeded by phases of psychic chaos that defy any form of rationality or control while still being the *conditio sine qua non* for the transformative mystery that is individuation:

> We recognized that the world comprises reason and unreason; and we also understood that our way needs not only reason but also unreason. ... But one can be certain that the greater part of the world eludes our understanding. We must value the incomprehensible and unreasonable equally, although they are not necessarily equal in themselves; a part of the incomprehensible, however, is only presently incomprehensible and might already concur with reason tomorrow. But as long as one does not understand it, it remains unreasonable. Insofar as the incomprehensible accords with reason, one may try to think it with success; but insofar as it is unreasonable, one needs magical practices to open it up. ... If one has done one's best to steer the chariot, and one then notices that a greater other is actually steering it, then magical operation takes place. ... But the condition is that one totally accepts it and does not reject it, in order to transfer everything to the growth of the tree.[62]

"The basic issue," writes Shamdasani, "... was how the problem of the opposites could be resolved through the production of the uniting or reconciling symbol. This forms one of the central themes of *Liber Novus*."[63] Both poles of each pair of opposites—good *and* bad, spirit *and* matter, reason *and* unreason, etc.—are to be acknowledged in life in order to gain a holistic worldview during the mysterious process of individuation. The world is a painting of opposites. Jung's perspective here, first and foremost, draws on Heraclitus and Nicolaus Cusanus. Together with the principles of *enantiodromia* and the transcendent function, the concept of opposites and the unification of opposites represent the foundation of Jung's later elaborations in Analytical Psychology.

The Coming Aeon: Jung strikes a prophetic tone in his *Red Book*. However, despite being certain that it is an important work of revelatory character eventually to gain a broader audience for its visionary elements, he does not see himself as a prophet. "I will be no saviour, no lawgiver, no master teacher unto you. You are no longer little children."[64] Upon further review, Jung's first picture at the beginning of the chapter, "The Way of What Is to Come," does hint at his notion of thinking in astronomic and astrological terms. His narrative of the individuation process directly corresponds to the insight that the Christian age, the Piscean Age, is coming to an end and that mankind is standing at the doorstep of a new age, the Aquarian Age. Humanity is experiencing birth-pains since a new image of God is unfolding.

The Red Book is a highly complex, and indeed an enormous, volume and anything but light reading. It does not offer itself for a quick skim, but rather it grows in substance for the persistent as with homeopathic doses and small bites. Although amenable to manifold perspectives and interpretations, it already is certain that *The Red Book* is going to call for a new view of Jung's life and oeuvre. Furthermore, one can confidently presume that Jung's rank in the intellectual history of the 20th century must be reevaluated since his searching for his "own myth" comes at an epochal turning point in human history and the history of human consciousness. In this sense, *The Red Book* serves as a document of Jung's discovery of his very personal myth—*life as the unfolding of the individuation process*—that simultaneously represents an account of the conditions necessary for the development of a much needed new collective myth. Put differently in the form of a thesis here: Jung's "personal individuation process" could resemble Lyotard's "*petit récit*," whereas the new myth of a "collective individuation process" has the potential to be Lyotard's "*grand récit*," a "grand narrative."

****

In a late letter to Sir Herbert Read dated 2 September, 1960, Jung writes:

> The great problem of our time is that we don't understand
> what is happening to the world. We are confronted with
> the darkness of our soul, the unconscious. It sends up its
> dark and unrecognizable urges. It hollows out and hacks
> up the shapes of our culture and its historical dominants.
> We have no dominants any more, they are in the future.
> Our values are shifting, everything loses its certainty, even
> *sanctissima causalitas* has descended from the throne of
> the axioma and has become a mere field of probability.
> Who is the awe-inspiring guest who knocks at our door
> portentously? Fear precedes him, showing that ultimate
> values already flow towards him. Our hitherto believed
> values decay accordingly and our only certainty is that the
> new world will be something different from what we were
> used to.[65]

It seems as if postmodern sensitivities, perplexities and intuitions are already shimmering through in this letter. Similarly, in the midst of Western spiritual and philosophical atony following the collapse of occidental metaphysics and political master ideologies, Jean-François Lyotard came to the philosophical realization that postmodernity does not offer a meaning-endowing and integrative metanarrative anymore. After the "end of modernity," he could find no "grand narrative" to provide people with an all-encompassing explanation for their position in the world. From today's point of view, one may argue that on a psychological level *The Red Book*, with its prototype of the concept of the individuation process, qualifies as a model for the development of a new collective myth in postmodern society. *The Red Book* encourages the discovery of the cosmos of the inner world and in it the birth of the "new god." With the help of the insights provided by Jungian psychology, one is aided in the "development" of one's own personal myth and in the rediscovery of the soul. Graf Dürckheim's fundamental maxim of "daily life as spiritual exercise" might serve as a trail marker to be followed on this path.[66]

"It is a fearful thing to fall into the hands of the living God."[67] In his self-experiment, Jung not only found his "own myth" but also the "new God" and a "new religion," about which he would remain silent for decades to come. *The Red Book* was made accessible only to some selected few of Jung's family and his inner circle, and for years it was kept private in his personal library. In retrospect, the experiences of the years 1912 through 1928 eventually turned into the foundation of Analytical Psychology, as Jung would write at the end of his life in *Memories, Dreams, Reflections*:

> It has taken me virtually forty-five years to distill within the vessel of my scientific work the things I experienced and wrote down at that time. As a young man my goal had been to accomplish something in my science. But then, I hit upon this stream of lava, and the heat of its fires re-shaped my life. That was the primal stuff which compelled me to work upon it, and my works are a more or less successful endeavor to incorporate this incandescent matter into the contemporary picture of the world.
>
> The years when I was pursuing my inner images were the most important in my life—in them everything essential was decided. It all began then; the later details are only supplements and clarifications of the material that burst forth from the unconscious, and at first swamped me. It was the *prima materia* for a lifetime's work.[68]

Although his *Red Book* was somehow intended for a future reader-ship, Jung was hesitant regarding its publication. Not until his near-death experience in 1944 and the visions witnessed there did the decision come to elaborate on his dialogue with the soul in his publication *Aion*:

> Before my illness (in 1944) I have often asked myself if I were permitted to publish or even speak of my secret knowledge. I later set it all down in *Aion*. I realized that it was my duty to communicate these thoughts, yet I doubted whether I was allowed to give expression to them. During my illness I received confirmation and I now knew that everything had meaning and that everything was perfect.[69]

Aion, therefore, can be read as Jung's commentary on his experiences put down in his *Red Book*.[70] Jung's initial painting in *Liber Novus*, found at the beginning of the first chapter, "The Way of What Is to Come," illustrates this "secret knowledge": After about 2,150 years, the Christian Aeon, the Piscean Age, is nearing its end. Humanity is now facing an epochal period of transition, the dawning of a new age. A closer examination of the painting on the first page of *Liber Novus* discloses Jung's view of the universe and of man's journey through time. In the middle of the picture, an old ship is ready to set sail; a medieval town is present in the background. Underneath the water's surface, inhabitants of the ocean's depth are discernable; below them lies the "fiery-fluid basalt" of the Earth's volcanic interior. At the top of the painting, a four-rayed sun is seen in the heavens, traveling on its ecliptic path through zodiacal signs. In Jung's illustration, the sun is positioned between the signs of Pisces and Aquarius, while one of the four rays reaches onward to the astrological sign of Aquarius, the coming age. Jung is here clearly referring to the astronomical pheno-menon of the zodiacal "precession of the equinoxes." Approximately every 2,150 years—a period know as a "Platonic Month"—this astronomical precession causes a gradual shifting of the vernal equinox into the preceding sign of the zodiac.[71] In the late Hellenistic Age, it was calculated that the equinox would move—or "precess"—through the entire circle of the 12 zodiacal constellations over a period of roughly 25,800 years. This period came to be called a "Platonic Year." (Recently, the International Astronomical Union calculated that the precession through the entire zodiac takes exactly 25,771.58 years.)[72] At the last turn of the times—which occurred around 200 B.C.E.—the vernal equinox transitioned from Aries into Pisces; this was the beginning of the Piscean Age. Now, over two millennia later, we have arrived at the end of the Piscean Age. Looking at these astronomical phenomena with an acausal syn-chronistic approach, Jung saw that humanity is on the threshold of a new age—the Aquarian Age. Within this difficult phase of aeonial transition, immense difficulties can be expected. Jung perceived that these epochal transitions between "Platonic Months" go hand-in-hand with a "metamorphosis of the gods." The period of transition between aeons is therefore always accompanied by pronounced anxiety, confusion, and melancholia:

> My thoughts about 'this world' were not—and are not—enjoyable. The drive of the unconscious towards mass murder on a global scale is not exactly a cheering prospect. Transitions between the aeons always seem to have been melancholy and despairing times, as for instance the collapse of the Old Kingdom in Egypt ... between Taurus and Aries, or the melancholy of the Augustian age between Aries and Pisces. And now we are moving into Aquarius ... And we are only at the beginning of this apocalyptic development! Already I am a great-grandfather twice over and see those distant generations growing up who long after we are gone will spend their lives in that darkness.[73]

> The development ... with its seemingly nihilistic trend towards disintegration must be understood as the symptom and symbol of a mood of universal destruction and renewal that has set its mark on our age. This mood makes itself felt everywhere, politically, socially, and philosophically. We are living in what the Greeks called the καιρός—the right moment—for a 'metamorphosis of the gods,' of the fundamental principles and symbols. This peculiarity of our time, which is certainly not of our conscious choosing, is the expression of the unconscious man within us who is changing. Coming generations will have to take account of this momentous transformation if humanity is not to destroy itself through the might of its own technology and science.[74]

The Christian age is coming to an end, and we are witness to this epochal turning point in human consciousness. The new age, the *Way of What Is to Come*, corresponds with the formulation of a new image of God. Jung's outlook points to the Paraclete, the Holy Spirit, who

> ... is the spirit of physical and spiritual procreation who from now on shall make his abode in creaturely man. ...

The future indwelling of the Holy Ghost in man amounts
to a continuing incarnation of God. ... It is the task of the
Paraclete, the 'spirit of truth,' to dwell and work in
individual human beings, so as to remind them of Christ's
teachings and lead them into the light.[75]

Thereby, the *incarnatio continua*, the continuing incarnation of the
Holy Spirit in mortal man, becomes the signature of a new spirituality
in the coming aeon:

We are still looking back to the pentecostal events in a
dazed way instead of looking forward to the goal the Spirit
is leading us to. Therefore mankind is wholly unprepared
for the things to come. Man is compelled by divine forces
to go forward to increasing consciousness and cognition,
developing further and further away from his religious
background because he does not understand it any more.
His religious teachers and leaders are still hypnotized by
the beginnings of a then new aeon of consciousness instead
of understanding them and their implications. What one
once called the 'Holy Ghost' is an impelling force, creating
wider consciousness and responsibility and thus enriched
cognition. The real history of the world seems to be the
progressive incarnation of the deity.[76]

The Age of the Holy Ghost: It certainly would be a worthwhile
endeavor to inquire as to the degree of influence the Calabrian abbot
Joachim of Fiore may have had on Jung's writings. With his "Theory
of Three Ages," Fiore's eschatological outlook had a significant
influence on the Western history of ideas. In a letter, Jung himself
directly refers to the age of the Holy Ghost:

The later development from the Christian aeon to the one
of the S. spiritus has been called the *evangelium aeternum*
by Gioacchino da Fiori in a time when the great tearing
apart had just begun. Such vision seems to be granted by
divine grace as a sort of *consolamentum*, so that man is not

left in a completely hopeless state during the time of darkness. We are actually in the state of darkness viewed from the standpoint of history. We are still within the Christian aeon and just beginning to realize the age of darkness where we shall need Christian virtues *to the utmost.*[77]

And taking Jung's remark further, Edinger notes in his *Aion Lectures*:

As it gradually dawns on people, one by one, that the transformation of God is not just an interesting idea but is a living reality, it may begin to function as a new myth. Whoever recognizes this myth as his own personal reality will put his life in the service of this process. Such an individual offers himself as a vessel for the incarnation of deity and thereby promotes the on-going transformation of God by giving Him human manifestation. Such an individual will experience his life as meaningful and will be an example of Jung's statement: 'The indwelling of the Holy Ghost, the third Divine Person, in man, brings about a Christification of many.'[78]

The individuation process—in psychological terms—resembles the "indwelling of the Holy Ghost" in the "vessel" of the individual. Jung did not only inscribe his "own myth" in his *Red Book*, but additionally formulated a new narrative, the process of individuation of man and mankind, which could be the special value of Jung's *Red Book* for our time, since this new narrative can be considered the antidote to Lyotard's analysis of our epoch. Inasmuch as Jung's life work lays out the cure of the current spiritual malaise, what is left as our "task of tasks"—for those who can sense and thus subscribe to the loss of "spiritual substance" within the contingencies of a postmodernity turned chaotic? In seeking to assist a patient in finding a way to her individuation process and the rediscovery of soul, Jung recommended creating a personal *Red Book*:

I should advise you to put it all down as beautifully as you can—in some beautifully bound book. It will seem as if you were making the visions banal—but then you need to do that—then you are freed from the power of them. If you do that with these eyes for instance they will cease to draw you. You should never try to make the visions come again. Think of it in your imagination and try to paint it. Then when these things are in some precious book you can go to the book & turn over the pages & for you it will be your church—your cathedral—the silent places of your spirit where you will find renewal. If anyone tells you that it is morbid or neurotic and you listen to them–then you will lose your soul—for in that book is your soul.[79]

"Your cathedral"—one's "own church" as an *ecclesia spiritualis*—this is the pressing issue today, according to Jung. We are in a period of turbulent transitions, in an interim of history. However, just how postmodern "radical plurality" and *incarnatio continua* are entangled with each other remains a mystery. Perhaps this logical contradiction is the sign of a deeper truth. Even if it took centuries, as Jung suspected, before the new god-image would constitute itself, the new collective myth already is delineated and the individual consequently called upon to actively contribute to the foundation of a "new religion" in the form of an "invisible church." As this is described in a dream and during an ensuing talk of Max Zeller with Jung himself:

A temple of vast dimensions was in the process of being built. As far as I could see ahead, behind, right and left there were incredible numbers of people building on gigantic pillars. I, too, was building on a pillar. The whole building process was in its very first beginnings, but the foundation was already there, the rest of the building was starting to go up, and I and many others were working on it.[80]

Jung said: "Yes, you know, that is the temple we all build on. We don't know the people because, believe me, they build in India and China and in Russia and all over the world. That is the new religion. You know how long it will take until it is built?" I said, "How should I know? Do you know?" He said "I know." I asked how long it will take. He said,

"About six hundred years." "Where do you know this from?" I asked. He said, "From dreams. From other people's dreams and from my own. This new religion will come together as far as we can see."[81]

So, where does the leave us? Sloterdijk is definitely right, of course, when he points out that no one has a grasp of the current situation with its technological titanism: We don't know what is happening to us; we are stuck too deeply in the process itself to be able to see it in its totality; we are caught flying blind, so to speak.[82] "Are the accelerated, energized and interconnected complexes we are living in able to do anything but a plunge forward? ... He who were able to discern between walking, drifting and plunging would have to be prophetically gifted. This is the state Heidegger hinted at when he made the remark that only a God can save us."[83] As Heidegger himself elaborates further during his famous interview with the German newspaper *Der Spiegel*: "The only possibility available to us is that by thinking and poetizing we prepare a readiness for the appearance of a god, or for the absence of a god in [our] decline."[84] Pointing at a previous, well-known "metamorphosis of the gods," Jean-Luc Nancy, a student of Jacques Derrida, states:

> We are in the situation the Romans were in during the 6th century after Christ: They knew that something was coming to an end—antiquity. Yet, the Christian Middle Ages were neither foreseeable nor conceivable. Just as much as we cannot imagine what may follow our current phase of upheaval. And this is exactly what creates so much confusion ...[85]

As we here have embedded the ongoing discussions of modernity, postmodernity, and "*posthistoire*"[86] within the broader context of Jung's speculation of an epochal turn, we also believe it is safe to say that he who experiences the objective psyche—whatever it reveals— will not fall prey to the assaults of philosophical deconstruction. In addition, from Jung's point of view, even amid the catastrophe-bearing turmoil of a paradoxical globalization and after the collapse of master narratives, we contemporaries are still left with opportunities and ways for experiencing the divine realm—new paths for mystical experiences, active imagination, dreams, and myth as modes of perception that can also be found in times of postmodern nihilism. To formulate this idea more clearly, Jung's "own myth" points back to late antiquity, and his psycho-historical excavations finally led him to a gnostic interpretation of the world, so that as a remedy for postmodern turbulences, it will be *gnosis* that represents the bridge toward what is to come. As Ernst Jünger put it: "We receive more life force than we can absorb for the time being, let alone manage: it is without specific qualities and originates out of the great depths that spread out into manifold phenomena—often just there, where it is not suspected by prognostics or utopianism. It can only be answered and contained from equal depths."[87] "Man lives in two worlds."[88]

Endnotes

This essay is dedicated to Dr. Maria Hippius-Gräfin Dürckheim (1909-2003; Existential-psychologische Bildungs- und Begegnungsstätte Todtmoos-Rütte, Black Forest, Germany) and Walter Schwery (1927-2016, Bern, Switzerland). It is a translated and slightly modified version of my German essay "Der Weg des Kommenden: Das Rote Buch und Jungs Ecclesia Spiritualis," in Thomas Arzt, ed., *Das Rote Buch: C.G. Jungs Reise zum "anderen Pol der Welt." Studienreihe zur Analytischen Psychologie,* Bd. 5 (Würzburg: Königshausen & Neumann, 2015), 13-38. Thanks also to Fabian Kanthak and Cita Lotz for the translation work and to Sonngard Doose for the inspirations.

1 Cited in C.G. Jung, *The Red Book: Liber Novus,* ed. Sonu Shamdasani, tr. John Peck, Mark Kyburz, and Sonu Shamdasani (New York, NY: W. W. Norton, 2009), 210.

2 Interview with Frank-Walter Steinmeier in the German newspaper *Handelsblatt* (09. 01. 2014).

3 Peter Sloterdijk, *Die schrecklichen Kinder der Neuzeit* (Berlin: Suhrkamp, 2014), 221.

4 Hartmut Rosa, *Beschleunigung. Die Veränderung der Zeitstrukturen in der Moderne* (Frankfurt/Main: Suhrkamp, 2005), 479.

5 Sloterdijk quotes Napoleon's mother, Laetitia Ramolino. See Peter Sloterdijk, *Die schrecklichen Kinder der Neuzeit,* 488.

6 Philipp Blom, *The Vertigo Years: Change and Culture in the West 1900-1914* (London: Orion Publishing Co., 2009).

7 Ibid., 2.

8 "Total Mobilization" is the english translation of an essay of Ernst Jünger, *Die Totale Mobilmachung* (1930). As a signature of modernity as well as "progress" Jünger describes the submission of all resources of modern society under *one* guiding principle, namely "work" and technology.

9 Heinz Bude, *Gesellschaft der Angst* (Hamburg: Verlag des Hamburger Instituts für Sozialforschung, 2014).

10 Joachim Radkau, *Das Zeitalter der Nervosität. Deutschland zwischen Bismarck und Hitler* (München: Propyläen, 1998).

11 Cited in Jung, *The Red Book,* 194.

12 "Gestell" is used by Martin Heidegger to describe what lies "behind" modern technology. Not only is the essence of technology represented by "Gestell," it decribes an all-encompassing view of technology and a mode of human existence. See Wikipedia on "Gestell".

13 My translation. See Hans Magnus Enzensberger, *Mittelmaß und Wahn: Gesammelte Zerstreuungen* (Frankfurt/Main: Suhrkamp, 1991), 264.

14 Jean-François Lyotard, *The Postmodern Condition: A Report on Knowledge* (Minneapolis: University of Minnesota Press, 1984).

15 Ibid., XXIV.

16 Rosa, *Beschleunigung*, 334.

17 Edward Edinger, *The Creation of Consciousness. Jung's Myth for Modern Man* (Toronto, Inner City Books, 1984), 9.

18 Ibid., 12.

19 "Yet if the last century has been called 'the Freudian century', there are reasons for thinking that this one could be Jung's. His time does seem to have come." *The Guardian* (01. 25. 2012). Also see Edward Edinger, *The Aion Lectures. Exploring the Self in C.G. Jung's Aion* (Toronto: Inner City Books, 1996), 192.

20 David Tacey, *The Darkening Spirit. Jung, Spirituality, Religion* (London/New York, NY: Routledge, 2013), 2.

21 Ibid., 130.

22 C.G. Jung, "The Spiritual Problem of Modern Man" (1933), in *CW*, vol. 10 (Princeton, NJ: Princeton University Press, 1964), par. 159.

23 Martin Heidegger, *Einführung in die Metaphysik*. Gesamtausgabe, Bd. 40 (Frankfurt/Main: Vittorio Klostermann, 1983), 41.

24 C.G. Jung, "Archetypes of the Collective Unconscious" (1954), in *CW*, vol. 9/I (Princeton, NJ: Princeton University Press, 1968), par. 50.

25 My translation. Ernst Jünger, *An der Zeitmauer*. Sämtliche Werke, Bd. 8 (Stuttgart: Klett-Cotta, 1981), 639.

26 See Tacey, *The Darkening Spirit*, 38f.

27 Richard Tarnas, *The Passion of the Western Mind: Understanding the Ideas that Have Shaped Our World View* (New York, NY: Random House, 1991), 440.

28 Jung, "The Spiritual Problem of Modern Man," *CW* 10, par. 175.

29 C.G. Jung, *Aion. Researches into the Phenomenology of the Self*, in *CW*, vol. 9/II (Princeton, NJ: Princeton University Press, 1968), par. 51.

30 Tacey, *The Darkening Spirit*, 62.

31 Jung, *The Red Book*, 232.

[32] Ibid.
[33] Ibid., 202.
[34] C.G. Jung, *Symbols of Transformation* (1952), in *CW*, vol. 5 (Princeton, NJ: Princeton University Press, 1967), Foreword to the Fourth Swiss Edition, XXIV.
[35] Cited in Jung, *The Red Book*, 210.
[36] Ann Conrad Lammers and Adrian Cunningham, eds., *The Jung-White Letters.* (London: Routledge, 2007), 117.
[37] Jung, *The Red Book*, 202.
[38] Ibid., 207.
[39] Wolfgang Giegerich, "*Liber Novus*, That is, The New Bible: A First Analysis of C.G. Jung's *Red Book*," *Spring: A Journal of Archetype and Culture* 83 (Spring 2010), 376.
[40] Jung, *The Red Book*, 207.
[41] Lance Owens, Stephan A. Hoeller, "Carl Gustav Jung and *The Red Book: Liber Novus*," in *Encyclopedia of Psychology and Religion* (New York/Heidelberg/Dordrecht/London: Springer Reference, 2014), 4.
[42] Jung, *The Red Book*, 229.
[43] Ibid., 232.
[44] Ibid., 231.
[45] Ibid., 232.
[46] Ibid., 233.
[47] Ibid., 229.
[48] Ibid., 242.
[49] Ibid., 230.
[50] Ibid., 254.
[51] Ibid., 202.
[52] Ibid., 279.
[53] Ibid., 281.
[54] Ibid., 354.
[55] Ibid., 299.
[56] Ibid., 354 n123.
[57] Ibid., 356.
[58] See Sanford L. Drob, *Reading the Red Book. An Interpretive Guide to C.G. Jung's Liber Novus* (New Orleans, LA: Spring Journal, 2012), 251.
[59] Jung, *The Red Book*, 245.
[60] Ibid., 356.
[61] Ibid., 248.

[62] Ibid., 314.

[63] Ibid., 210.

[64] Ibid., 231.

[65] Gerhard Adler, *C.G. Jung Letters*. Trans. by R. F. C. Hull. Vol. 2, 1951-1961 (Princeton, NJ: Princeton University Press, 1975), 590.

[66] Karlfried Graf Dürckheim, *Alltag als Übung* (Bern: Huber, 2012).

[67] *Hebrews* 10:31.

[68] C.G. Jung, *Memories, Dreams, Reflections*, ed. Aniela Jaffé (New York, NY: Vintage, 1963), 199.

[69] Quoted in Edinger, *The Aion Lectures*, 13.

[70] Lance S. Owens, "Jung and Aion: Time, Vision, and a Wayfaring Man," in *Psychological Perspectives: A Quarterly Journal of Jungian Thought* 54:3 (2011), S. 275.

[71] Ibid., 271.

[72] Capitaine, N., Wallace, P. T. and Chapront, J., "Expressions for IAU 2000 precession quantities," in *Astronomy & Astrophysics*, 2003, 412, 567-586. Also see https://en.wikipedia.org/wiki/Axial_precession (accessed July 17th, 2017).

[73] Adler, *C.G. Jung Letters*, Vol. 2, 1951-1961, 229.

[74] C.G. Jung, "The Undiscovered Self (Present and Future)" (1958), in *CW*, vol. 10 (Princeton, NJ: Princeton University Press, 1964), par. 585.

[75] C.G. Jung, *Answer to Job* (1952), in *CW*, vol. 11 (Princeton, NJ: Princeton University Press, 1969), pars. 692-696.

[76] Adler, *C.G. Jung Letters*, Vol. 2, 1951-1961, 436.

[77] Ibid., 136.

[78] Edinger, *The Creation of Consciousness. Jung's Myth for Modern Man*, 113. Elsewhere Edinger states: "Jung is the new Aion, he is the harbinger of the new aeon—what I call and what I think will in the future be called the Jungian aeon. ... If my reading of the symbolism is correct, the aeon of Aquarius will generate individual water carriers. The numinous reality of the psyche will no longer be carried by religious communities—the church, the synagogue or the mosque—but instead it will be carried by conscious individuals. This is the idea Jung puts forward in the notion of a continuing incarnation, the idea that individuals are to become incarnating vessels of the Holy Spirit on an ongoing basis." See Edinger, *The Aion Lectures*, 192. Russell A. Lockhart has a similar view on the coming age: "Is the 'Age of

Aquarius' this 'coming time'? Aquarius is pictured as a water bearer pouring water into a pool. I like to think of this as the image of the coming time when each and everyone of us brings to a common pool the water we have gathered from our unique and individual sources, from our encounters with the unconscious. By pooling together what we bring from these moments, by telling one another what we have experienced there, by acting on the hints we experience there ... we will, I trust, begin to create that song of welcome to the coming guest." See Russell A. Lockhart, *Psyche speaks. A Jungian Approach to Self and World* (Wilmette, Illinois: Chiron Publications, 1987), 79.

[79] Jung, *The Red Book*, 216.

[80] Tacey, *The Darkening Spirit*, 157f.

[81] Ibid. In *The Red Book*, chapter "The Three Prophecies," Jung speaks of 800 years: "How can I fathom what will happen during the next eight hundred years, up to the time when the One begins his rule? I am speaking only of what is to come." See Jung, *The Red Book*, 306 n236.

[82] Peter Sloterdijk, *Eurotaoismus. Zur Kritik der politischen Kinetik* (Frankfurt/Main: Suhrkamp, 1989), 26 and 298f.

[83] My translation. Peter Sloterdijk, *Die schrecklichen Kinder der Neuzeit*, 487f.

[84] My translation. Heidegger-Interview. *Der Spiegel*, No. 23, May 31st, 1976.

[85] My translation. Jean-Luc Nancy, DIE ZEIT, Nr. 12/2012, March 15th 2012.

[86] Besides the discussions about "modernity" and "postmodernity" that have been going on since World War II, there is a more radical school of thought (Arnold Gehlen, Francis Fukuyama, Jean Baudrillard etc.) proclaiming the "end of history"—in the "*posthistoire*" history has come to an end and within this phase of "cultural crystallization" no innovation is possible, indicating an overall cultural exhaustion. As Max Weber has already anticipated 1904 with his famous sentence: "No one knows who will live in this cage in the future, or whether at the end of this tremendous development entirely new prophets will arise, or there will be a great rebirth of old ideas and ideals, or, if neither, mechanized petrification, embellished with a sort of convulsive self-importance."

[87] My translation. Ernst Jünger, *Typus, Name, Gestalt*. Sämtliche Werke, Bd. 13 (Stuttgart: Klett-Cotta, 1981), 172.

[88] Jung, *The Red Book*, 264.

"The Way of What Is to Come":
Jung's Vision of the Aquarian Age

Liz Greene

When we speak of the new Aquarian type of person, we are actually referring to human beings through whom will be released ... the energies, the faith, the downflowing enthusiasm and revelations of the new Age ... These true 'Aquarians'... are mouthpieces for the new spirit, and many of them may almost be called born 'mediums' for the release of that spirit at the beginning of the new cycle.[1]

Dane Rudhyar

When the month of the Twins had ended, the men said to their shadows: 'You are I' ... Thus the two became one, and through this collision the formidable broke out, precisely that spring of consciousness that one calls culture and which lasted until the time of Christ. But the fish indicated the moment when what was united split, according to the eternal law of contrasts, into an underworld and upper-world ... But the separated cannot remain separated forever. It will be united again and the month of the fish will soon be over.[2]

C.G. Jung

The Idea of the "New Age"

In the last few decades, a considerable amount of scholarly literature has been dedicated to Jung's influence on so-called New Age beliefs and practices.[3] Olav Hammer, following Richard Noll, uses the term "Jungianism" to describe a form of "modern psycho-religion" based on the cultlike role assigned to Jung as a New Age guru.[4] Paul Heelas has identified Jung as one of three key figures in the development of

New Age thought, the other two being Helena Petrovna Blavatsky (1831-1891), founder of the Theosophical Society, and Georges Ivanovich Gurdjieff (1866-1949), whose spiritual system, referred to as the "Fourth Way," focuses on the development of higher states of consciousness.[5] Wouter Hanegraaff, also following Noll, views Jung as a "modern esotericist, who represents a crucial link between traditional ... esoteric worldviews and the New Age movement."[6]

There are certainly broad parallels between Jung's psychological models and those currents of "New Age" thought that emphasise the enlargement of consciousness in a dawning new epoch. This can be explained, in part, by the fact that both Jung and the late 19th-century occult revival, which provided the basis for many of the most potent New Age ideas, drew on the same pool of sources: Hermetic, Platonic, Neoplatonic, Gnostic, and Jewish esoteric speculations and practices, along with liberal dashes of Hindu and Buddhist thought. Many New Age religious approaches had thus already been fully formed by the end of the 19th century. Roderick Main, in a paper on the relationship between Jung's ideas and New Age thought, comments:

> It is possible to construe that Jungian psychology, even as originally expounded by Jung, may itself have been influenced by New Age thinking. ... While Jung certainly influenced the New Age movement, he may himself have been influenced by New Age religion or was even one of its representatives.[7]

The idea of the New Age as an astrologically defined epoch—assumed, in modern times, to be the incoming "Aquarian Age"—began to take shape in the late 18th century, crystallised in the 19th, and is still popular today. The American astrologer Dane Rudhyar (1895-1985) believed that the Aquarian Age would commence in 2060, although he thought that its "seed period" had begun between 1844-46.[8] The historian Wouter Hanegraaff, in his important work, *New Age Religion and Western Culture*, refers to the New Age *in sensu strictu*: those currents of ideas which focus on the expectation of an imminent Aquarian Age and an accompanying radical shift in consciousness reflecting the meaning of the astrological constellation. Hanegraaff then discusses the New Age *in sensu lato*: an innovative movement "in a general sense" which does not necessarily bear a specifically astrological connotation.[9]

This is a useful approach through which to explore many contemporary spiritualities. But it is difficult to find agreement among authors about just what constitutes New Age in the broad sense. Many of the ideas that form the basis of New Age thought are very ancient and have not been significantly altered by another exceedingly ambiguous term, "modernity." They might equally be viewed as "Old Age," as they reflect certain consistent cosmological and anthropological themes that possess great agency and immense cultural adaptability, while maintaining a structural integrity for more than two millennia. These ideas have not necessarily been "secularised" in the sense that their present-day adherents have become "irreligious," nor in the sense that they eschew a specific organised form of religion. Jung viewed such ideas as archetypal: They belong to the "spirit of the depths," as he called it in *The Red Book*, and not, as might be assumed, the "spirit of this time."

New Age ideas—particularly the conviction that self-awareness and God-awareness are indistinguishable, and that God can be found within—are assumed by some scholars to be unique to "modern" spiritualities, in which category Jung's own ideas are often included. This assumption is not supported by textual evidence. The equation of "god-knowledge" with "self-knowledge" is clearly expressed in late antique Hermetic, Neoplatonic, Gnostic, and Jewish esoteric literature.[10] In this sense, Hanegraaff's assumption of the modernity of New Age thought may be misleading, creating sharp artificial divisions between historical periods, cultures, and spheres of human expression where a more nuanced perspective might be more helpful. But however problematic the definitions of New Age *in sensu lato* might be, Jung's thinking about the incoming New Age clearly belongs in the category Hanegraaff calls *in sensu strictu*; for it seems that Jung believed wholeheartedly that a new epoch reflecting the symbolism of the constellation of Aquarius was about to dawn and that his psychology might make a significant contribution to the conflicts inevitably arising in the face of such a profound shift in the collective psyche.

The God in the Egg

In 1951, following two heart attacks, Jung wrote a work called *Aion*.[11] For the frontispiece, he chose a second-century C.E. Roman sculpture of the Mithraic god known to scholars variously as Aion, Aeon, Kronos, Chronos, or Zervan:[12] a winged, lion-headed being with a human body, encircled by a serpent and standing on, or emerging from, an egg. By the time he wrote *Aion*, Jung had been familiar with Mithraic beliefs and iconography for at least 40 years. While he worked on *The Red Book*, Jung relied in large part on Albrecht Dieterich's German and G.R.S. Mead's English translations of a late antique magical text known as the *Mithras Liturgy*.[13] He also acquired two books on Mithraism by the Belgian religious historian Franz Cumont: *Die Mysterien des Mithra* and the earlier, much lengthier *Textes et monuments figurés relatifs aux mystères de Mythra*.[14] Jung referred to Cumont as "the foremost authority on the Mithraic cult."[15] But Cumont rejected the central importance of astrology in Roman Mithraic worship, viewing its astrological iconography as properly belonging to the earlier, "Chaldaean" form of the cult, and blaming this older "Oriental" religious current for infecting Western beliefs with astrology's "long train of errors and terrors."[16] It seems that Jung did not agree.

In recent years, Roger Beck and David Ulansey have challenged Cumont's assumptions, focusing specifically on the astrological foundations of Roman Mithraism.[17] Mithraic archaeological finds have provided the chief source for these examinations; the cult's initiations were a well-kept secret, and no body of literature exists produced directly by its members. Only allusions have survived, often based on hearsay, in the writings of late antique authors such as Origen and Porphyry.[18] But numerous images of Aion have survived the centuries, discovered in Roman Mithraea throughout Europe. They typically present the same figure Jung used as his frontispiece: a winged, lion-headed male figure, usually holding a staff, enveloped in the coils of a serpent, and frequently—although not invariably—surrounded by, or bearing on his body, the signs of the zodiac.[19]

The Greek word *aionos* has a number of different meanings and usages, all of which are relevant to Jung's understanding of the imminent collective psychic change he envisioned in *The Red Book*.[20] Homer and Herodotus used the word to describe the lifetime of an individual.[21] Euripides, in common with some Hermetic treatises, personified Aion as a divine being, calling him the "child of time" who "brings many things to pass."[22] Aeschylus and Demosthenes used the word to describe both an epoch and a generation.[23] Sophocles understood it as one's destiny or lot, akin to the idea of *moira* or Fate.[24] Hesiod used it to define an age or era, such as the Age of Gold or the Age of Iron.[25] Paul used it to refer to the present world, as well as an era or epoch.[26] In Plato's *Timaeus*, *aionos* constitutes eternity, while *chronos* expresses *aionos* temporally through the movements of the heavenly bodies:

> Now the nature of the ideal being was eternal, but to bestow this attribute in its fullness upon a creature was impossible. Wherefore he resolved to have a moving image of eternity [αιονοσ], and when he set in order the heaven, he made this image eternal but moving according to number, while eternity itself rests in unity; and this image we call time [χηρονοσ].[27]

Jung seems to have favoured the idea of an aion as both an astrological epoch—lasting roughly 2,165 years, or one-twelfth of what he believed to be the great "Platonic Year" of 26,000 years—and a god-image, emerging out of the human religious imagination and embodying the specific qualities of that epoch. These astrological epochs are reflected by the astronomical phenomenon of the precession of the equinoxes: the gradual backward movement of the point of the spring equinox (the moment each year when the Sun enters the zodiacal sign of Aries) through the stars of the twelve zodiacal constellations.[28]

The Gnostic text *Pistis Sophia*, with which Jung was familiar in Mead's English translation, describes the aions as both celestial powers ruling over specific regions of the cosmos and the regions themselves: zodiacal constellations with doorways or gates through which the redeemer-god passes as he accomplishes his task of salvation.[29] In contrast, the *Mithras Liturgy* presents Aion, not as a zodiacal constellation, a planetary archon, or an epoch of time, but as a fiery primal divinity, also called Helios-Mithras: as Jung understood it, an image of the libido, or life force.[30] A vision of this eternal being is the goal of the ritual, leading to the temporary "immortalisation" of the initiate.[31]

> For I am to behold today with Deathless Eyes—I, mortal,
> born of mortal womb, but [now] made better by the Might
> of Mighty Power, yea, by the Incorruptible Right Hand—
> [I am to see today] by virtue of the Deathless Spirit the
> Deathless Aeon [αθανατον Αιωνα], the master of the
> Diadems of Fire.[32]

Later in the ritual, prayers are offered to the "seven Fates of heaven," the planetary divinities governing *Heimarmene*, or astral fate. An invocation is then addressed to Aion that names his primary attributes and functions:

> Light-giver [and] Fire-sower; Fire-loosener, whose Life is
> in the Light; Fire-whirler, who sett'st the Light in Motion;
> Thou Thunder-rouser; O Thou Light-glory, Light-in-
> creaser; Controller of the Light Empyrean; O Thou
> Star-tamer![33]

Aion the "star-tamer" emanates and controls the heavenly spheres, and the vision vouchsafed the initiate in the *Mithras Liturgy* allows an identification with divinity that, at least for a time, breaks the power of *Heimarmene*.[34] Jung associated this freedom from the bonds of astral compulsion with the integrating potency of a direct experience of the self; but like the *Liturgy*, he stipulated no guarantee of the permanence of the state. A comparison of Aion in the *Liturgy* with the words of the giant Izdubar in *The Red Book*, who rises out of a fiery egg revealed as the Sun-god, suggests how profoundly the *Mithras Liturgy* affected Jung's understanding of solar power as the symbol of both a divine cosmocrator and a central individual self.

> Streams of fire broke from my radiating body –
> I surged through the blazing flames –
> I swam in a sea that wrapped me in living fires –
> Full of light, full of longing, full of eternity –
> I was ancient and perpetually renewing myself ...
> I am the sun.[35]

Jung's description of Aion included the name Kronos (Saturn), but
he elided it with *chronos* (time) and emphasised the leonine attributes
of the figure:

> We come across in the Mithraic religion, a strange God of
> Time, Aion, called Kronos or Deus Leontocephalus,
> because his stereotyped representation is a lion-headed
> man, who, standing in a rigid attitude, is encoiled by a
> snake. ... In addition to that, the figure sometimes bears
> the Zodiac on his body. ... He is a symbol of time, most
> interestingly composed from libido-symbols. The lion, the
> zodiac sign of the greatest summer heat, is the symbol of
> the most mighty desire.[36]

Paradoxically, Jung associated this "Deus Leontocephalus" not only
with the Sun, but also with the Gnostic archon Ialdabaoth and the
archon's planet, Saturn.[37] Aion was many things for Jung: a fiery
libido-symbol embracing all opposites; a symbol of time expressed
through the solar pathway of the zodiacal round; and a personification of the planetary deity Saturn-Kronos, his own horoscopic
ruler, as he was born with the Saturn-ruled sign Aquarius rising in
the east. Aion may thus also be understood as the universal or
collective aspect of Jung's "personal daimon" Philemon, the "Master
of the House" or ruler of the horoscope in Hellenistic astrology.[38] And
Aion, for Jung, also embodied an astrological age—that of Aquarius—
which combines, in its imagery and meaning, the human form of the
Water-bearer with its opposite constellation of Leo, the Lion. William
Butler Yeats, preoccupied with the same zodiacal polarity, described
his own vision of the approaching New Age in his poem, *The Second
Coming*, written just after the Armageddon of the Great War, with a

prophetic pessimism not unlike Jung's own: a terrifying being with a lion's body and the head of a man, that "slouches toward Bethlehem to be born" in the midst of chaos and the disintegration of social order.[39]

In *The Red Book*, Jung described his own transformation into a leontocephalic deity encircled by a serpent, with "outstretched arms like someone crucified."[40] Later, he explicitly related this vision to the Mithraic iconography of Aion:[41]

> The animal face which I felt mine transformed into was the famous [Deus] Leontocephalus of the Mithraic mysteries. It is the figure which is represented with a snake coiled around the man, the snake's head resting on the man's head, and the face of the man that of the lion.[42]

This allusion suggests a deeply personal significance underlying Jung's choice of the frontispiece for *Aion*. The vision in *The Red Book*, like that of the *Mithras Liturgy*, describes a transient, although profoundly transformative, inner experience resulting in an enlarged consciousness and, in Jung's terminology, a fuller integration of the personality. In Jung's natal horoscope, as he was well aware, the opposites of Aquarius and Leo dominate. Aquarius was rising at the moment of Jung's birth, and the Sun was placed in Leo. It is not surprising that he felt the symbolism of Aion was relevant, not only for the collective psyche, but for his own.

The Age of Aquarius

The first image on the first page of *The Red Book* incorporates the letter D, illuminated in the style of a medieval German manuscript, and introduces the opening sentence of the work: *Der Weg des Kommenden* ("The Way of What Is to Come").[43] An astrological "strip" can be seen at the top of the image; it is painted in a blue lighter than that of the sky with its heavenly bodies.[44] Along this strip the zodiacal constellations, represented by their traditional glyphs, run in counterclockwise order, beginning with Cancer at the far left, followed by Gemini, Taurus, Aries, and Pisces, and concluding with Aquarius at the far right. A large four-rayed star is placed at the precise meeting point between the constellation represented by the glyph of Pisces and the constellation represented by the glyph of Aquarius. The star evidently represents the Sun at the moment of the annual spring equinox. This equinoctial point, slowly creeping backward through the constellations over the centuries, has, according to Jung, now reached the end of the constellation of Pisces and is about to enter its 2,165-year journey through the constellation of Aquarius. Jung referred to this astronomical event as the new Aion, the "Way of What Is to Come." He later called it "καιρος—the right time—for a 'metamorphosis of the gods.'"[45]

The major theme of the book *Aion* is the shift in human consciousness and a simultaneous shift in the god-image, reflected in the ending of the Piscean Aion. In Jung's view, Pisces is associated with the Christian symbols of Jesus and Satan as the two Fish, and the advent of the Aquarian Aion is associated with a new symbol: humanity as the Water-bearer. In *The Red Book*, the god who presides over this new Aion is Phanes, the ancient Orphic androgynous primal deity who reconciles all opposites. Lance Owens has suggested that it is necessary to cross-reference *Aion* with *The Red Book* in order to understand both: *Aion* is Jung's effort, late in life, to provide a rational exegesis of the revelations of *The Red Book*, and the two works are "fundamentally wed."[46] *Aion* appears to offer a more impersonal involvement with astrology than Jung's preoccupation with his own horoscope, a pursuit evident from the number of natal and progressed chart interpretations found in his private archives and provided for him by astrological practitioners such as John Thorburn and Liliane Frey at his request.[47] But Jung's approach to collective cycles incorporated the same psychological models as his perception of psychic dynamics in the individual: archetypes, typologies, complexes, and astrological significators as symbols of the qualities of time. Jung believed that each of the great shifts represented by a new astrological Aion is reflected in the imagery of the presiding zodiacal constellation and its planetary ruler:

Apparently they are changes in the constellations of psychic dominants, of the archetypes, or 'gods' as they used to be called, which bring about, or accompany, long-lasting transformations of the collective psyche. This transformation started in the historical era and left its traces first in the passing of the aeon of Taurus into that of Aries, and then of Aries into Pisces, whose beginning coincides with the rise of Christianity. We are now nearing that great change which may be expected when the spring-point enters Aquarius.[48]

While *Aion* discusses the historical nature of these transformations as they are expressed in the religious representations of the Piscean era, *The Red Book* reveals Jung's understanding of his own role in the imminent shift into Aquarius, in accordance with his conviction that every individual is part of the collective and that the future of the collective depends on the consciousness of each individual.[49]

There has been considerable speculation as to where Jung acquired the idea of a New Age in relation to the movement of the vernal equinoctial point. This seems to be particularly important because Jung has been credited with being the first person in modern times to disseminate the idea that the long-anticipated New Age would be Aquarian. The idea of an Aquarian Age is rooted in the late 18th-century Enlightenment, when a number of scholarly works were produced that focused on the Christian figure of Jesus as one of a long line of solar deities.[50] According to Nicholas Campion, the ideas presented in these works can be divided into three distinct categories. First was the attempt to establish a common origin for religions. Second came the theory that this shared origin lay in the worship of the celestial bodies, especially the sun. Third was the use of the precession of the equinoxes to establish the dating of the Indian sacred texts known as the Vedas.[51] Although none of the authors of these 18th-century works provided the kind of interpretations offered by astrologers contemporary with Jung, all of them emphasised the importance of the precessional cycle in the historical development of religious images and ideas.

In 1775, the French astronomer and mathematician Jean Sylvain Bailly (1736-1793) proposed an astral origin for all religious forms.[52] Bailly was followed by a French lawyer and professor of rhetoric, Charles François Dupuis (1742-1809), who, in his *Origine de tous les cultes*, argued that all religions sprang from sun worship and that Christianity was simply another form of solar myth.[53] Dupuis, like Jung himself over a century later, noted the parallels between the astrological constellation of Virgo and the mother of the solar messiah. Describing the engraving he commissioned for the frontispiece of his book, Dupuis noted: "A woman holding a child, crowned with stars, standing on a serpent, called the celestial Virgin. ... She has been successively Isis, Themis, Ceres, Erigone, the mother of Christ."[54]

Dupuis' frontispiece engraving combines the idea of a universal solar religion with religious themes related to the precession of the equinoxes. At the upper left corner, in the heavens, is a strip displaying the images of the zodiacal constellations of Aries (the Ram) and Taurus (the Bull), with the Sun shining on the midpoint between them. The vernal equinoctial point is thus crossing from Taurus to Aries, reflected in the shift from various Taurean religious forms represented in the engraving (Mithras slaying the cosmic bull, the Egyptian Apis-bull, the Golden Calf) to those of Aries (Zeus enthroned as the god of heaven, the Israelite High Priest before the Ark of the Covenant). At the top centre of the frontispiece are the symbols of the Christian dispensation: the "Celestial Virgin" crowned with stars, and the Christ-child as the newborn Sun. Although the engraving focuses primarily on the shift from Taurus to Aries rather than from Pisces to Aquarius, there is a striking similarity between Dupuis' illustration of the Sun at the midpoint between the constellations of Taurus and Aries and Jung's four-pointed solar star at the midpoint between the constellations of Pisces and Aquarius on the opening page of *The Red Book*. Jung never mentioned Dupuis in his published work, nor is a copy of *Origines* listed in his library catalog. But the similarity between the images of equinoctial precession is so close that it is probable that he was familiar with Dupuis' book.

Speculations on a link between the precession of the vernal equinoctial point and the changing of religious forms continued throughout the late 18th and 19th centuries. François-Henri-Stanislas de l'Aulnaye (1739-1830), who authored two books on Freemasonry, produced a text in 1791 called *L'histoire générale et particulière des religions et du cultes*.[55] This work was the first to consider the implications of the precession of the vernal equinoctial point into Aquarius, which de l'Aulnaye believed had taken place in 1726.[56] Godfrey Higgins (1772-1833), a religious historian whose work exercised a major influence on H.P. Blavatsky,[57] declared in his *Anacalypsis*, published in 1836, that the equinoctial shift from Taurus into Aries was the time when "the slain lamb" replaced "the slain bull."[58] In the late 19th century, Gerald Massey (1828-1907), an English poet and self-educated Egyptologist, offered a detailed scheme of the evolution of religious forms according to the precession of the equinoxes through the zodiacal constellations.[59] It is in one of Massey's papers, "The Historical Jesus and the Mythical Christ," privately published in 1887, that the first reference to the Age of Aquarius appears in the English language:[60]

> The foundations of a new heaven were laid in the sign of the Ram, 2410 BC.; and again, when the Equinox entered the sign of the Fishes, 255 BC. Prophecy that will be *again* fulfilled when the Equinox enters the sign of the Water-man about the end of this [nineteenth] century.[61]

All of these authors—Dupuis, Delaunaye, Higgins, and Massey—utilised mythic images to illustrate vast collective changes in religious forms and perceptions, and linked the myths to particular zodiacal constellations in the cycle of precession. Although Jung did not cite any of their writings in his own published work, nevertheless the same ideas are central to both *Aion* and *The Red Book*. That no one seems to have agreed on the date for the start of the new Aquarian Aion is not surprising. As Jung himself stated: "The delimitation of the constellations is known to be somewhat arbitrary."[62]

Ancient Sources for the New Age

Texts explicitly relating the dawning of a New Age to the precession of the equinoxes may only have begun in the modern era. But Jung believed that earlier sources supported his belief that a new astrological Aion was about to begin. His quest for historical evidence of the idea of the incoming Aquarian Age sometimes led him to assume connections that a 21st-century scholar, nervous of speculation of a "universalist" kind, might well avoid. But Jung's intuitive leaps seem to have been valid more often than they were misguided, even when his historical data lacked precision. An example of Jung's search to find validation for the Aquarian Age in alchemical texts is provided by the 16th-century alchemist and physician Heinrich Khunrath (1560-1605),[63] who declared that an "age of Saturn" would begin at some unspecified point in the not-too-distant future and that it would usher in a time when alchemical secrets would become available to everyone:

> The age of Saturn is not yet, in which everything that is private shall become public property: for one does not yet take and use that which is well meant and well done in the same spirit.[64]

Khunrath does not mention either the precession of the equinoxes or the zodiacal constellation of Aquarius anywhere in his text. Nor does the idea appear in any other alchemical literature of the early modern period, steeped in astrology though it was. But Jung believed that Khunrath was referring to the Age of Aquarius because this constellation is traditionally ruled by Saturn. In a lecture given at the ETH Zurich in 1940, Jung cited Khunrath's statement, and then commented:

> Khunrath means that the age of Saturn has not yet dawned. ... Obviously the question is: what does Khunrath mean by the age of Saturn? The old alchemists were of course also astrologers, and thought in an astrological way. Saturn is the ruler of the sign of Aquarius, and it is quite possible that Khunrath meant the coming age, the age of Aquarius, the water carrier, which is almost due now. It is conceivable that he thought mankind would be changed by that time, and would be able to understand the alchemists' mystery.[65]

Jung found in this influential alchemist's work what he perceived as evidence that the Age of Aquarius would be concerned with revelations of an esoteric and psychological nature, "secrets" that had either been lost or had never been known, and whose emergence into collective consciousness would result in an important transformation in human self-awareness. Despite his pessimism about the capacity for global self-destruction inherent in the interiorsation of the god-archetype, Jung was guardedly optimistic about the psychological potential of the New Age.

In Gnostic literature, Jung may also have found similar "evidence" of a belief in precession as a herald of great religious changes—although here, as in Khunrath's writings, there are no explicit references about the astrological aions in relation to the precession of the equinoctial point. The Gnostic text known as *Trimorphic Protennoia* speaks of a great disruption in the domains of the archons and their powers. Horace Jeffery Hodges, in a paper discussing the Gnostic preoccupation with *Heimarmene*, suggests that this prophecy of great change in the celestial realms reflects the Gnostics' knowledge of the moving of the vernal equinoctial point from the constellation of Aries into the constellation of Pisces.[66] Since precession had already been recognised by 130 B.C.E., astrologically inclined Gnostics of the first centuries C.E. might have been aware of it, although there is no surviving textual evidence that they connected it with either the "Platonic Year" or the astrological aions. However, even if *Trimorphic Protennoia* really does refer to precession, Jung would not have known about it in the early decades of the 20th century, as the only extant copy of the treatise was found at Nag Hammadi in 1945. But two other Gnostic texts, to which Jung did have access, concern themselves with a great "disturbance" in the heavenly realms. The *Apocryphon of John*, as described by the second-century Christian heresiolgist Irenaeus,[67] speaks of the breaking of the chains of astral fate by the advent of the Redeemer:

He [Christ] descended through the seven heavens ... and gradually emptied them of their power.[68]

Pistis Sophia also provides descriptions of a great "disturbance" in the heavens. But like the *Apocryphon of John*, there is no explicit reference to equinoctial precession in the text.

David Ulansey has argued that the precession of the equinoxes provided the basis for the central image of the Mithraic mysteries: the Tauroctony, or slaying of the cosmic bull.[69] But Ulansey's work was not published until 1989, twenty-eight years after Jung's death. However, even before his break with Freud, Jung had linked the symbolism of the bull in the Mithraic mysteries with the polarity of Taurus and its opposite constellation, Scorpio, describing them as "sexuality destroying itself" in the form of "active libido," and "resistant (incestuous) libido."[70] By the time he published *Psychology of the Unconscious* (*Wandlungen und Symbole der Libido*) in 1912,[71] Jung was well aware of the movement of the equinoctial point through the constellations:

> Taurus and Scorpio are equinoctial signs, which clearly indicate that the sacrificial scene [the Tauroctony] refers primarily to the Sun cycle ... Taurus and Scorpio are the equinoctial signs for the period from 4300 to 2150 B.C. These signs, long since superseded, were retained even in the Christian era.[72]

By 1912, Jung had thus already begun to arrive at certain insights regarding the precession of the equinoxes in relation to the significance of Mithraic iconography. But the scholarly literature on Mithraism available to him at the time—primarily the works of Cumont and Richard Reitzenstein,[73] and Dieterich's translation of the *Mithras Liturgy*—did not discuss precession. Nor did Mead in his own exegesis of Mithraism. Nevertheless, Jung seems to have been convinced that Taurus and Scorpio—the astrological aions he believed to have governed the period from 4300 to 2150 B.C.E.— were, although "long since superseded," still relevant as potent symbols of generation and regeneration even in the Piscean era, when the Roman cult of Mithras first arose.

The so-called "Platonic Year" of 26,000 years was never described by Plato, as precession had not been discovered in his time. Plato defined the "perfect year" as the return of the celestial bodies and the diurnal rotation of the fixed stars to their original positions at the moment of creation.[74] The Roman astrologer Julius Firmicus Maternus, echoing Plato, discussed a great cycle of 300,000 years, after which the heavenly bodies will return to those positions that they held when the world was first created.[75] Firmicus Maternus seems to have combined Plato's "perfect year" with the Stoic belief that the world undergoes successive conflagrations of fire and water, after which it is regenerated. But the Stoics did not describe any transformations of consciousness, as Jung did—only a precise replication of what had gone before.[76] Various other authors of antiquity offered various other lengths for the Great Year, ranging from 15,000 years to 2,484 years. But none of these speculations was based on the movement of the vernal equinoctial point through the constellations.[77] Although Jung was familiar with Firmicus Maternus' work as well as that of many other ancient authors, it was in modern astrological, Theosophical, and occult literature that he found inspiration for his own highly individual interpretation of the Aquarian Aion.

New Sources for the New Age

Jung's unique understanding of the meaning of Aquarius as the constellation of the incoming Aion is not traceable to any ancient or medieval source. His chief perception of the Aquarian Aion rested on the idea of the union of the opposites, the interiorisation of the god-image, and the struggle to recognise and reconcile good and evil as dimensions of the human psyche.

> We now have a new symbol in place of the [Piscean] fish: a psychological concept of human wholeness.[78]

In a letter to Walter Robert Corti, written in 1929, Jung prophesied a time of confusion preceding the new consciousness:

> We live in the age of the decline of Christianity, when the metaphysical premises of morality are collapsing. ... That causes reactions in the unconscious, restlessness and longing for the fulfilment of the times. ... When the confusion is at its height a new revelation comes, i.e. at the beginning of the fourth month of world history.[79]

The "fourth month of world history" is the Aion of Aquarius; "world history" in Jung's context began with recorded history in the Aion of Taurus, which Jung believed had occurred between 4300 and 2150 B.C.E. The imminent collective transformation will, in Jung's view, require a long and potentially dangerous process of integration, as it must occur in each individual. *The Red Book*, with its opening image of the movement of the equinoctial point into Aquarius and its frequent references to Phanes-Abraxas, the androgynous, dark-light god of the new aion, might be understood as a highly personal narrative of precisely that integrative process within Jung himself. Jung's interest in Nietzsche's work is likely to have contributed to the idea that the celestial Water-bearer—one of only three zodiacal images bearing a human form[80]—might be a symbol of the *Übermensch*, the "Beyond-Man" who transcends the opposites. Nietzsche's conviction that humanity was progressing toward a goal that lay "beyond good and evil" hints at the idea of the fully individuated human being whom Jung hoped would emerge in the new Aion.[81] But Nietzsche never associated his *Übermensch* with Aquarius.

An obvious modern source for Jung's expectations of a transformation of consciousness based on the precession of the equinoxes might seem to be the Theosophists, who certainly promulgated the idea of an imminent New Age. Blavatsky was familiar with authors such as Higgins and Massey. But she did not equate her New Age with the entry of the vernal equinoctial point into the constellation of Aquarius, preferring to use what she referred to as "the Hindu idea of cosmogony" (the concept of the Yugas) combined with certain fixed stars in relation to the equinoctial point.[82] According to Blavatsky, twelve transformations of the world will occur, following a partial destruction by water or fire (a lift from the Stoics) and the generation of a new world with a new twelvefold cycle. She identified this idea as "the true Sabaean astrological doctrine," which describes these twelve transformations as reflections of the twelve zodiacal constellations.[83] But this approach does not involve precession, and the twelve transformations do not comprise a precessional cycle of 26,000 years; they comprise the entire history of the planet over many millions of years.

In an article on the history of the idea of the New Age, Shepherd Simpson points out that Jung, whom he credits with the first promulgation of the idea of an "Aquarian Age" in modern times, could not have gotten the idea from Blavatsky.[84] The German esotericist Rudolf Steiner, whose Anthroposophical Society rejected the Eastern inclinations of the Theosophists but retained many of their ideas, likewise subscribed to the idea of a New Age and referred to it as the "Age of Christ's Second Coming." But this New Age, which, in Steiner's view, began in 1899, is not Aquarian.

> There is much talk about periods of transition. We are indeed living just at the time when the Dark Age has run its course and a new epoch is just beginning, in which human beings will slowly and gradually develop new faculties. ...What is beginning at this time will slowly prepare humanity for new soul faculties.[85]

These "new soul faculties" do indeed belong to the Aquarian Age, but they are only in preparation. According to Steiner's idiosyncratic reckoning, the Age of Aquarius will not begin until 3573, and the world at present is still living in the Piscean Age, which began in 1413.[86] Steiner wrote extensively about the problem of evil; like Jung, he believed evil to be a reality rather than a mere "deprivation of good," and, also like Jung, he was fascinated with but also repelled by Nietzsche's ideas.[87] Steiner also understood the necessity for humans taking responsibility for evil:

> Until now, the gods have taken care of human beings. Now, though, in this fifth post-Atlantean epoch, our destiny, our power for good and evil, will increasingly be handed over to us ourselves. It is therefore necessary to know what good and evil mean, and to recognize them in the world.[88]

But Steiner was much closer to Gnostic perceptions than Jung was and understood evil to belong to the incarnate world and the dark spiritual potencies (Lucifer and Ahriman) who, like the Gnostic archons, work to inflame the innate selfishness and destructiveness of the human being. Nor did Steiner associate the integration of good and evil with an imminent Aquarian Age. Although Jung was well acquainted with Steiner's work, Steiner was no more likely a source for Jung's understanding of the new Aion than Blavatsky was.

In 1906, Mead offered his own version of the New Age:

> I too await the dawn of that New Age, but I doubt that the Gnosis of the New Age will be new. Certainly it will be set forth in new forms, for the forms can be infinite. ... Indeed, if I believe rightly, the very essence of the Gnosis is the faith that man can transcend the limits of the duality that makes him man, and become a consciously divine being.[89]

This idea of a resolution of the problem of duality is much closer to Jung's formulation, and Mead may have contributed important ideas to Jung's vision of "The Way of What Is to Come." In *Aion*, Jung elaborated on Mead's description in a psychological context:

> The approach of the next Platonic month, namely Aquarius, will constellate the problem of the union of opposites. It will then no longer be possible to write off evil as the mere privation of good; its real existence will have to be recognized. This problem can be solved neither by philosophy, nor by economics, nor by politics, but only by the individual human being, via his experience of the living spirit.[90]

Jung's view of the incoming new Aion was full of foreboding and bears little resemblance to the sentimentalised presentations of the "Age of Aquarius" that emerged during the 1960s, exemplified by Broadway's first "concept" musical, *Hair*, in which the dawning New Age will be one of "harmony and understanding, sympathy and trust abounding."[91] The romantic idealism of these lyrics and their cultural context belong to a more optimistic and less cynical era. It is not surprising that Jung—who, in 1913, a year before the outbreak of the Great War, experienced a terrifying vision of "rivers of blood" covering the whole of northern Europe[92]—initially anticipated the opening of the new Aion as a mortal struggle requiring recognition of the "real existence" of evil. But although Mead referred to the "cycles of the Aeon,"[93] he did not link these cycles with the precession of the equinoxes in his published work. The New Age, whatever it might be, was apparently not, for Mead, an Aquarian Age. While Jung turned to Mead's work for insights into many of the texts of late antiquity, it seems he looked elsewhere for ideas about the meaning of the Water-bearer.

Two much likelier sources for Jung's ideas about the Age of Aquarius were the two Theosophically inclined astrologers who provided Jung with much of his knowledge of astrology: Alan Leo and Max Heindel.[94] Leo embraced Blavatsky's idea that humanity was at the midpoint of its millennia-old evolutionary cycle. But as an astrologer he could not ignore the significance of the precession of the equinoxes, and he directly associated the New Age with the constellation of Aquarius. In *Esoteric Astrology*, first published in 1913—the year that Jung began work on the *Red Book*—Leo declared:

> I am actuated by the primary motive of expressing what I believe to be the true Astrology, for the New Era that is now dawning upon the world.[95]

There is no mention of Aquarius in this statement. But two years earlier, Leo had declared explicitly that he believed the Age of Aquarius would begin on 21 March, 1928.[96] Leo did his best to reconcile Blavatsky's idea of the Hindu Yugas with precession, but his conclusions were, in the end, closer to Jung's:

> The constellation of Taurus was in the first sign of the zodiac [i.e., Aries] at the beginning of the Kali Yuga, and consequently the Equinoctial point fell therein. At this time, also, Leo was in the summer solstice, Scorpio in the autumnal equinox, and Aquarius in the winter solstice; and these facts form the astronomical key to half the religious mysteries of the world—the Christian scheme included.[97]

In Leo's view, the great cycle of precession is concerned with spiritual evolution, and the dawning Aquarian Age will mark the turning point of the cycle: the beginning of humanity's slow ascent back to the realm of pure spirit.[98] Although Jung used psychological models and wrote about wholeness and the integration of opposites rather than a return to a perfected world of pure spirit, it seems that, in principle, he agreed.

Leo described the Aquarian Age in general terms. Max Heindel was more specific. His statement about the purpose of his Rosicrucian Fellowship, made in 1911, emphasises the Aquarian character of the New Age:

> It [the Rosicrucian Fellowship] is the herald of the Aqua-
> rian Age, when the Sun by its precessional passage through
> the constellation Aquarius, will bring out all the intellectual
> and spiritual potencies in man which are symbolized by
> that sign.[99]

These burgeoning "intellectual and spiritual potencies" did not, for Heindel, involve the psychological problem of the integration of good and evil. In *The Rosicrucian Cosmo-Conception*, published in 1909, Heindel provided a detailed explanation of the precession of the equinoxes, calling the entire cycle a "World-year."[100] In accord with the general tendency to disagree about when the New Age would commence, Heindel declared that the Age of Aquarius would not begin for "a few hundred years."[101]

Heindel's *The Message of the Stars* may have been more useful to Jung, as it describes the astrological ages in relation to the polarity of each zodiacal constellation with its opposite. Heindel's view that the Age of Aquarius contains the attributes of Leo, the opposing constellation, must have been of considerable interest to Jung, who was inclined to view the workings of astrology, as well as human psychology, as a dynamic tension between opposites. Heindel had presented this theme in 1906, in *Message of the Stars*:

> There are two sets of three pairs of signs, the first being
> Cancer and Capricorn, Gemini and Sagittarius, Taurus and

Scorpio. In these pairs of signs we may read the history of human evolution and religion. ... This is also divisible into three distinct periods, namely: THE ARYAN AGE, from Moses to Christ, which comes under Aries-Libra;[102] the PISCEAN AGE, which takes in the last two thousand years under Pisces-Virgo Catholicism; and the two thousand years which are ahead of us, called the AQUARIAN AGE, where the signs Aquarius and Leo will be illuminated and vivified by the solar precession.[103]

Heindel also discussed the religious symbolism of the astrological ages:

In the New Testament we find another animal, the Fish, attaining great prominence, and the apostles were called to be 'Fishers of Men,' for then the sun by precession was nearing the cusp of Pisces, the Fishes, and Christ spoke of the time when the Son of Man (Aquarius) shall come. ... A new ideal will be found in the Lion of Judah, Leo. Courage of conviction, strength of character and kindred virtues will then make man truly the King of Creation.[104]

Heindel's "Son of Man," with his Leonine "courage" and "strength," abounds with echoes of Nietzsche's *Übermensch*. Jung, like Heindel, developed the idea that an astrological age reflects the symbolism of two opposing constellations.[105] But he was not as optimistic as Heindel about the new aion. Jung did not assume the union of the opposites to be a smooth passage into a higher and more loving stage of spiritual consciousness, as did the Theosophists and the "New Age" proponents of the late 20th century. He foresaw "a new advance in human development,"[106] but he viewed the transition into the Aquarian Aion as a dangerous time fraught with the human potential for self-destruction. In a letter to Father Victor White, written in April 1954, Jung stated that the shift into the Aion of Aquarius

... means that man will be essentially God and God man. The signs pointing in this direction consist in the fact that the cosmic power of self-destruction is given into the hands of man.[107]

With even more overt pessimism, he wrote a year later to Adolf Keller:

> And now we are moving into Aquarius, of which the Sibylline books say: *Luciferi vires accendit Aquarius acres* (Aquarius inflames the savage forces of Lucifer). And we are only at the beginning of this apocalyptic development![108]

In light of the history of the 20th century and the opening decades of the 21st, it seems that Jung's dark prophecy was uncomfortably relevant.

The Timing of the New Aion

There has never been any accord among authors about the date for the commencement of the New Age. At the end of the 18th century, de l'Aulnaye believed that the Aquarian Aion had begun in 1726. At the end of the 19th century, Gerald Massey insisted that the Age of Pisces began in 255 B.C.E. with the "actual" birth of Jesus, and that the equinoctial point would move into the constellation of Aquarius in 1901.[109] Alan Leo offered the very specific date of 21 March, 1928—the day of the vernal equinox of that year—while Dane Rudhyar, writing in 1969, suggested the Aquarian Age had begun in 1905.[110] And Rudolf Steiner, in the early decades of the 20th century, was convinced the Age of Aquarius would not start until 3573.

Jung was initially equally precise, and equally independent, about the date on which the new Aion would begin. In August 1940, he wrote to H. G. Baynes:

> This is the fateful year for which I have waited more than 25 years ... 1940 is the year when we approach the meridian of the first star in Aquarius. It is the premonitory earthquake of the New Age.[111]

This date did not come from esoteric literature, but from a young Dutch Jewish astronomer named Rebekka Aleida Biegel (1886-1943), who had moved to Zürich in 1911 to take her doctorate in astronomy at the university.[112] "Betty" Biegel became Jung's patient and then trained with him, giving papers at the Association for Analytical Psychology in Zürich between 1916 and 1918. One of these papers, presented in 1916, was titled "Die Mathematische Parallele zur Psychoanalyse"; based on the observations made in her paper, Jung credited Biegel with the term "transcendent function,"[113] which he described soon afterward, in an essay written in the same year, as "comparable in its way with a mathematical function of the same name," and which he defined as "the union of conscious and unconscious contents."[114] In 1917, he further noted that he had only recently discovered "that the idea of the transcendent function also occurs in the higher mathematics."[115]

In 1918, while Biegel was working at the Zürich Observatory, then located in Gloriastrasse in the centre of the city, she sent Jung, at his request, an envelope of materials which he marked "Astrologie" and kept in his desk at home.[116] Biegel went to considerable trouble to prepare a lengthy list of calculations indicating when the vernal equinoctial point—the moment when the Sun enters the first degree of the zodiacal sign of Aries each year—aligned with each of the stars in the constellations of both Pisces and Aquarius. Along with these calculations, Biegel's covering letter offered three possible dates for the beginning of the Aquarian Aion: 1940 (when the equinoctial point aligned with the midpoint between the last star of Pisces and the first star of Aquarius); 2129; and 2245 (when the equinoctial point aligned with two different stars in the constellation of Aquarius, either of which might be considered the "beginning" of the constellation).[117] What Jung called the "premonitory earthquake" of the Aquarian Aion, according to Biegel's first suggested date of 1940, coincided with some of the worst chapters of the Second World War. Germany invaded and occupied Norway, Denmark, Belgium, the Netherlands, and France; Hitler signed his Axis pact with Mussolini; the Blitz began in London; and the largest concentration camp, Auschwitz-

Birkenau, was opened in Poland, where over a million people would be murdered in the course of the next five years.

Jung later became less certain about the date of the commencement of the Aquarian Aion. In an essay titled "The Sign of the Fishes," written in 1958,[118] he stated that the equinoctial point "will enter Aquarius in the course of the third millennium."[119] In a footnote to this paragraph, Jung explained that, according to the preferred starting point, the advent of the new Aion "falls between AD 2000 and 2200," but that "this date is very indefinite" because "the delimitation of the constellations is known to be somewhat arbitrary."[120] But the "indefinite" and "arbitrary" nature of the date did not deter Jung from his lifelong conviction that the Aquarian Aion was coming soon and that its initial impact within the collective psyche would not be pleasant.

The Birth Chart of Jesus

Jung was as preoccupied with discovering the birth date of Jesus, whom he believed to be the avatar and chief symbol of the Piscean Aion, as he was with the date of the beginning of the aion itself. He was not alone in this quest, although his understanding of its importance in relation to archetypal patterns in the collective unconscious was unique. Jung had a wide range of references from the late 18th century onward which had already made an explicit link between Christ, the zodiacal image of Pisces, and the fish as a major symbol of Christian belief. These references included a work called *The Zodia* by E.M. Smith, published in 1906, in which Smith declared: "Modern astrological speculation ... associates the Fishes with Christ."[121]

The search for the "true" nativity of Jesus, although understandably not of particular interest to pagan astrologers in late antiquity, began in the Arab world in the eighth century and has continued to the present day.[122] But it has not always involved the equation of Jesus' horoscope with the advent of the Piscean Age. Arab astrologers were more interested in Jesus' birth in relation to the "great mutation cycle" of Jupiter and Saturn. These planets are aligned in conjunction along the ecliptic roughly every 20 years, but they take 960 years to return to a conjunction in a sign of the same element. This "great mutation cycle" of nearly a millennium was based on early Sassanian Persian astrological theories that the conjunctions of Jupiter and Saturn underpinned the great cycles of world history and the rise and fall of kings. As Jung was familiar with the work of Arab astrologers such as Abu Ma'shar, the Jupiter-Saturn cycle did not escape his notice.[123]

Nor did Jung neglect the writings of the 13th-century astrologer and magus Albertus Magnus, who insisted that Virgo was rising when Jesus was born,[124] or the speculations of the 14th-century Cardinal Pierre d'Ailly, who agreed.[125] Jerome Cardanus, another of Jung's favoured early modern astrologers, also prepared a horoscope for Jesus, using the traditional date of 25 December, just after the winter solstice. Cardanus proposed a birth year of 1 B.C.E., with Libra rather than Virgo rising.[126] Jung compared all these "ideal horoscopes for Christ" in *Aion*[127] and concluded that the "correct" birth date for Jesus was, in fact, 7 B.C.E., as the conjunction of Jupiter and Saturn in Pisces in that year, with Mars in opposition from Virgo, was "exceptionally large and of an impressive brilliance."[128] But rather than accepting 25 December as the date of birth, Jung followed the calculations of the German astronomer Oswald Gerhardt and proposed 29 May, the date on which the configuration of Jupiter, Saturn, and Mars had been exact.[129] This resulted in Jesus' Sun-sign as Gemini: the "motif of the hostile brothers" that Jung believed to be one of the dominant archetypal themes of the Piscean Aion.

In Jung's discussions about the symbolism of the Fishes, he revealed a perspective on astrological images that is firmly focused on the archetypal meaning of a zodiacal symbol rather than its characterological qualities, and on its relationship with the god-image— synonymous with the image of the self—as it appears in the human psyche.

> As the highest value and supreme dominant in the psychic hierarchy, the God-image is immediately related to, or identical with, the self, and everything that happens to the God-image has an effect on the latter.[130]

The religious symbols of each zodiacal Aion thus faithfully reflect in imaginal form the "highest value and supreme dominant" in the collective psyche for a particular epoch of history. At the beginning of *The Red Book*, Jung emphasised the importance of this changing god-image:

> It is not the coming God himself, but his image which appears in the supreme meaning. God is an image, and those who worship him must worship him in the images of the supreme meaning.[131]

Rebekka Biegel had indicated 4 B.C.E. as the beginning of the Piscean Aion, based on the movement of the equinoctial point. Jung's interest in the Jupiter-Saturn conjunction of 7 B.C.E., just three years earlier, led him to conclude that this configuration was the "star of Bethlehem" that had appeared as the augury of Jesus' birth:

> Christ was born at the beginning of the aeon of the Fishes. It is by no means ruled out that there were educated Christians who knew of the *coniunctio maxima* of Jupiter and Saturn in Pisces in the year 7 B.C., just as, according to the gospel reports, there were Chaldaeans who actually found Christ's birthplace.[132]

Jung amalgamated the image of Christ as the "supreme meaning" of the incoming Piscean Aion with the *coniunctio maxima* of Jupiter and Saturn in the zodiacal sign of Pisces.[133] He viewed the approaching Aquarian Aion as the epoch when individuals would interiorise the god-image; thus he did not anticipate a new avatar for the new Aion who would manifest "out there." He declined to adopt Steiner's belief in a "Second Coming" of Jesus, or Annie Besant's expectation of a "New World Teacher."

> …we now recognize that the anointed of this time is a God who does not appear in the flesh; he is no man and yet is a son of man, but in spirit and not in flesh; hence he can be born only through the spirit of men as the conceiving womb of the God.[134]

Nor is Phanes, the new aionic god of *The Red Book*, in any way human; this god-image is androgynous and spherical, like Plato's World Soul.[135] Jung did not believe any single person would personify the spirit of the new dispensation; the Water-bearer "seems to represent the self."[136] It was this insistence on individual responsibility that seems to have coloured Jung's expectations with profound misgivings about the human capacity to cope with the lack of an external divine object on which to project the god-image. He understood his own role as important, but as an individual, not an avatar, who could help to illuminate the difficult psychological process of interiorisation through his published work. Jung's understanding of the Aquarian Aion ultimately mirrors that of Alan Leo, who insisted that "the inner nature and destiny of this sign is expressed in the one word HUMANITY."[137]

It seems that Jung understood himself to be an individual "vessel" for the polarity of the new Aion, and the work he pursued for his own integration was also work on behalf of a collective that he feared was already beginning to struggle blindly and destructively with the same dilemmas: the rediscovery of the soul; the acknowledgement of good and evil as inner potencies, and the terrible responsibility that comes with that acknowledgement; and the recognition of a central interior self which alone can integrate the opposites. That Jung took his task very seriously, and felt he had failed in it as he moved toward the close of his life, is reflected in a letter he wrote to Eugene Rolfe in 1960:

> I have failed in my foremost task: to open people's eyes to
> the fact that man has a soul and there is a buried treasure
> in the field and that our religion and philosophy are in a
> lamentable state.[138]

Perceiving oneself as a vessel is not the same as attempting to found a solar cult, as Richard Noll has claimed. Jung appears to have viewed not only himself, but all those individuals with whom he worked and all those who might be influenced by his ideas in the future, as potential vessels who could, through their individual efforts to achieve greater consciousness, help to facilitate the collective transition into an astrological aion in which humans would be faced with the terrifying challenge of interiorising and integrating good and evil as inherent dimensions of a previously projected duality of God and the Devil. Attempting to define the nature of his psychology to Aniele Jaffé, Jung commented:

> The main interest of my work is not concerned with the treatment of neurosis, but rather with the approach to the numinous ...The approach to the numinous is the real therapy.[139]

The Red Book, as is obvious to any perceptive reader, records a highly individual journey, fraught with conflict and suffering as well as important transformations and the integration of previously rejected or unfamiliar elements in Jung's personal psychological world. But *The Red Book* also portrays a collective voyage, and its opening image places the ship that sails toward "what is to come" beneath a sky that reveals, clearly and inarguably, the shift from the dying Aion of Pisces to the birth of the Aion of Aquarius. Jung was not encouraging about the global problems that this shift would entail. He placed his hopes, not in mass political or social movements, but in the capacity of the individual to recognise the enormity of the responsibility involved and to develop the willingness to engage in the inner struggle to achieve greater consciousness. At the present time, Jung's dark forebodings seem to be entirely justified. Whether or not resolution and transformation are eventually possible on a collective level remained unknown to Jung—as it does to all of us—because the fate of the collective, in his view, rests on the shoulders of every individual:

> If things go wrong in the world, this is because something is wrong with the individual, because something is wrong with me.[140]

Endnotes

This essay is adapted from a chapter in my book, *Jung's Studies in Astrology: Prophecy, Magic, and the Qualities of Time* (Abingdon: Routledge, 2018)

1. Dane Rudhyar, *Astrological Timing* (New York, NY: Harper & Row, 1969), 166-167.
2. C.G. Jung, *The Red Book: Liber Novus*, ed. Sonu Shamdasani, tr. John Peck, Mark Kyburz, and Sonu Shamdasani (New York, NY: W. W. Norton, 2009), 314-15. All citations by Jung in the following pages are referenced by the paragraph number and volume of the *Collected Works*, or by the abbreviated title in the case of works by Jung not included in the *Collected Works*. Full publishing information is given in the Bibliography.
3. For a useful overview including references, see David John Tacey, *Jung and the New Age* (Hove: Brunner-Routledge, 2001).
4. Olav Hammer, *Claiming Knowledge: Strategies of Epistemology from Theosophy to the New Age* (Leiden: Brill, 2004), 67-70; see also 437-440 for Hammer's discussion of Jung's concept of the archetypes, which "resembles a hermetic concept of correspondences rather than a psychological theory in the usual sense of the word." Richard Noll uses the word "Jungism"; see Richard Noll, *The Jung Cult: Origins of a Charismatic Movement* (Princeton, NJ: Princeton University Press, 1994), 7-9 and 291-94.
5. Paul Heelas, *The New Age Movement* (Oxford: Blackwell, 1996), 46. For Gurdjieff's own work, see G. I. Gurdjieff, *Meetings With Remarkable Men* (London: E. P. Dutton, 1964). See also P. D. Ouspensky, *In Search of the Miraculous* (New York, NY: Harcourt, Brace, 1949).
6. Wouter J. Hanegraaff, *New Age Religion and Western Culture: Esotericism in the Mirror of Secular Thought* (Leiden: Brill, 1996), 497.
7. See Roderick Main, "New Age Thinking in the Light of C.G. Jung's Theory of Synchronicity," *Journal of Alternative Spiritualities and New*

Age Studies 2 (2006), 8-25, on p. 9; Hanegraaff, *New Age Religion*, 521-22.

8   Rudhyar, *Astrological Timing*, 167.

9   Hanegraaff, *New Age Religion and Western Culture*, 94.

10 See Hanegraaff, *New Age Religion and Western Culture*, 421-513; Alex Owen, "Occultism and the 'Modern Self' in Fin-de-Siècle Britain," in Martin Daunton and Bernhard Rieger (eds.), *Meanings of Modernity* (Oxford: Berg, 201), 71-96. The idea that God can be found within, and that "God-knowledge" is "self-knowledge," is stated explicitly in Plotinus, Ennead I:6.7 and Ennead VI:9.11, in Plotinus, *The Enneads*, trans. Stephen MacKenna, 6 volumes (London: Medici Society, 1917-30; repr. London: Faber & Faber, 1956).

11 C.G. Jung, *Aion. Researches into the Phenomenology of the Self*, in *CW*, vol. 9/II (Princeton, NJ: Princeton University Press, 1968), originally published as *Aion: Untersuchungen zur Symbolgeschichte* (Psychologische Abhandlungen VIII, Rascher Verlag, Zurich, 1951).

12 *Aeon* is the Latin spelling of the Greek word *Aion* (Αιων). Kronos (Κρονος), as described in Hesiod's *Theogony*, is the ancient Greek Titan who became ruler of the gods after he castrated his father Ouranos. Kronos became associated with the Roman god Saturn, and it is the name used for the planet Saturn in Ptolemy's *Tetrabiblos*, which was written in Greek. *Chronos* (χρονος) is the Greek word for time. Zervan (or Zurvan) is a Persian pre-Zoroastrian deity whose name, like the Greek *chronos*, means "time"; he is lord of the finite time of history as well as "boundless time", the primordial light out of which everything has emanated. This deity bears many similarities with the Orphic Phanes; see Liz Greene, *The Astrological World of Jung's Liber Novus* (Abingdon: Routledge, 2018), Chapter Six.

13 Albrecht Dieterich, *Eine Mithrasliturgie* (Leipzig: Teubner, 1903); G. R. S. Mead, *A Mithraic Ritual*, Volume 6 of *Echoes from the Gnosis* (London: Theosophical Publishing Society, 1907).

14 Franz Cumont, *Textes et monuments figurés relatifs aux mystères de Mythra* (Brussels: Lamertin, 1896).

15 C.G. Jung, *Psychology of the Unconscious*, trans. Beatrice M. Hinkle (New York, NY: Moffat, Yard & Co., 1916), par. 83.

16 Franz Cumont, *The Mysteries of Mithra*, trans. Thomas J. McCormack (Chicago, IL: Open Court, 1903), 125-26.

¹⁷ David Ulansey, *The Origins of the Mithraic Mysteries* (Oxford: Oxford University Press, 1991); Roger Beck, *Planetary Gods and Planetary Orders in the Mysteries of Mithras* (Leiden: Brill, 1988); Roger Beck, *The Religion of the Mithras Cult in the Roman Empire* (Oxford: Oxford University Press, 2006).

¹⁸ See Origen, *Contra Celsum*, trans. Henry Chadwick (Cambridge: Cambridge University Press, 1953), 6:21-22; Porphyry, *De antro nympharum*, in Thomas Taylor (ed. and trans.), *Select Works of Porphyry* (London: Thomas Rodd, 1823), 5-6.

¹⁹ See Cumont, *The Mysteries of Mithra*, 105.

²⁰ See Lance S. Owens, "Jung and Aion: Time, Vision, and a Wayfaring Man," in *Psychological Perspectives: A Quarterly Journal of Jungian Thought* 54:3 (2011), 268.

²¹ Homer, *Iliad* 5.685, 16.453, 19.27, 22.58; Homer, *Odyssey* 5.160; Herodotus, *Histories*, 1.32. These and the following translations are available at <http://www.perseus.tufts.edu>.

²² Euripides, *Heracleidae*, trans. Ralph Gladstone (Chicago, IL: University of Chicago Press, 1955), 900; Brian P. Copenhaver (ed. and trans.), *Hermetica: The Greek Corpus Hermeticum and the Latin Asclepius in a New English Translation* (Cambridge: Cambridge University Press, 1992), 11.

²³ Aeschylus, *The Seven Against Thebes*, ed. and trans. David Grene, Richmond Lattimore, Mark Griffith, and Glenn W. Most (Chicago IL: University of Chicago Press, 2013), 219; Demosthenes, *On the Crown*, trans. A. W. Pickard-Cambridge, in A. W. Pickard-Cambridge (ed. and trans.), *Public Orations of Demosthenes*, 2 volumes (Oxford: Clarendon Press, 1912), 18.199.

²⁴ Sophocles, *Trachiniae*, 34.

²⁵ Hesiod, *Theogony*, 609.

²⁶ Paul, *Romans*, 12.2.

²⁷ Plato, *Timaeus*, 37d.

²⁸ Zodiacal constellations (made up of fixed stars) and zodiacal signs (divisions of the ecliptic) are not identical; this has been known to astrologers since the 2ⁿᵈ century B.C.E. For an explanation of the phenomenon of precession, see Patricia Viale Wuest, *Precession of the Equinoxes* (Atlanta, GA: Georgia Southern University, 1998).

29 G. R. S. Mead, *Pistis Sophia* (London: Theosophical Publishing Society, 1896), 14.

30 See Jung, *Psychology of the Unconscious*, pars. 104-5; 110-11; 500 n21; 520 n14.

31 See Hans Dieter Betz (ed. and trans.), *The "Mithras Liturgy": Text, Translation and Commentary* (Tübingen: Mohr Siebeck, 2003), 1.

32 Mead, *A Mithraic Ritual*, II.3. See also Betz, *The "Mithras Liturgy"*, 518-521, 51.

33 Mead, *A Mithraic Ritual*, V.3. See also Betz, *The "Mithras Liturgy"*, 591-603, 53.

34 "This immortalization takes place three times a year": Betz, *The "Mithras Liturgy"*, 748, 57.

35 Jung, *Liber Novus*, 286.

36 Jung, *Psychology of the Unconscious*, pars. 313-14. Compare with Mead, *The Mysteries of Mithra*, 70-71.

37 See Jung, *Aion, CW* 9/II, pars. 128 and 325; C.G. Jung, *Alchemical Studies*, in *CW*, vol. 13 (Princeton, NJ: Princeton University Press, 1967), par. 275. Jung's remarks about the lion-headed Ialdabaoth and Saturn were first published in 1949, but the identity of the planet and the Gnostic archon is stated in Wolfgang Schultz, *Dokumente der Gnosis* (Jena: Diederichs, 1910), 103, where Jung would have encountered it no later than his painting of Izdubar in 1915. Jung later gave as his own references Origen's *Contra Celsum*, Bousset's *Hauptprobleme der Gnosis*, and Mead's translation of *Pistis Sophia*. As the former was cited in *Psychological Types* (1921) and the latter two in *Psychology of the Unconscious* (1911-12), Jung was already familiar with the idea of Saturn as the *Deus Leontocephalus* while he was working on *Liber Novus*. See above, n751.

38 For Philemon as a Saturnian-solar figure in *The Red Book*, see Greene, *The Astrological World of Jung's Liber Novus*, Chapter Six. For the Neoplatonic idea of the planetary ruler of the horoscope as the personal daimon, see Greene, *The Astrological World of Jung's Liber Novus*, Chapters Three and Four.

39 William Butler Yeats, *The Second Coming* (1919), in *Collected Poems of William Butler Yeats* (London: Macmillan, 1933), 211.

40 Jung, *Liber Novus*, 252.

41 For the leontocephalic being as Ialdabaoth in Gnostic iconography, see M. J. Edwards, "Gnostic Eros and Orphic Themes," *Zeitschrift für Papyrologie und Epigraphik* 88 (1991), 25-40.

42 C.G. Jung, *Analytical Psychology: Its Theory and Practice* (London: Routledge & Kegan Paul, 1968), 98.

43 Image in Jung, *Liber Novus*, 229.

44 For the observation that the image portrays the precession of the equinoctial point from Pisces into Aquarius, see Sonu Shamdasani, *C.G. Jung: A Biography in Books* (New York, NY: W. W. Norton, 2012), 117; Owens, "Jung and Aion," 271.

45 C.G. Jung, "The Undiscovered Self (Present and Future)" (1958), in *CW*, vol. 10 (Princeton, NJ: Princeton University Press, 1964), par. 585.

46 Owens, "Jung and Aion," 253.

47 See Liz Greene, *Jung's Studies in Astrology* (Abingdon: Routledge, 2018), Chapter Two. For a compilation of Jung's statements about astrology, see C.G. Jung, *Jung on Astrology*, selected and introduced by Keiron le Grice and Safron Rossi (Abingdon: Routledge, 2017).

48 C.G. Jung, "Flying Saucers. A Modern Myth of Things Seen in the Skies" (1959), in *CW*, vol. 10 (Princeton, NJ: Princeton University Press, 1964), par. 589.

49 See Jung, "The Undiscovered Self," *CW* 10, par. 536.

50 For more recent works exploring this theme, see David Fideler, *Jesus Christ, Sun of God: Ancient Cosmology and Early Christian Symbolism* (Wheaton, IL: Quest Books/Theosophical Publishing House, 1993); Herbert Cutner, *Jesus* (New York, NY: The Truth Seeker Co., 1950), 129-64.

51 See Nicholas Campion, *Astrology and Popular Religion in the Modern West* (Farnham: Ashgate, 2012), 22.

52 Jean Sylvain Bailly, *Histoire de l'astronomie ancienne* (1775); Jean Sylvain Bailly, *Traite de l'astronomie indienne et orientale* (1787).

53 Charles Dupuis, *Origine de tous les cultes, ou religion universelle* (Paris: H. Agasse, 1795).

54 Charles Dupuis, *Planches de l'origine de tous les cultes* (Paris: H. Agasse, 1795), 6.

55 François-Henri-Stanislas de L'Aulnaye, *L'histoire générale et particulière des religions et du cultes* (Paris: J. B. Fournier, 1791).

[56] Campion, *Astrology and Popular Religion*, 22-23. See also Joscelyn Godwin, *The Theosophical Enlightenment* (Albany, NY: SUNY Press, 1994), 69 and 82.

[57] See William Emmette Coleman, "The Sources of Madame Blavatsky's Writings," in Vsevolod Sergyeevich Solovyoff, *A Modern Priestess of Isis* (London: Longmans, Green, and Co., 1895), Appendix C, 353-66.

[58] Godfrey Higgins, *Anacalypsis*, 2 volumes (London: Longman, Rees, Orme, Brown, Green, and Longman, 1836), II:110-111.

[59] Gerald Massey, "The Hebrew and Other Creations, Fundamentally Explained," in *Gerald Massey's Lectures* (London: private publication, 1887), 105-140, on p. 114.

[60] See Campion, *Astrology and Popular Religion*, 24; Hammer, *Claiming Knowledge*, 248-49.

[61] Gerald Massey, "The Historical Jesus and Mythical Christ," in *Gerald Massey's Lectures*, 1-26, on p. 8.

[62] Jung, *Aion*, CW 9/II, par. 149, n84.

[63] For more on Khunrath, see Peter Forshaw, "Curious Knowledge and Wonder-Working Wisdom in the Occult Works of Heinrich Khunrath," in R. J. W. Evans and Alexander Marr (eds.), *Curiosity and Wonder from the Renaissance to the Enlightenment* (Farnham: Ashgate, 2006), 107-130.

[64] Heinrich Khunrath, *Von hylealischen, das ist, pri-materialischen catholischen, oder algemeinem natürlichen Chaos, der naturgemessen Alchymiae und Alchemisten* (Magdeburg, 1597), 36, cited in *Jung, Modern Psychology*, Vol. 5-6, p. 156. Jung acquired Khunrath's work in the original 1597 edition.

[65] C.G. Jung, *Modern Psychology: Notes on Lectures Given at the Eidgenössische Technische Hochschule, Zürich by Prof. Dr. C.G. Jung, October 1933-July 1941*, 3 volumes, trans. and ed. Elizabeth Welsh and Barbara Hannah (Zürich: K. Schippert & Co., 1959-60), Vol. 5-6, p. 156.

[66] Horace Jeffery Hodges, "Gnostic Liberation from Astrological Determinism", *Vigiliae Christianae* 51:4 (1997), 359-73.

[67] Irenaeus, *Irenaei episcopi lugdunensis contra omnes haereses* (Oxford: Thomas Bennett, 1702), I:29-30.

[68] Irenaeus, *Haer.* I:30.12.

⁶⁹ Ulansey, *The Origins of the Mithraic Mysteries*, 49-51, 76-81, 82-84.

⁷⁰ Letter to Sigmund Freud, 26 June 1910, in Sigmund Freud and C.G. Jung, *The Freud-Jung Letters*, ed. William McGuire, trans. Ralph Manheim and R. F. C. Hull (London: Hogarth Press/Routledge & Kegan Paul, 1977), 336. See also C.G. Jung, *Symbols of Transformation*, in *CW*, vol. 5 (Princeton, NJ: Princeton University Press, 1967), par. 665, n66; Richard Noll, "Jung the Leontocephalus," in Paul Bishop (ed.), *Jung in Contexts: A Reader* (London: Routledge, 1999), 51-91 on p. 67. Compare Jung's description of Taurus with Mead's in *The Mysteries of Mithra*, 63: "The 'God who steals the Bull' [Mithra] occultly signifies generation." See also Jung's letter to Sigmund Freud, 22 June 1910, in *The Freud-Jung Letters*, 334.

⁷¹ *Psychology of the Unconscious* is the original English translation, published in 1916, of *Wandlungen und Symbole der Libido*, first published in German 1912 and later revised, retranslated, and published in English as *Symbols of Transformation* (*CW* 5) in 1956. Beatrice Hinkle's original English translation was released as Supplementary Volume B to *The Collected Works*.

⁷² Jung, *Psychology of the Unconscious*, pars. 226-7 and par. 523, n60. The Tauroctony is the characteristic cult image of Mithras slaying the bull.

⁷³ Richard Reitzenstein, *Poimandres: ein paganisiertes Evangelium: Studien zur griechisch-ägyptischen und frühchristlichen Literatur* (Leipzig: Teubner, 1904); Richard Reitzenstein, *Die hellenistische Mysterienreligionen* (Leipzig: Teubner, 1910); Richard Reitzenstein, *Mysterienreligionen nach ihren Grundgedanken und Wirkungen* (Leipzig: Teubner, 1910).

⁷⁴ Plato, *Timaeus*, 39d.

⁷⁵ Julius Firmicus Maternus, *Of the Thema Mundi*, in Taylor, Thomas, (trans.), *Ocellus Lucanus, On the Nature of the Universe; Taurus, the Platonic Philosopher, On the Eternity of the World; Julius Firmicus Maternus, Of the Thema Mundi; Select Theorems on the Perpetuity of Time, by Proclus* (London: John Bohn, 1831).

⁷⁶ For Stoic cosmology, see A. A. Long, *From Epicurus to Epictetus* (Oxford: Oxford University Press, 2006), 256-84; John Sellars, *Stoicism* (Berkeley, CA: University of California Press, 2006), 99-100.

[77] Macrobius proposed 15,000 years; Aristarchus proposed 2,484 years. See the discussion in J. D. North, *Stars, Mind, and Fate* (London: Continuum, 1989), 96-115.

[78] Jung, *Aion, CW* 9/II, par. 286.

[79] Jung, Letter to Walter Robert Corti, 12 September 1929, in Gerhard Adler, *C.G. Jung Letters*, 2 volumes, trans. R. F. C. Hull (Princeton, NJ: Princeton University Press, 1973-75), Vol. 1, 69-70.

[80] The other two are Gemini (the Twins), and Virgo (the Virgin). All the other constellations are represented by animals except Libra, the inanimate Balance or Scales.

[81] See Friedrich Nietzsche, *Also sprach Zarathustra* (Chemnitz: Ernst Schmeitzner, 1883-84). There are various English translations of this work.

[82] For Blavatsky's discussions of the "Ages," see H. P. Blavatsky, *Isis Unveiled: A Master-Key to the Mysteries of Ancient and Modern Science and Theology*, 2 volumes (London: Theosophical Publishing Co., 1877), II:443, 455-56, 467-69; H. P. Blavatsky, *The Secret Doctrine: The Synthesis of Science, Religion, and Philosophy*, 2 volumes (London: Theosophical Publishing Co., 1888), II:198-201.

[83] Blavatsky, *Isis Unveiled*, II:456.

[84] http://www.oocities.org/astrologyages/ageofaquarius.htm, October 2009. This URL is now out of date but is archived.

[85] Rudolf Steiner, *The Reappearance of Christ in the Etheric* (Spring Valley, NY: Anthroposophic Press, 1983), 15-19.

[86] See Nicholas Campion, *Astrology and Cosmology in the World's Religions* (New York, NY: NYU Press, 2012), 194-95.

[87] Rudolf Steiner, *Friedrich Nietzsche. Ein Kämpfer gegen seine Zeit* (Weimar: E. Felber, 1895).

[88] Rudolf Steiner, *Evil*, ed. Michael Kalisch (Forest Row: Rudolf Steiner Press, 1997; original publication, *Das Mysterium des Bösen* (Stuttgart: Verlag Freies Geistesleben, 1993), 56.

[89] Mead, *Echoes*, I:47.

[90] Jung, *Aion, CW* 9/II, par. 142.

[91] *Hair* (1967), book and lyrics by James Rado and Gerome Ragni, music by Galt MacDermot.

[92] Jung, *Memories, Dreams, Reflections*, 199-200.

[93] Mead, *Echoes*, I:46.

94 For a detailed exploration of Jung's reliance on the works of Alan Leo and Max Heindel, see Greene, *Jung's Studies in Astrology*, Chapter Two.

95 Alan Leo, *Esoteric Astrology* (London: Modern Astrology Office, 1913), p. v.

96 Alan Leo, "The Age of Aquarius," *Modern Astrology* 8:7 (1911), 272.

97 Alan Leo, *Dictionary of Astrology*, ed. Vivian Robson (London: Modern Astrology Offices/L. N. Fowler, 1929), 204.

98 For more on Leo's idea of the Aquarian Age, see Nicholas Campion, *What Do Astrologers Believe?* (London: Granta Publications, 2006), 36.

99 Max Heindel, *The Rosicrucian Mysteries* (Oceanside, CA: Rosicrucian Fellowship, 1911), 15.

100 Max Heindel, *The Rosicrucian Cosmo-Conception, or Mystic Christianity* (Oceanside, CA: Rosicrucian Fellowship, 1909), 159-60.

101 Heindel, *The Rosicrucian Cosmo-Conception*, 305.

102 Heindel's ellision of "Aryan" with "Arian" may reflect his own socio-religious agenda, but the former spelling has nothing to do with the zodiacal constellation of the Ram.

103 Max Heindel, *The Message of the Stars: An Esoteric Exposition of Medical and Natal Astrology Explaining the Arts of Prediction and Diagnosis of Disease* (Oceanside, CA: Rosicrucian Fellowship, 1918), 12.

104 Heindel, *Message of the Stars*, 25-27.

105 See Jung's various discussions of Pisces and its opposite constellation, Virgo, in Jung, *Aion, CW* 9/II.

106 Jung, *Aion, CW* 9/II, par. 141.

107 Letter to Father Victor White, 10 April 1954, in *C.G. Jung Letters*, II:167.

108 Letter to Adolf Keller, 25 February 1955, in *C.G. Jung Letters*, II, 229.

109 Gerald Massey, *The Natural Genesis*, 2 volumes (London: Williams & Norgate, 1883), Vol. 2, 378-503.

110 Rudhyar, *Astrological Timing*, 115.

111 Letter to H. G. Baynes, 12 August 1940, in *C.G. Jung Letters,* I, 285.

112 Biegel's dissertation on Egyptian astronomy, *Zur Astrognosie der alten Ägypter*, was published three years after her correspondence with Jung (Göttingen: Dieterichsche Universitäts-Buckdruckerei, 1921).

For more on Biegel, see A. C. Rümke and Sarah de Rijcke, *Rebekka Aleida Beigel (1886-1943): Een Vrouw in de Psychologie* (Eelde: Barkhuism, 2006).

[113] Personal communication from Sonu Shamdasani, 28 July 2014.

[114] C.G. Jung, "The Transcendent Function," in *CW*, vol. 8 (Princeton, NJ: Princeton University Press, 1969), par. 131.

[115] C.G. Jung, "On the Psychology of the Unconscious", in *CW*, vol. 7 (Princeton, NJ: Princeton University Press, 1966), par. 121, n1.

[116] This material has never been included in any official archive. Andreas Jung kindly allowed me to examine the documents, and stated that the material must have been of great personal importance to Jung because it had not been filed with other papers, but was kept in a special place in his desk.

[117] Jung amended Biegel's calculations by the time he wrote *Aion*. In Jung, *Aion, CW* 9/II, par. 149, n84, he gave the date as 2154 "if the starting-point is *Omicron* Pisces," and 1997 "if the starting-point is *Alpha* 113, which accords with the star-list in Ptolemy's *Almagest.*" Biegel also stated that the equinoctial point had arrived at the first star in the constellation of Pisces in 4 B.C.E, a date which Jung initially accepted as the "true" birthdate of Christ, but which he later amended to 7 B.C.E.

[118] Jung, *Aion, CW* 9/II, par. 127 149.

[119] Ibid., par. 149, n88.

[120] Ibid., par. 149, n84.

[121] E. M. Smith, *The Zodia, or The Cherubim in the Bible and the Cherubim in the Sky* (London: Elliot Stock, 1906), 280, cited in Jung, *Aion, CW* 9/II, par. 149, n85.

[122] See James H. Holden, "Early Horoscopes of Jesus", *American Federation of Astrologers Journal of Research* 12:1 (2001).

[123] For Jung's discussion of the Jupiter-Saturn cycle and Abu Ma'shar's *De magnis coniunctionibus*, see Jung, *Aion, CW* 9/II, pars. 130-138.

[124] For an English translation of Albertus Magnus' *Speculum astronomiae*, which discusses Jesus' birth horoscope, see Paola Zambelli, *The Speculum astronomiae and its Enigma* (Dordrecht: Kluwer Academic, 1992). For Jung's references to Albertus Magnus, see Jung, *Aion, CW* 9/II, pars. 130, 133, 143, 404.

[125] Pierre d'Ailly, *Tractatus de imagine mundi Petri de Aliaco* (Louvain: Johannes Paderborn de Westfalia, 1483). For d'Ailly's horoscope of Jesus, see Ornella Pompeo Faracovi, *Gli oroscopi di Cristo* (Venice: Marsilio Editori, 1999), 104. For Jung's references to d'Ailly, see Jung, *Aion, CW* 9/II, pars. 128, 130, n35, 136, 138, 153-54, 156.

[126] Faracovi, *Gli oroscopi di Cristo*, 130.

[127] See Jung, *Aion, CW* 9/II, par. 130, n39.

[128] Jung, *Aion, CW* 9/II, par. 130.

[129] Oswald Gerhardt, *Der Stern des Messias* (Leipzig: Deichert, 1922).

[130] Jung, *Aion, CW* 9/II, par. 170.

[131] Jung, *Liber Novus*, 229. For Jung's distinction between the god-image and the ontological existence of God, see Jung, *Liber Novus*, 229 n7.

[132] Jung, *Aion, CW* 9/II, par. 172. "Chaldaeans" is an ancient synonym for "astrologers," see Cicero, *De divinatione*, II:44.93.

[133] Jung, *Aion, CW* 9/II, pars. 147 and 162.

[134] Jung, *Liber Novus*, 299 and n200.

[135] For the spherical nature of the World Soul, see Plato, *Timaeus*, 37d.

[136] Jung, *Memories, Dreams, Reflections*, 372.

[137] Alan Leo, *Astrology for All* (London: Modern Astrology Office, 1910), 44.

[138] C.G. Jung, Letter to Eugene Rolfe, in Eugene Rolfe, *Encounter with Jung* (Boston, MA: Sigo Press, 1989), 158.

[139] Aniela Jaffé, *Was C.G. Jung a Mystic?* (Einsiedeln: Daimon Verlag, 1989), 16.

[140] C.G. Jung, "The Meaning of Psychology for Modern Man" (1934), in *CW*, vol. 10 (Princeton, NJ: Princeton University Press, 1964), par. 329.

Abraxas: Jung's Gnostic Demiurge in *Liber Novus*

Stephan A. Hoeller

C.G. Jung possessed an intense and sympathetic interest in the early alternative Christian tradition now known as Gnosticism. Both in his published writings and in his private reminiscences, one finds frequent and insightful comments about Gnostic tradition, although during much of Jung's life the subject of Gnosticism was virtually unknown to all but a few scholars of religion.

One of the key documents bearing early testimony to Jung's vital Gnostic interest was his finely designed book, *Septem Sermones ad Mortuos*—"Seven Sermons to the Dead." Jung had the work privately printed in 1916 and over subsequent decades gave copies of it to a select number of friends and associates. With Jung's approval, H.G. Baynes translated the text of the Sermons into English, and this edition was privately printed in 1925.[1] Again, Jung distributed the English edition only to persons whom he felt to be properly prepared for its message.

What remained generally unknown was that around 1917 Jung also transcribed a much-expanded version of the *Septem Sermones* into the third and final portion of his draft manuscript of *Liber Novus*, the section titled *Scrutinies*. There the Sermons appear as the summary revelation of *Liber Novus*. Jung never publicly revealed the existence of this longer form of the Sermons, and until the publication in 2009 of *The Red Book: Liber Novus* this version of the Sermons remained entirely inaccessible.[2]

Those who were fortunate enough to become acquainted with *Septem Sermones ad Mortuos* usually found it intriguing, but they were often somewhat puzzled by its contents. Authorship of the book was attributed not to Jung, but to a historical Gnostic teacher named Basilides. And its place of composition was stated to be "Alexandria, the city where East and West meet." Over ensuing years, those who had read the book sometimes referred to it as Jung's Gnostic revelation. But of course, during Jung's life few people knew much about Gnosticism, nor did they understand what really made this little book "Gnostic." Nonetheless, following the publication of *Liber Novus,* it has become evident that the Sermons are indeed the revelation of C.G. Jung's Gnostic myth. The Sermons might even be seen as the heart of his New Book—*The Red Book: Liber Novus.*

Since Jung's death in 1961, a great deal more information regarding Gnosticism has become available, and it has become a subject of wide popular and academic interest. A major impetus to this awakened attention was the publication in 1977 of the Nag Hammadi library of Gnostic scriptures, the most extensive collection of original writings of the ancient Gnostics discovered thus far.[3] The Nag Hammadi texts have shed new light on many details of the Gnostic mythos that were previously obscure. They also help place Jung's Gnostic tract into a broader context.

The *Septem Sermones ad Mortuos* has proved over past years to be a difficult book to categorize. Some writers have termed it a "cosmology," but that remains an inadequate formulation. The document might perhaps more accurately be termed a "psychocosmology." Since Gnostic scriptures typically approached their psychospiritual themes in the form of myths, one might propose that the *Septem Sermones* exemplify the contemporary formulation of a Gnostic myth. Though Jung's text is not identical with any preexisting Gnostic myth, it is nonetheless related in form to many ancient Gnostic texts that have come to light over the last century.

The Gnostic themes in the *Septem Sermones* are further amplified by another document created by Jung during the period in which he recorded the Sermons. In early 1916, Jung constructed a detailed and artistically impressive image—or mandala—that diagrammatically represented many of the elements discussed subsequently in the Sermons. He titled it *Systema Munditotius,* "the system of the entire world." Jung did not include this image among the many illustrations within his *Red Book.* Much later in life he did, however, allow it to be published—it appeared in a 1955 issue of the German periodical *Du* that was dedicated to the Eranos conferences (Jung did not, however, allow his name to be given explicitly as the image's creator). The illustration was subsequently included as a full-page plate in *C.G. Jung: Word and Image.*[4] The *Systema Munditotius* is now reproduced beautifully in *The Red Book: Liber Novus*, where it appears in Appendix A.[5] The amplified text of the Sermons present in *Liber Novus* and the diagram of *Systema Munditotius* together provide a foundation for the following discussion.

Statements substantiating Jung's affinity with Gnostic tradition run throughout his published writings. Jung held the view that during much of the history of Western culture, the reality of the psyche and its role in the transformation of the human being had received scant recognition. In contrast, the Gnostics of old and their later covert progeny—which in Jung's view included the alchemists and other alternative spiritual movements—affirmed the revelatory importance of the psyche. Jung plainly stated: "For the Gnostics—and this is their real secret—the psyche existed as a source of knowledge." In response to the recurrent question of whether or not Jung was a Gnostic, one must reply: "Certainly he was, for 'Gnostic' means 'knower,' and by his own statements Jung was *one who knew.*" The visions, myths, and metaphors of the Gnostics confirmed Jung's own experiences recorded in *Liber Novus,* and this circumstance created a bond that joined him with Gnostics of all ages and places.

Myth of the Demiurge

The myth of the demiurge originated with Plato. In his *Timaeus,* Plato postulated the existence of a creator deity, or "demiurge," who fashioned the material universe. The term *demiurge* is derived from the Greek word meaning "craftsman." Although a craftsman and fashioner, it must be understood that the demiurge was not identical with the monotheistic creator figure; the demiurge and the material from which the demiurge fashioned the universe were both secondary consequences of another primary factor. The demiurge is thus an intermediate architect, not a supreme source.

In ancient times, Plato was regarded as the paragon of all wisdom, and his model of a demiurge, or cosmic fashioner, was further elaborated and adapted within many subsequent schools of thought, including in the myths of the Gnostics.[6] Gnostics envisioned the demiurge as a subordinate supernatural power that was not identical with the true, ultimate, and transcendent godhead. The presence of a myth about this demiurge became a signal characteristic of Gnostic systems. Taking note of the sometimes distasteful character and conduct of the Old Testament deity, Gnostics frequently identified the latter as the demiurge—a being that was not evil, but still of questionable moral stature and limited wisdom.

It has long been apparent to some students of Jung that in *Answer to Job* he characterized the divine tyrant who tormented Job as a classic Gnostic demiurge. This divinity, as described by Jung, was a being who lacked wisdom due to having lost or forgotten his feminine side—his *Sophia* ("wisdom"). Notwithstanding this and other evidence, some readers of Jung previously argued that his mythos in the *Septem Sermones* did not include the controversial Gnostic figure of the demiurge, and therefore it should not be properly called Gnostic. Publication of *The Red Book: Liber Novus* now makes it abundantly clear that the demiurge *is* present in Jung's myth. Indeed, *Answer to Job* is unmistakably a reformulation of the Gnostic myth disclosed to Jung in *Liber Novus* and within the *Septem Sermones*.[7]

Prior to the availability of the expanded version of the Sermons found in *Liber Novus*, the figure of Abraxas—as portrayed in the published 1916 edition of the Sermons—remained ambiguous. In my book, *The Gnostic Jung and the Seven Sermons to the Dead,* first published in 1982, I offered an initial commentary on the locus of Abraxas in Jung's myth.[8] With the long-sequestered text of *Liber Novus* finally available, I now wish to amend and expand those prior comments composed nearly four decades ago. Based on documentation in *Liber Novus*, the figure Jung identified as "Abraxas" has finally and indisputably been divulged as a classic Gnostic demiurge.

The mysterious being called "Abraxas" first appears in *Septem Sermones* in the latter part of the Second Sermon; passages describing him continue throughout the Third Sermon and into the Fourth Sermon. Initially, he is there characterized as "a god about whom you know nothing, because men have forgotten him." This statement can certainly be taken to apply to an intermediate deity, as is ubiquitous in a large number of Gnostic scriptures.

For some 2,000 years, Western and Middle Eastern cultures have been dominated by the monotheistic god-image familiar to us today. Prior to the first several centuries of the current era, however, many Mediterranean cultures accommodated religions of a pluralistic nature wherein the image of an ultimate, impersonal divine reality coexisted with a number of lesser or intermediate deities. In such ancient pluralistic systems, the image of a materially powerful but morally and spiritually impaired demiurge often played an important role.

Scholars now widely affirm that the incipient Christian religion harbored various alternative forms; those movements in early Christianity that included a myth of the demiurge are usually categorized collectively as "Gnostic." While the name Abraxas does occur in a few ancient Gnostic texts (where he is usually identified as a great archon), no evidence exists that the demiurge of classical Gnosticism was specifically called Abraxas. Jung's assignation of the ancient name Abraxas to the demiurge was thus his own imaginative appropriation.[9]

Abraxas and the Demiurge

So, was Abraxas the demiurge in Jung's myth? Jung's *Black Book* journal entry dated January 16, 1916, and reproduced as Appendix C in *Liber Novus,* removes all question about this issue: Abraxas was the demiurge in Jung's myth. As Dr. Lance Owens has previously noted, this journal entry—written around the same time Jung sketched the *Systema Munditotius,* and about two weeks before he scribed his initial journal version of the *Septem Sermones*—records the following words spoken to Jung by the Soul, who assumed the voice of the Gnostic *Sophia.*[10] Her address to Jung is inarguably a rendition of the primal Gnostic myth of the demiurge, here named Abraxas:

> *You should worship only one God.* The other Gods are unimportant. *Abraxas is to be feared.* Therefore it was a deliverance when he separated himself from me.

Note that the separation of the demiurge from *Sophia*—"when he separated himself from me"—is a key element of the classic Gnostic myth of *Sophia* and the Demiurge.[11] She then exhorts,

> You do not need to seek him. He will find you, just like Eros. He is the God of the cosmos, extremely powerful and fearful. He is the creative drive, he is form and formation, just as much as matter and force, therefore he is above all the light and dark Gods. He tears away souls and casts them into procreation. He is the creative and created. He is the God who always renews himself in days, in months, in years, in human life, in ages, in peoples, in the living, in heavenly bodies. He compels, he is unsparing. If you worship him, you increase his power over you. Thereby it becomes unbearable. You will have dreadful trouble getting clear of him. ... So remember him, do not worship him, but also do not imagine that you can flee him since he is all around you. You must be in the middle of life, surrounded by death on all sides. Stretched out, like one crucified, you hang in him, the fearful, the overpowering.[12]

This journal entry unambiguously identifies the figure of Abraxas, who a few weeks thereafter appeared in Jung's initial journal version of the Sermons as the demiurge of classical Gnostic mythology. The identification of Abraxas with the demiurge is further established in the draft manuscript of *Liber Novus,* where in several passages Jung substituted the term "ruler of this world" for the name "Abraxas" that was originally recorded in his *Black Book* journal.[13]

At its beginning, Jung's Gnostic theogony in the Sermons describes an ultimate, utterly transcendental source called the Pleroma, and then a number of intermediate deities, including God-the-Sun, the Devil, Eros, and The Tree of Life. In addition to these figures, the entire

Third Sermon is devoted to introducing the demiurgic figure of Abraxas. In the Fourth Sermon, Jung summarizes:

> Immeasurable, like the host of stars, is the number of gods and devils. Every star is a god, and every space occupied by a star is a devil. And the emptiness of the whole is the Pleroma. The activity of the whole is Abraxas; only the unreal opposes him.[14]

The version of the Sermons included in *Liber Novus* contains several crucially important additions to the original text that was printed in 1916. In this expanded 1917 manuscript version, Philemon is identified as the speaker presenting the Sermons to the dead (Basilides was the speaker of the Sermons in the printed version). The text incorporates questions that Jung asks Philemon about each sermon, along with Philemon's answers. Philemon also adds extended homiletic commentary upon the content of his sermons. All of this additional material enriches and further explicates the meaning of the Sermons.

After the First Sermon, Jung's initial question addressed to Philemon voices concern that the teachings in the Sermons might be regarded as "reprehensible heresy." (This query bears the characteristic of a rhetorical question.) Philemon replies that the audience to whom the Sermons are addressed—"the dead"—are Christians whose now-abandoned faith long ago declared these teachings to be heresies. This commentary might be interpreted to further imply that a large number of people in our culture are now abandoning their traditional religion and are thus prepared to listen to ancient heresies, wherein they may find answers to their own portentous questions. Philemon's statement is clear and to the point:

> Why do I impart this teaching of the ancients? I teach in this way because their Christian faith once discarded and persecuted precisely this teaching. But they repudiated Christian belief and hence were rejected by that faith. They do not know this and therefore I must teach them ...[15]

Philemon's words are eminently applicable to the problem of religion in contemporary Western culture. Religion in much of Europe has reached an unprecedented low point in its history, and allegiance to the Christian tradition in the U.S. appears to be diminishing. Jung frequently pointed out that the god-image in a religion and culture is of crucial importance to the well-being of the collective psyche, and therefore also to the well-being of the individual. A major factor inducing the decline of the Christian religion in the West is unquestionably the disappointment people have come to feel with the traditional monotheistic god.

Prophecy of a New Age and a New God-Image

Jung's epochal *Liber Novus* is, in the consensus view of informed readers, a book of prophecy. On the initial folio of *Liber Novus*, Jung presents an image of a complex landscape surmounted by a zodiac and showing forth the aeonial passage of the sun from the sign of Pisces into that of Aquarius. This image points forward to his title, *The Way of What Is to Come*. The reader then encounters several prophetic quotations from the writings of the prophet Isaiah and from the prologue to the Gospel of John. Jung's *Liber Novus* thus sets the stage for disclosure of its new prophecy.[16]

Throughout both *Liber Primus* and *Liber Secundus* of *Liber Novus*, we find recurring references to the coming of the new age of Aquarius. In an impressive section that Jung titled "The Three Prophecies," his Soul reveals to him three periods in the forthcoming age: War, Magic, and Religion.[17] In commentary on this vision, Jung wrote:

> These three mean the unleashing of chaos and its power, just as they also mean the binding of chaos. War is obvious and everybody sees it. Magic is dark and no one sees it. Religion is still to come, but it will become evident. ... I felt the burden of the most terrible work of the times ahead. I saw where and how, but no word can grasp it, no will can conquer it. ... But I saw it and my memory will not leave me alone.[18]

Examining the numerous prophetic passages in *Liber Novus*, it becomes clear that at the heart of Jung's experience there abides a vision of the formation of a new god-image. But what indications did Jung give regarding the nature of this new god-image and, moreover, how may contemporary persons facilitate the arising of a new god-image in their own natures and in the new religion that is to come?

Liber Novus offers several statements that refer to the coming god-image. The tone is set in the early part of *Liber Primus*; Jung there recounts several visions that he experienced which foretold of the time when "the great war broke out between the peoples of Europe." He then declares:

> Within us is the way, the truth, and the life. ... The signposts have fallen, unblazed trails lie before us. Do not be greedy to gobble up the fruits of foreign fields. Do you not know that you yourselves are the fertile acre which bears everything that avails you?[19]

It is clear from the beginning of Jung's mysterious prophetic book that the future god-image is none other than the divine essential Selfhood indwelling in the human soul. Here, again, we must turn to the expanded version of the Sermons for a clarifying commentary. At the conclusion of the First Sermon, Philemon instructs his audience to strive for what he calls their *essences*. He continues:

> At bottom, therefore, there is only one striving, namely the striving for one's own essence. If you had this striving, you would not need to know anything about the Pleroma and its qualities, and yet you would attain the right goal by virtue of your own essence. Since, however, thought alienates us from our essence, I must teach you that knowledge with which you can bridle your thoughts.[20]

Many Gnostic writings explicitly state that the *essence* of the human is the fragment of the ultimate reality residing at the center of its being. When it is possible for the human to gain access to this essence, all other religious or spiritual endeavors are redundant. It is largely the fault of the demiurge—or so Jung's old friends, the Gnostics, believed—that this access is so fraught with difficulty. In the Sermons, Jung's spirit mentor Philemon offers advice regarding the judicious way in which humans may free themselves from the yoke of the demiurge. Unlike some of the more radical Gnostics of old, Philemon advises us to neither flee from the demiurge Abraxas nor to seek him. In one passage in the Sermons, Philemon says about Abraxas, "to resist him not is liberation."

The Gnostic demiurge, by whatever name he may be called, is omnipresent in the outer world. While humans are in terrestrial embodiment, they must both accept the demiurge's presence and equally endeavor to counterbalance his influence by contacting their own indwelling essence. This indwelling essence is described in the Seventh Sermon as the "solitary star" in the heavens. This statement is supplemented by the revelation Jung recorded in his *Black Book* journal on January 16, 1916, wherein his Soul admonished him:

> You have in you the *one* God, the wonderfully beautiful and kind, the solitary, starlike, unmoving, he who is older and wiser than the father, he who has a safe hand, who leads you among all the darknesses and death scares of dreadful Abraxas. He gives joy and peace, since he is beyond death and beyond what is subject to change. He is no servant and no friend of Abraxas.[21]

What then is the principal deficiency in the god of the old Aeon, the god who is to be overcome? Employing the nomenclature of the Sermons and other statements by Jung, we might say that the god of the monotheistic religions is a compound in which the ultimate god (called the Pleroma in the *Septem Sermones*) is *unconsciously* combined with the demiurge, named by Jung as Abraxas.

Based on the numerous paradoxical and even downright evil deeds and utterances of the Old Testament deity, and the fact that this deity was carried forward into orthodox Christianity, one is tempted to conclude (as Jung did in *Answer to Job*) that the Judeo-Christian god is at best a being who embodies both arrogance and un- consciousness. It seems quite impossible to believe that this god is both almighty and good—for his goodness would thus have to be combined with impotence, or alternatively, his omnipotence would be joined to his absence of goodness. A considerable portion of humanity has thus reached the point where it can no longer endure the unconscious tension embodied by a blind belief in an utterly enigmatic and derisory god-image. This circumstance is causing an unprecedented upsurge of atheism and secularism in Western culture.

Throughout the 20th century, humanity experienced a multitude of terrible events; these undermined many people's ability to have faith in a benevolent god. The medieval brutality of modern-day terrorists motivated by commitment to a monotheistic god has only reinforced the rejection of such traditional god-mages in secular society. Our age cries out for a new understanding of divinity and a new god-image. This was Jung's prophesy in *Liber Novus*. As he also noted, this development may take centuries. Until a new god-image constellates, we will pass through an epoch of chaos and violence.

When Christendom cast out the salvific myth of Gnosis in favor of an unimaginative literalism, it became spiritually impoverished. Our impoverishment has now reached its terminus. We await the formation of our new myth—a myth that rediscovers the primordial images and myth of Gnosis. As Jung declared:

> I hope the reader will not be offended if my exposition sounds like a Gnostic myth. We are moving in those psychological regions where, as a matter of fact, Gnosis is rooted. The message of the Christian symbol is Gnosis, and the [response to it] by the unconscious is Gnosis in even higher degree. Myth is the primordial language natural to these psychic processes, and no intellectual formulation comes anywhere near the richness and expressiveness of mythical imagery. Such processes are concerned with the primordial images, and these are best and most succinctly reproduced by figurative language.[22]

The Self, the Demiurge, and the New God-Image

The issue of the coming god-image has captured the attention of several of Jung's students in recent decades. Edward Edinger made perhaps the most complete statement concerning Jung's declaration in his pioneering book, *The New God-Image*.[23] As Edinger noted, Jung avowed an ancient and esoteric image of a deific consciousness dwelling in the soul. This affirmation is present in *Liber Novus* and is restated in various ways throughout all of Jung's subsequent writings. In *Liber Novus,* Jung offered a startling prophecy: The long neglected indwelling god-image would eventually become the orienting god-image of the future. On the first page of *Liber Novus,* he made it plain that this prediction was coordinated with the synchronous passing of the world from the astrological age of Pisces into that of Aquarius.

It is now evident that the essential foundation of Jung's science and psychological language reposed in his long-concealed *Liber Novus*. A key revelation present within *Liber Novus* that later emerged as a core affirmation in his psychology—and as a spiritual and archetypal declaration—was the assertion of the presence within the human psyche of a central archetype, around which other archetypes constellate. He called this central principle, or archetype, the "self." In *Psychology and Alchemy*—published in 1944, and based on lectures given in 1935—Jung stated:

> I have found myself obliged to give [this] archetype the psychological name of the 'self'—a term on the one hand definite enough to convey the essence of human wholeness and on the other hand indefinite enough to express the indescribable and indeterminable nature of this wholeness. … Hence in its scientific usage the term 'self' refers neither to Christ nor to the Buddha but to the totality of the figures that are its equivalent, and each of these figures is a symbol of the self. This mode of expression is an intellectual necessity in scientific psychology and in no sense denotes a transcendental prejudice. On the contrary … this objective attitude enables one man to decide in favour of the determinant Christ, another in favour of the Buddha, and so on.[24]

While the existence of a divine image internal to the psyche, termed by Jung the "self," is widely accepted among followers of Jung, the opposing archetype of the demiurge is far less known. Jung claimed that at the heart of early Christianity there existed the insight of Gnosis; he himself had met this Gnosis in the experiences recorded in his *Black Book* journals, and thence in *Liber Novus* and in the *Septem Sermones*. An essential part of the archetypal mythos of Gnosis is the presence of a duality both inwardly in the soul and outwardly in the cosmos. This duality is composed of a divine spark within the deepest recesses of the soul and of an outer demiurgic power. *Self and Demiurge stand in opposition.*

This symbolic opposition is illustrated clearly in Jung's 1916 mandala, *Systema Munditotius.*[25] At the lowest point of the circular mandala, seated on the exterior circle, is a being with the lower body of a large serpent, surmounted by a light-colored torso, and topped by the golden head of a lion crowned with a ten-rayed golden halo. On the opposite pole of the mandala, at the apex of the design, we find a winged egg within which stands the figure of the child-god Phanes. The serpent-lion is described as *abraxas dominus mundi* (Abraxas, Lord of the World). This powerful demiurge dominates the lower creation, while the child-god Phanes above is about to attain to his full stature. The undifferentiated, primitive god-image is about to be replaced by the still developing child-god of promise.

The *Systema Munditotius* is further populated by images of archetypal beings that arrange themselves in pairs of opposites on the poles of the mandala. These include *deus sol* (god the sun) and *deus luna satanus* (god the moon, Satan). We also find paired a winged rodent identified as *scientia* (science), and a winged worm named *ars* (art). Despite the abundance of these symbolic images—many of which later appear as figures in the text of the *Septem Sermones*—the two principal focal points of the diagram are clearly Abraxas and Phanes.

A picture compensates for many words, and Jung's images here illuminate the nature and role of the archetypes depicted, particularly of the primordial demiurge Abraxas and of Phanes, the new god-image awaiting birth. Of course, in conjunction with this image, the verbal descriptions of Abraxas in the *Septem Sermones* are also instructive:

Abraxas is the god whom it is difficult to know. His power is the very greatest, because man does not perceive it at all. He is magnificent even as the lion at the very moment when he strikes his prey down. His beauty is like the beauty of a spring morn.[26]

To see him means blindness; To know him is sickness; To worship him is death; To fear him is wisdom; Not to resist him means liberation ... Such is the terrible Abraxas ... He is both the radiance and the dark shadow of man. He is deceitful reality.[27]

As Jung noted in the Second Sermon, people know nothing about the demiurge because they have forgotten him. This forgetting was aided by the self-declared architects of the early Christian centuries: the heresiologist Church Fathers of orthodoxy. The very thought of a demiurge thereafter became a heretical abomination to orthodox Christendom. Jung's insights recorded in the *Liber Novus,* and particularly in the Sermons, declared that in order to move toward greater wholeness we must look to the coming new god-image. But to do this, we need also recognize the forgotten demiurge, the god whom Jung declared "difficult to know."

Present-day humanity is gradually becoming aware of an inner psychic reality, a centering fact Jung identified as the salvific archetype of the self. In *Liber Novus,* he prophetically proclaimed that a new god-image is developing in humanity—and perhaps a new god-image has already awakened in some individuals of our age, as it did in Jung. This incipient aeonial development demands further conscious awareness and a conscious union of the opposites. Using the language of *Liber Novus* and the *Systema Munditotius*, we might proclaim that Phanes is now stirring and is about to break out of the egg. For this to happen, however, human beings must also consciously recognize the reality of his opposite entity, the demiurge Abraxas.

Western culture has suffered too long from a ruinous one-sidedness. A powerful element in this one-sided perspective is a militant unwillingness to acknowledge the effective reality of the demiurge. With singular symbolic insight, the ancient Gnostics noted how the human spirit is confined on earth by a prison constructed of perplexing opposites. A demiurgic reality has placed us behind these prison bars, which alternatingly assume form in the inexorable struggle of light and dark, good and evil, or wise and unwise components. Denying the reality of this fact merely continues our confinement.

Our extraverted immersion in the world, both in its natural and cultural aspects, perpetuates servitude to the forgotten Abraxas. His fiery, mesmerizing, and infinitely creative powers enthrall us. We worship the terrible Abraxas in the baleful political ideologies of our epoch. Ever increasingly, he holds us captive in the magically scintillating web of modern technology. Only an increase of psychological awareness, leading to the individuation of our psyches, offers a path to liberation from the domination of the internal complexes and external fascinations that are the essence of Abraxas. It is incumbent upon us to accept the reality of this archetypal force, for in the words of the Sermons, "to worship him is death; to fear him is wisdom, not to resist him means liberation."

The time has come when we must incorporate Jung's epochal insights into our lives. The teachings of *Liber Novus* must be met as a form of spiritual discipline. A few months before his death in 1961, Jung wrote to an acquaintance:

> I was unable to make the people see what I am after. I am practically alone. There are a few who understand this and that, but almost nobody sees the whole ... I have failed in my foremost task: to open people's eyes to the fact that man has a soul and there is a buried treasure in the field and that our religion and philosophy are in a lamentable state.[28]

Today, after the publication of his monumental spiritual classic, *Liber Novus*, we may be able to finally reply to Jung that he has not failed at all; that inspired now by his visionary message, we too are ready "to give birth to the ancient in a new time."[29] In some mysterious archetypal locale, the sage Dr. C.G. Jung awaits such a response to his great work.

Endnotes

I wish to thank Dr. Lance Owens for his editorial collaboration in the preparation of this article, and Vicky Jo Varner for her assistance in correcting the final text.

[1] H. G. Baynes' English translation of *Septem Sermones ad Mortuos* appears as an appendix in C.G. Jung, *Memories, Dreams, Reflections*, Aniela Jaffé, ed. (Rev. ed., New York, NY: Vintage Books, 1965).

[2] C.G. Jung, *The Red Book: Liber Novus*, ed. Sonu Shamdasani, tr. John Peck, Mark Kyburz, and Sonu Shamdasani (New York, NY: W. W. Norton, 2009); hereafter cited as *Liber Novus*. For Jung's expanded version of the *Septem Sermones*, see *Liber Novus*, 346-354.

[3] Marvin Meyer, ed., *The Nag Hammadi Scriptures: The International Edition* (San Francisco: Harper, 2007).

[4] Aniela Jaffé, ed., *C.G. Jung: Word and Image* (Princeton, NJ: Princeton University Press, 1979).

[5] *Liber Novus*, Appendix A, 364.

[6] Margaret Barker has asserted that a demiurge figure was also a component in primitive Judaic mythology; Margaret Barker, *The Great Angel: A Study of Israel's Second God* (Louisville, Kentucky: Westminster/John Knox, 1992).

[7] Sonu Shamdasani has described Jung's *Answer to Job* as an articulation of the theology of *Liber Novus*; Sonu Shamdasani, "Foreword to the 2010 Edition," *Answer to Job* (Princeton, NJ: Princeton University Press; Reprint edition, 2010), ix.

[8] Stephan A. Hoeller, *The Gnostic Jung and the Seven Sermons to the Dead* (Wheaton, IL: Quest, 1982).

[9] There exists considerable ambiguity in Gnostic scriptures regarding the archetypal-mythological being called Abraxas. Some speculative writing, mostly originating in nineteenth century popular scholarship, represented Abraxas as the supreme deity of the Gnostics. More authoritative sources, including two Nag Hammadi treatises, *The Hypostasis of the Archons* and *On the Origin of the World,* indicate that the deity represented as Abraxas, and also as Sabaoth, is at times

perceived as a demiurgic figure and at other times as a converted
demiurge who became a benign ruler of the Seventh Heaven.

10 I thank Dr. Lance Owens for these notes on the journal entries: Lance
    S. Owens, "Foreword" in Alfred Ribi, *The Search for Roots: C.G. Jung
    and the Tradition of Gnosis* (Los Angeles: Gnosis Archive Books,
    2013), 26-27.
11 For a discussion of the Gnostic myth of *Sophia* and the Demiurge, see
    Stephan A. Hoeller, *Jung and the Lost Gospels: Insights into the Dead
    Sea Scrolls and the Nag Hammadi Library* (Wheaton, IL: Quest, 1989).
    62-77, 136-152.
12 *Liber Novus,* Appendix C, 370.
13 These entries in *Black Book* 5 came on January 18, two days after the
    January 16, 1916 commentary on Abraxas, above. The name Abraxas
    would have been meaningless to readers; thus Jung substituted a
    descriptive term for the demiurge, "ruler of this world." *Liber Novus,*
    245 n75.
14 Hoeller, *The Gnostic Jung,* 53; here and below I used my translation
    of Jung's 1916 edition of the *Septem Sermones ad Mortuos*; for my
    complete translation, see *The Gnostic Jung and the Seven Sermons to
    the Dead,* 44-58.
15 *Liber Novus,* 348.
16 For a detailed discussion of this material, see: Lance S. Owens, "Jung
    and *Aion*: Time, Vision and a Wayfaring Man"; *Psychological Per-
    spectives* (Journal of the C.G. Jung Institute of Los Angeles, 2011)
    54:253-89.
17 *Liber Novus,* 305.
18 Ibid., 306.
19 Ibid., 231.
20 Ibid., 348.
21 Ibid., Appendix C, 370.
22 C.G. Jung, *Psychology and Alchemy* (1935/1936), in *CW*, vol. 12
    (Princeton, NJ: Princeton University Press, 1968), par. 28.
23 Edward F. Edinger, *The New God-Image* (Wilmette, IL: Chiron Pu-
    blications, 1996).
24 Jung, *Psychology and Alchemy, CW* 12, par. 20.
25 *Liber Novus,* Appendix A, 364.

[26] Hoeller, *The Gnostic Jung*, 50.

[27] Ibid., 52.

[28] Letter of Nov 13, 1960. Eugene Rolfe, *Encounter with Jung* (Boston, MA: Sigo Press, 1989), 158.

[29] Jung wrote in *Liber Novus*, "To give birth to the ancient in a new time is creation. This is the creation of the new, and that redeems me. Salvation is the resolution of the task. The task is to give birth to the old in a new time." *Liber Novus*, 311.

C.G. Jung and the Prophet Puzzle

Lance S. Owens

The Red Book: Liber Novus is a volume that defies categorization or comparison; it resounds with voices beyond our common ken.[1] Though a singularly modern document, it is nevertheless transcribed and presented in the form of a medieval manuscript. And since its belated publication in 2009, it has proved to be a work that perplexes most people who venture into its visionary domain. Whether one approaches *Liber Novus* as a historian, a psychologist, a literary critic, or simply as an interested reader, the puzzle is the same: What was Carl Gustav Jung doing, what was happening to him? Is this record to be interpreted as an imaginative literary creation, the product of an incipient psychosis, or a psychological work veiled in prophetic language?

Of course, *Liber Novus* is none of those latter things. To meet this book, one must apprehend that C.G. Jung elaborated *Liber Novus* in the form of a revelation; it is a message to mankind at a critical juncture in human history. This is a visionary work in the most fundamental sense of those words: Jung fashioned the book from his journal accounts of visionary and imaginative experiences, events he originally chronicled between 1913 and 1916. Though he labored at calligraphically transcribing the text into his illuminated red leather-bound folio volume for over 16 years, and though he asserted the book was the foundation of all his later work, it is a manuscript he chose never to publicly disclose. He knew it would not be understood by men of his time. Now, nearly a hundred years later, it has finally been revealed. Will people of this time understand it? Can this age comprehend a man who experienced and carefully recorded visions, ultimately regarded them as a revelation, and recognized in them the prophecy of a vast new coming age?

Vision, revelation, prophecy: How will the "spirit of this time" decipher such archaic words? And how will coming generations meet this strange tome, elaborated as a revelation and implicitly addressed as a message to them? I cannot prophesy how the future will view this book, but I do now know that *Liber Novus* and the lifework of C.G. Jung are inextricably intertwined. Any understanding of *Liber Novus* inevitably demands an engagement with Jung and his tireless efforts toward awakening modern consciousness to the ancient and mysterious fact of the soul.

The Hermeneutics of Vision

Dr. C.G. Jung certainly struggled with his own understanding of the visionary and imaginative experience that erupted in the fall of 1913 and continued nearly nightly into the spring of 1914.[2] Early on, he accepted the possibility that it might be a path into insanity. It began in October 1913 with two separate spontaneous visions of a wave of blood consuming Europe. Confronted with prolonged visual hallucinations, Jung conceded that interior powers he could neither resist nor ignore were demanding his attention. He interpreted his predicament firstly in personal terms, as a summons to engage lost, rejected, or hidden aspects of himself. In the opening words of his journal on 12 November 1913, he petitioned reunion with his "almost forgotten soul." Throughout four subsequent weeks of rigorous nightly introspection, a voice from the depths began to answer him. He listened.

As a physician with extensive clinical training, he committed himself to keeping a contemporaneous and carefully documented record of his nightly endeavors. In December 1913, two months after beginning his exploration, Jung described the journal in clinical terms, calling it "the book of my most difficult experiment."[3] In this and the five journal volumes that followed, he meticulously narrated what he saw and heard, and what he said in response. It was an experiment, a perilous journey of discovery into unknown psychic terrain.

Ten years later, Cary Baynes recorded Jung's description of his approach to the imaginative encounters, recounted to her privately in 1924:

You said some of it hurt your sense of the fitness of things terribly, and that you had shrunk from putting it down as it came to you, but that you had started on the principle of 'voluntariness' that is of making no corrections and so you had stuck to that.[4]

Jung's initial interpretive challenge was "putting it down as it came," recording in his journal the voice of the depths in dialogue, in visionary scene, and in image. This was an extraordinary initial hermeneutic task.[5] He described his effort at the outset of *Liber Novus*: "I speak in images. With nothing else can I express the words from the depths."[6]

"In the beginning, when I wrote these things," Jung told Aniela Jaffé in 1957, "there was this voice whispering to me, 'this is art.'" But he would not accept it. He forcefully countered "that it was not art, that it was nature."[7] This is an enigmatic distinction, and it needs further explanation. Jung perceived that through a concentrated engagement with imagination, fantasy and vision, he had gained entry into an autonomous realm of nature. It was real, it was independent of his will, and it had a tale to tell. What he recorded was not *his artistic creation*. Though his illuminated folio volume can certainly be viewed as a work of art, whatever artfulness materialized within *Liber Novus* was—in Jung's understanding—a voice of *nature*.

During the early months of 1914, the events he recorded often presented with a portentous prophetic tone. But by spring the visions slowly abated and then ceased entirely with the coming of summer. Jung recognized he had been gifted with something extraordinary; however, what he should do with it, or how to further interpret it, remained obscure. When the First World War erupted in August 1914, his interpretation of the experience and his journal record took a radical turn. Jung immediately recognized that what he had seen, heard, and recorded over the preceding months did indeed contain a prophecy: By willful engagement with the autonomous natural functions of vision and imagination, he had been shown the way of what is to come. Jung now confronted strong evidence that his visionary venture had not been of solely personal or subjective import. It was epochal; the account he had recorded was a revelation. It was the core of a new book, to be addressed to a new age.

Over the ensuing months Jung composed a thousand-page handwritten draft of this new book. Into it he transcribed the visionary events recorded in his journals, adding to them an additional layer of reflection and commentary. This was the culmination of Jung's initial hermeneutics of the visions—the essential condensation of his visionary experience into sensuous form. His interpretative journey with this primary record would, however, move through several further phases—indeed, this hermeneutic enterprise became his life's hidden work.

The revelation was not, however, finished in 1914—as Jung may have then supposed. After concluding the initial drafts and beginning the formal calligraphic transcription of his record, in late summer 1915 a second wave of visionary and imaginative experiences commenced. During this latter period, which extended in his manuscript record through 1916, the revelatory and prophetic tenor of the account was further augmented. This latter part of the revelation is recorded in the final section of *Liber Novus*, titled "Scrutinies," which Jung drafted in 1917. During this period, Philemon became a central figure in his imaginative encounters. The nature of Jung's relationship with Philemon was hinted at in *Memories, Dreams, Reflections*. Jung stated in that memoir, "At times he [Philemon] seemed to me quite real, as if he were a living personality. I went walking up and down the garden with him, and to me he was what the Indians call a guru."[8]

However, in private comments to Cary Baynes in 1923, Jung described Philemon as something ineffably greater. He was, in multiform manifestations, an avatar of "the Master … the same who inspired Buddha, Mani, Christ, Mahomet—all those who may be said to have communed with God."[9] Above Philemon's image on folio 154 of *The Red Book*, a page completed around 1924, Jung penned an appellation in Greek: "Father of the Prophets, Beloved Philemon."[10] A few years later, on the enormous mural painting of Philemon at his Bollingen Tower, Jung added a similar tribute: "Philemon, the Prophets' Primal Father."[11]

A Book of Revelation

Is *Liber Novus* a revelation? During several decades lecturing and teaching about C.G. Jung's life and work, I have found that the words *vision, revelation,* and *prophecy* are noxious reactants when cast into any alembic of academic discourse, even when added in homeopathic dilution. These words reek of rancid superstition. They have long since passed, it seems, their scholastic "sell by" date. Nonetheless, in the *Black Book* journals, and in comments transcribed by Aniela Jaffé in 1957, Jung did speak of *Liber Novus* as having been elaborated in the form of a revelation. He did avow that he had seen visions, and later in life he did expound at length on the prophetic message of his New Book.[12]

To say Jung rejected the archaic role of prophet is, of course, both accurate and completely insufficient. This is a crucial issue in understanding Jung, his *Liber Novus*, and his hermeneutics of vision. Simply proclaiming, "No, he didn't do *that*" is no solution at all.

Among the previously unseen source materials Dr. Sonu Shamdasani provided in the editorial apparatus of *Liber Novus* is a section from Jung's journal dated 5 January 1922, in which Jung entered a conversation with his soul about his vocation.[13] At the time of this journal entry, Jung had worked for seven years on the transcription and illumination of his *Liber Novus* manuscripts into the big, red leather-covered folio volume. He would continue the effort for at least seven more years. This journal entry illustrates how he perceived his book in the midst of that labor.

Jung had been unable to sleep and addressed his Soul, asking why. She said there was no time to sleep; he had great work to begin; he must go to "a higher level of consciousness." Jung asked, "What is it? Speak!"

> *Soul:* You should listen: to no longer be a Christian is easy. But what next? For more is yet to come. Everything is waiting for you. And you? You remain silent and have nothing to say. But you should speak. Why have you received the revelation? You should not hide it. You

concern yourself with the form? Is the form important,
when it is a matter of revelation?
Jung: But you are not thinking that I should publish what
I have written [*Liber Novus*]? That would be a misfortune.
And who would understand it?[14]

Three days later, his Soul explained further: "You know everything that
is to be known about the manifested revelation, but you do not yet live
everything that is to be lived at this time. ... The way is symbolic."[15]

He had received the manifest revelation, but still he struggled with
the proper form for its expression. Thirty-five years after that journal
entry, Jung affirmed to Aniela Jaffé, "The Red Book is an attempt at an
elaboration [of the imaginal events] in the sense of Revelation."[16]

An Ethical Obligation

In his introduction to *Liber Novus*, Sonu Shamdasani documented
that during the early 1920s Jung continued correcting and emending
the typescript drafts of *Liber Novus*, and publication of the book was
then still under consideration.[17] But there was an insurmountable
impediment to publication: "Who would understand it?"

Around 1928, Jung began to realize that another course was
both possible and necessary. Before his book could be exposed, he
needed to establish a hermeneutics—a new interpretive approach—
to visionary works such as his own. Sonu Shamdasani has described
the following years of labor as Jung's effort to elucidate a "psychology
of the religion-making process,"[18] and to produce a "comparative
study of the individuation process."[19]

This period of work, extending until about 1944—the fateful
year of Jung's grave illness and near-death visions—may constru-
ctively be understood as the essential next phase in Jung's hermeneutic enterprise.[20] The foundational task was the crystallization of
his visionary experience into word and image. But in order for
coming generations to comprehend *Liber Novus*—the molten
magma of vision he worked to form and from which he extracted

his science—an entirely new interpretive approach to imaginative experience was required.

Essentially everything Jung wrote from 1916 onward was oriented to creating an interpretive modus that could meet the seeming madness of his *Liber Novus*. What emerged in this next phase of Jung's work was an organic development—a necessary additional stratum—in his extended hermeneutics of vision. His writings during this time constitute a major portion of the published *Collected Works*; readers of those volumes, however, were heretofore granted little understanding of what the man was actually doing or why he was doing it.

In remarks recorded by Aniela Jaffé on 3 October 1957, Jung stated that the development of his science—which implicitly included his comparative study of the individuation process and the religion-making process—was in fact an *ethical obligation* laid upon his shoulders by *Liber Novus*.

In preparation for her biography of Jung, between September 1956 and May 1958 Aniela Jaffé conducted a series of interviews with him. Jaffé made careful stenographic records of Jung's spontaneous and wide-ranging statements during these sessions (her transcript of Jung's remarks fills 391 typed pages, and is available in the Library of Congress). Unfortunately, many things Jung said to Jaffé were excluded from the heavily edited text of *Memories, Dreams, Reflections*. The transcript of the session on 3 October 1957 includes several examples of crucially important remarks that were not conveyed in the now quasi-canonical memoir Jaffé compiled.

Jung began his comments that day by stating his visions had taken him in mind or spirit (*geistig voraus genommen*) a few hundred years into the future. He added, "That is why I am considered 'wise.'"[21] Jung recounted that by engaging in his visions, he had figuratively fallen into an immense hole; his merit was, he supposed, that he had not been lost in it. From the visions and dreams his science came into being. Science was the "frightful means" by which he "wriggled out of the hole."[22]

Nonetheless, he added, images such as he had met imposed a tremendous obligation. "They come to a man with supremacy." If one does not regard the knowledge imparted by such things as an ethical obligation, one falls into the trap of magic. When the ethical obligation is not seen, the knowledge thereby gained can be destructive—it can destroy the person and others.[23]

Jung continued, describing to Jaffé several events in *Liber Novus*: his fear during the visionary encounter with the devil;[24] and his struggle to heal Izdubar—the god from the East whom he had stricken unto death with his modernity.[25] Concluding, he gave a summary description of his *Red Book*:

> The Red Book is an attempt at elaboration [of the visions] in the sense of Revelation. It was my hypothesis that if I were faithful to the call, doing the best I could, I would then free myself.

Nonetheless, his elaboration of the revelation and faithfulness to the call were insufficient. There remained his ethical obligation, and that demanded a further hermeneutic step. He continued:

> But only then I saw that this [elaboration as Revelation] did not bring liberation. It became clear to me that I had to return to the human side. I understood that I had to go back to solid land, and that is science. From the insights I had to draw concrete conclusions. I have given my life for it. The elaboration in the Red Book was necessary, but this also led to an insight into the ethical obligation. I have paid with my life, and I have paid with my science.[26]

To that statement, Jung added a final verdict: "The first thing freed me, one way or the other."[27]

The elaboration of *Liber Novus* in the form of a revelation freed Jung—he had been "faithful to the call." It also encumbered him with heavy obligations, which he disbursed over the following 40 years with his life and with his science. In accepting the ethical onus laid upon him by *Liber Novus*, Jung gave birth to an extraordinary hermeneutics of human imagination and its unbounded psychic source.

Three Prophecies

Over the course of his life Dr. Jung said many strange things. Among them was the above quoted statement to Aniela Jaffé that he had mentally been taken several hundred years into the future. How will one interpret such words? Was this a form of madness, a delusion? Was it a bald-faced falsehood? Was it the testimony of a seer and revelator? Was it an event of consciousness that future generations will interpret in yet unseen ways? These are questions that must be engaged in a close reading of *Liber Novus*, and in a vigilant evaluation of the man Carl Gustav Jung.

Jung's sense of having seen into the future is documented in *Liber Novus*. There are several such junctures in his journals, but perhaps the most impressive is the account he titled "The Three Prophecies." He began his transcription of this section into *Liber Novus* with an introductory comment:

> Wondrous things came nearer. I called my soul and asked her to dive down into the floods, whose distant roaring I could hear. This happened on 22 January of the year 1914, as recorded in my black book. And thus she plunged into the darkness like a shot, and from the depths she called out: 'Will you accept what I bring?'[28]

This is the only place in the text of *Liber Novus* where Jung specifically references both his *Black Book* journal account and the exact date when the event occurred—those facts attest to the importance with which he endowed this experience.

His Soul dived into the depths. She brought back three images: War, Magic, and Religion.

> From the flooding darkness the son of the earth had brought, my soul gave me ancient things that pointed to the future. She gave me three things: The misery of war, the darkness of magic, and the gift of religion. ...
> These three mean the unleashing of chaos and its power, just as they also mean the binding of chaos. War is obvious

and everybody sees it. Magic is dark and no one sees it. Religion is still to come, but it will become evident. Did you think that the horrors of such atrocious warfare would come over us? Did you think that magic existed? Did you think about a new religion? I sat up for long nights and looked ahead at what was to come and I shuddered. Do you believe me? I am not too concerned. What should I believe? What should I disbelieve? I saw and I shuddered.

But my spirit could not grasp the monstrous, and could not conceive the extent of what was to come. ... I felt the burden of the most terrible work of the times ahead. I saw where and how, but no word can grasp it, no will can conquer it....

I would like to avert my eyes, close my ears and deny all my senses; I would like to be someone among you, who knows nothing and who never saw anything. It is too much and too unexpected. But I saw it and my memory will not leave me alone.[29]

Had Jung seen into the future? Whether or not one might now believe him, he rejoined, "I am not too concerned. What should I believe? What should I disbelieve? I saw and I shuddered."

War, Magic, and Religion. War is obvious, and it continues. But magic? What is that? In his journal record, it is apparent that at the time Jung was struggling to grasp the nature of magic. The next night, 23 January 1914, the Soul compounded his confusion by presenting him with a mysterious magical gift.[30] In bewilderment he inquired, "Magic! What should I do with magic? I don't believe in it, I can't believe in it." The Soul replied, "Magic will do a lot for you." Four nights later his imaginative journey led on to the garden gate of an old magician named Philemon.[31] Philemon had more to teach about magic.

In his publications during later years, Jung frequently mentioned magic, usually in the context of primitive peoples' perception and interpretation of psychic phenomena. He explained in a 1928 essay,

"'Magical' is simply another word for 'psychic.'"[32] But of course for enlightened ones, "magic is dark and no one sees it."

"And religion is still to come, but it will become evident." The singular, overarching theme of Jung's revelations in *Liber Novus* is that we stand at the threshold of a new age. Synchronous with the turning of the heavens and the passage of the astrological age of Pisces, the two millennia-long aeon dominated by Christianity is now approaching its terminus. In the coming age—the new aeon of Aquarius—a new god-image and a new religion will eventually take form. This is the proclamation Jung presented on the first folio page of the *Red Book*; it is "The Way of What Is to Come."[33]

Tertium non datur

Jung took his role as a natural scientist very seriously; throughout the central years of his life, he frequently addressed himself specifically to the scientific medical and psychological communities of his time. But those communities never really embraced or understood Jung, and have now relegated him mostly to historical footnotes.

Many of Jung's writings focused on "experience of the numinous" and the nature of symbol formation in the development of religion. Furthermore, over the course of several decades, he engaged in dynamic and influential dialogues with prominent 20th-century scholars of both Eastern and Western religious traditions. Nonetheless, Jung's deliberations now find faint welcome in the curricula of academic religious studies programs. And, of course, within the theological cloisters of orthodox religion, Jung is generally spurned as an occultist or neognostic heretic.

It appears that Jung's perception of psychic reality positioned him within a shadowy domain now disowned within both the academies of science and religion. Why is that?

Wouter Hanegraaff recently identified a fundamental fault line in secular and religious scholarship, and I believe his analysis helps explain Jung's "nonreception" by either province. Dr. Hanegraaff—a professor at the University of Amsterdam and a prominent academic voice in hermetic and religious studies—contends that the normative prototypes for the study of religion "are grounded in monotheistic, more specifically Christian, even more specifically Protestant, theological biases about 'true' religion."[34] Religion is further positioned as being in opposition to secular studies. However, both fields share a problematic blind spot:

> They both think that 'religion' stands against 'the secular.' However, the historical record shows that these two defined themselves not just against one another but, simultaneously, against a *third* domain…. This third domain that they both rejected has been referred to by different names, but the most well-known are *superstition* and *magic*.[35]

Religion and secular science positioned themselves in a dyadic or oppositional relationship, but in fact both defined themselves not only explicitly against each other, but implicitly against magic and superstition. For both domains, this other territory is a *tertium non datur*—a third and unexamined fact. "Magic is dark and no one sees it."

Hanegraaff employed the terms "superstition" and "magic" as shorthand for a range of alternative, nonorthodox currents in culture, potentially including folk magic, shamanic practices, Hermetic *magia*, alchemy, Paracelsian medicine, Mesmerism, 19th-century Spiritualism —and perhaps even the 20th-century science of C.G. Jung. Whether or not that latter name is properly appended to this list, Jung was nonetheless immensely interested in *all* of the former subjects.

"Did you think that magic existed?"

Jung's conception of the psyche encompassed—and reified—a domain of human experience articulated by terms such as "superstition" and "magic." He allowed that "magical" was simply another term for "psychic." As he perceived it, psyche was the preternatural fact pervading nature—and it was undeniably spooky. In the early 1950s,

Jung mused on its mystery using conceptual terms gleaned from theoretical physics[36]:

> Psyche can function as though space did not exist. The psyche can thus be independent of space, of time, and of causality. This explains the possibility of magic.[37]

> If we consider the psyche as a whole, we come to the conclusion that the unconscious psyche ... exists in a space-time continuum, where time is no longer time and space no longer space. Accordingly, causality ceases too.[38]

The psyche was both the boundless underpinning of consciousness and, imaginably, also its primal source. In commentary on *The Tibetan Book of the Great Liberation* composed in 1939, Jung asserted,

> The psyche is therefore all-important; it is the all-per-vading Breath, the Buddha-essence; it is the Buddha-Mind, the One, the *Dharmakāya*. All existence emanates from it, and all separate forms dissolve back into it.[39]

In the section of *Liber Novus* titled "The Three Prophecies," Jung asked future readers, "Did you think that magic existed?" One might now additionally inquire, "Do you think psychic reality exists?" Jung's views on the reality of the psyche certainly stand beyond what the "spirit of this time" accepts. But at the speculative edges of quantum theory, cognitive studies, and theoretical physics, eminent scientists have recently forwarded unitive panpsychic theories of consciousness and matter no less uncanny than Dr. Jung's.

Jung's affirmation of psychic reality was, nonetheless, not grounded in philosophical or quantum theoretical speculations. It grew organically from, and in an ethical obligation to, unique observations of psychic processes. Those observations were, of course, subjective; Jung confessed this ultimate subjectivity of his work on several occasions. Speaking in London at the Tavistock Clinic in 1935, he stated: "Never forget that in psychology the *means* by which you judge and observe the psyche is the *psyche* itself. ... In psychology the observer is the observed."[40] At the Eranos Conference in 1946, Jung explained further,

> The tragic thing is that psychology has no self consistent mathematics at its disposal, but only a calculus of subjective prejudices. ... There is no medium for psychology to reflect itself in: it can only portray itself in itself, and describe itself. That, logically, is also the principle of my own method: it is, at bottom, a purely experiential process. ...[41]

His method of science was "a purely experiential process." Experiences that Jung vigilantly recorded in his *Black Book* journals had apparently granted him vision into a vast continuum of time—to the coming of wars, of magic, and of the emergence of a new religion. In that context, his statements about the psyche being "independent of space, of time, and of causality," or existing "in a space-time continuum, where time is no longer time and space no longer space," are revealed as having a *subjective* empirical foundation.

I have read the section of *Liber Novus* titled "The Three Prophecies" many times, and I have on occasion sat into the night pondering his words: *War, Magic, and Religion.* Jung concluded his account of that vast future with grim words, "I saw and I shuddered." I do not, of course, know *what* he saw, nor do I fathom *how* he saw it. But following his path, I have seen foreshadowed there "the way of what is to come."

War is obvious, and everybody sees it. In 1914, Jung realized that his visions had foretold the coming of war. But was it just *one war*? I peer out across the continuum of time and sense that war is not done. War is yet to come. The horrendous wars waged by peoples of the West during the last three centuries were typically provoked by quests for geopolitical dominance, or by political ideologies and nationalistic agendas. Do we now approach an epochal conflagration evoked in the service of ancient gods at the twilight of their time? I see and I shudder.

Magic is the second mysterious movement within Jung's "Three Prophecies." What is this dark and unseen power, and what role does it play in his vision of the future? Again, lacking answers, I can only offer intuitions. In *Liber Novus*, Jung was forced to give magic focused attention. He subsequently described it as an aspect of the psyche. The "magic" of the psyche grants vision into past, present, and future and opens states of consciousness where "time is no longer time, and space no longer space." Throughout human history, however, magic has been portrayed as following two divergent paths, each with very different objectives. Magic could be used to manipulate matter and people for personal gain; historically, this was labeled black, low, or *goetic* magic. In contradistinction, the higher road of magic sought knowledge about the self and its relation to divinity; this was the objective of *theurgic* magic. What magic awaits people of the future? Which of these two ancient paths will be pursued?

Imagination is the doorway into the psychic realm, as Jung affirmed.[42] It is an infinitely creative source; it can foreshadow things not yet materially existent. And, like magic, it can be plied to very different purposes. Modern technological culture has made every effort to monetize the power of creative imagination. The results now abound. They enwrap us like a web. But does a magical hungry spider weave this web? It so, it feeds off our attention and, ultimately, it sucks the blood of human life. Vampiric feeding is a squalid legacy of *goetia*, the black magic method to *means*.

The psyche can be milked; it offers nourishment to human creativity. But its nature and ultimate source remain a mystery to our age. Perhaps when Jung looked into the future, he saw a coming time that comprehended the psyche's fundamental reality and acknowledged, "All existence emanates from it, and all separate forms dissolve back into it." Whether mankind follows a high or low road into the future, Jung envisioned that a confrontation with the magic of the psyche loomed on the way.

"A new religion is still to come, but it will become evident." This is the last movement in Jung's "Three Prophecies." Throughout *Liber Novus*, Jung looked toward that coming religion, and he associated it with a heritage of so-called heresies rejected by the passing age— suppressed nonorthodox traditions that had affirmed the indwelling mystery of divinity in humankind. "What will come to you lies within yourself. But what lies there!" When a future new religion does finally form, it will evolve in reflection of that indwelling wonder.

In conclusion to this profound prophetic outpouring, Jung exclaimed in exhaustion:

> How can I fathom what will happen during the next eight hundred years, up to the time when the One begins his rule? I am speaking only of what is to come. … The future should be left to those of the future. I return to the small and the real, for this is the great way, the way of what is to come. I return to my simple reality, to my undeniable and most minuscule being.[43]

The Prophet Puzzle

It is difficult to prophesy, especially about the future.[44] Nonetheless, during his 9 October 2009 address on occasion of the publication of *The Red Book: Liber Novus*, Sonu Shamdasani was asked to prophesy about the effect this work would have on the future. He replied:

> I think, donning my prophet's garb, I would say that I feel quite certain, in ten years hence, this will indeed transform our understanding of Jung, such that no one will bother with the biographical literature of the previous period, and there will be a whole new translation of Jung's scholarship. … I am certain this will completely transform the under-standing of Jung.[45]

I agree with Dr. Shamdasani. However, surveying the situation now nearly 10 years henceforth, it appears the time frame foreseen in his prophecy was far too short. Entrenched interpretations are not displaced in a decade. The transformation of our understanding of C.G. Jung—now freshly illuminated by *Liber Novus*—is unavoidably a multigenerational task.

Jung elaborated *Liber Novus* as a revelation. It was crystalized from the molten magma of visionary experience. It contained a prophecy of a coming new age and the coming of a new religion. Who (except a proper prophet) can foretell how such facts will affect future understanding of Jung or of the future itself? And inevitably, the above assertions evoke a further disquieting question: Was Jung a prophet? What might the archaic word "prophet" signify to our own time or to a coming new age? These are all pieces of the insoluble "prophet puzzle" bequeathed us by Carl Gustav Jung. In *Liber Novus,* Jung proffered a vision of the way to come. But only time can tell its tale.

Endnotes

I thank Vicky Jo Varner for her expert editorial assistance with this essay.

1. C.G. Jung, *The Red Book: Liber Novus*, ed. Sonu Shamdasani, tr. John Peck, Mark Kyburz, and Sonu Shamdasani (New York, NY: W. W. Norton, 2009), 264. Hereafter cited as *Liber Novus*. This work is often referenced simply as the "Red Book." For clarity, a distinction must be made between the terms *Liber Novus* and the "Red Book." The *Red Book* is the illuminated calligraphic red-leather-bound volume into which Jung eventually transcribed about two-thirds of his draft manuscripts of *Liber Novus*. When speaking hereafter about the "Red Book," I specifically reference the physical folio volume transcribed and illuminated by Jung. Citations to *Liber Novus* reference the published edition of Jung's manuscripts, as edited and compiled by Sonu Shamdasani.

2. For a detailed introduction to these events, see Lance S. Owens, "The Hermeneutics of Vision: C.G. Jung and *Liber Novus*," *The Gnostic: A Journal of Gnosticism, Western Esotericism and Spirituality*, Issue 3 (July 2010), 23–46. (Online edition available.)

3. *Black Book 2*, 58; *Liber Novus*, 200 n67; C.G. Jung, *The Black Books of C.G. Jung (1913-1932)*, ed. Sonu Shamdasani, (Stiftung der Werke von C.G. Jung & W. W. Norton), forthcoming.

4. Cary F. Baynes papers; *Liber Novus*, 213.

5. Owens, "The Hermeneutics of Vision: C.G. Jung and *Liber Novus*."

6. *Liber Novus*, 230.

7. X. Roelli translation of "Memories Protocols," pg. 31; Carl G. Jung Protocols, Box 1, Library of Congress.

8. C.G. Jung, *Memories, Dreams, Reflections*, Aniela Jaffé, ed. (Rev. ed., New York, NY: Vintage Books, 1963), 183.

9. Cary F. Baynes papers, Jan 26, 1924; *Liber Novus*, 213.

10. This image of Philemon in *Liber Novus* was probably completed in late 1924 or early 1925; at some point Jung added in the margin beside the painting an English quote from the Bhagavad-Gita about the nature of the avatar: "The bhagavadgita says: whenever there is a decline of the

law and an increase in iniquity, then I put forth myself. For the rescue of the pious and for the destruction of the evildoers, for the establishment of the law I am born in every age." *Liber Novus*, 317 n281.

11 Jung began construction of the Tower at Bollingen in 1923. It is unknown when he painted the mural of Philemon, but it was probably before 1930. The Greek inscription on the Tower mural reads: "ΦΙΛΗΜΩΝ ΤΩΝ ΠΡΟΦΗΤΩΝ ΠΡΟΠΑΤΩΡ." The final word, *Propator*, implies both "forefather" and "the very first" or primal father.

12 Jung's last four major works, which I have called the "Last Quartet," are all a mature commentary on *Liber Novus*. For a discussion of Jung's "Last Quartet" see Lance S. Owens, *Jung in Love: The Mysterium in Liber Novus* (Gnosis Archive Books, 2015), 7-9; "Jung in Love: The Mysterium in *Liber Novus*," in Thomas Arzt, ed., *Das Rote Buch: C.G. Jungs Reise zum "anderen Pol der Welt." Studienreihe zur Analytischen Psychologie*, Bd. 5 (Würzburg: Königshausen & Neumann, 2015), 215-7. (Online edition available.)

13 *Liber Novus*, 211-2.

14 Ibid.

15 Ibid.

16 "Das Rote Buch ist der Versuch einer Elaboration im Sinne der Offenbarung." Jaffé's typescript of her September 1956 to May 1958 interview sessions with Jung is available in the Library of Congress; "Memories Protocols, " Carl G. Jung Protocols, Box 1, Library of Congress, p. 148; hereafter cited as MP. All translations and paraphrases of MP are my own; in notations I have included the original Jaffé transcription of key sections, in the original German.

17 Shamdasani, *Liber Novus*, 212-15.

18 *Liber Novus*, 212.

19 *Liber Novus*, 219.

20 The near-death visions in 1944 reoriented Jung; on the nature of his work in the following period; see Lance S. Owens, *Jung in Love: The Mysterium in Liber Novus* (Gnosis Archive Press, 2015), 6-10; and "Jung and *Aion*: Time, Vision and a Wayfaring Man," *Psychological Perspectives* (Journal of the C.G. Jung Institute of Los Angeles, 2011) 54:259-266. (Online editions available.)

21 3 October 1957, MP, 147; Jaffé transcribed: "Ich habe ja geistig einige 100 Jahre voraus genommen, das heisst, es hat mich um einige 100 Jahre in die Zukunft versetzt. Darum gelte ich für 'weise.'"

22 The German text has been redacted at the request of the Foundation for the Collected Works of C.G. Jung. As of the date of publication of this edition the source material awaits publication.

23 The German text has been redacted at the request of the Foundation for the Collected Works of C.G. Jung. As of the date of publication of this edition the source material awaits publication.

24 *Liber Novus*, 288-9.

25 *Liber Novus*, 277-88.

26 The German text has been redacted at the request of the Foundation for the Collected Works of C.G. Jung. As of the date of publication of this edition the source material awaits publication.

27 Ibid.

28 *Liber Novus*, 305.

29 *Liber Novus*, 306.

30 *Liber Novus*, 307.

31 *Liber Novus*, 312.

32 C.G. Jung, "The Relations between the Ego and the Unconscious," in *CW*, vol. 7 (Princeton, NJ: Princeton University Press, 1966), par. 293.

33 For an extended discussion of Jung's vision of the new aeon, see Lance S. Owens, "Jung and *Aion*: Time, Vision and a Wayfaring Man," *Psychological Perspectives* (Journal of the C.G. Jung Institute of Los Angeles, 2011) 54:253-89. (Online edition available.)

34 Wouter J. Hanegraaff, "Reconstructing 'Religion' from the Bottom Up," *Numen: International Review for the History of Religions,* 63 (2016), 577–606.

35 Ibid., 577, 591.

36 Jung had a close and influential association with the Nobel Prize winning physicist Wolfgang Pauli, a founder of quantum theory; their personal relationship extended from 1932 until Pauli's death in 1958. Each man highly valued the insights of the other. See Suzanne Gieser, *The Innermost Kernel: Depth Psychology and Quantum Physics - Wolfgang Pauli's Dialogue with C.G. Jung* (Berlin: Springer, 2005).

37 Journal of Suzanne Percheron in *C.G. Jung, Emma Jung and Toni Wolff - A Collection of Remembrances* (The Analytical Psychology Club of San Francisco, 1982), 62.

38 Gerhard Adler, ed., *C.G. Jung Letters* (Princeton, NJ: Princeton University Press, 1973), Vol. 1, 547.

39 C.G. Jung, "Psychological Commentary on 'The Tibetan Book of the Great Liberation'" (1939), in *CW*, vol. 11 (Princeton, NJ: Princeton University Press, 1969, par. 771.

40 C.G. Jung, "The Tavistock Lectures" (1935), in *CW*, vol. 18 (Princeton, NJ: Princeton University Press, 1976), par. 277.

41 C.G. Jung, "On the Nature of the Psyche" (1946), in *CW*, vol. 8 (Princeton, NJ: Princeton University Press, 1969), par. 421.

42 C.G. Jung, *Mysterium Conjuntionis*, in *CW*, vol. 14 (Princeton, NJ: Princeton University Press, 1963), par. 752.

43 The first statement appears only in the draft manuscript; *Liber Novus*, 306 & n236.

44 This Danish adage has been attributed to numerous persons over the last fifty years, but never to C.G. Jung.

45 My transcription; Sonu Shamdasani, 9 October 2009 address at the New York Academy of Medicine, New York City.

In a World That Has Gone Mad, Is What We Really Need ... A Red Book?

Plato, Goethe, Schelling, Nietzsche, and Jung

Paul Bishop

In his papers in the Library of Congress, William McGuire records the reaction of Richard Hull, the translator of Jung's works, when Aniela Jaffé showed him the *Red Book*: Hull described it as "full of real mad drawings with commentaries in monkish script; I'm not surprised Jung keeps it under lock and key!"[1] This reaction is an understandable one, and for many years the work did indeed remain under lock and key—not just during Jung's lifetime, but for several decades afterward, until finally Sonu Shamdasani published his edition of *The Red Book* in 2009.

And madness is a key theme in *The Red Book* itself. In "The Way of What Is to Come," Jung admits to the spirit of the time, "It is true, it is true, what I speak is the greatness and intoxication and ugliness of madness"; in "Descent into Hell in the Future," he asks, "But who can withstand fear when the divine intoxication and madness comes to him?"; and when, in "The Sacrificial Murder," Jung is invited by his soul to eat the liver of the murdered child, he responds (quite understandably) by asking, "What are you demanding? This is absolute madness."[2] In "Nox secunda," Jung is literally carted off to a madhouse and—stripped of his clothes—he ponders that "the problem of madness is profound":

> Divine madness—a higher form of the irrationality of the life streaming through us—at any rate a madness that cannot be integrated into present-day society—but how? What if the form of society were integrated into madness? At this point things grow dark, and there is no end in sight.[3]

As we shall explore, this theme of madness points not just to *The Red Book*'s relevance for today, but also to its intellectual roots—notably, its roots in Plato, Goethe, Schelling, and Nietzsche. One of the great achievements of Jung's work in general and his *Red Book* in particular is to open up and make relevant these earlier works in the Western tradition.

Plato

Although in Book 9 of the *Republic* Socrates expresses reservations about the way in which desire manifests itself in dreams (571c-d), in another of the middle dialogues, the *Phaedrus*, he cites the view of Stesichorus of Himera that "the greatest blessings come by way of madness"; this kind of madness is "heaven-sent" (244a).[4] Basing himself on Stesichorus, Socrates distinguishes between four types of madness: first, divinely inspired prophecy: "It was when they were mad that the prophetess at Delphi and the priestesses at Dodona achieved so much for which both states and individuals in Greece are thankful." (244b)[5] This kind of madness is called *mantic* or *oionoistic* (244d). Second, there a madness which, "when grievous maladies and afflictions have beset certain families by reason of some ancient sin," appears and, "breaking out into prophecy," has "secured relief" (244d-e).[6] This kind of madness secures relief "by recourse to prayer and worship, and in consequence thereof rites and means of purification were established, and the sufferer was brought out of danger, alike for the present and for the future." (244e)[7]

Third, there is a form of possession or madness of which "the Muses are the source," (245a) a kind of madness that "seizes a tender, virgin soul and stimulates it to rapt passionate expression, especially in lyric poetry" and in this form glorifies "the countless mighty deeds of ancient times for the instruction of posterity." (245a)[8] And fourth, there is the madness of love—"sent from heaven for the advantage both of lover and beloved [...] a gift of the gods, fraught with the highest bliss." (245b-c)[9] In different ways, all these kinds of madness are exemplified by Jung's *Red Book*, but especially the third kind.

Further on in the *Phaedrus*, Socrates resumes, consolidates, and modifies his argument as a distinction between two kinds of madness, one "resulting from human ailments," the other resulting from "a divine disturbance of our conventions of conduct," (265a) and subdividing the divine kind into four types ascribed to four gods: "the inspiration of the prophet to Apollo, that of the mystic to Dionysus, that of the poet to the Muses, and a fourth type which we declared to be the highest, the madness of the lover, to Aphrodite and Eros." (265b)[10] Now love, or *eros*, turns out to be a major theme of Jung's *Red Book*, although it is arguably not its only or most important theme. For Jung's stance on love is, one might say, in a state of constant equivocation. In "On the Service of the Soul," Jung recalls Christ's teaching that "God is love" (cf. 1 John 4: 16), but he adds that "you should know that love is also terrible."[11] In "The Conception of the God," he reprises this view, asking: "But what is more ambiguous than love?" and declaring: "Love is the way of life, but your love is only on the way of life if you have a left and a right."[12] Citing the motto that *Eindeutigkeit ist Einseitigkeit* (to have one meaning is to be one-sided) and "leads to death," Jung praises ambiguity as "the way of life": It allows us to move forward, just as using first one foot, then the other, does.[13]

This ambiguity is reflected in Jung's relationship to Salome, governed as it is by love and fear in equal measure,[14] and it goes on to become a constantly repeated theme. In "The Magician," Jung holds in his hand a golden, royal crown bearing the inscription "Love never ends" (cf. 1 Cor. 13: 8), and while hanging, Odin-like, from the tree, he ponders "ominous things that are dangerously ambiguous" and the distinction between "heavenly and earthly love," or what he calls "the mystery of the crown and the serpent."[15] (This entire episode anticipates Jung's later meditation on the slogan *amor vincit omnia* in *Memories, Dreams, Reflections*.)[16] In fact, in one of the most devastating monologues of *The Red Book*, Jung sets up a distinction between love and life, declaring that he will speak no more "for the sake of love, but for the sake of life"—that "love seeks to have and to hold, but life wants more" and that "the beginning of things is love, but the being of things is life," a distinction he describes as "terrible."[17]

When in *Scrutinies* he returns to the theme of love, Jung's tone becomes decidedly Nietzschean as he protests that "what you call love oozes with self-interest and desirousness."[18] In *Thus Spoke Zarathustra*, Nietzsche had inveighed in no uncertain terms against the "love of one's neighbour," when his Zarathustra declared: "You crowd together with your neighbours and have beautiful words for it. But I tell you: Your love of your neighbour is your bad love of yourself. You flee away from yourselves and would like to make a virtue of it: but I see through your 'selflessness.'"[19] Precisely this stance echoes in Jung's critique of "selfless love" and in the disgust shown by the shadow of the dead one for how "these hypocritical preachers speak of love, divine and human love, and use the same gospel to justify the right to wage war and commit murderous injustices."[20] In fact, the only way in which Jung can find a way to "unite hate and love" is through a kind of technique of madness, that is, through "remain[ing] true to love," "suffer[ing] the dismembering," and thus "attain[ing] bonding with the great mother [*die Kindschaft der großen Mutter*], that is, the stellar nature [*die Sternnatur*]," so that, "liberat[ed] from bondage to men and things," he is able to accept "all the joy and every torment of my nature and remained to my love, to suffer what comes to everyone in their own way."[21]

Goethe: Theme of madness in *Faust*

At the time when Goethe was completing his work on *Faust II*, he wrote in a letter to Wilhelm von Humboldt on 1 December 1832: "By means of a mysterious psychological transformation, [...] I believe that I have elevated my mind to a kind of productivity which brought all this forth in a full state of consciousness and which pleases me still, [...] a productivity which Aristotle and other prosaic minds would ascribe to a kind of madness."[22] The passage to which Goethe here refers is in the *Poetics,* where Aristotle claims that "poetry demands a man with a special gift for it, or else one with a touch of madness in him." (chapter 17, 1455a 32)[23] Subsequently, Wilhelm Dilthey explored precisely this theme in his lecture, *Poetic Imagination and Madness* (1886), making reference to Goethe's ability to conjure up in his mind's eye the picture of an imaginary flower.[24] (This is an example of the power of the imagination that caught Jung's interest, too.)[25]

This kind of creative madness is explicitly thematized in *Faust* itself, a work that was so highly influential on Jung. (Incidentally, *Faust* is not the only work by Goethe that thematizes mental illness; one thinks of *The Sorrows of Young Werther* (1774; 1787) and *Torquato Tasso* (1790), for instance).[26] In Part Two, Act II, Faust falls into conversation with Chiron the centaur, whom he tells about his obsession with Helen (ll. 7435-7445). In Chiron's eyes, however, Faust has simply gone mad: "Dear stranger, as man you are enthused, / To spirits, though, your mind appears confused" (*Mein fremder Mann! als Mensch bist du entzückt; / Doch unter Geistern scheinst du wohl verrückt*).[27] So in order to cure him, Chiron proposes to take Faust to Manto, the daughter of Asclepius (the Greek god of healing and medicine). Manto herself describes Faust as someone who "craves beyond his reach," (*Unmögliches begehrt*) (l. 7488) and she compares him to Orpheus, before conducting Faust on a descent to the underworld and the realm of Persephone—a repetition of Faust's earlier descent to the Mothers (and, in fact, a scene which Goethe never wrote). As one commentator has recently observed, Goethe "thus raises Faust to his own rank by endowing him with the 'Muses' madness' that Plato declares to be the mental state which alone permits poetic creation."[28]

Faust's descent to the Mothers (described by Mephisto in Act II) and his Orpheus-like descent to Persephone serve as a model for Jung's own descent into the unconscious in his *Red Book*, and in both cases, classical and world mythology are reimagined and experienced anew. And Goethe was not the only figure in the age of German classicism and Romanticism who revived the ancient discourse on creative madness.

Schelling

In his "Stuttgart Seminars" (1810), F.W.J. Schelling defined madness as a "most horrible specter," originating or rather *emerging* when "communication between the understanding and the soul breaks down."[29] At the same time, he describes madness as "the most profound essence of the human spirit" and, indeed, as "the highest state of clairvoyance."[30]

In his later work, his unfinished project titled *The Ages of the World* (1811), Schelling returned to the theme of madness. (The current relevance of this work is indicated by the interest shown in it by the Slovenian psychoanalytic philosopher, Slavoj Žižek).[31] Toward the end of his *Ages of the World*, Schelling turns to a discussion of the "divine and holy madness," of which the ancients "did not speak idly."[32] The context of this remark is the rites of the god Dionysos, whose chariot is drawn by panthers or tigers, a fitting representation of "the wild, ecstatic enthusiasm into which nature comes at the sight of the essence, which the ancient nature worship of prescient peoples celebrated in the drunken feasts of Bacchic orgies."[33] In these rites, Schelling believed he had discovered something fundamental, namely that "that self-lacerating madness is still the innermost character of all things and, when ruled and justified, as it were, by the light of a higher reason [*durch das Licht eines höheren Verstandes*], it is the real power of nature and of all its products."[34] With reference to Aristotle (who was not mentioned in his Stuttgart lectures) Schelling writes:

> Since Aristotle it is even customary to say of man that no one accomplishes anything great without an admixture of madness. Instead of this we should like to say: There is no greatness without a continual solicitation to madness which, while it must be overcome, must never be completely lacking.[35]

On the basis of this principle, Schelling goes on to develop a classification of human beings (or what one might even call a typology), arguing that "one might profit by classifying men in this respect."

First of all, there are people in whom there is "no madness at all"—these are the so-called *Verstandesmenschen*, and they might sound rather familiar to us:

These would be the spirits which are uncreative, incapable of begetting anything, those who call themselves sober and are the so-called men of intellect [*Verstandesmenschen*] whose works and deeds are nothing but cold works and deeds of the intellect [*kalte Verstandes-Werke und -Thaten*]. Some people in philosophy have quite strangely misunderstood this expression. For, because they heard talk of intellectuals [*Verstandesmenschen*] as being inferior, as it were, or worse than others, and therefore themselves did not want to be such, they good-naturedly opposed reason [*Vernunft*] to intellect [*Verstand*] instead of to madness [*Wahnsinn*]. But where there is no madness, there is, to be sure, also no real, active, living intellect [*kein rechter, wirkender, lebendiger Verstand*] (whence the dead intellect, dead intellectuals [*der todte Verstand, todte Verstandes-Menschen*]).[36]

Here, Schelling brings out the importance of madness for creativity, or what one could call a certain *necessity of madness*, as he asks: "For wherein is intellect to prove itself but in the conquest, mastery, and ordering of madness?" and concludes: "Hence complete lack of madness leads to another extreme, to imbecility (idiocy) [*Blödsinn* (*Idiotismus*)], which is an absolute absence of all madness."[37]

Second, there are people in whom there "really is madness," but who "rule" this madness and show "the highest strength of intellect just in this conquest."[38] And third, there are people in whom there "really is madness" but who are ruled *by* it: These are "people who are really mad [*die eigentlich Wahnsinnigen*]." "One cannot strictly say," Schelling observes, "that madness originates in them; it only comes forth as something which is always there (for without continual solicitation to madness there would be no consciousness) but which now is not subdued and ruled by a higher power."[39]

Thus for Schelling it is a question of recognizing madness and accepting it, but also ruling or governing it and not allowing oneself by to be ruled or governed by it. This would seem to be Jung's position, too, when in "Descent into Hell in the Future" he says:

"When the desert begins to bloom, it brings forth strange plants. You will consider yourself mad, and in a certain sense you will in fact be mad. [...] Take note of what the ancients taught us in images: madness is divine."[40]

Nietzsche

The figure of Dionysos, associated by Schelling with madness, would become an important motif in the work of Nietzsche (and, indeed, Jung). In *Beyond Good and Evil* (§156), for instance, Nietzsche observed (in an aphorism whose relevance for our own time hardly needs underlining) that "madness is rare in individuals—but in groups, parties, nations, and ages it is the rule."[41] In a draft of this aphorism Nietzsche appended the comment, "and this is why historians up to now have not talked about madness. But at some stage medical doctors will write history."[42] And Nietzsche saw himself as just such a medical doctor, writing in 1881 that "moral judgements are epidemics, which have *their time*,"[43] and offering in *On the Genealogy of Morals* a psychological account of the history of morality.[44] Equally, in *The Anti-Christ* Nietzsche tried to describe the history of Christianity in medical terms, writing: "To be physicians *here*, to be inexorable *here*, to wield the scalpel *here*—that is *our* part, that is *our* love of man, that is how *we* are philosophers, we *Hyperboreans*." (§7)[45]

In fact, in an earlier work, *Daybreak*, Nietzsche had already investigated the significance of madness in some detail (§14).[46] In the course of a long aphorism titled "Significance of madness in the history of morality," Nietzsche explicitly refers to the passage in the *Phaedrus* where Plato describes madness as the means through which the greatest good things have come to Greece (cf. 244a-b).[47] He also alludes to the discovery of the dithyramb through Archilochus of Paros in the seventh century B.C.E., recorded in a fragment preserved by Athenaeus of Naucratis in his *Deipnosophistae* 14.24 (628a-b), "I know how to lead the fair song of Lord Dionysus, the dithyramb, when my wits are fused with wine."[48] Now this idea recurs an early Platonic dialogue, the *Ion*, where Socrates maintains that the Muse "first makes men inspired, and then through these inspired ones others share in the enthusiasm," and so "a chain is formed, for the epic poets, all the good ones, have their excellence, not from art, but are inspired, possessed, and thus they utter all these admirable poems," and "so it is also with the good lyric poets; as the worshipping Corybantes are not in their senses when they dance, so the lyric poets are not in their senses when they make these lovely lyric poems." (533e-534a)[49] On this account, the poet becomes a voice for the deity: "Herein lies the reason why the deity has bereft them of their senses, and uses them as ministers, along with soothsayers and godly seers"— it is in order "that we listeners may know that it is not they who utter these precious revelations while their mind is not within them, but that it is the god himself who speaks, and through them becomes articulate to us." (534d)[50] For evidence of this worked in practice, Socrates points to the case of Tynnichus of Chalcis, who "never composed a single poem worth recalling, save the song of praise which everyone repeats, well-nigh the finest of all lyrical poems, and absolutely what he called it, an 'Invention of the Muses.'" (534d-e)[51]

Nietzsche recalls an episode recorded by Plutarch in his *Life of Solon* (§8) in which Solon had recourse to this convention when he incited the Athenians to reconquer Salamis:

> Once when the Athenians were tired out with a war which they were waging against the Megarians for the island of Salamis, they made a law that no one in future, on pain of death, should move, in writing or orally, that the city take up its contention for Salamis. Solon could not endure the disgrace of this, and [...] he pretended to be out of his head, and a report was given out to the city by his family that he showed signs of madness. He then secretly composed some elegiac verses, and after rehearsing them so that he could say them by rote, he sallied out into the market-place of a sudden, with a cap upon his head. After a large crowd had collected there, he got upon the herald's stone and recited the poem which begins:—

> "Behold in me a herald come from lovely Salamis,
> With a song in ordered verse instead of a harangue."
> [...] When Solon had sung it, his friends began to praise
> him, and Peisistratus in particular urged and incited the
> citizens to obey his words. They therefore repealed the law
> and renewed the war, putting Solon in command of it.[52]

This raises for Nietzsche—rather poignantly, given his fate, the reasons for which remain often misunderstood—the following question: "How can one make oneself mad when one is not mad and does not dare to appear so?"[53]

In response to this question, Nietzsche provides a brief cross-cultural survey—from Indian medicine men and Christian saints to magic priests in Greenland and Brazilian pajees—and draws up a recipe to make oneself mad, involving "senseless fasting, perpetual sexual abstinence, going into a desert, ascending a mountain or pillar, or 'sitting in an aged willow tree which looks upon a lake' and thinking of nothing at all except what might bring on an ecstasy and mental disorder."[54] In Jung's case, stimulating—or simulating?— mental disorder was remarkably easy: as he put it in *Memories, Dreams, Reflections*, "Then I let myself drop."[55] Yet in *The Red Book* he invokes some of these madness-inducing traditions, notably going into the desert (in the chapters titled "The Desert," 'Experiences in the Desert," and "The Anchorite").[56]

In *Thus Spoke Zarathustra*, Nietzsche plays almost incessantly with the idea of madness (perhaps one reason why so many Germanists ignorantly dismiss this work as simply mad). In his "Prologue," (§3) Zarathustra asks: "Where is the lightning to lick you with its tongue? Where is the madness, with which you should be cleansed?" before he declares: "Behold, I teach you the Superman: he is this lightning, he is this madness!"[57] In "Of Reading and Writing," Zarathustra reflects that "there is always a certain madness in love," but "also there is always a certain method in madness."[58] And in "Of the Bestowing Virtue," (§2) he announces that "not only the reason of millennia—the madness of millennia too breaks out in us" and proclaims that "it is dangerous to be an heir."[59]

These and other passages have prompted Herbert Theierl to interpret the figure of the *Übermensch* as referring, not to an individual, but to a condition, so that the *Übermensch* "describes a condition of mystical ecstasy."[60] It is in this sense that the *Übermensch* is, in Zarathustra's words, "a *going-across* and a *down-going*,"[61] a down-going, descent, or *nekyia* that Theierl compares with the *Untergang* that is described by no less a figure than Meister Eckhart when he writes that "the highest delight that is granted to the soul is to flow back again into the nothingness of its primordial image and—as the self—to be entirely lost there."[62] In this respect, *Thus Spoke Zarathustra* forms an arc back to Nietzsche's earliest work, *The Birth of Tragedy*, which asked, as Nietzsche himself pointed out in his later "Attempt at a Self-Criticism," "And what, then, is the significance, physiologically speaking, of that madness out of which tragic and comic art developed—the Dionysian madness?" And this question prompted Nietzsche to ask the further ones: "Is madness perhaps not necessarily the symptom of degeneration, decline, and the final stage of culture? Are there perhaps—a question for psychiatrists [*Irrenärzte*]—neuroses of *health*?"[63]

Madness in Our Time

As T.W. Adorno and Max Horkheimer argued in *Dialectic of Enlightment* (1944; 1947), the relationship between myth and enlightenment is not simply one of opposition, but rather reciprocity; or in their terms, dialectical. "Just as myths already entail Enlightenment," they wrote in the 1940s, "with every step enlightenment entangles itself in myth."[64] This is so because Adorno and Horkheimer identify reason (*Vernunft*) with instrumental rationality (*instrumentelle Vernunft*), that is to say, with a form of reason that seeks less to understand and more to control the world around it. The problem here is that instrumental rationality can, as a form of technological fantasy, easily be harnessed for regressive ends, as Jung realized and as we have seen in our own times. As Walter Benjamin, another prominent member of the Frankfurt School, memorably put it in his

famous essay, "The Work of Art in the Age of Mechanical Reproduction" (1936), "instead of draining rivers, society directs a human
stream into a bed of trenches; instead of dropping seeds from
airplanes, it drops incendiary bombs over cities; and through gas
warfare the aura is abolished in a new way."[65] In this respect,
Analytical Psychology and the Frankfurt School have much in
common, not just with each other, but also—despite Jung's caustic
dismissal and Adorno's savage critique of existentialism and the
"jargon of authenticity"—with Martin Heidegger's view of the
dangers of technology.[66]

Yet neither Critical Theory nor Heidegger can see myth in the
way that Analytical Psychology can: namely, as a resource. As the
anthropologist Bronisław Malinowski (1884-1942) argued (in a
passage cited by Karl Kerényi in the prologue to his and Jung's *Essays
on a Science of Mythology* [1941]), myth is not "an explanation put
forward to satisfy curiosity," but rather "the rearising of a primordial
[i.e., archetypal] reality in narrative form."[67] Of course, it is precisely
such a primordial or archetypal dimension (as found, for instance, in
The Red Book, albeit in a surprising and possibly unexpected form)
that so many cultural commentators neglect or reject, in itself a
reflection of the "totally administered world" we currently inhabit;[68]
we, the dwellers in the "iron cage," as Weber called it, of bureaucracy
against which, in *The Red Book*, Jung repeatedly and painfully chafes.

And so, in "Nox tertia," Jung's soul calls on him to "accept
madness," to let its light "shine," and to "give it life."[69] Since life itself
is full of craziness and at bottom utterly illogical," humankind strives
toward reason only in order to be able to "make rules."[70] In "The
Magician," Jung comes to the realization that "madness and reason
want to be married," and in his encounter in this chapter with the
mysterious Cabiri, these deities of Samothrace present Jung with two
symbolic gifts, a "flashing" sword and a "devilish, skillfully twined
knot"—gifts whose symbolization they explain to Jung as follows:
"The entanglement is your madness, the sword is the overcoming of
madness."[71] In *Scrutinies*, Jung confesses that he dreads "the madness
that befalls the solitary," but his soul tells him: "You do not need to
be afraid of madness."[72] (The reference to Brimo in *Scrutinies* recalls

the figure of Hecate, the goddess who is the sender of madness.) In this way, Jung revives Schelling's distinction between the person overcome by and the person who governs madness.[73]

Conclusion

In the weeks and months leading up to his decision to start work on his *Red Book*, Jung had a series of dreams, fantasies, and visions, beginning in 1912. During the period 1913-1914, 12 fantasies have been identified by Sonu Shamdasani as likely to have been regarded by Jung as precognitive and anticipating the outbreak of the First World War.[74] Profoundly shaken by these disturbing fantasies, Jung apparently feared that he was going mad, as he later recounted to Mircea Eliade. At the time Jung was preparing to give a paper on schizophrenia to a congress in Aberdeen, and he wondered whether he would be speaking about himself! Then, on July 31 1914, immediately after his lecture, he learned from the newspapers that war had broken out: "Finally I understood. And [...] nobody was happier than I."[75]

For now we must lay aside the fascinating question as to whether or not Jung's fantasies had actually predicted what would happen, not to *him*, but to Europe and to the world. (As Shamdasani has speculated, this raises the prospect that, had the war not broken out, then the *Red Book* itself might never have been compiled.)[76] But it is hard not to reflect on whether the actual publication itself of *The Red Book* heralds a new age of turmoil, given the attack on the Twin Towers of 2001, the subsequent growth of terrorism and militarism, the financial crisis of 2008, the annexation of Crimea in 2014, the situation in Ukraine, the civil war in Syria, and the refugee crisis—to say nothing of more recent developments that may be summarized in the neologism "Brexit" and the monosyllable "Trump." Or should we rather remember that in the words of Walter Benjamin, "the concept of progress is to be grounded in the idea of the catastrophe" and that "things just go on *is* the catastrophe"?[77] This idea, that "hell [...] is not something that lies before us, but *this life here*," is one that we also find expressed by Jung in his *Red Book*. For in "Descent into Hell in the Future," Jung says:

> He who journeys to Hell also becomes Hell; therefore do not forget from whence you come. The depths are stronger than us; so do not be heroes, be clever and drop the heroics, since nothing is more dangerous than to play the hero. The depths want to keep you; they have not returned very many up to now, and therefore men fled from the depths and attacked them. What if the depths, due to the assault, now change themselves into death? But the depths indeed have changed themselves into death; therefore when they awoke they inflicted a thousandfold death. We cannot slay death, as we have already taken all life from it. If we still want to overcome death, then we must enliven it.[78]

Yet at the same time *The Red Book* also includes a positive message:

> Therefore on your journey be sure to take golden cups full of the sweet drink of life, red wine, and give it to dead matter, so that it can win life back. The dead matter will change into black serpents. Do not be frightened, the serpents will immediately put out the sun of your days, and a night with wonderful will-o'-the-wisps will come over you.[79]

This tension between the madness of insanity and the insanity that characterizes the totally administered society of our contemporary world makes Andrew Samuels's comments on *The Red Book* made shortly after its publication so prescient, then as now: "It's not just an archival document, it's a very contemporary document: it says a lot about what's wrong with modern society. ... It's about why living in the kind of society we've got right now drives you crazy—because the inner world, what you've got going on inside you, is not listened to, not wanted on board. We live in a flattened, regulated, controlled society that's also actually out of control, as the economic crisis shows"[80]—and as many global events that have unfolded in the meantime have confirmed.

Endnotes

1 C.G. Jung, *The Red Book: Liber Novus*, ed. Sonu Shamdasani, tr. John Peck, Mark Kyburz, and Sonu Shamdasani (New York, NY: W. W. Norton, 2009), 221.
2 Jung, *The Red Book*, 230, 238, and 290.
3 Jung, *The Red Book*, 295.
4 Plato, *Collected Dialogues*, ed. Edith Hamilton and Huntington Cairns (Princeton, NJ: Princeton University Press, 1989), 491.
5 Ibid.
6 Ibid., 492.
7 Ibid.
8 Ibid.
9 Ibid.
10 Ibid., 510-11.
11 Jung, *The Red Book*, 235.
12 Ibid., 244.
13 Ibid.
14 Ibid., 246.
15 Ibid., 325-326.
16 C.G. Jung, *Memories, Dreams, Reflections*, ed. Aniela Jaffé (New York, NY: Vintage Books, 1963), 387.
17 Jung, *The Red Book*, 327.
18 Ibid., 334.
19 Friedrich Nietzsche, *Thus Spoke Zarathustra* (Harmondsworth: Penguin, 1969), 86.
20 Jung, *The Red Book*, 338 and 341.
21 Ibid., 343 and 356.
22 In Johann Wolfgang Goethe, *Faust: A Tragedy*, ed. Cyrus Hamlin, trans. Walter Arndt (New York, NY: W. W. Norton, 1976), 548.
23 Aristotle, *Complete Works*, ed. Jonathan Barnes (Princeton, NJ: Princeton University Press, 1984), vol. 2, 2329.
24 Wilhelm Dilthey, "Dichterische Einbildungskraft und Wahnsinn," in *Die geistige Welt: Einleitung in die Philosophie des Lebens*, vol. 2 [*Gesammelte Werke*, vol. 6] (Stuttgart; Göttingen: Teubner; Vandenhoeck & Ruprecht, 1994), 90-102. For further discussion, see

Frederick Burwick, *Poetic Madness and the Romantic Imagination* (University Park, PA: Pennsylvania State University Press, 1996).

25 C.G. Jung, "On the Psychology and Pathology of So-Called Occult Phenomena," in *Psychology and the Occult* (London: Ark, 1987), 6-91 (17).

26 For further discussion, see Sylvia P. Jenkins, "The Depiction of Mental Disorder in *Die Leiden des jungen Werthers* and *Torquato Tasso* and its Place in the Thematic Structure of the Works," *Publications of the English Goethe Society*, NS 62 (1991-1992): 96-118.

27 Goethe, *Faust*, 211.

28 Gisela Brude-Firnau, "From *Faust* to Harry Potter: Discourses of the Centaurs," in Hans Schulte, John Noyes, and Pia Kleber (eds.), *Goethe's "Faust": Theatre of Modernity* (Cambridge: Cambridge University Press, 2011), 113-128 (122).

29 F. W. J. Schelling, *Idealism and the Endgame of Theory: Three Essays*, ed. Thomas Pfau (Albany, NY: State University of New York Press, 1994), 233.

30 Schelling, *Idealism and the Endgame of Theory*, 233 and 238.

31 Slavoj Žižek, *The Abyss of Freedom; Ages of the World* (Ann Arbor: University of Michigan Press, 1997).

32 Schelling, *The Ages of the World*, trans. Frederick de Wolfe Bolman, Jr. (New York, NY: Columbia University Press, 1942), 227.

33 Ibid., 227.

34 Ibid., 228.

35 Ibid., 228.

36 Ibid., 228-229.

37 Ibid., 229.

38 Ibid., 229.

39 Ibid., 229.

40 Jung, *The Red Book*, 238.

41 Friedrich Nietzsche, *Basic Writings*, ed. Walter Kaufmann (New York, NY: Modern Library, 1968), 280.

42 Friedrich Nietzsche, *Nachlaß 1882-1884* [*Kritische Studienausgabe*, vol. 10], ed. Giorgio Colli and Mazzino Montinari (Munich; Berlin and New York: dtv; de Gruyter, 1999), 72.

43 Friedrich Nietzsche, *Nachlaß 1880-1882* [*Kritische Studienausgabe*, vol. 9], ed. Giorgio Colli and Mazzino Montinari (Munich; Berlin and New York: dtv; de Gruyter, 1999), 483.

44 See Andreas Urs Sommer, *Kommentar zu Nietzsches "Jenseits von Gut und Böse"* [*Nietzsche-Kommentar*, vol. 5/1] (Berlin and Boston: de Gruyter, 2016), 465.

45 Friedrich Nietzsche, *The Portable Nietzsche*, ed. Walter Kaufmann (New York, NY: Viking Penguin, 1968), 574.

46 Friedrich Nietzsche, *Daybreak*, trans. R.J. Hollingdale (Cambridge: Cambridge University Press, 1982), 14-15. For a detailed commentary on this passage, see Jochen Schmidt; Sebastian Kaufmann *Kommentar zu Nietzsches "Morgenröthe"; Kommentar zu Nietzsches "Idyllen aus Messina"* (*Nietzsche-Kommentar*, vol. 3/1] (Berlin and Boston: de Gruyter, 2015), 91-100.

47 Plato, *Collected Dialogues*, 491.

48 Thomas J. Mathiesen, *Apollo's Lyre: Greek Music and Music Theory in Antiquity and the Middle Ages* (Lincoln and London: University of Nebraska Press, 1999), 71; cf. M.S. Silk and J.P. Stern, *Nietzsche on Tragedy* (Cambridge: Cambridge University Press, 1981), 136.

49 Plato, *Collected Dialogues*, 220.

50 Ibid.

51 Ibid.

52 *Plutarch's Lives*, vol. 1, trans. Bernadotte Perrin (London; New York, NY: Heinemann; Macmillan, 1914), 421 and 423.

53 Nietzsche, *Daybreak*, 14.

54 Ibid.

55 Jung, *Memories, Dreams, Reflections*, 203.

56 Jung, *The Red Book*, 235-237 and 267-270.

57 Nietzsche, *Thus Spoke Zarathustra*, 43.

58 Ibid., 68.

59 Ibid., 102.

60 Herbert Theierl, *Nietzsche—Mystik als Selbstversuch* (Würzburg: Könighausen & Neumann, 2000), 14.

61 Nietzsche, *Thus Spoke Zarathustra*, 44.

62 Theierl, *Nietzsche—Mystik als Selbstversuch*, 13; cf. Meister Eckehart, *Schriften und Predigten*, ed. Herman Büttner (Jena: Diederichs, 1921), vol. 1, 143.

[63] Nietzsche, *Basic Writings*, 21.

[64] Theodor W. Adorno and Max Horkheimer, *Dialectic of Enlightenment: Philosophical Fragments*, ed. Gunzelin Schmid Noerr (Stanford, CA: Stanford University Press, 2002), 8.

[65] Walter Benjamin, "The Work of Art in the Age of Mechanical Reproduction," in *Illuminations*, trans. Harry Zorn (London: Cape, 1970), 211-244 (235).

[66] Martin Heidegger, "The Question Concerning Technology," in *Basic Writings*, ed. David Farrell Krell (London: Routledge, Kegan and Paul, 1978), 307-41.

[67] See Karl Kerényi, "Prolegomena," in C.G. Jung and Karl Kerényi, *Essays on a Science of Mythology*, trans R.F.C. Hull (New York: Princeton University Press, 1969), 1-24 (6); cf. Malinowski, "Myth in Primitive Psychology" [1926], in *Magic, Science and Religion and other Essays* (Garden City, NY: Doubleday, 1948), 72-123.

[68] For further discussion, see Harvey C. Greisman and George Ritzer, "Max Weber, Critical Theory, and the Administered World," *Qualitative Sociology* 4, no. 1 (Spring 1981): 34-55.

[69] Jung, *The Red Book*, 298.

[70] Ibid.

[71] Ibid., 317 and 321.

[72] Ibid., 336.

[73] Ibid., 321 n314.

[74] Ibid., "Introduction," 202.

[75] William McGuire and R.F.C. Hull (eds.), *C.G. Jung Speaking: Interviews and Encounters* (Princeton, NJ: Princeton University Press, 1977), 225-36 (233-234).

[76] Jung, *The Red Book*, "Introduction," 202.

[77] Benjamin, "Central Park," trans. Lloyd Spencer and Mark Harrington, *New German Critique* 34 (Winter 1985): 32-58 (50).

[78] Jung, *The Red Book*, 244.

[79] Ibid.

[80] BBC Radio 4, *Today*, broadcast on 28 October 2009.

Confronting Jung: *The Red Book* Speaks to Our Time

John Hill

What happened to Jung when writing his *Red Book*? I witnessed his labors when invited to act in a theatre production on passages from *The Red Book* together with Dariane Pictet, Paul Brutsche, and Murray Stein. We performed in various countries. Not only did we read the book but learned passages by heart and embodied them in action. I was given three roles: Elijah, Izdubar, and Philemon.

Drama is a wonderful experience to experiment with one's identity—who we are, who we are not. *The Red Book* performance encouraged us to explore Jung's vision of the psyche as an arena of multiple personalities that stimulates the imagination and provides a stage for the dissociated parts of the self to emerge and gain presence in the conscious mind. Following Jung's odyssey through the labyrinth of his inner world, we began to see his journey as a process to confront, understand, and partially integrate the hidden subpersonalities that rule over our lives when we least expect them.

Playing the roles of Elijah, Izdubar, and Philemon was a challenge. The prophet, the warrior, and the magician are powerful archetypal figures. I had to invest all my energy in the roles to make them come alive. This was the work of imagination. Inevitably, it created dissociation, even inflation. After I had finished each role, I needed several minutes of silence. The interval gave me a chance to recover and click into the next role. I had to struggle to gain control over the roles so that they would not control me. For several days after each performance the words and emotions of Elijah, Izdubar, or Philemon would spontaneously emerge, and I would find myself in a state of dissociation until I could finally shake them off and go about my usual business. Nevertheless, some parts of me are "prophet," "warrior," and "magician." It was helpful to remember that these roles were not identical with the conscious ego. They belong to the collective heritage of humankind and influence each one of us according to our level of consciousness and how they play out in fate or destiny.

In enacting each role, I noticed how they underwent transformation after each performance. I believe this was largely due to the exchanges with my colleagues Paul Brutsche and Dariane Pictet, who performed the roles of Jung and Salome, respectively. Playing the roles gave me the opportunity to connect with Jung from inside of those other personalities that judged him, loved him, challenged him, humiliated him, and inspired him. It was like seeing Jung within the larger framework of his own psyche, seeing the one from the many, the ego from the complexes, the self reflected in a pleroma of archetypes. I will end with some reflections on what the exchange with these three figures could have meant for Jung, for psychology, and for our time.

Elijah

In enacting Elijah, I had to identify with the Old Testament prophet. I was omniscient, a semigod who knew the secrets of the universe. I was severe and was going to tell Jung exactly what he had to do. But already in the opening of *The Mysterium* scene, I felt incomplete. I was united with darkness, embodied in the blind Salome, as evident when I said: "Consider this: Her blindness and my sight have made us companions through eternity."[1] These words immediately reminded me of a biblical text in the *Book of Proverbs* (8: 22-24). The text refers to *Sophia* as the eternal feminine, embodying God's wisdom that existed before creation:

> The Lord possessed me in the beginning of his way before
> he made anything from the beginning. I was set up from
> eternity, before the earth was made. The depths were not
> as yet, and I was already conceived …

With each performance as Elijah, I felt more attached to and protective of my blind daughter, Salome. I was becoming gentler and less judgmental. I was sure Salome was Jung's soul that had become blind. I had to be patient, especially when Jung continued to identify Salome with her New Testament counterpart as when he said: "Was she not vain greed and criminal lust ... [who] shamefully shed [the prophet's] blood?" I knew that if he could only accept the loving yet blind part of his soul, he would be ready to embrace the new message. Hence, I reminded him of this mystery: "But she loved a holy man ... she loved the prophet who announced the new god to the world."[2]

Eventually, I saw that the mysteries of the new god-image were too much for him. He needed time to accept them. He was still too identified with the spirit of the times. He still believed he could solve everything with his intellect by reducing Elijah and Salome to some kind of intellectual symbols. Elijah, however, responded with a powerful voice: "We are real, not symbols."[3]

Reflection

In *Liber Primus*, Jung was working through both the personal and collective dimensions of his psyche. He was certainly aware of an inner connection between the blind Salome he discovered in his inner world and biblical *Sophia*. So I wondered what had happened to *Sophia* and why she had become Salome, who asked for the head of John the Baptist. Whose head was to be sacrificed? Was it Jung's head, the head that had identified with science, perhaps embodied in his admiration of Freud? Jung admits that by the time he was creating this work, he had achieved all that men could desire: fame, wealth, and knowledge. He had to go through a process of purgation and let go of his devotion to the ideals of the time: his love of science and his "joy in ordering and explaining things."[4] Some pages later in *The Red Book* this sacrifice is imaged in the killing of Siegfried, the Germanic semidivine hero. For Jung, Siegfried was "my power, my boldness, my pride"[5] and represented the belief: "Where there is a will there is a way."[6]

Further, I was intrigued about a possible link between the patriarchal Elijah and Freud.[7] We know that Freud was a father figure for Jung. Had Jung's psyche transformed Freud into an Old Testament prophet? Was Jung's psyche reaching into the deeper levels of the collective unconscious? Having been dismissed by father figure Freud on a personal level, Jung could approach father figure Elijah on an archetypal level. In this way he could continue to develop psycho-analysis and apply it to the biblical God in ways entirely different from what Freud expressed in *Totem and Taboo*. This project eventually manifested in the transformational potential of the god-image, the main theme of the much later work, *Answer to Job*.

It also occurred to me that the blind Salome might be connected with Sabina Spielrein. If you have read Jung's few letters concerning the relationship and compare them with the many letters of Spielrein, you can only conclude that Jung was overwhelmed by the encounter. He was highly defensive, yet obviously fascinated by his young Jewish patient. Eros was constellated, and Jung could not maintain boundaries or respond to the challenge in a differentiated way. Was he in the grips of an anima who had lost her sight? It took many years before he could accept the significance of that experience, as witnessed in his later work on the psychology of transference.

Toward the end of "Mysterium: Encounter," Elijah reveals to Jung a new god-image that will eventually bring healing to the feminine component of his psyche, a step that the agnostic Freud could not take. Jung's psyche transforms the Old Testament prophet into a prophet who is inseparably linked with the soul that has lost its way in the world, a prominent narrative in Gnosticism and Neo-Platonism. In *Liber Primus*, the soul's redemption finds expression in the restoration of Salome's sight. For Jung the soul, as the principle of life and love, now represents a force independent of the intellect. As we read through *The Red Book*, this figure continues to challenge him in no uncertain terms.

In Jung's *Collected Works*, we hear no more about Salome. She does, however, reappear in *Memories, Dreams, Reflections*, where she is identified with Eros. In *Answer to Job*, Jung identifies *Sophia* with Eros.[8] So there is a link between the two figures. *Sophia* is the Hebrew *Ruach*, representing God's feminine spirit that accompanies God at the beginning of creation. According to Jung, God has forgotten *Sophia* and is more in league with Satan. In *Answer to Job*, the tribal Yahweh comes up against a man who stands against him. In the drama between a man and his God, God's status begins to change when God remembers his original alliance with his playmate *Sophia*.

As Eros, she reveals herself to humans as their friendly helper and advocate against Yahweh. By so doing, she transforms the wrathful Yahweh into a "kind, just, and amiable" God. *Sophia* and God enter a new *hieros gamos*. *Sophia* in *Answer to Job* represents a further redemption of the Salome of *The Red Book*. She becomes an integral part of a new god-image. In the stretch between Salome and *Sophia*, Jung seems to be in a process of overcoming his rejection by Freud and laying the foundation of an attitude to God that is less patriarchal, less rigid, more loving, more mysterious.

While onstage I could fully sympathize with Jung's confusion when Salome announces that she is his sister, Maria is their mother, and he is Christ. At first this sounds mad, both theologically and psychologically. Christians would interpret this statement as heresy, and psychologists would see it as an example of inflation. But if I was to stay in the role of Elijah, I had to find a way of supporting the mystery, even though it was at variance with my own beliefs. Clearly, the text indicates that this process was not the creation of an ego. Jung on the cross with the head of a lion and a serpent coiled around his body resembles more the Mithraic Aion than an Orthodox Christ. He already wrote about this god in 1912, one year before the first entries in the *Black Books*. In *Psychology of the Unconscious* he links the winged *Deus Leontocephalus* ("lion-headed god"), an important god of the Mithraic hierarchy and ancient Egypt, with time, the great transformer. The image represents a union of opposites, evident in the union of the solar lion with the chthonic serpent, an outcome of the Mithraic struggle of the "sun with the dragon."[9] For Jung, this implies that "the division of the God into many parts ceases, and the divine unity is restored."[10] Or, as he says later in *Mysterium Coniunctionis*: "These concepts ... naturally imply the renewal of the aging god."[11]

Linking the lion-headed god with the sacrificed Christ suggests the inevitable death and renewal of the soul's imagery. Jung's image of Christ was not immutable or literal. It changes in the course of time and is subject to shifting cultures of human history. For Jung, Christ's sacrifice could not be imitated. It represented a process of submitting to the warring opposites of the soul. Jung entered a liminal space between "what is past and what is to come." From this crucified state, the new emerged. Jung had now to think with the heart and love with the head.[12]

The lion-headed god on the cross represents a struggle with the instinctual heritage of humankind in order to raise it to higher level of consciousness. As an age-old syncretic figure (the lion-headed figure found in Germany is dated 40,000 B.C.E., and probably is the oldest sculpture of humankind), it represents an attempt to embrace the heritage of pre-Christian religions, thereby reversing a history of their brutal suppression. This strange image suggests a source of unity that could link dissociated components of Jung's soul.

Here, one might ask if Jungian psychology is a religion that will eventually replace the older religions. Despite Jung's gothic language, the answer is no. Jungian psychology is a psychology of religion. Jung does not expect us to worship these images. He uses them to indicate how our images of god change. He does not ask us to believe. He focuses on core aspects of religious experiences that are necessary for the health and wholeness of the psyche. As a nonconfessional approach to religious experience, Jungian psychology can act as a bridge between the various religious traditions. Theoretically and ontologically, it is important to distinguish Jung's deeper self from a metaphysical God. Jung implies this in a letter to Fritz Burri: "I don't by any means dispute the existence of a metaphysical God. I permit myself, however, to put human statements under the microscope."[13]

Izdubar

Of all the roles I played, Izdubar was the most interesting. The story of Izdubar occupies three chapters of Liber Secundus, "First Day," "Second Day," and "The Incantations." The role was less stereotyped than those of Elijah and Philemon. As Izdubar, I opened the scene (Liber Secundus) as the mighty bull warrior, huge and all-powerful, ready to smash the skull of anyone who dared challenge me. As soon as Jung spoke of a world of which I have no knowledge, fear overcame me. Izdubar, the mighty one, was broken. Like the Aztec king Montezuma of Mexico, I could not fight a force that I recognized to be more powerful than the world I had never questioned. Bewildered and confused, my whole mythological belief system came crashing down. How could I give up my ancestral belief in a divine cosmos where the sun descends to an immortal land to be reborn each new day?[14] If the cosmos is but an eternal void where we can "never reach the sun," and the only knowledge we have of it is through arithmetic measurement, then there is little hope for life after death. I tried to argue with the powerful Jung, but when he showed me matches, a watch, and mentioned that he had a machine that can fly like a bird, my cause was lost.

For me, this was one of the most moving scenes, especially when I took Jung's watch and asked if he was immortal. At that moment, I felt like a member of an endangered indigenous tribe that had never encountered modern civilization. Vulnerable as I was, I only wanted to return to the East, "Where the pure source of life-giving wisdom still flows."[15]

When Jung lights a fire and I responded with "The holy fire warms me,"[16] I felt gratitude. Like the Zoroastrians, I regarded fire as holy and found that I had something in common with Jung, a sign that the sacred and the profane were closer than ever before. I felt fascination, curiosity, and even trust when he showed me the wonderful things that science had invented. But I reverted to mistrust when he intimated that the Western world had lost its belief in the gods and replaced it with words that have no mythological or religious power.

As Izdubar, I resisted Jung almost to the very end, as evident when I called him "a tormenting devil."[17] Finally, in a state of helplessness and anger, I surrendered to become a fantasy that he put in his pocket. It took me a long time to find resonance with the words "If it helps, yes," which created feelings of rage and defeat. This felt like an anticlimax and a humiliation. There seemed to be no other option, perhaps expressing the hubris of all belief systems when faced with the challenge of modernity that scoffs at mythic belief. Was I reliving a conflict that was familiar to Jung?

Reflection

Izdubar was a very authentic role, perhaps the most human of them all. Having been reduced from the status of a semidivine being to that of a wounded human, I could appeal to Jung and to the audience to sympathize with me as I faced an uncertain future.

Apparently Jung, while working on *The Red Book*, intended to divest religious and mythological belief of its literalism. All too often such systems tend to reify the symbolic, claiming the right to possess an all-exclusive truth, eventually to fall into the trap of fundamentalism. When these systems threaten those who are of a different creed, we witness a state of rigid social dissociation. Jung, however, tells Izdubar about two kinds of truth, inner and outer, and Izdubar responded by saying: "That was a salutary word."[18] At the end of the Izdubar story, Jung emphasizes the inner, symbolic aspect of a belief system when he changes Izdubar into a fantasy. If we follow the sequence in *The Red Book,* which was not part of our performance, Izdubar is placed in an egg. The egg becomes a womb for God's rebirth in the human soul. Izdubar is healed, and the sacred cosmos with its promise of immortality becomes a psychological reality.

By 1913, Jung had become disenchanted with the canons of collective consciousness, especially its belief in science as the exclusive possessor of truth. He came to realize that at the core of every ideology there lies a belief in some kind of absolute truth, often embodied in a god, idol, hero, or method. In order to come to terms with his previous unquestioned adherence to science, he went into the desert and appealed to his soul as a living reality, as witnessed in what is perhaps the most appealing passage of *The Red Book*: "My soul, where are you? Do you hear me? I speak, I call you."[19] And some lines later he asks his soul: "Who are you child? My dreams have represented you as a child and as a maiden. ... Are you God? Is God a child, a maiden?"

Jung intimates that each one of us in our own way has to go into a desert and call out to the soul, there to encounter a child, a maiden, or a god. This expresses an attitude that has little in common with Nietzsche's "death of God" or with Freud's notion of God as a guilt-atoning substitute for the son's crime of patricide. Jung is intent on celebrating God's rebirth in the soul. The human psyche is a womb through which we gain awareness of a deeper self that is intimately connected with the sacred. The task is to link the ego with the self, to differentiate it and incarnate it, at least partially, in our daily life.

Izdubar's final transformation represents Jung's attempt at bridging East and West, the former representing the world of myth, the latter of science. Of course, this is not only an East-West, but also a North-South and an inner Below-Above encounter. It represents a transcultural approach to the indigenous age-old human belief systems within us all. It is a way of connecting with earlier layers of civilization that we hold in common. In allowing the soul to achieve an existence that is independent of the conscious intellect, Jung indicated a way of restoring the sacred beliefs of our ancestors, perhaps allowing us to imagine ways of bridging the barriers that the more sophisticated cultures have erected between us.

Izdubar dies; Izdubar is reborn. Embodying this strange figure, I could eventually reconcile myself with Jung. Representing a warrior god, I could deflate and befriend the man who was trying to endow me with new inner significance for our time. I no longer needed to act out.

Philemon, the Sophist

In our performance, Philemon had two distinct roles, that of a Greek Sophist ("The Magician," *Liber Secundus*) and a Gnostic seer (*Scrutinies*). As the Sophist, I enjoyed playing with the naïve Jung who still believed he could solve everything with his mind. I teased him, distracted him, and put obstacles in his way. In the end, I could only admire his tenacity not to give up the pursuit of magic. For Philemon, magic implied a way of serving the soul, nature, and the mysteries of the cosmos. I had to find a way of undoing Jung's unquestioned belief in the superior power of the intellect. In the course of our discussions, I felt sympathy for this young academic who was desperately trying to grasp another approach to reality, which cannot be achieved with the intellect alone. I knew he had to be broken so that he could let go and be open to a reality that can never be fully understood. At one stage, Jung asks Philemon: "Surely you don't want to take your secrets to the grave, do you?" And Philemon answers: "It would be better if everything would be buried with me. It can always be rediscovered later. It will never be lost to humanity, since magic is reborn with each and every one of us."[20]

Reflection

Philemon conveys to Jung what was to become a fundamental aspect of his psychology, one which makes it radically different from other kinds of psychoanalysis. Jungian psychology is not only a scientific project with its special terms, its history, and its different schools. Nor can its approach be limited to fixed dates or tracing historical development. We are asked to focus on how this psychology is continually reborn in each of us in order to preserve its living character. It is not just a method—it is a way of life.

Philemon, the Seer

As Philemon the Gnostic seer, who appears in several places in *The Red Book*, predominantly in the third part of *Liber Novus*, *Scrutinies*, I felt connected to some ultimate mystery that cannot be grasped with the five senses. I had to answer the quandaries of the unredeemed "souls of the dead" who have returned from Jerusalem and did not find what they sought. The dead did not want to be stuck in fixed theological belief systems but sought the paradoxical light that Philemon embodied. In playing the role of Philemon, unlike in playing Elijah, I was more of a trickster who has freed himself from all those who claim to possess an exclusive truth or fall victim to dogmatic literalism. I have learned to accept the world of paradox and have liberated the gods from their fixed attributes. This is what was meant when I said: "You must not forget that the Pleroma has no qualities. We create these through thinking. ... Therefore I must teach a God to whom nothing can be attributed, who has all qualities and therefore none."[21]

Yet with these words alone the dead were not yet free. On the seventh night, they wanted Philemon to teach them about the human being. Enacting this final passage as Philemon, I truly became a seer, a poet, and a metaphysician. I began by saying, "Man is a gateway, through which you pass from the outer world."[22] In uttering these lines, I felt something begin to open up in me as I caught a glimpse of further horizons. Internalizing "the open gateway," I entered another plane of existence that transcended the commonplace divisions between inner and outer, between life and death. Inspired by this image, it became possible to invest energy into the numinous passages that followed.

For playing this role, modern technology came to my assistance. I focused on one of the ceiling lights that seemed far away, like a star of the heavens "at an immeasurable distance." Having gained a feeling of farsightedness into the unending cosmos, I could turn to Jung, encased in his body and crouched at his desk. He seemed so infinitesimally small and limited when compared to the immensity of the universe that surrounded him. And yet I felt my role was to serve as a link between the two, between the individual soul and "his lone guiding god." In other words, I had to make Jung aware of the greater world beyond earthly life. In that way, I felt that the souls of the dead or the unredeemed complexes in Jung himself could finally achieve freedom and liberation. I made him aware of the bridge between the living and the dead. I intimated to him that the only adequate expression of this union is none other than prayer. I was deeply moved when facing the once-mighty Jung. I placed my arm on his shoulders and supported him in overcoming his fear and resistance. Opened to the immensity of all that is, earthly things seemed like passing shadows: "Here nothing but darkness and clammy cold, there total sun."[23]

As you can imagine, it was not easy to shake off this particular role. It was helpful to remember Jung's words:

> You cannot get conscious of these unconscious facts without giving yourself to them. If you can overcome your fear of the unconscious and can let yourself go down, then these facts take on a life of their own. You can be gripped by these ideas so much that you really go mad, or nearly so.[24]

Paul Brutsche, encouraging us to learn the lines, said it was at least a good way to avoid senile dementia.

Reflection

If Jung's individuation process had stopped after completing the *Black Books*, he might have remained a follower of Gnosticism and Neo-Platonism. In those creeds, the sole purpose of life is to free the soul from the shackles of earthly life, considered to be the source of evil. In enacting the second role of Philemon who catches a glimpse of the vastness of the afterlife, I could feel the misery of what Jung later called "the box-system." Philemon's thoughts, however, seem to go in another direction that is very different from creeds that fix good and evil within the framework of spirit and matter, thus creating a split world. Perhaps this is implied when, as Philemon, I said, "In Him (God) everything that man withdraws from the great world shines resplendently."[25] Or when Salome utters: "Touch the earth, press your hand into matter, shape it with care."[26]

These words seem to intimate that our individual earthly existence is not dismissed, but raised to the higher plane of spirit, to become more luminous, more whole, more beautiful. This kind of journey is perhaps best compared with Rilke's ninth *Duino Elegy*:

> … Yet the wanderer too doesn't bring from mountain to valley
> A handful of earth; of for all untellable earth,
> But only a word he has won …
> Praise this world to the Angel, not the untellable:
> You can't impress him with the splendor you've felt; in the cosmos
> Where he more feelingly feels you're only a novice.
> So show him
> Some simple thing, refashioned age after age,
> Till it lives in our hands and eyes as part of ourselves.[27]

Rilke implies that a numinous experience by itself does not impress the spiritual beings of the Beyond. They are much more interested in knowing what you have done with the earth, "the untellable earth." Have you made something from it? A pot, a rope, a word, a poem? If you have put the beauty of your individual soul into these creations, they and you will shine resplendently in this life and beyond. I believe this is precisely what Jung attempted to do in extracting the concepts of analytical psychology from those earlier experiences.

The premonitions of Jung and Rilke hint at another, more embracing belief system, which comes closer to Jung's final conception of the religious function of the human psyche. In one of his last great visions, which happened while recovering from a heart attack, he became a witness to the Cabalistic marriage of Malchuth and Tifereth. This took place in a garden of pomegranates in the presence of a nurse who is transformed into an old Jewish woman, preparing kosher dishes. Later he remembers he asked this same figure to forgive him if she were harmed, which is significant, considering some of his statements made in the 1930s. This vision was followed by the marriage of the Lamb and is an example of the *hieros gamos*, an archetypal motif common to most religions of the world, signifying a union of heaven and earth. For Jung these visions embraced an entirety that filled his soul with an ineffable joy.

What We Still Have to Say

In the roles of prophet, warrior, sophist, wise man, and Salome, we confronted Jung, humiliated him, and inspired him. Through us, he learned to understand the mysteries of an inner life. As Elijah, I opened his eyes to the nature of his loving soul. He helped me as Izdubar to survive in a godless society. As Philemon, I teased him about his know-all attitude and opened a gateway to the greater life. We gave him a hard time. He learnt to respect us as radically Other, as non-ego. Indeed, Jung's attitude of service to the greater whole resonates with statements of Emmanuel Levinas, concerning otherness: "In the responsibility for the other … commands me and ordains me to the other. ... All my inwardness is invested in the form of a despite-me, for another. ... It is the very fact of finding myself while losing myself."[28] In the encounter with Salome, Jung saw that life is not just about "the love of wisdom" but rather about "the wisdom of love," to use another expression of Levinas.

Do you hear our voices in the new book? We are thankful that Jung, with the finest pen and brush, wrote, painted, and put into calligraphy our message to humanity.

And now it is time to derole, an important technique in psychodrama. I am no longer Elijah, Izdubar, or Philemon. Calling to mind one of Jung's opening lines of *The Red Book*, I return to cultivating my own garden: "My path is not your path therefore I cannot teach you. The way is within us, but not in Gods, nor in teachings, nor in laws."[29]

For our Time?

The Red Book presents us with a plethora of strange figures, which can be unsettling for the average reader. Recent research by Maria Wimber at the University of Birmingham with 6,000 adults has shown that the push-button culture of our time prevents the buildup of long-term memory, which many consider to be essential in creating a core identity.[30] The brain strengthens a memory each time we recall it and forgets irrelevant memories that distract it. The process of building up long-term memory cannot function if we stop learning to memorize events and information and just move on from one bit of information to another, without interiorizing them. This was certainly not the case when we had to learn all those lines for a theatre performance, but I understand the reader might be over-whelmed when immersed in *The Red Book's* manifold imagery.

Some consider *The Red Book's* material as an example of Jung's schizoid personality. That could be a reason why Jung appealed to the New Age and LSD cultures and why today's video clips, artists and DJ's delight in the unconnected, fragmentary, and contradictory aspects of life. David Bowie's work and life were infinitely changeable and heterogeneous. Most of his songs were about the outsider: the alien, the misfit, the sexual adventurer, and the faraway astronaut. We also meet this kind of mentality in the brilliant wit of James Joyce, in James Hillman's celebration of dream consciousness that converts the ego into metaphor by divesting it of materiality,[31] or even in the contradictory statements of Donald Trump, who can attract crowds with statements that conflate fact with fiction. Perhaps it is an expression of our times, a playful, inspiring, but at times confusing compensation to a world that is becoming increasingly controlled, systematized, and standardized. When the essential dissociability of the psyche is not recognized as its inner primordial structure, it will manifest in destructive ways in the outer world. Identifying with it can enhance the mind's tendency to radical dissociation. One floats on a sea of imagery and thoughts without building up a coherent narrative about self and the world.[32]

The overall drama of *The Red Book* is not only about dissociation, but also about deep personal confrontation with the splitoff, unlived, or hidden potentials of the psyche. In the long conversations recorded in *The Red Book,* Jung attempted to come to terms with, understand, and partially integrate those strange figures of his soul. One of the book's key themes is expressed in a series of dramatic confrontations with opposites that yield a new attitude. This struggle continued throughout his life and became elaborated and refined in his later works. It represents a coherent narrative of self and the world, a blossoming of Jung's true self.

Jung's confrontation with "Philemon" and "Salome" made him aware of the wisdom and animating forces of the unconscious, later termed "self" and "anima." If Jung had just stayed with the images, his experiences would have remained mysterious, fragmentary, and private. He did not advocate a premodern belief system of "Philomites" or "Salomites," adherents of a cult inspired by *The Red Book's* visionary power, as Richard Noll would have us believe. In search of a universal significance of the symbolic, he opted for distance from his own material. He first created a symbolic space, which allowed him to paint, play, and, like a child, built miniature stone buildings on the lakeside of Zurich. It took the rest of his life to find parallels, classify, compare, and finally formulate generalized symbolic forms in order to communicate those discoveries to his colleagues and to the world. Jung once intimated that he created analytical psychology as a language to end his isolation.

Analytical Psychology rests on a foundation in which there is a continual encounter with estranged components of the personality. *The Red Book* has clinical implications. Jung's encounters with the radical Other provides an example how to develop sensitivity and empathy for the hidden subpersonalities in our clients and in ourselves. I believe if one can do this in an authentic way, as later outlined in Jung's concept of Active Imagination, then a process of reconciliation with the stranger can take place. Inwardly, this might be experienced as a new beginning. Outwardly, it becomes a solid and convincing foundation for an authentic encounter with the stranger without. An attitude of this magnanimity is sorely needed in our much-troubled world.

I end with a quote from the *Memories, Dreams, Reflections*:

My science was the only way I had of extricating myself from that chaos. Otherwise the material would have trapped me, strangled me like jungle creepers. I took great care to understand every single image, every item of my psychic inventory. And to classify them scientifically ... and, above all, to realize them in actual life.[33]

Endnotes

1 C.G. Jung, *The Red Book: Liber Novus*, ed. Sonu Shamdasani, tr. John Peck, Mark Kyburz, and Sonu Shamdasani (New York, NY: W. W. Norton, 2009), 246.
2 Ibid.
3 Ibid.
4 Ibid., 229.
5 Ibid., 242.
6 C.G. Jung, *Memories, Dreams, Reflections*, ed. Aniela Jaffé (New York, NY: Vintage Books, 1963), 180.
7 Sonu Shamdasani draws attention to a synchronous link in the *Black Book* 2 between Freud, Jung, and Elijah. Jung remarks that his Elijah resembles Michelangelo's *Moses* in Rome's San Pietro in Vincoli, which was also a subject of study by Freud, finally published in 1914. See Jung, *The Red Book*, 248 n187.
8 C.G. Jung, *Answer to Job* (1952), in *CW*, vol. 11 (Princeton, NJ: Princeton University Press, 1969), pars. 613-642.
9 C.G. Jung, *Psychology of the Unconscious*, in *CW*, vol. 5 (London: Kegan Paul, Trench, Trubner, 1919 [1912]), 314. This book was revised and renamed as *Symbols of Transformation*, in *CW*, vol. 5, trans, R. F. C. Hull (Princeton, NJ: Princeton University Press, [1956] 1969).
10 Ibid., 313.
11 C.G. Jung, *Mysterium Coniunctionis* (1955), in *CW*, vol. 14 (Princeton, NJ: Princeton University Press, [1955] 1963), par. 379.
12 Jung, *The Red Book*, 253.
13 Gerhard, Adler, *C.G. Jung Letters*. Trans. by R. F. C. Hull. Vol. 2, 1951-1961 (Princeton, NJ: Princeton University Press, 1975), 64.
14 Jung, *The Red Book*, 278.
15 Ibid., 279.
16 Ibid., 278.
17 Ibid., 282.
18 Ibid., 278.
19 Ibid., 232.
20 Ibid., 312-13.
21 Ibid., 348-49.

22 Ibid., 354.

23 Ibid., i.e.

24 Ibid., 252 n211.

25 Ibid., 354.

26 Ibid., 345.

27 Rainer Maria Rilke, "The Ninth Elegy," in Rilke: Selected Poems, trans. J. B. Leishman (London: Penguin, 1988), 63-64.

28 Emmanuel Levinas, *Otherwise than Being or Beyond Essence* (Pittsburgh, PA: Duquesne Univ. Press, 1998), 11.

29 Jung, *The Red Book*, 231.

30 Maria Wimber, "Digital dependence eroding human memory," http://www.bbc.com/news/education-34454264.

31 James Hillman, *The Dream and the Underworld* (New York, NY: Harper and Row, 1979), 95.

32 Daniel Siegel, *The Developing Mind* (New York and London: The Guilford Press, 1999), 4-5.

33 Jung, *Memories, Dreams, Reflections*, 218.

On the Impact of Jung and his *Red Book*:
A Personal Story

J. Marvin Spiegelman

Upon receiving an invitation to participate in this project discussing the impact of Jung's astonishing years-long active encounter with the unconscious in *The Red Book,* I was actually rereading that marvel and took this as a synchronicity, one encouraging me to accept the offer, despite being just two months shy of my 91st birthday. When I was permitted to be personal in my essay, I pondered whether I was being presumptuous or inflated and decided that old age gave me leeway, plus the fact that I have been an avid reader of Jung since the age of 22 and an acolyte since undertaking analysis at 24. I will be showing similarities and differences in our experience as I am able. The large extent of the former is surprising since almost all of my work precedes publication of *The Red Book* and much of it is even independent of his *Memories, Dreams, Reflections.* This suggests a common connection with the "spirit of the depths," as Jung termed it, along with the desired individuality emerging as a consequence. The main conclusion, providing a continuing inspiration for our time, is that the contemporary person "in search of a soul" can do no better than follow Jung's example to find the "divine within."

My own encounter with the unconscious, like Jung's, begins in early childhood. Shortly before my fourth birthday, I was seated on my little tricycle outside my parents' bungalow in East Los Angeles, just awakening from a nap and a dream in the midday sun. I was powerfully made aware that I was a son of the sun, connected with God and, marveling at this fact, feeling that I was competent on the tricycle and could steer it well. The sun was California warm, and there was a glow in my body, too. In contrast, my mother was in the cottage, and she was dark and unpredictable. (My later adult self could understand that this poor extraverted woman of 22 was cooped up while my father was working most of seven days a week to support both us and, with his brother, his parents and his two maiden sisters.)

Next door, though, lived my good friend, Gracie, two years older than I, with whom I played every day and we even attended kindergarten together at times. Her little cousin, however, scandalized me by scratching me for no good reason and even defecated on the driveway. Within weeks, I moved away. Gracie, now a widowed mother, living in a home for the aged, would find me 80 years later. She, my wife, and I enjoyed a few lunches together but, alas, she died before we could visit our old neighborhood.

This early sun experience of what Jung would later call Abraxas was gradually forgotten, but I would remember it again many years later, in the second year of my analysis when I was 25 (more about that later).

Before the recall of the son of the sun incident, in the first year of my analysis, I had several impressive—to me—dreams and visions which began the construction of my myth. The first came after my first active imagination. In the waiting room of Dr. Max Zeller, I found several volumes, recently arrived, of the important Kabbalistic text, *The Zohar*. Opening one volume at random, I read a page and was startled to see that it strongly resembled my initial active imagination! I trembled as I went up to the office, but stayed away from reading that book until I was 40, only then discovering that one was advised against such study until one had indeed arrived at that age. The Kabbalistic *Tree of Life* was ultimately to be a central image for me.

Shortly after that, I found a halt to my analytic work. I had the image of a great wall that blocked my way. My analyst suggested that I talk to this wall (indeed, many years later I would experience an intense numinosity when I visited the Western Wall in Jerusalem) and, remembering that my mother used to say that talking to me was like "talking to a wall," I heard a powerful voice speak:

> Where in the thunder of the Name is the ghost?
> Go back to the place where you found the Worm.
> Look for it there behind the Tree,
> Holy man, hollow man; Solo-man, Solomon.

With this pronouncement, I recalled a dream that I had when I was around 11, at the time of first adolescent sexual arousal. I dreamed that I was about to have intercourse with my maiden aunt (the rather soft one, in comparison with my Mother's strength) when a Worm crawled out of her vagina, menacingly. Naturally, I was terrified but spared this bit of incestuous union. This recalled dream did bring me in touch with the phallic god of Jung as well as the *Tree of Life* (as I was later to learn) from the Voice, so I could validate for myself these similarities to Jung's experience as revealed in *The Red Book*. Individuation (solo-man) and overcoming external authority (hollow man) were hinted at as well.

The recollection of my earliest experience, however, came a few months later, after I had spent a kind of hermit summer, in vacation from the university and my teaching assistant job. I dreamed:

> I was sailing the seas with Marco Polo (I was in the Merchant Marine in World War II) when suddenly a whirlwind blew me into the Underworld. I there encountered a huge Snake, green in color, spitting yellow fire and challenging me. I struggled with this creature—how I did so I do not know— and ultimately subdued it, leaving me utterly exhausted. I was then transported from this scene of intense color to a black and white background of a medieval European city. Suddenly a door opened up and two Knights, dressed in green mail with a golden sun on their chests, dragged me into a circular room with many people, including a loving French couple and my university professor. As I was brought into the room, I was beaten—as initiation, not punishment—with branches of a tree by each of the Knights. Inside the room was a huge jewel-bedecked crown. Apparently, I was to be crowned. Recognizing that this crown was overwhelmingly large for me, I stepped back, at which a chorus said, "He is not worthy" or "He is too young."

I awakened sobbing, remembering the first appearance of the Knight in me when I was on that tricycle, weeks before my fourth birthday. The rejection by the chorus devastated me, but I was mollified many years later when I discovered that the "crown" in Kabbalah was indeed larger than any individual and belonged to the highest *sephira* in the *Tree of Life*, the center where the divine begins to come into manifestation. Yet, the rejection was true in that my leadership role in life has always remained "uncrowned," in the background and subtle. Good enough.

Jung's archetypal Snake certainly emerged for me at this point, and the dream struggle has been repeated, as it was for him, many times indeed! The Knight, as we shall see, continued to be a central carrier of a self-image for me later on. I now believe that my hero image, unlike Jung's, had me in search of God and was not to be overcome as was his power-driven Siegfried. This was confirmed later on, as we shall see. The dream also emphasized the Tree symbolism, which was to be central for me in my myth. I here also encountered the phallic God so important to Jung. These similarities seem significant to me, especially since this experience took place decades before I read Jung's *Red Book*.

A further difference from Jung's myth was made clear in a dream I had not long after this "big" one. It was during the Christmas season, and I had been humming the "Three Kings" carol during the day. I dreamed that night that a divine child was being born and that he was accompanied by three kings who were, respectively, a Jewish rabbi, a Christian priest, and a Buddhist priest. This successor to the Christ child is now over 65 years old and has been my leader/co-pilot in analytic work, in authoring 20 books and over 100 articles, lecturing in 25 American cities and a half-dozen foreign countries, and in living out what became my Psycho-Ecumenical myth.

Later came more analysis, marriage, and service as a Medical Service Corps officer in the United States Army during the Korean War. I was then granted the G.I. Bill and fellowships, allowing me to study at the C.G. Jung Institute in Zurich, a high point of my life. Attendance at lectures with gifted speakers such as von Franz and association with like-minded students from all over the world was a longed-for gift that satisfied me deeply. Lectures and a seminar with Jung plus a final private session with him wherein I received a requested blessing, to match the familial one I had got from my

Hassidic grandfather when I went to sea in World War II, made it all perfect.

My final dream in analysis, in 1959, was the following: I am wrestling with my analyst, C.A. Meier, generating heat and light, at the end of which we bow to each other. I leave, saying goodbye to my friend, the secretary of the institute. I then see my maternal grandmother, who points significantly to a one-room building open at the roof to a star-filled night sky above it while sunshine fills the rest of the atmosphere elsewhere. Inside the building is a dark man sitting at a table and writing furiously, stopping at times to argue with God. Impressed, I am next on a ship wherein I am chief-mate and serving a captain who is largely a presence rather than a person. We are amidships, on a circular deck which slowly rotates around a center. The ship somehow goes over the Alps to the Mediterranean and then sails around South America, arriving at the port of Los Angeles. The ship now becomes a truck, and we drive to Santa Monica, dropping off a sailor in Pasadena (On returning to Los Angeles with my pregnant wife, I was quite without funds and took a job—thanks to a friend I had assisted years before—as a psychological consultant with a firm serving industry, something for which I was quite unqualified. This allowed me to start a practice and care for my family. I quit this job after a year, after dreaming that my wealthy Swedish friend, Mrs. Kate Hillman, [Jim's wife] initially looked beautiful but then haggard when she saw me using the telephone as part of my job, which was to find lush places to live for clients. When I told her that I was now used to this job, she nodded despairingly in the affirmative. Naturally, I resigned the next day, recognizing that acculturation was the "sin").

The Captain (now a person) and I then reached the Pacific Palisades and looked out across the Pacific Ocean, watching the sun rising, *contra naturam*, in the East. I thought of the Land of the Rising Sun, but also saw that a woman had died in a fire nearby.

This dream was also predictive. Not only did I (the sailor) take a job in Pasadena when I returned, but only months later, in the fall of 1959, when I was teaching at UCLA, a Fulbright scholar from Japan, Hayao Kawai, came to work with me in analysis for the next two years. He then returned to Japan, completed his doctorate, and went to Zurich to train. He subsequently founded Jungian psychology in Japan, trained many and was even appointed to a post in the national cabinet. Dr. Kawai referred a number of men and women from Japan to me for analysis over the years. I visited and lectured there several times and was most cordially received. Land of the Rising Sun indeed! Furthermore, alas, the flame-torn woman of the dream occurred in time, connected with a tragic analytic work in which I was engaged. All survived, thank goodness, but with great distress.

An ending of my personal Jungian analysis took place in 1963, when I returned to Zurich for—as I put it—my 100,000-mile checkup. After two weeks of intense work, I had a dream that led me to do a series of paintings. I began with a forest scene and a central tree from which emerged a hero figure. He grasped a branch, phallic in nature, and proceeded to traverse cities, deserts, and seas in search of a way to deal with that energy, finally planting it in the earth under the Eye of God. Lightning and thunder then came forth from that Eye, terrifying, yet tears then poured forth also, watering that stick compassionately until it became a beautiful Tree. The Eye then fell into the center of that Tree, which changed into a mandala. This, then, was my sign for ending personal analytic work.

Three years later, my relation with my local analytic society came to an end when I resigned in protest against what I felt to be serious injustices (I returned 14 years later). At the same time, I began studying Kabbalah in earnest (now the age of 40!) and I dreamed significantly again, now with the Knight in warrior mode, dressed in black with the golden sun on his chest. We were on a field of battle, I think in Macedonia, which reminded me of Philip, the father of Alexander. The Knight told me that we no longer had a cause to serve in the outer world, implying Jungian psychology. I sadly agreed.

Shortly thereafter, I was engaged in an active imagination wherein for some months I had been in a cave with an old wise man who did not speak, a woman, and a young boy. Suddenly, the Knight appeared and rode off with the young woman. When I caught up with him, he explained that he was trying to get my attention. He and some others like him had stories to tell, not just for me but for a larger public also. Would I be willing to join him? I had always had an interest in writing, so I was intrigued. I told him that I had a wife and children plus a busy practice but could devote Wednesday afternoon and much of Saturday to such work, and the Knight agreed.

For the following four years, I was passionately engaged in writing these stories (enacting the dream figure), producing three large volumes called, sequentially, *The Tree*, then *The Quest*, and finally, *The Love*, later published as *Passions of the Soul*. The first book contained stories of 10 different people, representing different religious or spiritual attitudes, all ultimately finding their own symbol of the self on the *Tree of Life*. The first story was that of the Knight himself, a Gnostic tale of being called to help restore the unity of God the Humpty-Dumpty, confronted in His/Her/Its fragmentation and requiring total effort of union, of man with himself and with the Divine. The second story was that of a Muslim Arab, overcome with guilt, sailing the seas to find redemption for his transgressions. The third tale was that of a Japanese Ronin, a samurai warrior without a Lord and, using the Zen Ox-Herding pictures as a structural guide, achieved Buddhist *Satori*.

After three stories of men, *The Tree* continued in presenting three tales of women. The first, Julia the Atheist-Communist, a psychologist, sought redemption of her lack of maternal capacity in the Land of Israel, achieving her own individuation as well as generativity. Following Julia came the tale of Sibylla, the Nympho-maniac, who had to reconcile strands in her psyche of warring nations and religions, causing uncontrollable lust in her sexuality, finding redemption in the desert with an equally troubled rabbi and then bringing healing to others. This polytheistic tale was followed by the story of Maria the Nun, whose incestuous sexual transgression and struggle with her faith also found redemption in the desert.

The final four tales were, first, that of an African-American writer meeting his *soror mystica* in Ethiopia and engaging, with her, in an alchemical journey; second, Maya the Yogini undertakes a full *Kundalini* work alone, with her inner guru; third, an old Chinese man dialogues with the *I Ching* in Taoist fashion; fourth, Sophie-Sarah, a

Medium, dialogues with God about the Holocaust. These 10 seekers meet in Paradise, finding their individual self-symbols on the *Tree of Life*. Some individual "Psalms" round out the work.

Hardly had this book been completed when a second figure, calling himself the Son of the Knight, appeared with a new book. He was the initial boy of the Cave and started out on a path to find his mother, accompanied by Dog. This book, in contrast to the individual paths of *The Tree* people, was a work in pairs, exploring Greek and other themes, resulting in divinization of Dog and a resolution of the questions and uncertainties in that Cave. The two Knights of the "big" dream when I was 25 thus fulfilled the initiation begun at that time.

With this completion of the book of the Son of the Knight, there appeared yet a third figure, who called himself the Grandson of the Knight. His book was initially called *The Love* (later published as *Jungian Psychology and the Passions of the Soul*) and undertook an exploration of that theme in literature (e.g., Don Juan), fairy tales (e.g., Bluebeard), and religion (Christianity, Judaism, Hinduism, Islam, Polytheism), concluding with a kind of magical Mandala, incorporating all of it in a *Tree of Life*/Kundalini diagram and schema.

As one can see, this four-year journey of active engagement with the unconscious parallels Jung's intense involvement but, as he would also desire, it is my own and, despite many similar themes, is quite different from his. First off, as I have already mentioned, the Hero was not destroyed in my case but employed. I saw it, finally, as if my ego was stationed at the lowest point of the Tree of Life, *Malkuth*, and looked up on the Middle Pillar to *Tifereth*, abode of the self. I could then inhabit the latter and undergo the adventures above that *sephira* or beneath it, at the physiological centers, via my heroes and heroines. I understood these qualities of the ego-self axis the way that the Buddhist master, Christmas Humphries, describes as ego, self, and SELF, with the first two as belonging more to the individual and the last as totally collective. Furthermore, my attitude was like that of my final dream when I was in training, namely I was first officer or copilot to a captain who was both abstract and a presence, but also very human as we undertook the voyage together. I was no mere amanuensis.

A recent dream of mine helps me to understand my difference from Jung. In it, Elijah the Prophet appears and says that he has things to tell me. In active imagination, he told me that his appearance in Jung's work was accurate for him and that the latter's task was to overcome all the authorities/holy men to arrive at a full apprehension of the "God-Within" but he, Jung, was wrong about the Prophet being transcended.

"He fell victim," Elijah went on, "to the prejudice of the monotheisms, less so now in Judaism, that their belief superseded the earlier dispensation, forgetting, for example, that I reappear every year at Passover time to each and every Jewish household, to enjoy wine and reminding all to welcome the Stranger, in every sense of the term. For Jung, all authorities rightly had to be overcome for him to mightily demonstrate the role of the individual finding and forming the divine within himself. But that is not true for your myth, which has a Jewish root, in contrast to Jung's Christian root." Finally, Elijah called to mind that he spoke of God appearing, not in earthquakes and fire but as the still, small, inner voice. Anticipating Jung?

These comments of my inner Elijah reminded me of what the great medieval Jewish physician and theologian Maimonides said to his pupils when they queried him as to why God went on to "choose" Christians. Maimonides replied that God wanted to spread the monotheistic idea and presence and needed to do so with others who had little or no similarity with the psyche of the Jewish people.

I was also mollified with the realization of that prejudice when my paper on *Jung's Answer to Job: Fifty Years Later* was greeted with disdain when it was sent out for comment. In that paper, published online, I suggested that the Holocaust may have indeed been a crucial event in the inauguration of the new Aeon. I noted that the 6 million murdered Jews may have constituted a symbolic multiplication of the traditional 600,000 who heard the word of God at Mount Sinai. That initial collective experience of the divine was followed by an individual dispensation in Jesus for the then-new aeon, further realized in depth by the knowing of God within via Jung. It might now also be seen as a possibility of a forthcoming collective experience of the Godhead. The numbers 600,000 to 1 to 6,000,000 with the factor of 10 (one and zero) seemed potentially significant indeed. The combination of dismissal and vitriol suggested that I might have struck a nerve. Jung surely showed us the revolutionary view that the projection of the god-image could be retrieved and transformed back into the individual soul. Why, then, is the possibility of there once again being a collective vision so threatening? After all, many religions await a first or second coming of a messiah, do they not? Perhaps the achievement of the God-within is still not strong enough to withstand an addition.

Jung respectfully met and overcame a succession of hugely powerful figures, from Elijah and Salome to Amonius, the Christian anchorite, a devil, Izdubar and others, even the ultimately leading figure, Philemon, without taking the heroic stance of intending victory. The fact that he ultimately achieved inward focus and wholeness is a model for us all and is truly amazing. Finally, advising us to do what he did—take up our own inward challenge—is even more inspiring. I surely followed his example but arrived at my own Psycho-Ecumenical myth, as evidenced in both *The Tree* trilogy and in my books on the relation of Jungian psychology to the monotheisms, to Buddhism and Hinduism, and other spiritual paths. I shall describe the further development of that myth later on, but I need to preface that by several other significant events.

The first of these took place when I was suffering my difficulty in finding a publisher for my first book, *The Tree*. One morning, despairing and wondering if I was truly following the self in this Psycho-Ecumenical work, I took my bicycle—as I often did—up to Mulholland, a hill road between Los Angeles and the San Fernando Valley. Soon, I saw a man whom I had not seen since high school, walking his dog. He had become a famous psychologist after treating a world-renowned singer, publishing a book about his method. I got off my bike, of course, and greeted him. He then told me about his troubles, a publisher who did not treat him right, a difficult marriage, and an expensive holiday home in Europe. I got the point and rode off on my bike with a diminution of any envy I might have had and grateful for this synchronicity. Riding on for a few miles, I then encountered, to my amazement, a large stag, standing in the middle of the road. One sometimes saw deer in this area in those days, but never a stag and certainly not on the road. The stag and I looked at each other for what seemed like a long time. He held his head high, with antlers that impressed me deeply. I even imagined I saw a crown on his head. I bowed and it seemed that he did, too. He slowly turned and walked back into the hills. This deeper encounter with the alchemical self both calmed and reassured me. The dignity of this creature, living on the fringes of civilization, who was both connected and apart, manifested his own truth. Amen as example. With less astonishment than recognition, I was glad to find a publisher later.

This very meaningful synchronicity and resolution did not end the matter, however. I also had great difficulty with this publisher and felt the need to write about that, too. I had been reading the works of H. Rider Haggard again, as I had done in my adolescence, and had been delighted to learn that C.G. Jung also found this writer of *She* to be one who had encountered the anima; another author, Henry Miller, was a friend of mine who readily offered to write a blurb for me after he read *The Tree* with appreciation. I therefore titled my book, *Rider Haggard, Henry Miller and I: The Unpublished Writer*. This was, of course, a story about my troubles in publishing, plus an anima adventure with the deceased and celebrated author. This book was published more easily, later on, with a more reliable publisher who brought out many of my books subsequently.

In the meantime, a colleague and I, interested in Magick—as that spiritual discipline was called—discovered that the foremost living practitioner of that art, Francis Israel Regardie, was living in my own backyard—so to speak—in Studio City. When we went to him seeking instruction, he told us that the energies activated in that work were formidable and that it would be wise to undertake Reichian therapy as an accompaniment. My colleague and I were both aware that our Jungian therapy did not fully include the literal body and such investigation and experience could be helpful in any case, agreed to such an undertaking. This was in 1971, and I was 45 years old.

Regardie had undergone both Freudian and Jungian therapy in England, as well as qualifying as a Reichian practitioner. He had also, of course, been an assistant, as was well-known, to the famous-infamous Magickal personality Aleister Crowley. Regardie stuck to performing all the body work that Wilhelm Reich and his followers had devised to break down the "armor"—as he called it—of body resistance and memorial pain. This was substantial indeed, and I once again felt called upon to write a book about my first four years—of an eight-year treatment—under that discipline. My Jungian colleagues will understand when I characterize this phase of the work as *nigredo* and a merciless confrontation with the shadow, much like what Jung did in that part of *The Red Book* called *Scrutinies*. True to form, I wrote a book about those four years, this time titled, *Jung, Reich, Regardie and Me: The Unhealed Healer*. As in *Scrutinies*, the archetype of the Judge was relentless in demolishing any pretension or defense of the miserable ego, thus accomplishing what Jung did there and in his slaying of the archetypal hero earlier on.

The main positive consequence of that treatment was that my experience of the "subtle body"—as noted in alchemy and Jung's work—took on full substantiality, with the literal experience of that energy in a tingling in the hands, sometimes feet and full body, and awakening of the *Kundalini chakras*. This became manifest in my analytic practice with patients as a signal of the activation of the self in the work. It was also shown in my resumption of my Psycho-Ecumenical myth in writing again sometime later. Two other events intervened, however.

The first of these took place in the 1970s on the occasion of the visit of Marie-Louise von Franz to the Panarion conference, arranged by our local Jungian Society. I was still apart from that group but, wanting to see my old teacher (she had been my Control Analyst in Zurich), I wrote to her and asked for a meeting. She graciously invited me to dine with her at her hotel (paid for by my Society!), and just before meeting her I had two powerful dreams:

In the first dream, I was on a bridge in a medieval European city, headed toward a golden city in the distance to the east. Coming toward me was a crippled fellow on a kind of skateboard. His lower extremities hung lifelessly. As he greeted me, I returned the greeting, and he announced that he was God. Strangely agreeing to this, I bowed to him and invited him to a glass of wine at a kiosk on the side of the bridge, for which he thanked me. Then, before my eyes, he took on full bodily form, healthy and very tall. We then toasted each other, after which he held out his hands to me and from them flowed, into my own palms, silver and gold coins from every country and time. I awakened from this dream understandably exhilarated, noting that the self was now embodied and that my Psycho-Ecumenical myth was further affirmed.

That same night I dreamed again, this time in a less personal way, but still of the self. In the dream, I was told that God was a great Worm, his body was the universe itself, galaxies comprising his organs, and he was closed in on Himself in uroboric fashion. He was engaged in a great rhythmic breathing. I was also informed that many creatures, including me, were to be found in multiple points in that universe and that, at these points, one could have mystical experiences. I concluded that the second dream was revelatory of the Godhead and the first presented my personal self, something I later confirmed with *The Red Book*.

When I told these dreams to Dr. von Franz, she nodded solemnly and said that, with the Worm, I must have suffered greatly, which was certainly true and I appreciated the confirmation. She also supported my separation from the Society, and we enjoyed a lovely evening. Honoring the dream, I supplied the wine!

The second event was my founding of a Psycho-Ecumenical Group in the outer world. I had often led teaching groups, of course, but this one mirrored my initial dream of the divine child being born in the company of a Jewish rabbi, a Christian priest, and a Buddhist priest. The present group consisted of clergy who were also therapists, all of whom had been analysands of mine earlier on. They were an Orthodox Jewish rabbi, a Japanese Buddhist priest, a Roman Catholic priest, two Catholic nuns, an Episcopalian priest, a Protestant minister, plus occasional guests from other religious backgrounds. That group met monthly for 20 years, and I was delighted to hear from them that they often felt freer together than they did with their fellow clerics.

Around that same time, I realized that my two last books on the Unpublished Writer and Unhealed Healer were actually continuations of my inner ecumenical bent, and I then changed my ongoing journal writing into volumes chronicling the dream-sharing and texts-exploring of similar inner figures, now residing at the various *chakras*.

At the first center, Muladhara, dwelt the "Unfrocked" (self-imposed) Catholic Priest. At the second, dwelt a Japanese Buddhist woman, the "Empty Teacher." The third *chakra* carried the Muslim "Powerless Magician," while the fourth, the heart *chakra,* supported the "Unhealed Healer," a traditional Jewish man. At the fifth, throat center, was the "Unpublished Writer," a Hellenistic Jew, along with his Pagan Muse, Lady Tewfik of Tewfik Land. With Lady Tewfik, the "failures" ended, and the third-eye was the home of the Protestant, Jungian scholar, the "Baroness." And, at the top, the carryover from the very first book was the Hindu, Maya the Yogini. The title of the book, understandably, was *Failures and Successes.* When Henry Miller learned of this project, he was delighted, saying that he did his best work when he felt like a failure. All my Psycho-Ecumenicals were largely "inner" with some connection to the outer world, with the exception of Healer and Writer, with whom I identified outwardly as well, along with Teacher when I was engaged in lecturing. I am now in the 11th volume of that unpublished series, and they will linger in the archive that has been established in my name at the University of California, Los Angeles.

That brings me to the present, March 2017, close to the birthday of my beloved wife, Ryma, who died last June, age 84, after 63 years of marriage. This last event is decisive and brings my work closer to Jung as well, in unexpected ways. The first few months after her passing, I was totally devastated, grieving and mourning and weeping and sobbing, even calling out her name, more like a Middle Easterner than the native Californian that I thought I was. The grief and tears seemed endless, aided only by sharing with my daughter, Tamar, and by my listening to our favorite Mozart piano concertos. Gradually, though, I noticed that Love was making its powerful entrance in the tears. I felt opened up and wept at the appearance of love in spouses, lovers, family, Nature and even love of country. At Christmastime, I found myself weeping on witnessing the face of a young woman as she received a beautiful jewel from her beloved, in an advertisement of all things! At first, I thought this was from knowing that my wife had been a skilled Silversmith (maiden name was Silberstein!) and that in my dream the night before we wed, I had presented her with a large, uncut diamond, embedded in a stone. That self-image was indeed refined by her and by our love over the years. But now the love was manifest in tears, both alone and with patients when the self was constellated. Now, too, I realized that God was and is in the tears, as shown in Sufism, wherein our longing for God is the same as His longing for us and is revealed in those tears, both the emptiness and the fullness. Furthermore, I recalled that such tears are one of the Gates to Heaven in Jewish mysticism and, once opened, cannot be closed. So, like Jung and von Franz, I find that after a life in search of meaning, I discover that God is in the love and that we are, as the Hindus say, "two peas in a pod," just as are my beloved wife and I, as revealed in this recent dream:

> I am floating on the great sea with my wife, sensing that I am going to die and feeling happy as long as I am with her. A stone (Rock of Ages, Philosophers Stone?) then rises up from the depths, just big enough to hold us both. Realizing that this is temporary, we hold each other contentedly. Before long, a boat appears and helpfully brings us to a nearby island. The island seems to be a beach resort for families who have suffered tragedy or disruption or, on the other hand, have had unusual closeness and harmony. This is told us by an older man who says that this is a "Jerusalem Re-divivus" and constitutes one of many such places in the afterlife reality wherein people are healed, rewarded, or challenged to grow. Such heavens and hells are multiple and are temporary in that spaceless and timeless condition.

Upon awakening, I see how people in near-death experiences claim to have been with Jesus or in the "Happy Hunting Ground" of Native Americans, but I wonder how such multiple souls and conditions can be accommodated. I then hear the wise man say that this is what is meant by the infinite power and love of the Godhead. Psychic Reality is the key.

And Jung thought so, too, as revealed in *The Red Book* and in *Memories, Dreams, Reflections.* He may not have the deification envisioned by our colleague Edward Edinger as carrying the name of the Age of Aquarius, but he is certainly a great harbinger of that age, showing us how to relate to the Divine Within. Although not for everyone, of course, his example, a hundred years later, seems to me to be the best one available for many on the spiritual path. Thank you, Herr Professor Dr. Jung, for this gift that has been a lifetime guide in my search for Meaning and thanks to my wife, Ryma, who has shown me the path of Love. Together, the two comprise my outer guides in the inner path of the self, who has been present from the beginning.

The author passed away on September 22, 2017. This is the last work he authored.

Encountering the Spirit of the Depths and the Divine Child

Andreas Schweizer

Introduction: The Poor House in the Beyond

Carl Gustav Jung once called the tower, the house that he built for himself on the lakefront of the Upper Lake Zurich at Bollingen, "a confession of faith in stone."[1] Accordingly, we might say that the tower is the material equivalent of the *Red Book*, which I would call a confession of faith in an imaginary and symbolic form.

C.G. Jung recounted repetitive dreams in which he saw a rather poor house located on the opposite side of the lake from Bollingen on the upper part of Lake Zurich. This "house in the beyond" was not

The House at Bollingen (Photo by Andreas Schweizer)

actually on the lakefront but rather situated on a plateau in the midst of pastureland and luxuriant vegetation. Even though Jung knew that this house must have something to do with his personality Number 2, that is, with the eternal or whole man, this could never really satisfy him. He always had doubts and a bad conscience that he had neglected that house or even completely forgotten it. In short, the house was a bit characterless. Jung knew from his dreams that the key to this house was in the hands of an old countrywoman. Though Jung described the inside of the house quite precisely, it nevertheless remained somehow poor, because he had to "spare it," as he put it, which probably meant that he had not enough time to be alone and prepare for the house in the beyond.

For many years, Jung had no clear idea of what that unfinished house really meant. Then, one day—it was almost like enlightenment—he suddenly recognized: "Of course, that's it, it clicks! The *Red Book* also has never been finished!" He immediately realized that what he had recorded in his *Red Book* must now be shaped into another *form*. In the present form, he said, "it sounds like prophecy and this I really detest … for there is not *the whole human being* in it."[2]

"There is not the whole human being in it." After this insight, Jung became aware that he had not yet found the right language and that he still had to translate the text of the *Red Book* into something more concrete. "I saw that *so much fantasy needed firm ground underfoot*, and that I must first return wholly to reality."[3] And for him this reality meant, more than anything else, scientific comprehension. Only an *increase of consciousness*, that is a higher level of consciousness, can serve as the firm ground underfoot that brings fantasies into reality, into human reality.

We are quite fortunate that Jung struggled for decades to elaborate on the raw material as presented in *The Red Book* in order to bring it into a less archetypal or prophetic language. It was his creative daimon who *forced him* to formulate and reformulate the messages of the inner world in order to make it comprehensible for his contemporaries and for future generations. This was hard work indeed, which at times brought him to the edge of exhaustion and even of death. Until his old age, Jung was in the grip of that daimon that overpowered him again

and again, forcing him to continue with his writing. "A creative person",
he stated in his *Memories*, "has little power over his own life. He is not
free. He is held captive and driven by his daimon."[4]

This transformation of the images of the unconscious into the
language of Analytical Psychology was a tremendous creative task
that can hardly be overestimated. When I now read Jung's work, it
may happen that I recall this or that passage of *The Red Book*. "Aha,"
I say to myself, "that is where Jung's surprising idea stems from!" It is
as if we could now see the original unconscious images that lie behind
the psychological expression, or to put it in another way, as if the
theoretical or scientific way to express something became more alive
through the image in *The Red Book*. However, this is also true as seen
from the opposite side: The more familiar we are with Jung's *Collected
Works,* the better we can understand the imagery and symbolism of
Liber Novus. They mutually penetrate each other.

From Fantasy to Ethical Obligation

One might argue that being in the grip of a creative daimon holds
true for Jung's life since he was a genius, but as I am far from a genius,
I can hardly imagine that there is something like a creative daemon
in my life! After all I am not Jung, Picasso, Kandinsky, Shakespeare
or Rilke. This attitude, I believe, is a tricky self-delusion, a cheap
excuse to avoid the responsibility and burden of one's own individual
nature and destiny. So the question would be: How can *we* deal with
our own psychic raw material? I believe we are all happy when we
have a moving or numinous dream. But the dream image as such is
not yet the whole matter. The whole includes the understanding *and*
the realization of the inner images in actual life or, as Jung put it in
his Memoirs: "Insight into them [namely, the images of the
unconscious] must be converted into an *ethical obligation*. Not to do
so is to fall prey to the power principle ..."[5]

In his *Tavistock Lectures* given in London in 1935, Jung
beautifully described this ethical obligation or transformative work
as the "jewel of wholeness." I assume that it was in retrospect to his
experiences of the *Red Book* that he said:

The descent into the depths will bring healing. It is the way to the total being, to the treasure which suffering mankind is forever seeking, which is hidden in the place guarded by terrible danger. This is the place of primordial un-consciousness and at the same time the place of healing and redemption, because it contains *the jewel of wholeness.* It is the cave where the dragon of chaos lives and it is also the indestructible city, the magic circle or *temenos,* the sacred precinct where all the split-off parts of the personality are united.[6]

Wholeness requires accepting this dragon of chaos. In his *Red Book,* as well as in the tower of Bollingen, Jung created substantial vessels, both of which served him as a *temenos* for his entire scientific life's work.

The "Spirit of this Time" and the "Spirit of the Depths": *Liber Primus*

A painful standstill: In the first section of *The Red Book,* titled *Liber Primus,* we find the chapter heading: "Refinding the Soul." Here, Jung described his overpowering vision of the flood covering all the land between the North Sea and the Alps, which finally turned to blood:

When I had the vision of the flood in October of the year 1913, it happened at a time that was significant for me as a man. At that time, in the fortieth [thirty-ninth!] year of my life, I had achieved everything that I had wished for myself. I had achieved honour, power, wealth, knowledge, and every human happiness. Then my desire for the increase of these trappings ceased, the desire ebbed from me and *horror [Grauen] came over me.* The vision of the flood seized me and I felt the spirit of the depths, but I did not understand him.[7]

"Horror came over me"—this is the way the "spirit of the depths" often, if not always, announces itself in someone's life. Today, we would not call it horror anymore, but rather a traumatic experience. I am not a specialist in trauma theory, but I have the impression that these theories often miss the archetypal truth or message of trauma. The horrific experience of a trauma can transmute—if at least partially understood and accepted—into a realization of the "spirit of the depths," that is, into the first and often most terrifying experience of the dark side of God, of the *Deus absconditus*. From then on the daimon is awakened, the daimon that actually forces people to express their inborn creativity throughout their entire lives. I believe that many analysts have had such an experience of horror at least once in their life. It is an initial experience that *compels* someone to follow the path of the soul. That is what happened to Jung with his childhood dream of the subterranean phallus.[8] The text of *The Red Book* continues:

> Yet he [the spirit of the depths] drove me on with unbearable inner longing and I said:
> '*My soul, where are you? Do you hear me?* I speak, I call you—are you there? ... Should I tell you everything I have seen, experienced, and drunk in? Or do you not want to hear about all the noise of life and the world? But one thing you must know: the one thing I have learned is that one must live this life.
> This life is the way, the long sought-after way to the unfathomable, which we call divine. There is no other way, all other ways are false paths. I found the right way, it led me to you, to my soul...[9]

When Jung wrote this text, he was in his 40s. He had achieved practically everything a man can wish for himself. He had his family with healthy children, his practice flourished; he was at the crest of his fame. More and more Americans and people from all over the world came to see him. With the money of his wife he had built a huge and beautiful house for their growing family at the lake of Zurich, etc. But still, as he felt it, something was missing.

This feeling didn't change until that vision broke into his life and forced him to understand the "spirit of the depths." However brilliant the success, no human fortune or happiness could remove this almost unbearable inner longing, the longing for his Soul: "My soul, where are you?" It was a question of survival for him. He knew that he *must* find his soul. Much later, when he recalled that time of his life while sharing his thoughts with Aniela Jaffé, he suggested titling the chapter of the autobiography referring to the *Red Book:* "Lucky to have escaped death."[10] (As we know, this title did not appear in the book.) One thing became clear to him: If he couldn't find the courage to descend to the "spirit of the depths" and if he couldn't find access to the "spirit of the depths" as opposed to the "spirit of this time," he would not survive, for life would lose all meaning.

At that time Jung was a professor at the University of Zurich, but he decided to resign his chair. He realized that scientific work in the regulated setting of academic teaching at the university would always hinder him from connecting himself with the "spirit of the depths" and with his soul. To *talk about the soul* is by far not the same as having a vivid relationship *with* the soul. We should never forget this. As analysts, in our busyness and seeming self-importance, we are always in danger of talking too much about the soul, while neglecting the care for our inner life. Hopefully, a depression or some other so-called neurotic suffering will prevent us from this, so that we might be willing to turn back to our soul. Quite self-critically, Jung confessed at the beginning of *The Red Book*:

> I [then] still laboured misguidedly under the spirit of this time, and thought differently about the human soul. I thought and spoke much of the soul. I knew many learned words for her, I had judged her and turned her into a scientific object. I did not consider that my soul cannot be the object of my judgment and knowledge; much more are my judgment and knowledge the objects of my soul. Therefore the spirit of the depths forced me to speak to my soul, to call upon her as a living and self-existing being. I had to become aware that I had lost my soul.[11]

Jung gradually lost his passion for scientific discourse on the soul.
His journey to the inner world, or to be more precise, to the "spirit of
the depths," took away from him his belief in science, for only "he
whose desire turns away from outer things, reaches the place of the
soul."[12] Obviously, science was not able to express the *living* soul, to
express her often childlike vitality. Thus he came to the conclusion
that scholarliness "belongs to the spirit of this time, but this spirit in
no way grasps the dream, since the soul is everywhere that scholarly
knowledge is not."[13]

The "spirit of the depths" forced Jung to talk *directly* to his soul
and to enter an intimate dialogue with her. *The Red Book* is a most
impressive document of a Western man searching for the lost soul,
struggling with her and thus entering an increasingly deep encounter
with her.

The search for the "spirit of the depths" is the predominant topic
of *Liber Primus*, which is titled *The Way of What Is to Come*. In the
first sentences we already hear of this theme:

> I have learned that in addition to the spirit of this time
> there is still another spirit at work, namely that which rules
> the depths of everything contemporary. The spirit of this
> time would like to hear of use and value, I also thought this
> way, and my humanity[14] still thinks this way. ... But I did
> not consider that the spirit of the depths from time
> immemorial and for all the future possesses a greater
> power than the spirit of this time, who changes with the
> generations. ... He [the spirit of the depths] took away my
> belief in science, he robbed me of the joy of explaining and
> ordering things, and he let devotion to the ideals of this
> time die out in me. He forced me down to the last and
> simplest things.[15]

"He forced me down to the last and simplest things." This reminds
me of Jung's dreams of the poor, almost shabby house on the other
side of the lake. There, it was a *country woman* who had the key to
this house. The "spirit of the depths," or as we might also say, his soul,
forced Jung down to the last and simplest things of nature. Therefore,

it's of no surprise that she, the farmer's wife, knows about that "spirit of the depths." Toward the end of *The Red Book*, expressing somehow the goal or quintessence of the whole book, the same spirit of nature is addressed in a very moving way: First, we read, "When the God enters my life, I return to my poverty for the sake of the God. I accept the burden of poverty ..."[16] And not much later

> I return to my small garden that presently blooms, and whose extent I can measure. It shall be well-tended.
> The future should be left to those of the future. I return to the small and the real, for this is the great way, the way of what is to come. I return to my simple reality, to my undeniable and most minuscule being.[17]

"I return to my small garden that presently blooms" is an allusion and clear antithesis to the Faustian hubris that deeply concerned Jung throughout his entire life. Beside the big tower in Bollingen, along with the kitchen on the ground floor and the two small dormitories on the first floor, is a small tower that Jung added eight years later in 1935. This is the so-called chapel, Jung's place of meditation. Above the entrance door of this chapel, chiseled into the arch, we read *Philemonis Sacrum Fausti poenitentia*—the sacred place of Philemon the atonement of Faust. So whenever Jung entered the chapel to meditate, he was reminded of Faust's sin. But what *is* his sin? Even though I am aware that the beautiful story of Philemon and Baucis, as recounted in Ovid's *Metamorphoses*, is well-known, some stories are so true that they bear repeating again and again. So I offer it here once more.

> Jupiter and Mercury (Zeus and Hermes) decided to come down to earth, wandering around disguised as peasants. Wherever they knocked and begged for shelter, they were haughtily turned away. Finally when they came to the miserable hut of an old couple, Philemon and Baucis, they found an open door. The old people welcomed them and served them a meal. When they wanted to slaughter their only goose for their guests, the goose sought shelter in the

lap of one of the visitors and thus was spared from being
slaughtered. It was only much later, when Philemon and
Baucis saw that the wine jar was refilled magically, that
they recognized their divine visitors. The gods rewarded
them by granting them a wish and the two asked to stay
together until death and even afterwards. Thus when they
died the humble cottage was changed into a magnificent
temple where the two served as priest and priestess.[18]

So again, what is Faust's sin, and what is the sin of modern man? At
the end of *Faust II*, Faust, in order to increase his properties, carries
out his megalomaniac plans with great ambition and with an inflated
consciousness. In the midst of these properties, however, there was
still that small place, including the garden and the chapel of Philemon
and Baucis. Faust was annoyed at the sound of the church bells of
these pious people. Thus he gave an order to Mephistopheles to get
rid of them, whereupon Mephistopheles immediately killed the old
couple, which was not exactly Faust's conscious intension.

In the Epilogue of *Psychology and Alchemy*, Jung dealt with that
Faustian hubris. He said, with a side glance to Nietzsche's *Zarathustra*:
"In his blind urge for superhuman power, Faust brought about the
murder of Philemon and Baucis."[19] "An inflated consciousness is
always egocentric and conscious of nothing else but its own
existence."[20] Ever since the Age of Enlightenment, and in the era of
scientific rationalism, the psyche had become synonymous with
consciousness. "There was no psyche outside the ego."[21] Therefore,
Jung continued, we must repudiate "the arrogant claim of the
conscious mind to be the whole of the psyche, and to admit that the
psyche is a reality which we cannot grasp with our present means of
understanding."[22] The problem of modern man is, as Jung saw it, his
"god-almightiness" [*Gottähnlichkeit*], that is, the identification of the
ego with the objective psyche or the divine. We may say as well that
the sin of modern man is his inflation. As *The Red Book* strongly
suggests, as long as we are unwilling to return to poverty for the sake
of the God and as long as we are unwilling to accept the burden of

our spiritual poverty, then despite all our material wealth, there will remain a lack of inner happiness.

Up to his old age Jung was attracted to the simple life in the midst of nature. Only a few years after his descent to the depths in the *Red Book*, in 1923, he started to build the Tower at Bollingen. Whenever his schedule would allow, he lived a rather primitive life there with no electricity and no running water. He cooked all the meals on the open fire. There he felt at home, connected with the "spirit of the depths." "From the beginning," he said in his Memoirs, "I felt the Tower as in some way a place of maturation—a maternal womb or a maternal figure in which I could become what I was, what I am and will be. ... At Bollingen I am in the midst of my true life, I am most deeply myself. Here I am, as it were, the 'age-old son of the mother'."[23] Indeed, the "spirit of the depths" "forced him down to the last and simplest things." In the tower of Bollingen, living a most simple life, Jung had materialized these last and simplest things. This was the place he felt nearest to the soul.

The Murder of the Hero

Despite the increasing development of his career, Jung more and more realized that, in order to survive, a murder was required of him. Not the murder of Philemon and Baucis, but just the opposite: the murder of the hero![24]

Beginning with Chapter V of the *Liber Primus*, the problematic aspect of the *heroic* becomes more and more obvious. In other words, the way of the "spirit of the depths" necessarily leads to the murder of the heroic. How could one find the way into the depths if not through the sacrifice of the great and heroic within, which is still striving for power? This, by the way, includes the great and heroic that hides itself behind the mask of false modesty and, at times, even of a depression! The devil in angels' clothes is, as we know, the worst to fight with. The fact that someone suffers from such behavior does not exclude the reality that they are secretly identified with the heroic within. In other words, just because one suffers from depression, from

childhood memories, or from whatever does not necessarily mean
that one is not in the grip of a power complex!

When Jung became aware of his standstill, he had this impressive, and, as we will see, finally redeeming dream about the murder
of Siegfried, that is, the murder of the brilliant solar hero. In this
dream, he was in the company of an unknown, brown-skinned man,
a savage, when Siegfried, their mortal enemy, was coming high across
the mountains on a chariot made of the bones of the dead. He knew
that they had to murder him, and indeed they fired at the same time,
and Siegfried fell slain. Then a terrible rain swept down.[25]

We must be aware that Jung had this dream in December 1913,
before the catastrophes of the two World Wars. So even if it is a clear
anticipation of these disasters, we must look at it from a psychological
perspective rather than a purely historical one. We must ask what the
murder of the hero means in the life of Western man in general.

I am always puzzled by the fact that it is not clear who had finally
killed Siegfried. Was it Jung or his companion, or both of them? We
don't know. But what we *do* know is that after Jung had this dream,
he "went through a torment unto death." He immediately felt certain
that he must kill himself if he could not solve the riddle of the murder
of the hero. Unable to understand his dream, he tried to fall asleep
again, but a voice within him said, "You *must* understand the dream,
and must do so at once!" And not much later the voice added—now
really demanding, "If you do not understand the dream, you must
shoot yourself!"[26] This was not at all an empty menace, since Jung
always had a loaded revolver in the drawer of his night table!

Accepting the Absurd

I won't go into the interpretation of the dream that Jung gave in
Memories, Dreams, Reflections. In the context of *The Red Book,* the
dream has a slightly different meaning. As the title of *Liber Primus,*
"The Way of What Is to Come," suggests, Jung was striving for the
future spirit from the very beginning onward. We have seen that the
spirit of the future emerges from the "spirit of the depths" as opposed

to the "spirit of this time." Jung's dream forced him to murder everything heroic within him, in order to clear the way for the "spirit of the depths." Obviously, the blond solar hero takes no part in this *future spirit,* nor does he contribute anything to it. Rather, he is holding onto old values. So, we must ask, what exactly *is* the heroic that is to be sacrificed? If we follow *The Red Book,* we realize in amazement that it particularly has something to do with accepting that which makes no sense. Soon after the murder of the hero, Jung heard the redeeming word, when the "spirit of the depths" told him:

> The highest truth is one and the same with the *absurd.* [The German expression '*mit dem Widersinnigen*' is very difficult to translate. The sentence literally means: 'The highest truth is one and the same with that *which makes no sense* or even *with that which is opposed to any sense or meaning.*'] This statement saved me, and like a rain after a long hot spell it swept away everything in me which was too highly tensed.[27]

At the beginning of *The Red Book* we often hear of the "*Widersinn,*" of that which is opposed to or deprived of any meaning. The historical background of this idea must be sought in the writings of the Gnostics, to whom Jung felt quite attracted in those years, mainly because of their emphasis on paradox. I cannot go into this topic here even though the Gnostics have the most wonderful statements about the paradoxical truth of the psyche. However, these texts are rather difficult and at times confusing. It would lead us too far astray. Their core message, however, as I see it, is the following: Any true encounter with the "spirit of the depths" takes away from man the belief that he can rule his life by reason or by intellect; that is, it takes away the illusion that he can ever fully understand his life and the mystery of the world. Wholeness requires *conscious* acceptance of the paradox, of the *Widersinn,* of that which makes no sense to our mind. In other words, as we shall see, it requires us to accept *the madness of our own darkness.*

Just listen to the text at the beginning of Chapter V of *Liber Primus*, "Descent to Hell into the Future"[28] (Jung is still struggling here with the "spirit of the depths"):

> A loud voice called, 'I am falling ...' [Jung speaking to himself responded:] Should I entrust myself to this confusion? I shuddered. It is a dreadful depth. [And addressing the soul he continues:] Do you want me to leave myself to chance, to the madness of my own darkness? Whither? Whither? You fall, and *I want to fall with you, whoever you are.*[29]

It seems that he had lost the ground under his feet and was now completely exposed to the madness of his own darkness. Following his soul, he let himself fall into unknown depths. But it is obvious that this madness simultaneously relieved him. It was a redeeming revelation. Thus the text continues:

> The spirit of the depths opened my eyes and I caught a glimpse of the inner things, the world of my soul, the many-formed and changing.[30]

Finally, at the end of the same Chapter V, it becomes clearer what this commitment to one's own madness, which is, in fact, the madness of clinging to the heroic, implies:

> The heroic in you is the fact that you are ruled by the thought that this or that is good, ... that this or that goal must be attained in headlong striving work, ... Consequently you sin against incapacity [meaning you commit a sin by not admitting your incapacity or your impotence].[31]

The very moment when Jung let himself fall into the abyss, the "spirit of the depths" opened his eyes. He caught a glimpse of the inner world of his soul, of the psychic world beyond any Christian delusion. He now realized that "love, soul, and God are *beautiful and terrible*."[32] What a profound insight, indeed!

Now we must let go the illusion of knowing what is good for myself and for those to whom I feel close. Whoever pretends to know what is good and what is evil, thus says *The Red Book*, commits a sin against incapacity. And it is true, we are often convinced to do the good, but how can we really know which spirit is ruling us, the "spirit of the depths" or rather the "spirit of this time"? The cruelest deeds and the worst crimes have always been and still are perpetrated in the name of the good or even in the name of God. Therefore, I truly love Paul's passage in *Romans 7*, because it is deeply and eternally true:

> I do not understand my own actions. For I do not do what I want, but I do the very thing I hate... For I do not do the good I want, but the evil I do not want is what I do...
> (And realizing how painful this insight actually is, Paul finishes the chapter by exclaiming:) Wretched man that I am! Who will deliver me from this body of death?
>
> *(Romans 7:15.19 and 24)*

Paul was a wise man, indeed, full of Jewish wisdom! There is a beautiful passage in the last chapter of Jung's *Memories, Dreams, Reflections*, which, some forty years later, takes up this idea from the *Red Book* of not really knowing what is good and what is evil:

> The world into which we are born is brutal and cruel, and at the same time of divine beauty. Which element we think outweighs the other, whether meaninglessness or meaning, is a matter of temperament. ... Probably, as in all metaphysical questions, both are true: Life is—or has—meaning and meaninglessness. I cherish the anxious hope that meaning will preponderate and win the battle.[33]

This is what *The Red Book* calls *Widersinn*, that which is opposed to any meaning, the painful fact that life is deeply meaningful and at the same time without meaning and at times even spiritless. And this is what the "spirit of the depths" calls the highest truth. This truth, however, can only be accepted through the sacrifice of the solar hero, the sacrifice of everything too clear, too bright, too good, in short, the sacrifice of our illusion of control.

At the beginning of *The Red Book*, there is already a beautiful passage on sacrifice. These are the words of the "spirit of the depths":

> Sacrifice is not destruction, sacrifice is the foundation stone of what is to come. Have you not had monasteries? Have not countless thousands gone into the desert? You should carry the monastery in yourself. The desert is within you. The desert calls you and draws you back, and if you were fettered to the world of this time with iron, the call of the desert would break all chains. Truly, I prepare you for solitude.[34]

In the desert of solitude we can overcome the old gods, our highest ideals and convictions, which have ruled our life. However, old habits die hard. This is why *The Red Book* speaks of a *terrible* sacrifice that erupted with force sweeping away with a powerful wave everything unnecessary.[35]

Now at the very moment the murder is committed, a surprising twist happens: The cruel words of the "spirit of the depths" saved him, and like a rain after a long hot spell, they swept away everything in him which was too highly tensed. This rain is fructifying, and renewing the earth "it begets the new wheat, the young, germinating God."[36] This long expected God is Phanes, the divine child.

I summarize these reflections on the frightening fall into the abyss and the renewal from the depths of the earth with a passage from the *I Ching*. It stems from Hexagram 51, *Thunder*, which is a *yang* line beneath two *yin* lines ☳, or as Master Alfred Huang put it, *buried* underneath two yielding lines.[37] It is an explosion of *yang* energy from within the depth of the earth, thunder, which bursts forth from the earth like an earthquake. However, the ancient Chinese masters compared it with the explosion of the creative in spring. Richard Wilhelm gave a revealing comment on this image. "The shock that comes from the manifestation of God within the depths of the earth makes man afraid, but this fear of God is good, for joy and merriment can follow upon it."[38] So it is no surprise that Chapter VIII of *Liber Secundus*, following the "Murder of the Hero," talks about "The Conception of the God," that is, the birth of the divine child!

The Birth of the Divine Child

We have heard that the title of *Liber Primus* is "The Way of What Is to Come." Only gradually we learn that what is to come is nothing less than the divine child! It is the inner child that will be, or is to be, created in you! The human psyche is the dwelling place of that child. Humans become the birthplace of the new god-image. Therefore, the path of individuation is a path into the future since the child always means future life. *The Red Book* puts it beautifully:

> The spirit of the depths taught me that my life is encompassed[39] by the divine child. From his hand everything unexpected came to me, everything living. This child is what I feel as an eternally springing youth in me.[40]

However, we should not cherish any illusions about that child. In Chapter VIII, "The Conception of the God," we hear again about it, but this time of its rather ambiguous nature: "The divine child approached me out of the terrible ambiguity, the hateful-beautiful, the evil-good, the laughable-serious, the sick-healthy, the inhuman-human and the ungodly-godly."[41] Psychologically, this child refers to wholeness as the goal of the individuation process. Decades later, accordingly, C.G. Jung, in *Answer to Job*, interpreted the birth of the divine child, in the context of John's vision of the apocalyptic sun-woman (Revelation 12), "as the coming to consciousness of the self. … As a result, John became personally involved in the divine drama."[42] This is what happens to everyone who is confronted with the "spirit of the depths" and who is, as a consequence, embraced by the divine child. And this is how Jung, yearning for the new light, praises the divine child:

> My god, I love you as a mother loves the unborn whom she carries in her heart. … We need your light, O child. Since we go in darkness, light up our paths. May your light shine before us, may your fire warm the coldness of our life.[43]

Endnotes

1 C.G. Jung, *Memories, Dreams, Reflections*, ed. Aniela Jaffé (New York, NY: Vintage Books, 1963), 223.
2 This information stems partly from the *Protokolle* (*Protocols*), i.e., from C.G. Jung's interviews with Aniela Jaffé, which served as a starting point *Memories, Dreams, Reflections*.
3 Jung, *Memories, Dreams, Reflections*, 188.
4 Ibid., 290-291.
5 Ibid., 193.
6 C.G. Jung, "The Tavistock Lectures" (1935), in *CW*, vol. 18 (Princeton, NJ: Princeton University Press, 1976), par. 270.
7 C.G. Jung, *The Red Book: Liber Novus*, ed. Sonu Shamdasani, tr. John Peck, Mark Kyburz, and Sonu Shamdasani (New York, NY: W. W. Norton, 2009), 231.
8 Jung, *Memories, Dreams, Reflections*, 11-13.
9 Jung, *The Red Book*, 231. Emphasis mine.
10 This is in a footnote of the German edition, which is not in the English version. See Jung, *Erinnerungen, Träume, Gedanken*, 180 n4.
11 Jung, *The Red Book*, 232.
12 Ibid.
13 Ibid., 233.
14 Or *my humanness*—in German: *mein Menschliches*.
15 Ibid., 229.
16 Ibid., 303.
17 Ibid., 306.
18 See also M.-L. von Franz, "The Unknown Visitor," in *Archetypal Dimension of the Psyche* (London: Shambhala, 1999), 58.
19 C.G. Jung, *Psychology and Alchemy*, in *CW*, vol. 12 (Princeton, NJ: Princeton University Press, 1968), par. 561.
20 Ibid., par. 563.
21 Ibid., par. 562.
22 Ibid., par. 564.
23 Jung, *Memories, Dreams, Reflections*, 225.
24 Jung, *The Red Book*, 241-242.
25 Ibid. See also Jung, *Memories, Dreams, Reflections*, 180.

[26] Ibid.

[27] Jung, *The Red Book*, 242.

[28] In German the phrase "*Höllenfahrt in die Zukunft*" means: "Hellish Descent *into* the Future" – not "Descent to Hell in the Future."

[29] Jung, *The Red Book*, 237.

[30] Ibid.

[31] Ibid., 240.

[32] Ibid., 238.

[33] Jung, *Memories, Dreams, Reflections*, 358-359.

[34] Jung, *The Red Book*, 230.

[35] Ibid., 238.

[36] Ibid., 242.

[37] Huang, *The Complete I Ching*. On the *I Ching* see also: Andreas Schweizer, "The Book of the Play of the Opposites," in A. Schweizer and R. Schweizer-Vüllers (eds.), *Stone by Stone* (Einsiedeln: Daimon, 2017), 16-50.

[38] *The I Ching or Book of Changes*, trans. Richard Wilhelm, Hexagram 51.

[39] The German text has "*umschlossen*" meaning: "surrounded" or "embraced" by the divine child.

[40] Jung, *The Red Book,* 234.

[41] Ibid., 243.

[42] C.G. Jung, *Answer to Job*, in *CW*, vol. 11 (Princeton, NJ: Princeton University Press, 1969), par. 714.

[43] Jung, *The Red Book*, 286.

Imagination for Evil

Liliana Liviano Wahba

"Innocence was his blinder."
Herman Melville, *Billy Bud*

Jung considered modern society to be in urgent need of a collective conscience, and Analytic Psychology could provide a model of pragmatic intervention. Ideally, the process of individuation would stimulate widespreading actions to support individuals and society in building community with values and meaning linked to welfare, spiritual harmony, and nature, and paying due respect to integrity. Being familiar with the psyche and the somber components (shadow) that go along with the noblest of ideals, Jung foresaw certain hurdles and defenses that would affect groups and individuals not only in their very intimate and family relations but also as regards their community ties. Especially worried about the political leaders of the time and the deterioration that authoritarian regimes could cause to society, Jung dedicated much of his writings to the critique of dogmatism, inflation of the ego, psychopathic power, credulity, and unconsciousness of myopic followers of so-called "leaders." These works were largely in line with what he called "confronting the shadow" and often rooted in the religious theme of the struggle between good and evil in the representations of the divine and in psychic projections.

This paper sets out to knit together observations on evil and credulity and the importance of awareness of these polarities in these days of intensive conflicts of an ethnic, religious, and economic nature, all of whose symptoms of arbitrariness in the exercise of power, of technology stripped of any humanism, and suicidal despair endorse the fear that is born of a world in convulsion. Inspiration for the article was found in the expression used by Jung concerning the importance of remaining alert to the "imagination for evil."[1]

A recent tragic incident that took place in the interior of Brazil's southeastern region fits the proposed theme addressed to the power of evil when innocence—or ingenuousness—encounters cruel psychopathy. The incident involved a social worker just over 30 years of age, married and the mother of a child. She lent assistance to a 65-year-old man she called "grand-daddy." She went to his small farm on her own to teach him to read and write and even see to his personal needs, such as cutting his toenails. The catastrophe happened on her last visit: The man raped and killed her with a hammer blow to the head. Her husband was disconsolate, feeling guilty for not having foreseen that this fatality might occur and for not having protected her. The murderer kept a photograph with words describing her figure and several "I love you" notes. Both he and a neighboring farmer who acted as an accomplice had criminal records as rapists.

The tale of *Little Red Riding Hood* deals with a girl's initiation and the need to lose childhood innocence, for the wolves are hungry. What happens when the age of innocence is over yet still remains in an inappropriate form and even on behalf of good?

In our professional practices as psychotherapists we come upon patients who put the blame for their suffering on all that is alien to them and find it tremendously hard to perceive their own participation in what happens, or else they blame themselves so generically that they also remain unaware of the effects they produce on others. Here evil is diffuse, the world being made of traps into which they are bound to fall, so there is no point in their trying to become aware of these traps. So these patients are left regretting their guilt, be it external or internal. There is yet another condition, which is when a film of apparent innocence protects one from recognizing what would be considered evil. As an example, a patient aged 25 who was adopted attributed to her parents and her surroundings an aura of almost magical protection and felt it extremely difficult to understand situations of conflict. She was always surprised and disturbed in groups when for some reason she was ignored or someone spoke badly of her. Very intelligent and respected in her postgraduate studies and career, her face was that of a child, which also made her dream of a happy marriage, although she never got close to boys, not knowing what to do and how to act. She dreamed of a suitable and well-intentioned partner showing up one day. In this particular case, the defenses against feelings of abandonment and orphanhood added to this psychic state of absolute purity and innocence.

Regardless of the underlying psychological dynamic, malice and innocence appear to be factors that actually interpenetrate in dangerous games that can even lead to catastrophic outcomes, as seen in the newspaper incident.

The last of Herman Melville's works, his masterful novel *Billy Bud*, portrays the angelic character of a young man, innocent as a "flower child" and free of any malice, which leads to his destruction through the projections of a master-at-arms who is filled with envy, hate, and cruelty. Melville dramatically traces his fate in the play of two opposites: innocence and evil in the figures of the two characters.

Rollo May in his work *Power and Innocence* also mentions *Billy Budd* and endorses Arthur Miller's opinion that "the perfection of innocence, indeed, is madness."[2] He considers the attitude of innocence a way of refusing legitimate power, very often making a virtue of such an attitude. He provides the etymology in Latin: "*innocens:* not harmful. To be free from guilt or sin, guiltless, pure and in action it means without evil influence or effect, or not arising from evil intention."[3]

May distinguishes between two kinds of innocence: one has the quality of imagination, as for the poet and the artist, and preserves the childlike clarity in adulthood, leading to spirituality, therefore a source of purity and newness; the other is irresponsible childishness, when innocence that cannot include the daimonic becomes evil.

The first fits Jung's description of the child archetype. The second is pictured in Melville's character. It is rather pseudoinnocence, a kind of fixation in the past, childishness rather than childlikeness. This sort of pseudoinnocence leads to utopianism, where we do not need to face real danger, and even though it claims to be a virtue, it is not. It doesn't make things clear, only simple and easy to avoid the tragedies and complexities of life. In endorsing innocence, we cannot recognize the destructiveness in ourselves, leading to a sort of complicity with evil. Billy Bud wasn't capable of noticing enmity, not being suspicious or distrustful enough.

Although it dates from 1972, *Power and Innocence* still means a lot today. It remains a perspicacious description of how individuals and groups behave and made vulnerable by simplistic "life slogans" denying all desire for power and supposedly remaining above evil to avoid having to face—and assume—the reality of power. Such avoidance eludes responsibility and opens the way to explosions of violence: "The innocent person in religion, the one who lacks the 'wisdom of the serpents,' can do considerable harm without knowing it."[4] May also emphasizes, avoiding any religious premises, that Melville had already remarked that spirituality is opposed to innocence.

Like Jung, May advocates the urgent necessity to promote awareness of the good and evil in each one of us, inescapable from the experience of life and accepting responsibility and blame for human actions. In short, according to the author, the answer to the problem of evil in humanity will not be given through innocence and exemption from sins, but rather by accepting that evil will always be our adversary.

The problematic posed by evil and destructiveness permeates Jung's work, and even though he did not postulate the notion of a death instinct, he recognizes the aggressive-destructive polarity in psychic energy. In *Symbols of Transformation,* he wrote: "Libido is not only a ceaseless forward movement, an unending will of life, libido also wills its own descent, its own involutions—death,"[5] thereby circumscribing the life and death instincts within libido itself. Also, in *The Red Book* he writes: "You are not forced to live eternally but you can also die since there is a will in you for both. Life and death must strike balance in your existence."[6]

We can symbolize the death and life cycles, as well as the cycles of creation and destruction, within the myth of sacrifice that harbors pain transformed into an act of renovation, perhaps due to our capacity of resilience. And if, in fact, we observe complex psychic processes and deep needs for change that entail destruction in order to go forward to build new attitudes, we observe involutions—of a psychic nature—without any exit: psychopathic disorders, cruel behavior inflicted on someone rendered vulnerable, massacres, tyrant power, blind and deadly fanaticism, and myriad other expressions of what we may understand as incurable, unalterable evil. Psychiatry has tried to give a name to the noncomprehensible, to evil: *psychopathy*, although not all those considered to be psychopaths commit criminal acts.

Guggenbühl-Craig explored the theme of absence of moral sense and Eros in psychopathy,[7] while James Hillman suggested some deficiency of a constitutive nature, as if those deriving from a "bad seed" found in violence a mode of transcendence, a mode of going beyond the ordinary human so that it becomes inhuman.[8] In order to control "inhuman" demonic aggressiveness, he proposes that we need to find modes of ritual, through the arts and collective ceremonies, which allow excessive, extravagant, demonic force to find a way of expression.

Nevertheless, mercilessly annihilating one's fellow-man is likewise human, with or without a causal reason to justify such an act. And no matter what psychiatric nosology decides, a frightful, terrifying, and unfathomable attraction toward evil exists, throbs, and pulsates in the human being.

In particular, in the essays contained in volume 10 of the *Collected Works, Civilization in Transition* and in *Answer to Job*,[9] Jung reflects on the valence of evil in the psyche, in society, and even rooted in religion. The Second World War left its painful mark on thinkers of the time, and Jung witnessed the devastation of two terrible wars in the 20th century. On several occasions he expressed his deep concern for the future of humanity.

Murray Stein, in his extensive review of Jung's work on the subject of evil,[10] explores the meaning that Jung lends to evil. He shows that Jung understood how energy is manifested in the psyche and in nature in terms of cycles of structuring and dissolution. The question posed refers to the intrinsic nature of the unconscious and the archetypal reality of evil. According to Stein, Jung pursues a psychological vision of evil, adopting such notions as shadow, complexes, projection, and possession of the ego, all of which in some measure annul the capacity of moral discernment.

On the one hand, Jung understood evil as the product of consciousness rather than as having substance of its own whether in terms of a psychic, physical, or metaphysical nature. Accordingly, good and evil would be poles of contrasting discrimination used to differentiate experience, as well as a prerequisite for refining moral judgment by cognitive means. In other words, evil would not be intrinsic to human nature. On the other hand, however, by proposing the incarnation of the dark side of God and evil contained in the duality of the divine essence and consequently in that of human beings, evil would be of an intrinsic nature. Stein claims that Jung admitted the paradoxical nature of this contradiction.

We lack an answer, that is to say we shall remain at a loss as to whether evil springs from the shadow and is the product of archetypal possession and inflation, and if it is a judgment of consciousness or a reality in itself. Be that as it may, the effects of evil are always real, and some individuals seem endowed with intrinsic badness. Perhaps a scrutinizing consciousness—and not just reason—provides the appropriate vaccine or the antibiotic available to us, whether to face the evil that is in us or else to increase our chances of being protected from what is alien to us and often insoluble.

Knowing and exploring the depths of the psyche as he did, Jung understood that ingenuousness on the part of scientists and psychologists was unconscionable and that an attitude of confront-ation was necessary, indeed even indispensable, to cope with the destructive forces rooted in the human psyche. In *Answer to Job*, written in 1952, Jung warned about the scope of the power of destruction given to man and the necessity to "temper his will with the spirit of love and wisdom."[11]

Since his early personal experiences with the unconscious that resulted in his *Red Book*, the problematic of evil is present in Jung's work and receives thorough scrutiny. We shall refer to some important passages on this matter later. For the present, let us look at how Jung warns us about what has been described above whenever we are dealing with a state or attitude of innocence, pseudo-innocence, convenience, or childishness—"infantile cowardice"[12]—be it neurotic or merely opportunistic. In *Flying Saucers*, Jung describes the risk of a naive and unconscious person who could imagine avoiding sin as a childish illusion, when the danger of succumbing to evil is stronger by remaining unaware of it: "Unconsciousness is no excuse but is far rather a transgression, in the literal sense of the word."[13]

Like other thinkers of his era, including Freud,[14] Jung was preoccupied with the fanaticism and mental servility of large, undifferentiated groups dominated by uniform, unilateral premises. In extreme cases, this would lead to sociopathic leaders, as emphasized by Hannah Arendt in *The Origins of Totalitarianism*: regimes in which the totalitarian tendency is to make human beings superfluous, redundant, and dispensable as individuals.[15] Since the subject cannot be prevented from thinking, his thinking is made impotent and irrelevant as if his individuality has dissolved and *all men have become "One Man," an* undifferentiated mankind. By exerting pressure on everyone and turning each one against the other, total terror destroys the space between them and becomes a condition of a perfect totalitarian government, when radical evil emerges in connection with a system in which all men have become equally superfluous.

This phenomenon, however, does not occur only in situations of terror or totalitarian oppression. It frequently appears too in democratic contexts when conscious or unconscious dominating and subjugating forms of behavior are habitual.

Kant's notion of minority applies to the so-called mass mentality and relationships characterized by subjugation: "Enlightenment is the human being's emergence from his self-incurred minority."[16] Due to laziness and cowardice, so many people remain "minor" under other guardians and do not take the trouble to assume their responsibilities.

Here, the presupposition is that the direction exercised by another—whether by an imposing force or by free acceptance—reduces the capacity of full awareness of oneself and the surrounding world. The state of innocence would thus be one of the variables on a scale

when the individual—without anyone identified as his director—
remains at the mercy of actions or projections that he fails to perceive.

In this regard, in *The Undiscovered Self* Jung refers to a society
composed of deindividualized human beings (Arendt's "One Man")
completely at the mercy of ruthless dictators. He also points to the
unrealistic and infantile dream-state of the "mass man," slipping back
into the "kingdom of childhood, into the paradise of parental care,
into happy-go-luckiness and irresponsibility."[17] In short, in this work
he reflects on the tremendous importance of self-knowledge and
responsibility with regard to actually being capable of harming
oneself and others, and the importance of recognizing "humanity's
black collective shadow":

> In fact, this negligence is the best means of making him an
> instrument of evil. Harmlessness and naïveté are as little
> helpful as it would be for a cholera patient and those in his
> vicinity to remain unconscious of the contagiousness of
> the disease ... What is even worse, our lack of insight
> deprives us of the capacity to deal with evil.[18]

In this text, Jung uses the term "imagination for evil," and it is in *The Red
Book* that he inserts vivid pictures and visions to represent this imaginary
power that raises the strangest figures from the depths of the psyche,
figures known to poets, artists, and philosophers, and leave no doubt as
to the horror that dwells within us. He gives the name "spirit of the
depths" to what stands against the "spirit of this time" and proclaims: "…
what I speak is the greatness and intoxication and ugliness of madness."[19]
Here, Jung prepares us for the disturbing visions that follow and paves
the ground of the "imagination for evil" referred to above.

The crudeness of some of these visions raised criticism and
suspicion concerning the mental health of the author, who nevertheless
made it clear that the work was an experiment ("my most difficult
experiment"), an opening to the unconscious gathered through
intuitions to be confronted with consciousness. Paul Bishop refers to
the aesthetics of unacceptably horrendous and repulsive with shocking
passages and portraits of death, somewhat comparable to spiritual
exercises designed to contemplate death.[20] In Jung's view, the fantasies

described there are to be read symbolically rather than literally, that is to say, with a hermeneutic treatment of creative fantasies that accepts the irrational as a psychological factor.[21] The revelations of the unconscious should be understood from a scientific and ethical stance.

In the introduction to *The Red Book*, Shamdasani points out some themes from the work that he sees as an attempt to understand the individual's relationship with the social and as an effort to understand subjectivity itself.[22] He underscores the fact that Jung realized the contemporary malaise of spiritual alienation and dealt with the atrocities of war, manifestations of madness, and religious transformations. Cary Baines remarks that Jung told her that he had no respect for inspired ideas that had no impact on reality, which confirms his psychological philosophy of elucidating psychic phenomena and his desire to institute a psychological education for the individual in modern times.[23]

According to Jaffé, the unconsciousness of human beings and their submergence in a quite irresponsible mass disturbed Jung deeply, and he foresaw catastrophes threatening the existence of the human species. "With apprehension he saw the dangers which arise when the truth of the depths is not recognized, its darkness neither endured nor enlightened."[24]

If the paradox of the essence of evil may be in Jung's work often interpreted by the shadow, in other words by pointing to the differentiation of consciousness and, as we have seen, leaving evil in itself unsolved, in *The Red Book* the phenomenology of evil appears substantial, even haunting the author himself. What follows is a selection of quotations the better to appreciate Jung's thinking in *The Red Book*.

With regard to his preoccupation with man's aggressiveness toward his fellow men, see the description written between the wars as well as what Freud wrote in 1930.

> No one should be astonished that men are so far removed from one another that they cannot understand one another, that they wage war and kill one another. One should be much more surprised that men believe they are close, understand one another and love one another. Two things

are yet to be discovered. The first is the infinite gulf that separates us from one another. The second is the bridge that could connect us. Have you considered how much un-suspected animality human company makes possible?[25]

... men are not gentle creatures, who want to be loved, who at the most can defend themselves if they are attacked; they are, on the contrary, creatures among whose instinctual endowments is to be reckoned a powerful share of aggressiveness. As a result, their neighbor is for them not only a potential helperorsexual object, but also someone who tempts them to satisfy their aggressiveness on him, to exploit his capacity for work without compensation, to use him sexually without his consent, to seize his possessions, to humiliate him, to cause him pain, to torture and to kill him.[26]

Accordingly, if evil is inevitable and inherent to human nature, all we can do is to confront it as Jung incites us to do after observing that abysmal evil may come from man's stupidity and unconsciousness: "One of the toughest roots of all evil is unconsciousness."[27]

The Red Book contains several passages where the author now adopts a dialogue tone with the reader, and then a superior, affir-mative rhetoric as spokesman of this "spirit of the depths." What message does this convey? What transpires is the constitution of polarities of the ego, the necessity to renew and adjust consciousness and to confront the shadowy, destructive tendencies, but mainly to acknowledge that evil is absolutely "real," although we cannot under-stand it fully, for evil always eludes us. In other words, the thinker, the psychiatrist, seems to be warning us that any interpretation (like shadow or possession) will be partial and limited, and yet, even so, it is up to us to face the task.

In perusing this coming and going of fantasies, some of which are hermetic and incomprehensible, what one sees delineated is almost a manual on how to confront evil without succumbing to it. The author exhorts human beings to see themselves in their moral shortcomings and to realize the ambiguity of virtues. The almost prophetic tone of his words carries us to other realms that defy understanding. Vivid images are used, such as: "did you know what evil is?" "inevitable substance," "unsuspecting messenger," "the serpent hisses," "the bloodthirsty tiger."

> Did you ever think of the evil in you? Oh, you spoke of it, you mentioned it, and you confessed it smilingly, as a general human vice, or a recurring misunderstanding. But did you know what evil is, and that it stands precisely right behind your virtues, that it is also your virtues themselves, as their inevitable substance?[28]
>
> You smile innocently, my friend? Don't you see that a gentle flickering of your eye betrays the frightfulness whose unsuspecting messenger you are? Your bloodthirsty tiger growls softly, your poisonous serpent hisses secretly, while you, conscious only of your goodness, offer your human hand to me in greeting.[29]

We are shown that recurrent supports can be useless when faced with such mighty opposition, including blind confidence in faith. The illusion that makes us place ourselves in the hands of a benevolent facilitator God is dispelled as a help to combat human destructivity.

> The one eye of the Godhead is blind, the one ear of the Godhead is deaf, the order of its being is crossed by chaos. So be patient with the crippledness of the world and do not overvalue its consummate beauty.[30]

And if we are deeply disturbed by the injunction, "assimilate the dark God who also wants to become man,"[31] we are somewhat relieved when Jung also asserts that evil is necessary—equivalent here to destruction—in order to dissolve and renew established formations: "You will need evil to dissolve your formation and free yourself from the power of what has been."[32]

He then endeavors to orient us by announcing that—paradoxically—the infernal condition of the psyche, enveloped as it is in darkness and horror, can only be shed by confronting evil rather than denying it:

> He who does not want evil will have no chance to save his soul from Hell. So long as he remains in the light of the upper world, he will become a shadow of himself.[33]

Note that "Hell" is followed by a very striking, hermetic part that is difficult to understand and assimilate; "The Sacrificial Murder," in which a mutilated girl has her liver devoured by the protagonist at the request of the soul, symbolizes the sacrifice of the divine child and the soul's need for atonement. The innocent murdered child becomes divine after eating the liver. Each and every man is to blame for the horrors committed by men. Each and every man has to expiate and to feel remorse (the liver metaphor); in other words, our sense of ethical responsibility extends beyond the personal to the collective. We remain neither in innocence nor sin, just responsive to our deeds, be they virtuous or malicious, as well as acknowledging the deeds committed throughout history.

Considering the crude, "abominable"[34] description, we can understand Jung's doubts about the publication reported by Cary Baines, who feared jeopardizing his position as a scientist and respect as a human being, seeing as the book could be considered "sheer lunacy."[35]

Finally, after traveling the sinuous and irrational paths of fantasy and its intriguing and complicated metaphors, the warning message against evil and the ineffective attempt to ignore it seem coherent enough and in line with Jung's observation on the individual and collective psyche. The wisdom of the psychologist and humanist scientist is revealed here in the attempt to reach out to his and future generations not only in a rational manner, by clarifying prophylactic measures to draw our attention, since as an analyst he was aware that words of advice did not work by themselves. He therefore endeavored to transmit the message through the unconscious, a message that he hoped would echo in each one so as to avoid extreme destructiveness, cruelty, barbaric oppression, and annihilation, escape through death when life loses meaning, and also in order to avoid naiveté and denial.

The quotation below closes this essay. The notion of desire for evil that we bear within us is one of the strangest paradoxes of our consciousness, defying as it does all ethical sense. In rereading these lines, they strike us in a profound and defiant manner, inciting us to offer unique answers to a universal reality. It is not a question of surrender—that would be intolerable—but rather of an uncommon appropriation as a form of confrontation. What remains to be questioned is the feasibility of extending this individual confrontation to the collective:

> You suffer from evil because you love it secretly and are unaware of your love. You wish to escape your predicament, and you begin to hate evil. And once more you are bound to evil through your hate, since whether you love or hate it, it makes no difference: you are bound to evil. Evil is to be accepted. What we want remains in our hands. What we do not want, and yet is stronger than us, sweeps us away and we cannot stop it without damaging ourselves, for our force remains in evil. Thus we probably have to accept our evil without love and hate, recognizing that it exists and must have its share in life. In doing so, we can deprive it of the power it has to overwhelm us.[36]

Endnotes

This essay was translated by James Mulholland, Rio de Janeiro.

1 C.G. Jung, "The Undiscovered Self" (1956), in *CW*, vol. 10 (Princeton, NJ: Princeton University Press, 1964), par. 559.
2 Rollo May, *Power and Innocence* (New York, NY: W. W. Norton, 1972), 47.
3 Ibid., 48.
4 Ibid., 256.
5 C.G. Jung, *Symbols of Transformation*, in *CW*, vol. 5 (Princeton, NJ: Princeton University Press, 1967), par. 680.
6 C.G. Jung, *The Red Book: Liber Novus*, ed. Sonu Shamdasani, tr. John Peck, Mark Kyburz, and Sonu Shamdasani (New York, NY: W. W. Norton, 2009), 274.
7 Adolf Guggenbühl-Craig, *Eros on Crutches* (Texas: Spring, 1980).
8 Mary Nurrie Stearns, "The Soul's Code: An Interview with James Hillman," see http://www.personaltransformation.com/james_hillman.html.
9 C.G. Jung, *Answer to Job*, in *CW*, vol. 11 (Princeton, NJ: Princeton University Press, 1969), pars. 553-756.
10 Murray Stein, "Introduction," in *Jung on Evil* (Princeton, NJ: Princeton University Press, 1995), 1-21.
11 Jung, *Answer to Job*, *CW* 11, par. 745.
12 C.G. Jung, "Good and Evil in Analytical Psychology" (1960), in *CW*, vol. 10 (Princeton, NJ: Princeton University Press, 1964), par. 868.
13 C.G. Jung, "Flying Saucers. A Modern Myth of Things Seen in the Skies" (1958), in *CW*, vol. 10. (Princeton, NJ: Princeton University Press, 1964), par. 677.
14 Sigmund Freud. "Group Psychology and the Analysis of the Ego," in *The Standard Edition of the Complete Works of Sigmund Freud* (London: The Hogarth Press and the Institute of Psychoanalysis, 1953-74).
15 Hannah Arendt, *Origins of Totalitarianism* (New York, NY: Harcourt, 1976).

16 Immanuel Kant, "An Answer to the Question: What is Enlightenment?" See https://www.marxists.org/reference/subject/ethics/kant/enlightenment.htm.

17 C.G. Jung, "The Undiscovered Self" (1956), in *CW*, vol. 10 (Princeton, NJ: Princeton University Press, 1964), par. 538.

18 Ibid., par. 572.

19 Jung, *The Red Book*, 230.

20 Paul Bishop, "Jung and the Quest for Beauty," in (eds.) Thomas Kirsch and George Hogenson, *The Red Book: Reflections on C.G. Jung's Liber Novus* (London: Routledge, 2014).

21 C.G. Jung, "The Structure of the Unconscious," in *CW*, vol. 7 (Princeton, NJ: Princeton University Press, 1966), par. 497.

22 Jung, *The Red Book*, 207.

23 Ibid., 213.

24 Aniela Jaffé, *From the Life and Work of C.G. Jung* (Einsiedeln: Daimon Verlag, 1989), 186-87.

25 Jung, *The Red Book*, 289.

26 Sigmund Freud, *Civilization and its Discontents* (New York, NY: W. W. Norton, 1961), 58.

27 C.G. Jung, "A Psychological Approach to the Dogma of the Trinity," in *CW*, vol. 11 (Princeton, NJ: Princeton University Press, 1969), par. 291.

28 Jung, *The Red Book*, 274.

29 Ibid., 289.

30 Ibid., 231.

31 Jung, *Answer to Job*, *CW* 11, par. 742.

32 Jung, *The Red Book*, 287.

33 Ibid., 289.

34 Ibid., 290.

35 Ibid., 213.

36 Ibid., 288.

Movements of Soul in *The Red Book*

Dariane Pictet

After his breakup with Freud at the age of 37-38, Jung experienced a crisis that led him to consider his attitude to both the temporal, phenomenal world and to the timeless, inner realm.

> I had labored misguidedly under the spirit of this time, I thought and spoke much of the soul. I knew many learned words for her, I had judged her and turned her into a scientific object. Therefore the spirit of the depths forced me to speak to my soul, to call upon her as a living being. I had to become aware that I had lost my soul.[1]

The Red Book is the account of Jung's search for inwardness, or as he called it, his confrontation with the unconscious. Taking the form of awakened fantasies, he opened himself to the images that poured out from the depth and set them down into his black books. These were subsequently commented on and transcribed into his *Red Book*. In this very intimate work, Jung shows with humility not only his inner landscape but also the journey of a man in search for his soul. Jung later devised a psychology of relatedness with his theory of the anima, he said:

> The anima becomes, through integration, the Eros of consciousness ... the anima gives relationship and related-ness to a man's consciousness.[2]

Soul is associated with feeling, essence, depth, and matter, and relates us to core values. Classically, Anima is soul, seen and described from a male psychological perspective. My concern here will be to link Jung's theory of the anima with scenes of *The Red Book* and follow its development through the narrative out of which it emerged, leading to its highest fulfillment, the *anima mundi*. The *Red Book* was also, as we shall see, a seedbed for Jung's *Psychological Types*.

At the time of his writing the *Red Book* Jung wanted to find out what happened when he switched off ordinary consciousness and allowed expression to remote parts of his psyche. The "spirit of the depths" pointed him toward the recovery of his soul. He had served "the spirit of this time," a collective adaptation to the demands of society, culture, and outer reality, and, as a result, he felt a spiritual alienation that forced him into the depths of himself so as to regain an inner dimension. He realized that the "spirit of this time" leads to knowledge and scholarship, but the "spirit of the depths" leads to things of the soul, "a knowledge of the heart that gives deeper insight"[3]:

> The spirit of the depths took away my belief in science and
> … took my understanding and knowledge and placed it at
> the service of the inexplicable and the paradoxical.[4]

Understanding that he had been driven by worldly ambition, he resigned his professorship at the University of Zurich and the Psychoanalytical Society in April 1914 to focus on deepening his confrontation with the unconscious. This exploration of soul took place at night. During the day, his attention went to "things, to men ... I went to the desert only at night."[5] Later he commented that "depth and surface should mix, so that new life can develop."[6]

Jung's first encounter with Soul, as described in *The Red Book*, occurred in the autumn of 1913. He began a dialogue with what he deemed a primitive aspect of himself holding a different viewpoint from his own. This he experienced as being "in analysis with a ghost and a woman."[7] Whether she took the form of Soul, serpent, winged goddess, or Salome, this inner function led him through an imaginal landscape to deepen his understanding of an elusive faculty that animates life. As the anima dwells in collective unconscious, it is permeated with universal elements bringing with it an infinite potential and giving the irrational a presence in psychic reality.

> When Dr. Jung uses the word 'soul,' he defines 'soul' as the
> individual's attitude to the inner reality, the function of
> relationship between the inner and outer worlds, the
> bridge to the centre of our whole being.[8]

Is it significant that Vera van der Heyd does not genderize "soul"? There seems to be a difference in conceptualizing soul and anima—the first ungendered, the second only a male preserve, which I will consider specifically in the light of *The Red Book*. In Jungian psychology, the anima is both a personal complex and an archetypal image of woman present in the male psyche since birth and taking on the personal feeling tones associated with every unique individual. Anima is also the feeling engine that drives man's connection with the women in his life. If a man can recognize and work with his anima projections upon women, he can not only achieve a greater balance between his inner and outer realities, but can over time improve his overall relationship with women.

At the onset of *The Red Book*, we are told that Jung spent a period of loneliness and longing in the desert. The desert is a metaphor for aridity, lacking the renewal bestowed by the water of life. In the desert, we are also free from the agitation of mundane preoccupation, thus we can describe it as the entry point to inwardness. With silence as a backdrop, the mind's ceaseless agitation abates, and complexes from the depths come to the forefront of awareness. There, Soul spoke to Jung for the first time, and asked him to wait. It took another 19 days of this purifying atmosphere before Soul awakened from her shadowy life and approached him as a separate entity. Thus, he learned the value of patience without intentions—for a descent into the depths is not something that can be done hurriedly; it demands time and space. He entered a diffuse, mythopoetic awareness distinct from the focused awareness that comes with scholarship.

The anima archetype may be observed in the innumerable cultural representations of the feminine over time.

> There is [in man] an imago not only of the mother but of the daughter, the sister, the beloved, the heavenly goddess, and the chthonic Baubo. Every mother and every beloved is forced to become the carrier and embodiment of this omnipresent and ageless image, which corresponds to the deepest reality in a man.[9]

This archetype takes the form of Eve, the Great Mother who bestows, sustains and dissolves existence, then develops into Helen/Salome, Mary and *Sophia*.

> The first stage—Hawwah, Eve, earth—is purely biological; woman is equated with the mother and only represents something to be fertilized. The second stage is still dominated by the sexual eros, but on an aesthetic and romantic level where woman has already acquired some value as an individual. The third stage raises Eros to the heights of religious devotion and thus spiritualizes him: Hawwah[10] has been replaced by spiritual motherhood. Finally the fourth stage illustrates ... Sapientia ... wisdom.[11]

Jung speaks of the transformation of the anima as a process "whereby life acquires new meaning."[12] We can observe her transformation in Jung's relationship with the female figures of *The Red Book*. Each new development opens up new fields to consciousness. The anima complex tends to disrupt the ego's behavior: The dynamic part of the psyche that wishes to shake things up and change the status quo confronts the part that doesn't want things to change.

> If the encounter with the shadow is the 'apprentice-piece' in the individual's development, then that with the anima is the 'master-piece.'[13]

Through the stages of Eve, Helen, Maria and *Sophia*,[14] the image of an individuating man's inner feminine undergoes a process of transformation. Although we may think of it as a progression, it is also the case that at every stage the other anima images are present in the archetype *in potentia*. When you touch one aspect of an archetype, its other manifestations are always present, ready to be constellated at different moments of life. As Jung writes:

> The anima is bipolar and can therefore appear positive one moment and negative the next; now young, now old; now mother, now maiden; now a good fairy, now a witch; now a saint, now a whore.[15]

Ambivalence comes with all anima projections, and we can identify Jung's own changes of feeling toward anima in *The Red Book*. Yet, through all these changes, "the anima represents the connection with the spring or source of life in the unconscious."[16] She is always numinous and has that divine quality.

Eve

Anima at its most primordial level is Eve, the primeval mother who bestows all that is vital and bountiful. Here, man and nature are intertwined, undifferentiated, and in blissful symbiosis. In this first phase, and in intimate connection with Eve, anima appears also as a serpent, as "the earthly essence of man of which he is not conscious … since it is the mystery that flows to him from the nourishing earth mother."[17] The serpent is associated with the roots of being and symbolizes the chthonic aspects of earth that were split off from the wholeness of the mother archetype in the Abrahamic religions. Identified with Eve, anima is in an undifferentiated relationship with consciousness, meaning that man is subjected to her influence in an unreflected way.

Eve symbolizes the anima of life wanting consciousness, differentiation, and eventually individuation. In the biblical myth, Eve offers fruit from the tree of the knowledge of good and evil, and she is therefore the one who brings consciousness to the uroboric field. At first, there is an incestuous relationship to the Eternal Feminine, and she is indistinguishable from the personal mother. For Jung, symbolic incest with the Mother is a necessary stage. To become independent, the Terrible Mother must be confronted, the darkness faced, the fear of her power conquered, and the inertia that condemns one to compliance in relationships and emotional states, overcome.

In *The Red Book*, Jung is confronted with an emptiness that he described as a loss of soul. Much later in his life, Jung was to describe the experience in these terms:

Younger people ... can bear even the total loss of the anima without injury. The important thing at this stage is for a man to be a man ... After the middle of life, however, permanent loss of the anima means a diminution of vitality, of flexibility, and of human kindness. The result, as a rule, is premature rigidity, crustiness, stereotypy, fanatical one-sidedness, obstinacy, pedantry, or else resignation, weariness, sloppiness, irresponsibility, and finally a childish ramollissement [petulance] with a tendency to alcohol.[18]

When Soul first appears to Jung as a living presence in *The Red Book*, he tells her that his life has been hard and that he has suffered a lot. She answers like a woman who has been ignored for a long time and tells him that she is not interested in his lamentations or his self-pity. Here, we witness Jung taken in by an anima mood that makes him appear needy and a bit childish, relating to Soul as Eve, a mother who should understand him and tell him what to do. "You talk to me as if I were your mother, I am not mother,"[19] she adds derisively. She wants to be related to as a woman and wants him to take responsibility for his emotions.

He calls her hard but accepts her observation and proceeds to confess that he experiences scorn; he despises himself and despises others. Contempt is a superior attitude that presupposes inflation and an overemphasis on rationality, what he deemed to be a sacralization of the goddess Reason. Soul's response is to show him that by belittling her, he is belittling all things that have to do with interiority. Without a living connection to the inner world, man is bereft of a feeling connection to life, and he is literally in an emotional desert.

The Red Book next describes how Jung descended into the "Hell of the Future," where he realizes the wounds that doubt inflicted on his soul. Jung says: "Heal the wounds that doubt inflicts on me, my soul. ... I am still a victim of my thinking."[20] The anima compensates the outer attitude. He thus needs to disengage further with intellectual and rational attitudes and began to integrate a lunacy that connects him with the shifting moon, its subtle silvery light bringing shadowy perceptions and revealing long-lost secrets and encounters with strange characters. This he experiences as a divine madness, which is terrifying and confusing to him. In this section of *The Red Book*, we understand that his relationship with Soul is difficult; he listens to her but does not trust her. He understands the need to sacrifice the intellect, to refrain from thinking and to do without meaning:

> Keep it far from me, science that clever knower, that bad prison master who binds the soul and imprisons it in a lightless cell. But above all protect me from the serpent of judgment.[21]

The chthonic qualities of the serpent, not fully integrated, appear in the form of poor value judgments. We judge others harshly when we have not recognized our own primitive aspects, so we meet them in projection; we judge others according to our own ideas and ideals, yet they lack embodiment. We judge from on high, not from recognizing our shared humanity.

In a later scene, "The Slaying of the Hero," Jung is called upon to slay the heroic function that protects him from feeling an existential powerlessness that he calls "incapacity" and from the ability to recognize that limitations are real:

> When I was aspiring to my highest worldly power, the spirit of the depths sent me nameless thoughts and visions, that wiped out the heroic aspiration in me as our time understands it.[22]

The "spirit of the depths" points him to question the hero who rules with judgmental thoughts and ideas of perfection stemming from the "spirit of this time," from ambition and one-sided views. The hero within does not recognize that we are all brothers and sisters. We do not see the conflict inside our own soul, and instead we murder each other when what we need to do is to murder the hero in us.

After Jung's slaying of the hero and recognition of his "incapacity," Soul endeavors to teach him the value of solitude. As outer, collective values slip away, it becomes possible to focus on the source within that allows us to recognize our kinship with others:

> But now, if you are in your solitude, you can encounter
> your God and this can lead you to the God of others, and
> through that to the true neighbor, to the neighbor of the
> Self in others.[23]

As an inner figure, the anima functions to influence the man from within, shaping his moods. It is associated with emotional development and inner values. In the journey from unconscious to conscious, the anima, at this stage of development, is still partially regressive, the libido flowing partly toward mother, with its laziness tinged with oceanic feelings of oneness. Still, in a childlike relationship to the anima, the man can find it hard to take responsibility for his feelings; they victimize him. Jung describes the effect of such an anima on a man:

> The anima ... intensifies, exaggerates, falsifies, and
> mythologizes all emotional relations with his work and
> with other people of both sexes. The resultant fantasies and
> entanglements are all her doing. When the anima is
> strongly constellated, she softens the man's character and
> makes him touchy, irritable, moody, jealous, vain, and
> unadjusted.[24]

Salome/Helen

After the first encounters with Soul that enabled him to accept the wounds that heroic patterns of behavior bestowed on his capacity for genuine relatedness, the narrative takes us to the "Mysterium: Encounter." In this scene, Jung meets Soul in the form of Salome who, in the biblical narrative, danced and delighted King Herod and his guests but then requested and received the head of John the Baptist, the prophet who announced the coming of Jesus, the new god, the new awareness. This young girl, who evoked the sensuality and erotic temptation that culminated in the beheading of a holy man, fills Jung with horror. Yet he finds himself strangely attracted to her and discovers that she loves him and that this is significant. Must he love her too? Must he love his own desire?

Salome stands for desire and pleasure, a force without form or definition. Elijah, the older man who accompanies her in this scene, stands for a function of mind Jung calls "forethinking." Jung relates Salome and Elijah to Eros and Logos, and is told that these two principles have been together since the beginning of time. Elijah can see but inhabits a dark place, whereas Salome is blind and inhabits a bright place. Elijah, as forethinking, can see into the depths of the past and the future. In this encounter, Jung recognizes that "thoughts are natural events that you do not possess, and whose meaning you only imperfectly recognize."[25] Freeing himself gradually from the activity of mind allows Salome, as wild desire, eventually to lead him to the depth of love.

During this period, Jung began to elaborate his theory of psychological types, and later he wrote that the anima is also "the personification of the inferior function which relates a man to the collective unconscious."[26] But when he first visited the bright garden of Salome, of pleasure, Jung had to realize that, being a thinking type, his feeling remained in darkness, blind and primitive, and so appeared disgusting to him:

> I recognized the father because I was a thinker, and thus I did not know the mother, but saw love in the guise of pleasure, and called it pleasure, and therefore this was Salome to me. Now I learn that Mary is the mother, the innocent.[27]

This important differentiation between pleasure and love shows that the anima is now transforming his understanding of these two principles. Elijah tells him: "May the thinking person accept his pleasure, and the feeling person accept his own thought."[28] Otherwise, they are death to each other, just as John the Baptist found death at the hands of Salome. Clearly, thinking types fear Salome, as she wants their heads. As Jung came to accept that he desired Salome, he further integrated his feeling function and accepted pleasure as a dynamic force in nature. Soul is always close to embodiment and to what "matters." Salome, as the serpent of temptation, points him to the mysteries of earth, sensuality, and erotic love. Jung's reference here to Mary the mother points to the next development of anima. As his capacity to relate to his inner figures developed, so Jung's relationships with women changed, and it was at this time that he began an involvement with Toni Wolf.

Jung tells us: "I climbed down to my pleasure, but ascended to my love."[29] By sacrificing his highest function, thinking, he could develop a living relationship with his most primitive and unconscious function, feeling. By acknowledging pleasure and erotic impulses, he dethroned his thinking function from its lofty heights. This integration of darker, unknown aspects led to increasing consciousness.

> Love is empty without thinking, thinking hollow without love …[30]
> Love and forethinking are in one and the same place.[31]

Salome and Elijah appeared to Jung as companions; thinking and feeling are two complementary functions, the feeling nature of inner feminine soul providing a counterbalance to the logic of the outer-oriented masculine ego. The assumption of that time was that a man was more naturally oriented to logos, the spirit, and therefore has a lesser natural aptitude for relatedness. Similarly, a woman was said to be naturally oriented to relatedness and more primitive in her animus, her logos function. Social constructs, particularly in relation to women, have changed greatly since Jung began elaborating these concepts in 1912. At the time, in Switzerland, he would have observed that women did not often work or have an academic background. They were generally confined to the domestic sphere. Furthermore, having no equal rights in the running of their affairs or that of the world, they would be regarded as, and usually felt, dependent on a man for all outer things. Now this has greatly changed with the advent of woman's liberation, the right to vote, to study and work outside of the home, and with the modern climate of equality in the social arena. The social structure of the time mirrored an incomplete development of the anima, whereby women were kept in a demeaning and subservient role, yet their repressed power was greatly feared.

It is also important for us to remember that the anima is an archetypal symbol, not a genetic or gender-related biological reality. Gender roles have changed greatly since Jung elaborated his theory, with his own fear and ambivalence of the inner feminine evident in these early dialogues with Soul in *The Red Book*. Today, these stereotypes would not apply to gender roles as it is generally accepted that a man can have a developed Eros function or a woman a well-differentiated Logos function. A postmodern view could well be that we develop the contrasexual functions according to our own psychology.

The chapter, "Resolution," contains this dialogue:

> Salome says, 'Mary was the mother of Christ, do you understand?'
> I: 'I see that a terrible and incomprehensible power forces me to imitate the Lord in his final torment. But how can I presume to call Mary my mother?'
> S: 'You are Christ.'
> I stand with outstretched arms like someone crucified, my body taut and horribly entwined by the serpent: 'You, Salome, say that I am Christ?'
> It is as if I stood alone on a high mountain with stiff outstretched arms. The serpent squeezes my body in its terrible coils and the blood streams from my body, spilling down the mountainside. Salome bends down to my feet and wraps her black hair round them. She lies thus for a long time. Then she cries, 'I see light!' Truly, she sees, her eyes are open. The serpent falls from my body and lies languidly on the ground. I stride over it and I kneel at the feet of the prophet, whose form shines like a flame.[32]

The serpent, representing the opposition between good and evil, becomes ineffectual as a new consciousness takes form in Jung's psyche, and the anima as symbolized by Eve and Salome transforms further. When Salome says that Jung is Christ, his fear of madness increases, for identification with archetypal energies is a common sign of psychosis. We can also say that Salome evoked in him the *numinosum*, and she constellated the fear of evil that surrounds the repressed inferior function. In the text, he realizes the power of these images and their autonomy and comments:

> If you can overcome your fear of the unconscious and can let yourself go down, then these facts take on a life of their own ... They form part of ancient mysteries ...[33]

When the ego faces the dragon of the unconscious, the mythological Terrible Mother, and surrenders to the self, one becomes capable of a religious, connected attitude. With the anima as soul guide, mediator, and companion, mystical experiences of oneness become possible as the ego is strong enough to surrender to the depth and be impregnated by the generative imagery that emerges from the source. James Hillman writes:

> As mediatrix to the eternally unknowable she is the bridge both over the river and into the trees and into the sludge and quicksand, making the known ever more unknown.[34]

At the end of this scene, Jung understands that Salome is his sister and both are the children of Mary. Jung comments:

> Just as my thinking is the son of forethinking, so is my pleasure the daughter of love, of the innocent and conceiving mother of God ... forethinking is the procreative, love is the receptive.[35]

Mary

The mother of Christ is the archetypal feminine in its compassionate aspect that gave birth to the new god. Jesus, the light of conscious love in the world, is the Christ who brings the new covenant of brotherhood to our Western culture. Later, Jung wrote: "In Christian metaphor, Mary is the flower in which God lies hidden ..."[36] Compassion is born with the Heavenly Mother, who knows and suffers the darkness of existence. She is receptive, suspends judgment and accepts what is to come. Mary is the third development of the anima that is disclosed in spiritual growth, enabling a capacity for lasting relationships and a creative connection with the imaginal depths. The anima in a man can now love for its own sake, not for pleasure or gratification, and find value in feelings of closeness. Jung says: "Forethinking is singleness, love is togetherness."[37]

This development of the anima to the level of Mary takes place in The Red Book at the end of Liber Primus. In a scene titled "The Sacrificial Murder," Jung is asked to eat the liver of an abused and murdered girl. Soul appears as an ageless, cloaked woman who tells Jung that he shares in the guilt of the child's untimely death and that the murdered girl needs atonement. She thus intimates that he must sacrifice the idea that he is not involved in the murder and needs to take responsibility for all the impulses he murdered in himself and in the world. Sacrifice is rooted in the idea of "making sacred" and eating the liver symbolically brings a dimension of sacredness to Jung's relationship to mankind, both at inner and outer levels. Here, Soul teaches Jung that all humans share an individual responsibility for everything that happens in the collective, and each development of consciousness presupposes that we relinquish naiveté and separateness. This ritual, like the symbolic eating of the flesh of Christ in the mass, is a mystery that points to the ancient belief that we partake of the qualities of what we eat. By eating the child's liver, Jung himself became the murdered child. He symbolically absorbed and took into himself the qualities of the young feminine. Jung also described the liver as the seat of life, so we can infer that he is absorbing the very essence of life, oneness, in this ritual.[38] Atonement consists in realizing the brotherhood of all living things, and it opened Jung to the idea of the anima mundi, the world soul and the flowering of the anima principle.

Toward the end of the second part of The Red Book, Liber Secundus, Jung recognizes that all things are ultimately paradoxical:

> I loved the beauty of the beautiful, the spirit of those rich
> in spirit, the strength of the strong. I laughed at the
> stupidity of the stupid. I despised the weakness of the weak,

the meanness of the mean, and hated the badness of the bad. But now I must love the beauty of the ugly, the spirit of the foolish, and the strength of the weak. I must admire the stupidity of the clever, must respect the weakness of the strong and the meanness of the generous, and honor the goodness of the bad. Where does that leave mockery, contempt, and hatred?[39]

Salome, too, reappears at the end of *Liber Secundus* and prompts a further development of anima: No longer blind, she now offers him her love, but Jung replies that he is already married. In other words, he takes her offer of love literally and not as an inner quality that can enhance his psychic life. He cannot yet see that she is really offering him joy:

> Just as I had achieved pleasure in myself and power over myself, Salome had lost pleasure in herself but learned love for the other, and Elijah had lost the power of his wisdom but he had learned to recognize the spirit of the other. Salome thus lost the power of temptation and has become love. As I have won pleasure in myself, I also want love for myself. But that really would be too much and would bind me like an iron ring that would stifle me. I accepted Salome as pleasure, and reject her as love. But she wants to be with me. How, then, should I also have love for myself? Love, I believe belongs to others. But my love wants to be with me. I dread it.[40]

The scene further enables Jung to deepen his understanding of the feminine through his relationship to Salome. She is demanding an inner marriage. For that, he needs to open himself to the idea of self-love. Jung needs to be decapitated a third time, to sacrifice further his thinking function, so that freed from mental activity, he can dwell in the heart. The heart is the seat of true spirituality, a spirituality that knows that we are the only ones we can truly transform, that we are the ones who need help to develop the inner faculty of relatedness by relating to unhealed aspects of our psychology. This section ends with a further transformation of Salome, who asserts, "I haven't cried anymore, for good fortune and bad fortune are balanced in me."[41]

His deep concern for Salome transforms their relationship, and she no longer demands attention in a blind and needy way. Jung is then told that he is Salome and that her well-being depends on his growth: "You see, Salome is what you are. Fly, and she will grow wings."[42] This interdependency between Salome and Jung points to an inner marriage, between conscious and unconscious, potentially healing of the opposites in the psyche. The creative masculine and the sacred feminine can then work as partners on the journey to wholeness.

Jung's journey into greater embodiment and integration of feeling continues in *Scrutinies*, the final section of *The Red Book*, where he is initiated into ancient Egyptian mysteries. He is presented with the symbol Hap, the flesh spirit, the blood spirit. He encounters an Isislike goddess who appears with a red sun disk and whirring the song of her golden wings. She teaches him that "the enlightening thought comes from the body,"[43] and she asks him to drink blood. Reclaiming the repressed "son of the earth" goes hand in hand with the redemption of the dark feminine and the shadow of the instinctual realm. Thus, she teaches him the value of a joy that comes from fulfillment and not from longing.

Sophia

At the beginning of *The Red Book*, we are told that in the *Black Books*, Jung had commented thus on Soul: "... when the Above and the Below are not united, she falls into three parts—a serpent, the human soul, and the bird or heavenly soul, which visits the Gods."[44] In *Scrutinies*, Soul announces that she has "returned from above," thus appearing as *Sophia*, the celestial daughter and the wisdom side of the god archetype. In this ultimate stage of anima development, no human face can adequately contain the image of woman:

> When I looked up again, I saw my soul in the upper realms, hovering irradiated by the distant brilliance that streamed from the Godhead.[45]

Wisdom is the awareness that Soul encompasses the whole of life. This development of compassion and wisdom is not one that is often visible in today's world, as few can claim this level of consciousness. With *Sophia* constellated in the psyche, the anima's compassion has the differentiated attunement of wisdom. Wisdom is expressed in compassion. She connects us with immanence, which is the goal of individuation and the source of all love. Quality at that level can only be described through paradox and poetry.

> With the attainment of this goal it becomes possible to disengage the ego from all its entanglements with collectivity and the collective unconscious. Through this process the anima forfeits the daemonic power of an autonomous complex; she can no longer exercise the power of possession, since she is depotentiated. She is no longer the guardian of treasures unknown; no longer Kundry, daemonic Messenger of the Grail, half divine and half animal; no longer is the soul to be called 'Mistress,' but a psychological function of an intuitive nature, akin to what the primitives mean when they say, 'He has gone into the forest to talk with the spirits' or 'My snake spoke with me' or, in the mythological language of infancy, 'A little bird told me.'[46]

This is a return to simplicity, to the child whose curiosity and openness color all she encounters. The child archetype expresses the birth of a new awareness, or a new god who appears in *The Red Book* at the end of *Liber Primus* as Phanes.

With the return of Soul, Jung now sees soul in nature and the sparkling animating light that permeates all things, but he is troubled for he does not see this happening to the hearts of men and asks for her collaboration to change this. He urges her to work for the salvation of man: "I demand that you do this for the earthly fortunes of humankind."[47] The cooperation between soul and man, between conscious and unconscious, is one of the most solid tenets of Jung's psychology. To keep the balance and dialogue between inner and outer life is essential to his worldview.

The transformation of the anima is neither linear nor achieved once and for all; it is holographic and multidimensional. As shadow is deep and never conquered, man moves from one aspect of anima to another at different moments of life. Complexes will emerge and force one in and out of consciousness and offer opportunities for further development. The path of individuation developed in *The Red Book* describes one man's world, and the injunction is to take on the task of self-knowledge personally and deeply, thereby increasing compassion and wisdom in the world.

> I give you news of the way of *this* man, but not of your own way. My path is not your path, therefore I cannot teach you. The way is within us …Within us is the way, the truth, and the life … So live yourselves.[48]

Soul, in her *Sophia* aspect, finally emphasizes her connection to nature: "Touch the earth, press your hand into matter, shape it with care."[49] This implies taking responsibility for what we love. Unlike the paradigm described in *Genesis* 1, where man is given power over all living things, Soul asks him to embrace an ecological relationship to nature. Man's patriarchal attitude of power over the earth and the animals is as unsustainable and as pathological intrapsychically as it is for the world. Atonement is needed at all levels as all life forms share the same essential essence. The slaughterhouses that feed the world with battery chickens, pork, beef, and lamb bred in mechanistic warehouses devoid of all the basic necessities show the autistic relationship we have with nature. The same insensitivity is applied to alien economic or political refugees as well as to the more vulnerable parts of our own nature, bombarded with judgments and criticisms. Symptoms in the body echo the world's grief and difficulty with symbolic awareness.

In his conversation with Elijah, another character in *The Red Book*, Jung is told that he "cannot extricate himself from his law of his own nature"[50]. This idea is taken up again later when Jung states that "the development of the personality ... means fidelity to the law of one's being"[51]. It takes a very differentiated listening to attune to the spontaneous flow that runs through us. It may demand that we not follow social conventions of food, drink, or conversation. Individuation is the road away from collective pressures and demands an attuned ear to match the rhythms of our outer lives with that of own personal fate. The heroic and tyrannical ego capable of the destruction of life on a grand scale is incapable of perceiving the soul shining through all manifestations of life. As Philemon teaches:

> These dead have given names to all beings, the beings in the air, on the earth and in the water. They have weighted and counted things ... What did they do with the admirable tree? What happened to the sacred frog? Did they see his golden eye? ... Did they do penance for the sacred ore that they dug up from the belly of the earth? No, they named, weighed, numbered, and apportioned all things. They did whatever pleased them ... Yet the time has come when things speak.[52]

Sophia leads man to the *anima mundi*, the functioning and landscapes of world soul. In so far as we dwell in soul, and not that soul dwells in us, the *anima mundi* is the intelligence that resonates in all things, the vital force that contains us. We do not have a soul, we live in soul and are enlivened by her. The primary tensions of psychodynamics are now resolved. Thinking is no longer polarized and divisive; it becomes a practical tool, twinned with subtle intuitive certainties. The original unconscious ego locked in uroboric fusion with the Great Mother has reached a stage of conscious awareness of the unity of all things. Now consciousness dwells in soul, in wholeness. The I, the ego, is no longer experienced as separate but as an expression of interbeing. This new cosmic consciousness obliterates differences between soul and external things. Inner and outer worlds are both real, forming a continuum between the lightness of air and the density of matter, all expressions of Oneness. The world soul, *Sophia*, is a woman whose visible form becomes the universe, the prairies and the sky, the hollow of the neck and the curvature of the spine. Image, metaphor, and symbol emerge, bridging and uniting all aspects of experience. Feeling and wonder at the mystery embedded in all things nourish the imagination. Insight now finds best expression in paradox and poetry. Quantum mechanics are infused with it: What is matter? Is it light, is it wave? The imagination will take us to new wonderful descriptions of the world. Yet a deep ecology of soul maintains relationship to body, to nature, to inner images, forming and dissolving our understanding of reality. The wings of spirit travel through the dark earth and deepen the sacred connection to life, reenvisioning time and space and generating nonlocal, atemporal, awe-inspiring experiences.

And yet, before enlightenment, chop wood, work, sleep; after enlightenment, chop wood, work, sleep. ... Following the path of individuation is for the few and demands that the individual produce values that compensate for his absence from society. In Jungian psychology, nothing is truly developed until it is manifested in the world. Who we are and what we do become coherent and congruent. We no longer have soul, we dwell in her, then everything that we encounter through life takes on a new dignity, a new sacredness, and this shows itself in the presence we bring to life, to others, in the choices we make and the values we uphold. "The anima mundi is the innermost point and at the same time the encompasser of the world."[33]

The more conscious we are, the more ethical we become. This new sense of responsibility for all aspects of life is visible in increasing ecological awareness and the care we show in all our encounters. This is a difficult task as there is no guidebook to follow, each situation demanding an immediate feeling response, infused with experience and spontaneity. For this, we need to maintain a humble approach (the root of the word is *humus*, (which means "soil," "the earth") and know that for all that we know, just as much is unknown.

Endnotes

1 C.G. Jung, *The Red Book: A Reader's Edition* (New York, NY: W. W. Norton, 2012), 129.
2 C.G. Jung, *Aion. Researches into the Phenomenology of the Self*, in *CW*, vol. 9/II (Princeton, NJ: Princeton University Press, 1968), par. 33.
3 Jung, *The Red Book*, 133.
4 Ibid., 120.
5 Ibid., 151.
6 Ibid., 152.
7 Ibid., 21.
8 Vera van der Heydt, *The Psychology and Care of Souls* (London: Guild of Pastoral Psychology, 1954), 7.
9 Jung, *Aion*, *CW* 9/II, par. 24.
10 Hawaah means both snake and Eve in Hebrew.
11 C.G. Jung, "The Psychology of Transference" (1946), in *CW*, vol. 16 (Princeton, NJ: Princeton University Press, 1966), par. 361.
12 C.G. Jung, *Man and His Symbols* (New York, NY: Dell, 1964), 195.
13 C.G. Jung, "Archetypes of the Collective Unconscious" (1954), in *CW*, vol. 9/I (Princeton, NJ: Princeton University Press, 1968), par. 61.
14 Jung, "The Psychology of Transference," in *CW* 16, par. 361.
15 C.G. Jung, "The Psychological Aspects of the Kore" (1951), in *CW*, vol. 9/I (Princeton, NJ: Princeton University Press, 1968), par. 356.
16 Emma Jung, *Anima and Animus* (Dallas, TX: Spring Publications, 1985), 67.
17 Ibid., 180.
18 C.G. Jung, "Concerning the Archetypes with Special Reference to the Anima Concept" (1954), in *CW*, vol. 9/I (Princeton, NJ: Princeton University Press, 1968), par. 146.
19 Jung, *The Red Book*, 144.
20 Ibid., 148.
21 Ibid., 149.
22 Ibid., 155.
23 Ibid., 173.
24 Jung, "Concerning the Archetypes with Special Reference to the Anima Concept," in *CW* 9/I, par. 144.

25 Jung, *The Red Book*, 251.
26 C.G. Jung, "The Tavistock Lectures" (1935), in *CW*, vol. 18 (Princeton, NJ: Princeton University Press, 1976), par. 187.
27 Jung, *The Red Book,* 192.
28 Ibid., 183.
29 Ibid., 198.
30 Ibid., 200.
31 Ibid., 201.
32 Ibid., 197-98.
33 Ibid., 197 n211.
34 James Hillman, *Anima* (Dallas: Spring Publications, 1985), 133.
35 Jung, *The Red Book,* 192, (note 201: Draft).
36 C.G. Jung, "A Study in the Process of Individuation" (1950), in *CW*, vol. 9/I (Princeton, NJ: Princeton University Press, 1968), par. 577.
37 Jung, *The Red Book*, 199.
38 C.G. Jung, *Memories, Dreams, Reflections* (New York, NY: Vintage Books, 1963), 198.
39 Jung, *The Red Book*, 454.
40 Ibid., 439-40.
41 Ibid., 445.
42 Ibid., 446.
43 Ibid., 485.
44 Ibid., 46.
45 Ibid., 494.
46 C.G. Jung, "The Relations between the Ego and the Unconscious" (1938), in *CW*, vol. 7 (Princeton, NJ: Princeton University Press, 1966), par. 374.
47 Jung, *The Red Book*, 504.
48 Ibid., 125.
49 Ibid., 505.
50 Ibid., 185.
51 C.G. Jung, "The Development of Personality" (1934), in *CW*, vol. 17 (Princeton, NJ: Princeton University Press, 1964), par. 295.
52 Ibid., 526.
53 Jung, "A Study in the Process of Individuation," *CW* 9/I, par. 554.

Encounters with the Animal Soul:
A Voice of Hope for Our Precarious World

Nancy Swift Furlotti

Introduction

In the year 2000 I had a dream:

I am at the base of the large Buddhist temple in Indonesia
called Borobudur with Jung. With a holy and respectful
attitude, we slowly begin our ritual circumambulation of
the temple moving silently from level to level on this large
square and round vertical mandala that depicts the many
lives of Buddha and Buddhist cosmology, from the world
of desires to the world of forms to the formless world.
Our pilgrimage begins in a counterclockwise movement
around the temple spiraling up the nine levels until we
reach the top. There we have a magnificent view over-
looking the land. Off in the distance I see Prambanan,
which is the Hindu holy area filled with tall and beautifully
intricate temples dedicated to the Trimurti, consisting of
Brahma, God as the Creator; Vishnu, the Preserver, and
Shiva, the Destroyer. Jung and I lay down small prayer rugs
and kneel on them to pray, facing in the direction of the
Middle East. All the religions of the world are contained
within this large mandala. We are on a holy Buddhist
temple with a large number of Hindu temples in view. Jung
and I are representatives of the Judeo-Christian religions,
and the prayer rugs represent Islam. I realize we are
praying for the recognition and unification of all of them
into a new religion.

At the time of this dream, life seemed to have a perceivable order, but
all that changed a year later with the 9/11 attack on the World Trade

Center. We are now living in a new era. Not only have we lost our innocence, but the word "terror" itself now evokes anxiety to the core of our beings. Adding to this, the world is in a mad forward rush of technological change that leaves us fearful and unsettled, uprooted and alone. Violence seems on the rise, yet simultaneously it is reported that we actually live in a safer world now than ever before in history.[1] However, our perceptions and our subjective experiences say otherwise, and it is the subjective forces reflecting our inner state of being, manifesting our greatest fears, that to a great extent create our reality. If our moral and ethical stability is off balance, then the world is, too. Through our clouded lens, it seems our fast-paced world has tilted off its central axis and is listing toward destruction. The Science and Security Board, a group of concerned atomic scientists, shares this belief. It has recently reset the Doomsday Clock forward to two and a half minutes to midnight.[2] The old threat of nuclear war remains a feared ghost in the shadows, and to that we can add the increasingly dangerous effects of global climate change. Some might explain their fear by pointing to President Trump's erratic behavior, Putin's aggression, or Kim Jong-un's nuclear missile tests, but its source lies deeper in the unconscious layers of our psyches. In response to this fear, authoritarian and potentially dangerous leaders have been called up by our collective will as the ground beneath us no longer holds. As C.G. Jung reminds us: "The psychology of the individual is reflected in the psychology of the nation. What the nation does is done also by each individual, and so long as the individual continues to do it, the nation will do likewise. Only the change in the attitude of the individual can initiate a change in the psychology of the nation. ... If ever there was a time when self-reflection was the absolutely necessary and only right thing, it is now."[3] Fear of change drives us into a regression and "reactivates in the unconscious a more or less primitive analogue of the conscious situation."[4] Hence, we are drawn to authoritarian leaders under the illusion that a supposed hero or strongman can make life safer by stopping change.

The sense of stability in the United States prior to 9/11 that was suddenly shattered was not so dissimilar to 1913, when war was precipitously unleashed because of misunderstandings and missteps.

Its aftermath led to World War II. Through this painful and destructive history, the Western myth of progress has been shaved down to a thin membrane, and now after 9/11 it is no longer capable of holding us. My dream as cited above points to the need for a new myth that speaks not only to the Western world but embraces the entire global world. All the differing religious and cultural viewpoints need to be brought into respectful dialogue. The difficulty is that religious ideologies tend to separate people into groups and support the process of shadow projection onto "the other"—a defensive attitude that maintains misunderstandings and furthers aggression. It is quite lamentable that with our present levels of philosophical and psychological understandings, with science and reason making us masters of our world, our more or less unconscious animal instincts still control the levers of our actions. We have not fully integrated something big, and that is the reality of the psyche. It is the creative source of renewal capable of guiding us through this brave new world or leading us to destruction.

Edward Edinger focused with great concern on Jung's admonition about the dying Western myth and the need and possibility for a new one. He speaks of what it might be:

> A notable feature of the new myth is its capacity to unify the various current religions of the world. By seeing all functioning religions as living expressions of individuation symbolism, i.e., the process of creating consciousness, an authentic basis is laid for a true ecumenical attitude. The new myth will not be one more religious myth in competition with all the others for man's allegiance; rather, it will elucidate and verify every functioning religion by giving more conscious and comprehensive expression to its essential meaning. The new myth can be understood and lived within one of the great religions communities such as Catholic Christianity, Protestant Christianity, Judaism, Buddhism, etc. or in some new community yet to be created, or by individuals without specific community connections. The universal application gives it a genuine claim to the term 'catholic.'[5]

I believe we are in the midst of a struggle to achieve this potential consciousness and unity among humankind. Yet, we might not make it. John Dourley expresses the problem and his concern as follows:

> ... specific religions continue to threaten common survival. With the intimate dialectic that Jung's psychology establishes between the divine and the human, should any concretion of a divinely based and so archetypal absolute in conflict with others bring an untimely end to the historical process, both humanity and divinity would lose. Bringing up Father, redeeming and humanizing God in history, is fraught with peril. At least Jung has made us more aware of the potentially deadly, yet also immensely rewarding game we are collectively and individually playing. The redemption of God in history as the religiosity of a new millennium carries with it a new moral imperative. 'Everything now depends on man...' The integration in human consciousness of the living and potentially overwhelming antinomy humanity calls divinity is the basis of humanity's 'new responsibility.'[6]

The primary image in my dream is a mandala, a symbol of the self, representing the archetype of meaning and wholeness. It contains within it the unifying and healing potential. It seems in the dream my psyche was expressing the collective need for a new world order and was offering a symbol as the foundation for a new myth. First, though, since Jung and I in the dream circumambulate the temple "counterclockwise," it seems the old collective order of world religions has to descend into the unconscious to be dismantled before a renewal of individual and collective attitudes can take place.

One hundred years after what Jung foresaw in 1913 we, in the first quarter of the 21st century, are in the midst of a radical change similar to when Jung's psyche became activated and produced visions of a devastated world. His view of a vulnerable world in need of consciousness continued to his death. In 1913, he was perilously dragged down into the unconscious to reencounter his soul and through the arduous process of transformation to discover the way to a new symbol of wholeness. His journey in *The Red Book* speaks of his personal inner journey, but it also offers a collective template for renewal as well—helpful for us today to find our way through these perilous times.

Voices of the Soul: Jung's Template for Transformation

It is 1913, a troubling year. Jung had vision after vision of world catastrophe. Although at first he thought it was his own personal catastrophe at the possible onset of schizophrenia, it wasn't. It was his call to introversion and a precognition of World War I. Everything changed overnight and was turned upside down, and Jung was called back to find his soul, impelled by the "spirit of the depths."[7] Who is this soul? What murmurings arise from the depths to call Jung's attention to her? He had neglected her and objectified her in pursuit of science. He had lived a full and rich life but had missed the essence, and that was *her*.[8] She was familiar to him, having provided the safe enclave he inhabited as a child away from the conflicted instability of his parents. She was real, "a living and self-existing being. ... He whose desire turns away from outer things, reaches the place of the soul. If he does not find the soul, the horror of emptiness will overcome him."[9] In another work, Jung writes:

> To do this, one had to hang up exact science and put away the scholar's gown, to say farewell to his study and wander with human heart through the world, through the horror of prisons, mad houses and hospitals, through drab suburban pubs, in brothels and gambling dens, through the salons of elegant society, the stock exchanges, the socialist meetings, the churches, the revivals and ecstasies of the sects, to experience love, hate and passion in every form in one's body.[10]

After years of establishing himself as a prominent doctor and researcher, Jung found himself split off from a vital part of himself—

his feminine side. He had no choice but to embark on a personal exploration of the very real world of feelings and sensations, quite the opposite from his typical thinking, intuitive standpoint. For him the drama in images, with figures including animals and their voices, emerged as they would in a waking dream. *The Red Book* only contains eight dreams, and the rest of the narratives are visions. His first three dreams are quite similar, and while he may have later regarded them as precognitive, they certainly also carried personal subjective meaning for him. They gave a glimpse of not only what would befall Europe in World War I, but also his arduous descent into the unconscious, emerging with the healing elixir he sought only after experiencing his shadow in the frozen corners of himself. The dream he had in July 1914 set the stage for his experience of being summoned by the "spirit of the depths" to re-engage with his soul:

> I was in a remote English land. It was necessary that I return to my homeland with a fast ship as speedily as possible. I reached home quickly. In my homeland I found that in the middle of summer a terrible cold had fallen from space, which had turned every living thing into ice. There stood a leaf-bearing but fruitless tree, whose leaves had turned into sweet grapes full of healing juice through the working of the frost. I picked some grapes and gave them to a great waiting throng.[11]

In Jung's Draft of his *Red Book*, he states that in the dream he was with a friend who had a lack of foresight and who stupidly wanted to return home on a smaller and slower boat, unlike Jung's dream ego. The two did finally travel together.[12] This reflects two opposing parts of Jung's personality, his ego and shadow. Before and during the period of the *Red Book*, Jung struggled to make sense of typological differences among people and their resulting attitudes toward life. This first became evident to him in his interactions with Freud and Adler, and he saw that their personalities were reflected in the theories they created. Jung first began by differentiating the attitudes, extraversion and introversion, and then he refined his thinking to include the four functions: thinking, feeling, sensation, and intuition.

The structure he created to understand typological differences also revealed a general framework for the natural course of an individual's development toward increased consciousness and wholeness. In other words, it set up guideposts to help us know where we are along the path of individuation. As a thinking-intuitive type, Jung found his opposites in feeling-sensation. These functions would imbue the *flavor* of his underworldly task, the much-needed compensation for his personality and for his stance in the world. It was his soul who would spoon-feed him the sometimes distasteful medicine that would bring him to wholeness.

A voice spoke to Jung, whom he later recognized as his inner guide Philemon: "You open the gates of soul to let the dark flood of chaos flow into your order and meaning. If you marry the ordered to the chaos you produce the divine child, the supreme meaning beyond meaning and meaninglessness." Apprehensively Jung responded to this by saying: "I spoke to a loving soul and as I drew nearer to her, I was overcome by horror, and I heaped up a wall of doubt, and did not anticipate that I thus wanted to protect myself from my fearful soul... I had to recognize that I must submit to what I fear; yes, and even more, that I must even love what horrifies me."[13]

What a confusing concept: to love what horrifies and to submit to what is fearful. Such a task takes one beyond the bounds of one's perceived reality and safety zone, pushing at the limits of one's capacity to remain coherent and cohesive. This is consciously crossing the threshold into the irrational, twisting oneself into another form entirely, and yet, surprisingly finding what is hidden away in the depths of our own being, in the far reaches of the corners and closets of ancient inner rooms. The dark passageways filled with dust and ghosts is where soul resides. Jung realizes that

> If I am not conjoined through the uniting of the Below and the Above, I break down into three parts: the *serpent*, and in that or some other animal form I roam, living nature daimonically, arousing fear and longing. The *human soul*, living forever within you. The *celestial soul*, as such dwelling with the Gods, far from you and unknown to you,

appearing in the form of a bird. Each of these three parts then is independent.[14]

The one who whispers to us is the one we need to learn from in order to compensate for who we think we are. This brings us forward to our wholeness, uniting the three parts of our soul into one. With that we are able to live our own unique life, not afraid of ourselves and those dark and previously rejected parts of ourselves. We are not living a collective life or an imitated life, but our very own life. It may sound easy. No way! There is a big difference between thinking about embarking on one's inner journey and actually submitting to the reality of the psyche. It is a torture bed of abomination. Why would soul insist on this? It insists because that sweet, angelic, diaphanous entity that in our mind's eye may seem like the soul; that we think leads us to our salvation, delivers us from the evil and the sins of the world; that whispers softly, lovingly, creatively is *not* what soul is. "You'll never find a more disloyal, more cunning and heinous woman than your soul."[15] She seduces, tricks, beguiles, causes suffering, and demands his development. And she is essential for life: "A man who goes astray becomes an animal, a lost soul becomes a devil. Cling to the soul with love, fear, contempt, and hate, and don't let her out of your sight."[16]

Jung was led into the barren, dusty desert of his own soul and was told by the "spirit of the depths" that led him to her that if he turned to her, his creative force would become green like a fruit-bearing tree and take on the force of life. This adventure was the first of many he had to undertake at her behest. It was her intention to have him confront all those aspects of himself he ignored and despised, the ones that generally get projected onto others. Through projection, one does not live one's life but burdens others to carry what one would rather not. The journey always begins with the shadow, as Jung later explained after he translated his personal experience into a theory of the nature of the psyche and the individuation process.

Soul as that shadowy being begins her conversation with him in the barren place and is hard on him, telling him he must let go of all intention and preconception. Jung struggles with his scorn, vanity, and cleverness. Finally, after 25 days in the desert, his soul appears for the first time in free-standing form. This indicates that before this she was merely an inner voice. Now she is becoming more real to him. In the desert, he descends into *Hell in the Future*,[17] where he realizes he has no control over his thinking and judgment, and although it serves him in life, in this realm it becomes poison and death. He sees in the red light of a crystal the future of what is to come—murder. "The blond hero lay slain. The black beetle is the death that is necessary for renewal."[18] He sees what he will have to do—kill the extraverted hero in himself, which he does when he slays Siegfried. He discovers himself to be the sacrificer and the sacrifice at the same time. The black beetle is the symbol of renewal, like the dung beetle from Egyptian mythology that pushes the sun into the underworld to travel to its renewal as the sun emerges for a new day. Soul left Jung to his own hell, his own inner civil war. By killing his hero, he was beginning to dispose of his superior function, thinking, allowing the forces of the unconscious to be released. "When this happens, the feeling of relief is engendered. The crime is expiated because, as soon as the main function is deposed, there is a chance for other sides of the personality to be born into life."[19] But this was still to be accomplished.

Serpents and dragons in the depths rise up in Hell as "the threat to one's inmost self... points to the danger of the newly acquired consciousness being swallowed up again by the instinctive soul, the unconscious."[20] Here Jung approaches his serpent soul that accompanies the arrival of Elijah and Salome, a black snake that lies at Elijah's feet. It represents the "earthly essence of man of which he is not conscious,"[21] "not only a separating but unifying principle"[22]... "introverting libido. ... Inasmuch as the serpent leads into the shadows, it has the function of the anima; it leads you into the depths, it connects the Above and Below... the serpent is also the symbol of wisdom."[23]

This representation of soul is a mediating symbol sitting between the opposites with the potential of uniting them. It represents Jung's auxiliary function between his thinking and inferior feeling. "The thinker feels the disgust of feeling, since the feeling in him is mainly disgusting. ... So the serpent lies between the thinker [Elijah] and the one who feels [Salome]. They are each other's poison and healing."[24] It is a chthonic animal of the earth, of the Great Mother, out of which everything germinates and emerges. Like the Great Mother, it is twofold, masculine and feminine, capable of destruction and enmity as well as fecundity and growth. The serpent soul offers up desire, which begins the movement of change and development. Pleasure as an aspect of love was no temptation for Jung, who disparaged his feeling and emotion. "But man is domineering in his thinking, and therefore he kills the pleasure of the forest and that of the wild animals. Man is violent in his desire, and he himself becomes a forest and a forest animal."[25]

As he continues to struggle between these opposites within himself, he encounters two serpents—on the right side a black one representing the dark, night side, and on the left side a white one representing the white, bright day side. As the snakes wrestle, the upper part of the black one becomes white, showing that the opposites are beginning to intermingle in Jung. With the black snake on the right and the white one on the left—a reversal from what one would expect with left being the side of the unconscious and the right representing consciousness—we see how everything is turned upside down, the known is unknown, the expected is the unexpected. In the psyche, preconceived notions are broken down, our rules and order are challenged, black is white, and white is black. Through this disorientation a new order can be conceived. The serpent as the Mercurial trickster serves as the perfect guide, frequently acting as a *psychopomp*.[26]

In 1948, Jung described the soulful aspect of *Mercurius*: "As a life-giving power like a glue, holding the world together and standing in the middle between body and spirit ... The spirit of Truth, which is hidden from the world ... *anima mundi* ... the Holy Spirit, who was present at the Creation and played the role of procreator, impregnating the waters with the seed of life ..."[27] *Mercurius* consists of a duality of opposites as well as the unity of all. It is a hermaphroditic figure, revealer of divine secrets, messenger of the gods:

> 'He ascends from earth to heaven and descends again to earth, and receives the power of Above and Below. His power is complete when he has returned to earth.' So it is not a question of a one way ascent to heaven, but, in

contrast to the route followed by the Christian Redeemer, who comes from above to below and from there returns to the above, the *filius macrocosmi* starts from below, ascends on high, and, with the powers of Above and Below united in himself, returns to earth again. He carries out the reverse movement and thereby manifests a nature contrary to that of Christ and the Gnostic Redeemers ...[28]

The important essence of Jung's statement is that the *filius macrocosmi*[29] unites the opposites, above and below, and returns to reside on earth. This brings the locus of the deity into the human realm.

In the mandala drawing, *Systema Munditotius*, which Jung drew in conjunction with the *Septem Sermones* (*The Seven Sermons to the Dead*) that he wrote during this same period, he drew a set of circles that alternate between inside and outside, up and down, reflecting the process of descent and ascent, ascent and descent. It is the Mercurial serpent as soul, not masculine or feminine but consisting of the one and the many, both the raw material and the goal of its own transformation, the divinity itself that accompanies Jung on his journey. It is the daemon that is not a part of God but precedes God and was present in the beginning as the animating force of the creative process that brings divinity to life. The snake form we see here embodies the necessary energy needed to compensate Jung's rational, heroic, worldly stance and plumb the depths of his reservoir of shadow. It leads and animates the process of consciousness and transformation. The dove form of soul introduces him to the heavenly, wise aspect of God—*Sophia*—that appears at crucial moments. Yet, it seems the appearance of *Mercurius* as Jung's snake soul compensates for the image of Christ as logos, or reason. Being thoroughly pagan, it resides outside the split of good and evil, possessing "a natural undividedness which is impervious to logical and moral contradictions,"[30] therefore containing both energies as a dark nature deity. It is by no means the devil, but instead is the bringer of light from nature veiled in matter, the *lumen naturae*.

At the end of *Liber Primus,* Jung has an important vision of the opposites he has been struggling with and shows how the conflict is resolved. This is a beautiful example of a very real experience that he later describes as the work of the transcendent function:

> A wreath of fire shines around the stone. I am seized with fear at what I see: The coarse peasant's boot? The foot of a giant that crushes an entire city? I see the cross, the removal of the cross, the mourning. How agonizing this sight is! No longer do I yearn—I see the divine child, with the white serpent in his right hand and the black serpent in his left hand. I see the green mountain, the cross of Christ on it, and a stream of blood flowing from the summit of the mountain—I can look no longer, it is unbearable—I see the cross and Christ on it in his last hour and torment—at the foot of the cross the black serpent coils itself—it has wound itself around my feet—I am held fast and I spread my arms wide. Salome draws near. The serpent has wound itself around my whole body, and my countenance is that of a lion.[31]

Jung has been forced to endure the torment and crucifixion of Christ, as Christ.[32] The giant's undifferentiated energy of the primordial depths destroys the city, or we could say, Jung's conscious, collective viewpoint. The cross represents hanging between the opposites of forethought and love, logos and eros. Pulled apart in opposite directions, Jung suffers mightily while out of this horrendous depression and struggle emerges the new life, the divine child, holding the black and white snakes in the correct hands now, representing the resolution to the conflict, the conflict that is Jung himself. Finally, the snake coils itself around him in a deification initiation, to hold him in a protected *temenos*, a sacred precinct, where he is held together and does not fall into pieces, and is able to meet the unconscious. Here, Jung *is* the vessel in which the opposites reconcile and the new god will be born, his new symbol of divinity. His face is that of a lion, with snake and lion as opposites depicted in the pre-Christian god, Mithras. In this mystery, Jung becomes the two principles, love and forethinking, and two energies, serpent and lion. Through his self-sacrifice as Christ, he transformed eros from pleasure into love:

Mark that it is my bad pleasure which leads me to self-sacrifice. Its innermost is love, which will be freed from pleasure through sacrifice. Here the wonder happened that my previously blind pleasure, [represented by Salome] became sighted. My pleasure was blind, and it was love. Since my strongest willing willed self-sacrifice, my pleasure changed, it went into a higher principle, which in God is one with forethinking. ... Love wants what is furthest, the best and the fulfilling. ... And I saw something further, namely that the forethinking in me had the form of an old prophet. ... pre-Christian, [Elijah]... and transformed itself into a form that no longer appeared in a human form, but in the absolute form of a pure white light. ... This just happened in me. I just saw it.[33]

Jung had a transcendent experience, which he later came to understand to be a result of the Transcendent Function, the new bridging symbol between opposites. He experienced himself as the vessel for this transformation. This is a very important discovery, which he later discusses in *Answer to Job*, pointing to locating the God within as humans' role in the incarnation and transformation of the God-image. With his soul/anima in human form and able to see, she has moved from the unconscious into the human realm of consciousness. Acting as a guide to the many other encounters with parts of himself he has to experience, she becomes once again the chthonic snake who knows her way through the unconscious. Then, when he becomes overly humble and mocked, the soul comes in the form of a white bird to bring compensation from above for his lowly attitude. From white bird to snake, the up and down is the energetic movement of inflation and depression that is a continuous cycle in the journey to self. "He who does not want evil will have no chance to save his soul from Hell. So long as he remains in the light of the upper world, he will become a shadow of himself. But his soul will languish in the dungeons of the daimons."[34] Jung's task is to accept the reality of these different energies within himself that manifest as *real figures*.[35]

Soul gives Jung three things: the misery of war, the darkness of magic, and the gift of religion. Soul, as snake, and Jung quarrel as they walk a tenuous middle road between opposites, accepting and not accepting each other's viewpoints. It becomes clear to Jung that the human stands in between the snake and the bird. "If you want to become, [and not only to be] then a battle between bird and serpent breaks out."[36] Recognizing that she, the snake soul, has wisdom, Jung asks her many questions trying to elicit understanding for himself. What he learns, which is of great importance, is that when the opposites come together, everything stops, becoming motionless and rests at a standstill. The counterforce of Satan or darkness is required to keep the libido or creative energy moving. This points to the continuous process of becoming; it is ongoing and never-ending. The place of stillness is where one experiences the reality of the self, a state of transcendence and unification. These moments are fleeting before we fall back into our humanity once again where the opposites push each other apart. Individuation strives to bring more of what is unconscious into our conscious awareness. "Through drawing the darkness from my beyond over into the day, I emptied my beyond. Therefore the demands of the dead disappeared, as they were satisfied. … I am no longer threatened by the dead, since I accepted their demands through accepting the serpent."[37] The dead represent the complexes and unlived life left behind by past generations that become ours to carry and make conscious. It became Jung's task now to live his life rather than succumb to the pressures from the past or the collective.

Once again true to the cycle, the snake, after giving Jung hardness, wisdom, and magical power from below, is pulled upward into the form of a white bird, the spiritual soul, to find something important in Heaven for Jung, something he needs—a discarded, golden crown with the incised words, *Love never ends*.[38] The movement from below to above is balanced by the need again for Jung to hang on the tree of life for three days and three nights until he understands—hanging between Heaven and Hell, much like his hanging on the cross in *Liber Primus*. This time he hangs between the opposites of life and love; love wants to hold on like the mother who cares for the child, while life wants more. "The beginning of all things is love, but the being of things is life."[39]

Meanwhile Philemon impregnates Jung's soul, and she in turn gives birth to a monster, the son of frogs, the antichrist. Jung is furious seeing this despised, ugly creature and can hardly believe that *his* soul gave birth to this monster. Finally, as he calms down, he realizes his task is to love all that is ugly, foolish and weak, contemptuous and hated within himself. The crown he wears unites what is separated. Abraxas, his new God, is lord of the physical world, a Gnostic god that represents the union of Christ and Satan. He is the antithesis of the golden bird, the shining god, Phanes, born out of Izdubar's egg, the bliss beyond suffering and joy. Lamed and humiliated as Jung is now by the deeply felt realization that this too is his creation, the divine born from his soul, he reluctantly approaches his rejected god. Yet his God cannot stay; he grows wings and ascends, leaving Jung alone with himself as animal, human, and Divinity.

Conclusion

Jung discovered an antidote to loss of soul, not an easy remedy but one that results in the transformation of the personality, the coming home to the soul of one's being. Here one experiences solid ground rather than the illusionary quicksand that is the *terra* on which our fragmented and fearful post-post-postmodern culture rests. He experienced his own multiplicity within and shaped it into a unity, which he called the self. This process of healing is individual yet affects the greater collective whole, as well. With each person's increased consciousness, the larger culture changes, reflecting the alchemical dictum that "the microcosm is identical with the macrocosm."[40]

In Jung's early vision as cited at the beginning of this paper, out of the frozen land he is given the gift of a "leaf-bearing tree, but without fruit (my tree of life, I thought), whose leaves had been transformed by the effects of the frost into sweet grapes full of healing juices. I plucked the grapes and gave them to a large, waiting crowd."[41] His life task, his myth, was presented to him through this vision. It pointed to not only him personally but also to his relationship to the collective.

Grapes signify both fertility and sacrifice and are related to the Greek god Dionysus, who facilitates the re-membering of one's inner nature, one's soul. Dionysus was a dismembered, sacrificed God. To unleash the inner creative forces of our life, sacrifice is always required of us.

From the frozen land where nothing grows and all is stagnant, the *Tree of Life* emerges in his early dream and later vision where he is transformed. Out of depression emerges new life. Jung's vision was a foreshadowing of what was to become of Europe, but it also pointed to his own need to break through the frozen soulless aspects of himself and descend into the center of his being, to understand and assimilate his own shadow contents in the unconscious. While he was a pioneer in exploring his inner "cosmos," his example is a gift of sweet grapes for the larger "cosmos." Through his journey inward, Jung realized that his process mirrored the template for what he later called *individuation*, or the natural course of human development. He reminds us: "If you look into yourselves, you will see ... the world of the inner is as infinite as the world of the outer."[42] He challenges each one of us to embark on our own unique journey to find ourselves.

My dream of the Buddhist mandala located in the real world and the wish for the unification of the essence of all religions into our hearts and souls reflect the continuing need for each one of us to take up the arduous but vital task of bringing to birth the new symbols that may unify us rather than destroy us, along with our earth and its other inhabitants, the animals and plants. We are running out of time as our world increasingly suffers from climate changes, overpopulation, and the unleashing of a torrent of intolerance, fear, and aggression, a reflection of our increasing inner chaos. Jung's *Red Book* was written years ago, yet published at the dawn of postmodern chaos. This was no accident. He left his map of the unconscious for us to use to navigate the inner world of psyche, which is where the outer world is fundamentally conceived. This vital fact is forgotten in our one-sided logos- and science-based culture, as well as in its opposite—feeling-sensation-based fundamentalism. No doubt the snakes and birds will lead the stream of demons across our paths until we re-member, put our technological devises aside and descend into our own heaven and hell to find our own new myth of wholeness in-between.

Endnotes

1   "Whereas in ancient agricultural societies human violence caused about 15 percent of all deaths, during the twentieth century violence caused only 5 percent of deaths, and in the early twenty-first century it is responsible for about 1 percent of global mortality." Yuval Noah Harari, *Homo Deus: A Brief History of Tomorrow*, (New York, NY: Harper Collins Publishers, 2017), 14.

2   *Science and Security Board*, The Bulletin of the Atomic Scientists, 2017 Doomsday Clock Statement. The *Science and Security Board* decided in 2017 to move the clock forward to two and a half minutes to midnight to represent the Board's current appraisal of the earth's health and safety. Factors that impacted the decision were the threat of nuclear weapons, climate change, future technological innovations in biology, artificial intelligence, and the cyber realm that may also pose global challenges.

3   C.G. Jung, "On the Psychology of the Unconscious" (1917), in *CW*, vol. 7 (Princeton, NJ: Princeton University Press, 1966), 4.

4   C.G. Jung, *Psychological Types* (1923), in *CW*, vol. 6 (Princeton, NJ: Princeton University Press, 1971), par. 314.

5   Edward Edinger, *The Creation of Consciousness: Jung's Myth for Modern Man* (Toronto: Inner City Books, 1984), 32.

6   John Dourley, "Recalling the Gods: A Millennial Process," in *Psychology and Religion at the Millennium and Beyond* (Tempe, Arizona: New Falcon Publications, 1998), 34.

7   C.G. Jung, *The Red Book: A Reader's Edition* (New York, NY: W. W. Norton, 2012), 120.

8   *Her* refers to Jung's soul/anima.

9   Jung, *The Red Book*, 129.

10 C.G. Jung, "New Paths in Psychology" (1912), in *CW*, vol. 7 (Princeton, NJ: Princeton University Press, 1966), par. 409.

11 Jung, *The Red Book*, 124.

12 Ibid., 124 n17, 18, 19.

13 Ibid., 139.

14 Ibid., 577.

15 Ibid., 496.

16 Ibid.

17 Ibid., fol. iii(v), 146.

18 Ibid., 151.

19 Ibid., 161 n115.

20 Ibid., 169 n140.

21 Ibid., 180.

22 Ibid., 180 n172.

23 Ibid., 180 n173.

24 Ibid., 183.

25 Ibid., 192.

26 *Psychopomp* is a guide to the underworld.

27 C.G. Jung, "The Spirit Mercurius" (1943), in *CW*, vol. 13 (Princeton, NJ: Princeton University Press, 1967), par. 263.

28 Ibid., par. 280.

29 C.G. Jung, *Memories, Dreams, Reflections*, ed. Aniela Jaffé (New York, NY: Vintage Books, 1963), 211. Jung explains that the *filius macrocosmi* is another expression of the life-spirit, the *anima mundi*, the Anthropos that animates the whole cosmos.

30 Jung, "The Spirit Mercurius," *CW* 13, par. 295.

31 Jung, *The Red Book*, 196-197.

32 Jung refers to the Christ archetype, not the human. The Christ archetype encompasses suffering, redemption and transformation as well as being a symbol of the self, the archetype of orientation, meaning, and wholeness.

33 Jung, *The Red Book*, 206-207 n240.

34 Ibid., 318.

35 Ibid. Elijah tells Jung, "We are real and not symbol" (176). Jung later states regarding Izdubar: "He did not pass away, but became a living fantasy whose workings I could feel on my own body" (295). The figures in the unconscious are not merely inner fantasies but are real because they affect the real world. In *MDR*, Jung states: "The contents of the psychic experience are real, and real not only as my own personal experience, but as collective experiences which others also have" (194).

36 Jung, *The Red Book*, 417.

37 Ibid., 433.

38 Ibid., 441 n331.

39 Ibid., 448.

40 C.G. Jung, "The Philosophical Tree" (1954), in *CW*, vol. 13 (Princeton, NJ: Princeton University Press, 1967), par. 372.

41 Jung, *Memories, Dreams, Reflections*, 176.

42 Jung, *The Red Book*, 229.

The Red Book for Dionysus:
A Literary and Transdisciplinary Interpretation

Susan Rowland

Although not produced under artistic auspices, the distinctive qualities of Jung's *The Red Book*, invite a literary as well as multi-disciplinary approach. And yet the work is peculiarly dismembered if considered through the conventional criteria for literature, psychology, art, or science. Not published by its writer and painter, *The Red Book* is unauthorized, unfinished, and unclaimed by canons of literary genres or psychology's more rational aims. My chapter will suggest that *The Red Book* is Dionysian. It enacts the god in its raw tearing apart of disciplinary norms and artistic conventions.

The Red Book is fated to be re-membered by its home in the terrifyingly dismembering 21st century in which multinational, political, and institutional norms are being torn up. On the other hand, Dionysus, god of comic *and* tragic drama, also provides a pathway to a remembering of knowing and being that promises a renewed consciousness in touch with instinctual life, or *zoe*. Using James Hillman's analysis of Dionysus in Jung, I argue that *The Red Book* heralds a re-membered transdisciplinary future. Jung anticipates the 21st-century paradigm that reconciles a postquantum vision of reality with its social potential for a world of coevolving democratizing and personal fulfillment.

The Problem of Literature and *The Red Book*

The Red Book, with astonishing paintings and handwritten text, looks like a work of literature of an earlier era, that of medieval illustrated manuscripts. In so doing, as Mathew Spano and John Beebe superbly demonstrate, it corresponds to artistic innovation at the time of its composition. The literary modernism of the period 1910 to 1940 fragmented traditional forms and genres, showed a predilection for myth, challenged established norms of rationality, and made a point of returning to the past in order to reconfigure art for the new industrial and alienated *modern* age. In this sense, *The Red Book* is a lost work of literary modernism belonging to the artistic heritage of the early 20th century.

And yet, its author, C.G. Jung, was famously dissatisfied with its ultimate form. He neither finished nor published the work, writing in the posthumously published *Memories, Dreams Reflections*:

> In the Red Book I tried an aesthetic elaboration of my fantasies, but never finished it. I became aware that I had not yet found the right language, that I still had to translate it into something else...[1]

"Aesthetic elaboration" does not work for Jung, the psychologist, and so *The Collected Works* are the result of this decision to change the style of his writing. I have written elsewhere of the important epistemological consequences of the literariness of *The Collected Works* and here want to continue exploring the uncanny liminality of literature and Jungian psychology.[2] After all, a psychology dedicated to a psyche defined by possessing inherently creative archetypes, has something to say to our contemporary sense that literature is imaginative, largely fictional writing.

On the other hand, *The Red Book* is itself a clue that defining literature this way is a localized, historical accident. For the medieval period, indeed from the start of written culture, "literature" was valued writing and its major genre, poetry, the vehicle for history, philosophy, stories, legends, and the premodern science of alchemy. Not until the Romanticism of the 18th century cemented the split from the rationality of the Enlightenment by deliberately exploring fantasy, ecstatic poetry, the uncanny, and seeking new literary canons of the imagination did "literature" come to be associated entirely with the *fictional* imagination accident.[3]

The Red Book, while offering aesthetic forms from an age far removed from current disciplinary divisions between literature and psychology, was fated to be rejected by its author for not conforming to them. Yet it is worth looking more closely at what is at stake in these disciplinary divisions as they continue to haunt the success of the work as a 21ˢᵗ-century publication. For example, there is a crucial issue in how the category of literature as the fictional imaginal has come to be studied in universities.

Like psychology itself, "literary studies" was invented in the 19th century under the influence of the proliferation of disciplines sponsored by the dominance of empirical science. These new disciplines were the "Social Sciences," meant to employ the objectivity of science to human and cultural matters. Objectivity means just what *The Red Book* laments. That Jung had found the human soul: "I had judged her and turned her into a scientific object."[4]

Similar "objectivity" pervaded literary studies in the 20th century with the determination of its "New Criticism," that the text was an object, sufficient in itself to generate knowledge with no participation from either the personality of its author or its reader. Known as "the intentional fallacy" and "the affective fallacy," a literary work was not to be understood by reference to its author's *intentional* meaning, nor how it *affects* or makes the reader feel.[5] Rather the "close reading" inaugurated by the new criticism and still in use today insisted upon the primary reality of literature as object.

Here we see disciplinary division as a primary severing of being. For the new psychology, psyche or soul is the reality to be studied, with *The Red Book* itself showing the high cost of so-called scientific objectivity. For literary studies, the text is the primary reality. While new criticism is no longer the dominant literary theory in universities, being-as-textual remains its central concern. It is also fascinating to realize that these now parallel and split ways of knowing and being developed strikingly similar research strategies in the early 20th century.

For, in comparing Jung's "active imagination," a key ingredient in composing his *Red Book,* with new criticism's close reading, it is possible to see both working with the autonomy of the image. For Jung, the image is primarily psychic but can manifest in words. For the new critics, the image is in the words of the literary text but can inspire some psychic mobility. In effect, close reading combines Jung's active imagination and amplification as I have suggested elsewhere.[6]

What is in psychology, allowing the image to assume its own reality and being as in active imagination and then amplifying it by comparison to collective sources, becomes in literary studies the autonomy of images in the literary work that point to other literary works in the new critical practice. With parallel strategies divided by disciplinary dismembering, it is time to look at the myth of such atomizing of being in knowing.

Dionysus in Jung's Writings

Prior to the publication of *The Red Book,* James Hillman's essay "Dionysus in Jung's Writings" pointed out that C.G. Jung stresses "dismemberment" as his primary focus in the many myths of the god Dionysus. In Jung's treatment of the dismemberment of the divine being, Hillman sees a germ of psychic rejuvenation in the corporeal breaking apart of an aging god. He calls Christian modernity too Apollonian, too distancing, rational, and dualistic. So, in Hillman's view, an era dominated by one god, defined by rationality and disembodiment, is to be followed by dismemberment, which will release multiple stories of being in Hillman's preferred polytheistic approach to psyche. I here suggest that *The Red Book*, in its complex relations to literature and psychology, demonstrates that Jung's dismembering of Dionysus has possibilities unexplored by Hillman.

According to Hillman, Jung sees a two-stage dismembering process: First comes a division into opposites, such as the very notion of Apollonian and Dionysian itself, the gods incarnated. This separation is celebrated in Jung's love of opposites and polarities. On the other hand, Jung, the rebalancing psychologist of the modern western psyche, has to go further to posit something more fragmented. Here we glimpse his animism in the form of bisexual, embodied, ecstatic Dionysus. In the second stage of Jung's Dionysian dismemberment, the god is scattered in pieces.

Dualistic opposites become multiplicity, with a wider dispersal of the divine in matter, which both Jung and Hillman call archetypal. To Jung, archetypes are inherited psychic potentials for certain sorts of images, patterns, and meaning. They represent the possibility of diversity in psychic functioning, or as Hillman later puts it, a polytheistic psyche in which the goddesses and gods are multiple structures of consciousness in the world. Very importantly, Hillman insists that this second stage of Dionysian dismemberment changes the psyche profoundly. The Dionysian psychic process is an initiation into a new cosmos of fragments of the body of the god.[7] Distance from divinity becomes interiority and animistic multiplicity within the domain of the god.

In particular, Hillman notes that *zoe*, the life force of the body in Eros, is awakened by this process of divine dismemberment.[8] This new consciousness, or *zoe,* is an intimation of wholeness that does not erode differences. The new enlivening *zoe* is animistic in a particular way of awareness of its own *partial* consciousness, aware of itself as *parts.*

> Rather the crucial experience would be the awareness of the parts *as parts* distinct from each other, dismembered, each with its own light, a state in which the body becomes conscious of itself as a composite of differences. The scintillae and fishes eyes of which Jung speaks … may be experienced as embedded in physical expressions. The distribution of Dionysus through matter may be compared with the distribution of consciousness through members, organs, and zones.[9]

Dionysian re-membering is re-membering a body-oriented consciousness in touch with *zoe* as endless instinctual life. This consciousness is multiple, animistic, connected to the divine in matter and nature, but how connected? What does it really mean to exist in the realm of a dismembered god; to have the task of re-membering divine consciousness from within?

Jung's Dionysian enactment is the notion of the symbol, not in its common English meaning as a motif standing for some known meaning, but rather in his emphasis as an image expressing something not yet or possibly not ever fully known in the ego.[10] Jung saw symbols as expressing something unknown that wants to come into being. His symbols are dynamic and alive. They provide what Hillman calls *zoe,* an experience of instinctual life, in their rejuvenating of consciousness.

> A symbol really lives only when it is the best and highest expression for something divined but not yet known to the observer. It then compels his unconscious participation and has a life-giving and life-enhancing effect.[11]

A symbol's route to the unknown invokes the archetypal qualities of psyche; those capacities possess roots in the instinctual body while also extending to the realm of spirit and rational knowing.

In this context, even academic disciplinary concepts such as those founding a psychology or theories of literature can be symbols when they do *not* forget their connection to the "living mystery":[12]

> We have to break down life and events, which are self-contained processes, into meanings, images, concepts, well knowing that in doing so we are getting further away from the living mystery. ...[13]

Dionysus is the mythical embodiment of such "living mystery." It follows that if rational, *disciplined* knowing can break down life and events into parts that retain awareness of the living mystery, then that knowledge, written in symbols, is Dionysian dismemberment. I am suggesting that in the many disciplines that make up the modern Western university we have dismembered an aging god of being, "him," the masculine divine of monotheism that founded dualism, including the dualism of body and psyche. Dismembered into our many disciplines, this god is our being in materialistic rubble.

However, Dionysus haunts us in the Jungian symbol, which he suggestively wrote about mainly in terms of words, which included the words of science. "Since every scientific theory contains a hypothesis ... it is a symbol."[14] Where the words of a discipline can be imagined as Jungian symbols, they turn the dead meat of our divided disciplines into scraps of the enlivening body of Dionysus. If we can regard disciplines not so much as eternally divided but as *parts* that need to re-member their status as parts of one body of divine knowing and being, then we know *zoe*, renewed, instinctual consciousness, or, put another way, the vision of *The Red Book*.

The Red Book and Transdisciplinarity

Before looking at *The Red Book* as Dionysian in its span of disciplines such as literature, art, and psychology, I want to offer another perspective to academic research in the 21st century, one that originates in quantum science and theology.

Inaugurated by quantum physicist Basarab Nicolescu, transdisciplinarity means beyond disciplinary severing of being.[15] Transdisciplinarity rejects any possibility of a hyperdiscipline, one capable of subsuming all human knowing into a system of perfect knowledge, or ultimate truth. Rather, he emphasizes that reality, currently fragmented in many disciplines, *is itself multiple.* In this sense, a single godlike vision for total knowledge gives way to a polyvalent polytheism of knowing. Dionysus arrives.

By refusing a hyperdiscipline, Nicolescu does away with the traditional unified human subject of Western modernity. After the discoveries of quantum physics, he posits a new human subject for *all* research. No longer should research assume the primacy of the criteria of objectivity. Nicolescu's radically "open" unity means accepting that humans live on many levels of reality simultaneously. It will never be possible to rationally know all psychophysical realities, not least because some are neither measurable nor stable. Knowledge therefore will always be in a state of dismemberment.

Nicolescu offers three axioms of transdisciplinarity to replace those of traditional science that go back to Galileo. Hitherto, many scientific disciplines adhered to the following axioms, or fundamental assumptions:

i) The universe is governed by mathematical laws.
ii) These laws can be discovered by scientific experiment.
iii) Such experiments, if valid, can be perfectly replicated.

Of course, as Nicolescu emphasizes, such an approach to knowledge entails turning the human subject into an object by removing feeling and values. Nicolescu's fundamental principles, or three axioms for knowing in transdisciplinarity, are as follows:

i)   The ontological axiom: *There are, in Nature and in our knowledge of Nature, different levels of Reality and, correspondingly, different levels of perception.*

ii)   The logical axiom: *The passage from one level of Reality to another is insured by the logic of the included middle.*

iii)   The complexity axiom: *The Structure of the totality of levels of Reality or perception is a complex structure: every level is what it is because all levels exist at the same time.*[16]

This approach to knowledge amounts to a paradigm shift from competing disciplines with separate perspectives to one regarding universe as multidimensional. Reality is now complex. So are human beings. No one sense organ or academic discipline is capable of understanding all the other levels of reality. Whatever any particular knowledge claims, it will be incomplete or open. The single god of our historic privileging of rational objectivity is in pieces. "He" cannot be put together to make a perfect being. Here and now is Dionysus re-membered in disciplines now knowing themselves as parts of a whole that cannot be stitched together to exclude an "other."

The axioms of transdisciplinarity imply an *unus mundus*, records Nicolescu.[17] Knowledge in this cosmodernity is both unified and also multiple because of the new logic of transdisciplinarity. Instead of the dualistic traditional science model of subject versus object, we now have a subject, object, and hidden third, the invisible, connected quantum realm. This realm and the growing under-standing of quantum complexity infer radical interconnectedness, a "oneness" that cannot be rationally plotted. Hence the *unus mundus* of transdisciplinarity is Dionysian in disciplines as parts as *parts*. Threaded into one by the hidden, nonrational third, they also rightly enact the multiple levels of reality in the cosmos. As Nicolescu puts it: "[r]eality is simultaneously a single and a multiple One."[18]

Such a transdisciplinary reality can only be enacted by a new logic of the included middle to extend the binary of subject/object into subject, included-middle-that-is-both-subject-and-object, object. Revisioned in this new logic is language which in transdisciplinarity is considered in a ternary hermeneutics, not a binary one.[19] Language becomes a quantum phenomenon, the material enactment of the hidden third as the included middle. Put another way, *what Jung calls the symbol is what Nicolescu calls the symbol*: that word-image that opens into unconscious so unknown, nonrational reality.

Symbols in Jung and transdisciplinarity are dynamic, *living* scraps of the body of dispersed Dionysus to be re-membered in the soul (Jung), to be the included middle that invokes the hidden third of quantum reality (Nicolescu). For both, symbols are ultraprecise but never, never fully definable in rational terms; they are never absolute truth. Nicolescu here in his wonderful *From Modernity to Cosmodernity,* could be quoting Jung.

> A literal understanding of a symbol, turns it into a dead, static concept, without any function or value. … The indefinite number of aspects of a symbol does not mean at all that the symbol is imprecise, vague or ambiguous. On the contrary, a precise definition implies an inaccuracy of meaning, a *mutilation* of the symbol. Accuracy is present, though, the invariance hidden behind the indefinite multitude aspects of the symbol. … The symbol and the logic of the included third are intimately linked.[20]

Or, one could say that symbols enact the included middle between the disciplines of literature and psychology. It is time to return to *The Red Book* as a Dionysian and transdisciplinary work.

The Red Book and Dionysian Transdisciplinarity

"… I had judged [my soul] and turned her into a scientific object."[21] *The Red Book* begins with the problem addressed by Dionysian transdisciplinarity, that in privileging experimental material science, the subject/object paradigm has turned the humanity of human beings into objects. Written in the first person, *The Red Book* is a quest by "I" for both the reality of his soul and for a relationship to her. What he discovers is that "the wealth of the soul exists in images," or in those psychic manifestations arriving via active imagination, the transdisciplinary included middle that is both "I" and not "I."[22]

Almost immediately, "I" suffers a terrifying sense of dismemberment in losing the sense of interior and exterior. Traveling to hell in these visions is to exist as hell in a loss of bodily and psychic boundaries.[23] Like Dionysus, he is both murdered and murderer. The god both suffered dismemberment and enacts it on those who do not respect him as Penteus, torn apart by Dionysian maenads, discovers. Indeed, the most infamous episode in *The Red Book*, when "I" is told to eat part of the liver of a dead child, resembles dismembered child Dionysus as much as it parodies Christian Eucharist.

Significantly, *The Red Book*, begins and ends by stressing the reality of symbols. "I" meets Elijah and blind Salome with the prophet insisting on their reality *as* symbols.[24] Later, when "I" attests to partially merging with symbols and being changed by them, he might be articulating Nicolescu's emphasis on symbols as the language that invokes the hidden third, the quantum realm that connects everything in ways that cannot be rationally formulated. It is exciting to think of the characters in *The Red Book* as precise and radically incomplete forms of knowing. If "I" is undergoing a trial where he must make a transition from split-apart, unviable dualism into a ternary form of Dionysian re-membering, what might *The Red Book* do for the reader?

Where Jung mentions science as also symbolic, he anticipates Nicolescu suggesting that theories articulated in symbols are *permanent*, not because they are never modified, but rather because their symbolic nature renders them participant in reality and permanently open to extension without closure.[25] Here, *The Red Book* is of its time and also for all time as long as we use it as a living structure of knowing. It is *parts as parts* because symbols are scraps of a never to be rationally assembled whole: They are Dionysus. In reading *The Red Book* today, we are invited to enter the body of re-membering Dionysus.

Nicolescu is also helpful on the consequences of symbols functioning as the included middle for language as a whole. In a book published in 2014 and frighteningly relevant to the politics of 2017, he offers what *The Red Book* embodies, that symbols restore Dionysian *zoe* to language. Where understanding of reality is too fragmented, such as into wholly separate disciplines or society too fractured, language loses life and meaning. Symbols, on the other hand, by invoking multiple levels of reality and forming the included middle between disciplines, gradually restores meaning.

> Classical logic based on the separation between the different levels of Reality, inevitably implies the gradual *entropy* of language. … The symbol brings about a gradual decrease in the entropy of language, an increase in *order*, in information, and in comprehension.[26]

The Red Book, of course, bears witness to the decay of language in the suffering of desert hermit Ammonius. On the one hand, entropy is mobilized throughout *The Red Book* in the return of the dead. On the other hand, the dead have something to say to "I," while poor Ammonius appears to be the focus for the decline of writing to support the soul, for the loss of symbols. After exchanges between "I," and Ammonius, there is a lament for a now impossible language that would protect from dismemberment by single, unambiguous meanings; a language that would reject the symbolic.

> You cry out for the word which has one meaning and no other. … The word becomes your God. … The word is protective magic against the daimons of unending, which tear at your soul and want to scatter you to the winds.[27]

To refuse the symbol is to suffer dismemberment because the single meaning is dead, has forced out the sacred in sacrificing the "other" to its rational completeness. Hence, nonsymbolic language rends being and has no means of re-membering. Fortunately, the daimons of unending, here unending *interpretation*, are also the *zoe* of re-membering. Instead of a monotheistic single meaning "word" versus daimons becoming demons (because tearing down meaning), symbols are parts as parts, of a multiple, rejuvenating embodied divine.

In *The Red Book*, re-membering via symbols offers "supreme meaning," a notion usefully unpacked by Nicolescu.[28] He proposes three levels of meaning: The first is horizontal meaning looking at one level of reality, what most disciplines do. Here, psychology tries to formulate a discrete "psyche" and literary studies, the object-reality that is the text. A second level of meaning brings the symbol into being as the included middle between disciplines because it deals vertically with different levels of reality.

Ultimately, Nicolescu offers "meaning of meaning": … [I]nter-connections involving all of Reality: the Subject, the Object and the Hidden Third.[29] If *The Red Book* indicates that the "supreme meaning" is the godhead, then it brings us back also to Dionysian transdisciplinarity in the role of the sacred. Here the sacred is indigenous to transdisciplinarity because it is the marker of the irreducibly real.[30] We return to the core of the word "sacred" in sacrifice. Quantum physics, transdisciplinarity, and *The Red Book* teach that delusions of certainty, single meanings and disciplinary hierarchy must be sacrificed lest they result in utter destruction. The story of Penteus is instructive. He refused to worship Dionysus and was torn apart by the feminine form of the despised god in his maenads. The sacred is irreducible, real, and tasted in the symbol language that is re-membering Dionysus.

One form of the sacred in *The Red Book* is the feminine soul in Salome, as well as numerous female characters and the serpent. Nicolescu suggested that the ancient alchemical image of the tail-eating, fertilizing serpent, or *ouroboros,* is a vision conveyed by the quantum domain that fosters transdisciplinarity.[31] The universe appears to create itself and be self-organizing, just as the *ouroboros* entails. *The Red Book's* serpent reminds "I" of the dreadful plight of those like Penteus "who did not live [their] animal."[32]

One who does live his animal in *The Red Book* and fares badly when encountering disembodied modernity is Izdubar. This man-god is horrified to hear of objectified science from "I." Just a whiff of mainstream science with its predilection for abolishing the sacred and symbols is enough to send him into terminal decline. And yet "I" finds a solution in relocating Izdubar to his imagination. Instead of the well-worn argument that religion is fantasy dealing a death blow to religion, it actually keeps Izdubar alive until he can be reborn, like a serpent, from an egg.

Clearly Izdubar, whom we are told is another name for Gilgamesh, heralds the birth of Jung's archetypal theory. Divine consciousness is innate to the human psyche in archetypes and will renew being because such fantasy of the sacred is, as Nicolescu would put it, indicative of the irreducibly real. In *The Red Book,* "I" instructs Izdubar on two kinds of truth.

> Our truth is that which comes to us from the knowledge
> of outer things. The truth of your priests is that which
> comes to you from inner things.[33]

Not only is this an overt exposition of transdisciplinarity's levels of reality, it also enacts what Nicolescu calls the dialogue of science and Tradition.[34] Whereas mainstream science developed out of Christian dualism that posited God as entirely nonmaterial, so producing a model of truth that could be abstracted from matter and ultimately offered knowledge as subject versus object, "Tradition" is Nicolescu's term for knowledge that is tacit, embodied, intuitive, shamanistic, handed down for centuries, possessing qualities that are both culturally specific and universal, and amounting to the spiritual evolution of humankind.[35]

"Tradition"'s core motif of "*unity in diversity* and of *diversity through unity*—applies to Tradition itself," and, as Nicolescu shows, applies to the vision of the cosmos unfolding in quantum research.[36] While the modern science that works through objectivity and complete rationality may claim to have abolished Tradition as viable knowing, to have eliminated the sacred, in fact that rejected serpent is really an *ouroboros* returning as science discovers the quantum domain.

On the one hand, modern objective science grew out of a religion in Christian dualism. Now religion in the form of a Dionysian vision of a dispersed, yet irreducible sacred returns as science discovers levels of reality that cannot be condensed into one, or into oneness. "Tradition" actually speaks coherently and urgently, and to objective science it suggests transdisciplinarity because its forms of knowing in intuition, imagination, and embodiment are necessary to appreciate the multiple levels of reality. Izdubar is real, just not an object. Fantasy is real, just not an object that can be treated objectively.

Izdubar is a mythic being from 6,000 years ago. Fascinatingly, tablets containing his stories were discovered by the West rather close in time to the discovery of quantum particles. "He" returns in *The Red Book* to remind as re-minding, to rejuvenate as a Dionysian symbol of a new consciousness. "I" learns that he can save his dying god; he can save this incarnation of Tradition for modernity because he is real, just not on the level of reality that existing mainstream science addresses. Just as transdisciplinarity has the project of uniting science and Tradition as a unity in diversity and a diversity in unity, so too does *The Red Book* provide a process of connecting to ancient wisdom that is not dead so long as we can offer a model of reality that gives him a home.

The story of Izdubar and "I" is one of transformation, picaresque adventures, and the forming of a relationship. "I" is learning about the multiplicity of levels of reality. He is similarly implicated in most of the scenes in which he finds himself. Potential lover of the maiden in the forest, sole survivor of the lowly man who enjoys cinema and dies alone, he is conveyed, perhaps none too soon, to the madhouse. There a small fat professor pronounces "I" mad, and he has a conversation with an inmate who claims to be Nietzsche and Christ.[37]

"I" decides that he must accept what is "low," the depths in himself, and that acceptance may itself be a seed from which grows a tree to conjoin above and below.[38] There seems to be an urgency to extend being beyond one rational level. In a sense, the whole of *The Red Book* is an exposition of the suffering engendered by trying to live on one level of reality when it is, in fact, multiple, as trans-disciplinarity shows.

This is not to make a mistake by Jung's conjuring of moral depths for Nicolescu's multiple levels of being. It is not an error to see these as different perspectives for the same topic of multiple levels of being. Rather, *The Red Book* is exploring more fully than transdisciplinarity yet has achieved, the Dionysian ethical conflicts of a dispersed, differentiated reality. Put another way, where *The Red Book* focuses on the individual undergoing a dismembering and re-membering Dionysian rite, Nicolescu sees the social implications of transdisciplinarity as requiring a new global culture that is transreligious and transrational.[39] How that culture might *feel*, what the transition to it might entail on a psychological level, is the drama of *The Red Book*.

To a person and a society wedded to one rational reality and building psychological being in a sense of subject/object, the dismembering of such a severing from the "other" indeed could feel like hell. It *is* hell as the underworld, the denied realm of Izdubar, the madhouse, the world also of sentimental novels, those whose poverty denies them the reason that sees through cinematic illusion, wily Salome, enigmatic Elijah, the fat cook, et. al. "I" discovers that while hell hurts, it *is* survivable. That which is banished from polite, rational European society of 20th-century rational science is hellish because so firmly repressed, socially, morally, psychologically and by an episte-mology lacking connection that condemns it to unbearable loneliness.

No wonder so many of the inhabitants of *The Red Book*'s underworld reach out to "I" for meaningful connection that would transform hell for them—shut in this reality alone—to one of connectivity to other realities, truths, ways of being. What is needed, of course, are symbols: images that make room for the other. The Jungian symbol does not have to be a word image, but words make highly communicable symbols. They pull up the underworld.

> With words you pull up the underworld. ... In words the emptiness and the fullness flow together.[40]

Only symbols and not mathematical language, says Nicolescu, can express the simplicity of the interaction of all levels of reality.[41] This bestows an ethical imperative of radical connection in human affairs. "Togetherness" is what reality itself demands of us because it is how the universe is.[42] *The Red Book* teaches this ethics by showing that all the permutations of humanity, fantasy, nature, and the gods have a role in the making of the being of "I." A Dionysian rending of illusions of a single rational reality is met with a radical re-membering of transdisciplinarity's multiple levels.

Transdisciplinarity means "beyond" disciplines not in the sense of dismissing them but removing their intrinsic claims to a single knowable reality and epistemology. Transrational and transreligious are terms doing the same job for their domains that also have the habit of claiming single, supreme validity. Just as religions represent diversity in their unity (common themes) and unity in their diversity (indigenous variety), so too do various postrational psychologies, liberally supplied in *The Red Book*. Notably emphasizing the ethical dimension of postrationality is the feminine.

Salome and Elijah occur as a pair, related. Moreover, Salome's repeated erotic designs on "I" cement what Jung was later to conceptualize as Eros knowing as rightful, even *necessary*, companion to more rational and spiritually inclined Logos. It is also worth remembering (and re-membering) the fat cook from "the realm of the mothers," whose simple religious faith impresses "I."[43] Eros knowing and the feminine are not confined to the sexual in *The Red Book*. It is a major mode of Dionysian re-membering via the symbol.

The Red Book is not a deliberate or planned work of Dionysus or of transdisciplinarity. Such is its unique potency in its spontaneity. It is a work of the symbol, of discovering what Nicolescu calls the precision and permanent validity of the symbol so long as it remains open to what Jung would call the numinous, and transdisciplinarity, the sacred or hidden third. The old god of singleness as singleness is dead, and his death is loud in the lamentations of the dead in *The Red Book*.

The dead lament because they did not live their animal as *The Red Book* so eloquently reveals.[44] Dionysus is living your animal, dismembering and re-membering in order to find *zoe,* an embodied consciousness rejuvenated by symbols into tasting instinctual life. Re-membering parts as parts, disciplines as addressing parts of a reality with multiple levels, *The Red Book* is a literary and psychological revelation for the 21st century.

Endnotes

1 C.G. Jung, *Memories, Dreams, Reflections*, ed. Aniela Jaffe (New York, NY: Vintage Books, 1963), 213.

2 Susan Rowland, *Jung as a Writer* (New York and London: Routledge, 2005).

3 See Terry Eagleton, *Literary Theory: An Introduction* (Great Britain: Blackwell, 1983).

4 C.G. Jung, *The Red Book: Liber Novus*, ed. Sonu Shamdasani, tr. John Peck, Mark Kyburz, and Sonu Shamdasani (New York, NY: W. W. Norton, 2009), 128. Page numbers refer to the "Reader's Edition."

5 W. K. Wimsatt, and M. C. Beardsley, *The Verbal Icon: Studies in the Meaning of Poetry* (Kentucky: University of Kentucky Press, 1954), 21.

6 Susan Rowland, *Remembering Dionysus* (New York and London: Routledge, 2017), 89-109.

7 James Hillman, 'Dionysus in Jung's Writings,' in *Mythic Figures: Uniform Edition of the Writings of James Hillman, volume 6.1* (Putnam, Connecticut: Spring Publications Inc., 2007), 26.

8 Ibid., 29.

9 Ibid., 28.

10 For Jung's extensive treatment of the symbol see C.G. Jung, *Dictionary of Analytical Psychology* (London and New York: Ark paperbacks, 1987), 144-51.

11 Ibid., 147.

12 C.G. Jung, "On the Relation of Analytical Psychology to Poetry," in *CW*, vol. 15 (Princeton, NJ: Princeton University Press, 1966).

13 Ibid., par. 121.

14 Jung, *Dictionary of Analytical Psychology*, 146.

15 Basarab Nicolescu, *From Modernity to Cosmodernity: Science, Culture, and Spirituality* (New York, NY: SUNY, 2014).

16 Ibid., 6.

17 Ibid., 208-9.

18 Ibid., 209.

19 Ibid., 118-9.

20 Ibid., 31.

21 Jung, *The Red Book*, 128.

[22] Ibid., 130.

[23] Ibid., 153.

[24] Ibid., 187.

[25] Nicolescu, *From Modernity to Cosmodernity*, 34.

[26] Ibid., 31. Italics in original.

[27] Jung, *The Red Book*, 250.

[28] Nicolescu, *From Modernity to Cosmodernity*, 201.

[29] Ibid.

[30] Ibid., 106.

[31] Ibid., 109-10.

[32] Jung, *The Red Book*, 341.

[33] Ibid., 280.

[34] Nicolescu, *From Modernity to Cosmodernity*, 21.

[35] Ibid.,19-24.

[36] Ibid., 20.

[37] Jung, *The Red Book*, 349.

[38] Ibid., 356.

[39] Nicolescu, *From Modernity to Cosmodernity*, 213-15.

[40] Jung, *The Red Book*, 351-2.

[41] Nicolescu, *From Modernity to Cosmodernity*, 211.

[42] Ibid., 213.

[43] Jung, *The Red Book*, 363.

[44] Ibid., 341.

Appassionato for the Imagination

Russell A. Lockhart

Introduction

It was not a voice dream, nor was there a visual image. It was one of those "knowing" dreams, where you wake up with a sense of *revelation*, in this case, that what I was to write was to be an "appassionato for the imagination."

The previous day, Murray Stein had asked me if I would be interested in contributing an essay to a book that would be titled *Jung's Red Book for Our Time*—a project focusing on Jung's *Red Book* as a guiding resource for individuals trying to navigate the tortuous currents of the contemporary world.

I had not yet agreed to do this, but when I woke from this dream, I felt it necessary to say "yes," feeling excited as well as daunted by the task the dream implied.

I experience dreams as the intentionality of something *Other*.[1] I prefer to say, "something Other" rather than "the unconscious," as this latter term is tied to the limitations of the ego. I also call this the *presentational* psyche, because the dream presents itself, fully formed, *to* the ego of waking consciousness. I refer as well to the *invitational* psyche because dreams have a quality of "inviting" the participation of the conscious ego. I think of these qualities of *other*, of *presentation*, of *invitation*, as characterizing the *gravitational pull of the imagination*.[2]

I have dreamed "titles" before, and I have followed through and worked on projects that—until such dreams—I had no conscious knowledge of or intention of doing. I experience these dreams as "tasks," tasks dreamed up by the Other, and presented to me, giftlike. *Appassionato for the Imagination* is a title that I would not have come up with from my conscious standpoint or intentions. Giving the dream credence and credibility, and privileging it in this way, is a measure of the impact that Jung's psychology—as exemplified by his experiences recorded in *The Red Book*—has had on *me* both personally and as an analyst for more than 40 years.[3]

As I wrote the dream, I was aware of Beethoven's *Appassionata*, even hearing some passages from that groundbreaking work. Beethoven was losing his hearing but wrote what he heard in his imagination, wrote in such a way that no one could play it and no piano could endure it. As commentators note, Beethoven plumbed the depths of imagination more so than any other musician in spite of his deafness and the degree of his debilitating and dreadful physical illnesses.[4] This is why so much of his music was and is *unique*.[5]

As a teenager, my piano skills had reached recital level. Beethoven's *Moonlight Sonata* and his *Pathétique* were in my repertoire, but the *Appassionata* was beyond me—a personal failure. As I was mulling on this, two images came together: the unhearing Beethoven plunging into imaginal depths; and Jung plunging into imaginal depths fearing the loss of his mind. Both men, unbowed by their fears and afflictions, plunged ahead, bringing forth enormous personal and cultural riches.

The dream felt as if bringing Beethoven and Jung together was part of the intentionality of the Other. To what end? It was not, I sensed, to do a scholarly piece on the parallels between the two men—though there are many and that would be a worthy task. The more I pondered and let imagination, too, have its say, it became clear that what was central to the two men's lives is what I must explore: *art* and *imagination*. Doing so would constitute my answer to how Jung's *Red Book* would guide seekers in whatever "post-futures" await.

"That's not art!" … "That is art!"

March 4, 1913. Fresh from his defeat in the 1912 presidential election, former President Theodore ("Teddy") Roosevelt, strode into the International Exhibition of Modern Art, now referred to as the "Armory Show," and waved his arms wildly as he stomped through the galleries pointing at paintings and sculptures and shouting, "That's not art!"[6]

Unlike some presidents, Roosevelt was no cultural buffoon. Historians have noted that he had the finest mind since Jefferson. This Nobel Peace Prize-winning president wrote, read, and spoke five languages. He read two books a day on wide-ranging topics. He wrote constantly. And he wrote a scathing review of the Armory Show. A self-proclaimed "bull moose," he never minced words. He considered these modern art examples—particularly those of the Europeans—to be expressive of a lunatic fringe, as being pathological, as having no artistic merit, and not to be taken seriously. Roosevelt's views were expressing those of the clear majority of the more than a quarter-million visitors to the Armory Show. The exhibit aroused passions like no other before or since, and when it moved on to the Art Institute of Chicago, it met with riots.

While it is not possible to pinpoint the birth of modernism, it is, I believe, possible to pinpoint the public awareness of modernism as *threat*—to this exhibit. Roosevelt saw and felt and articulated the threat. In his view, the purpose of art was to serve the progressive development of a nation. No president did more for the arts in assuring that this would be the case in America. He believed that economic and military power were not sufficient for the triumph of the American spirit, that *cultural* power was essential. He meant upholding, representational, figurative, and decorative arts as being the preeminent and necessary mode for achieving this triumph.[7] What he witnessed was the possible derailment of the cultural engine necessary for achieving America's manifest destiny, no matter how that was to be defined.[8]

What did Roosevelt see? Nothing expressing the hopes and desires of a nation, or of other nations' emulating the success of America. Instead, he saw the expression of individual and diseased minds, minds that had become dissociated from the "facts of the world," had lost all connection with the "reality" of representation, and glorified the pathology of extremist and dangerous individuals. He would agree with Leila Mechlin, then editor of *Art and Progress* at the time, who went so far as to ask: "Why do we so blithely tolerate these crimes in art?"[9]

Passions ran high as the negative press drew larger and larger crowds. Into this cacophony stepped another luminary: C.G. Jung.[10] Jung made it a habit to visit art galleries, exhibitions, and museums, both in his native Switzerland and in his foreign travels. Attending the Armory Show would not have been unusual for him. Jung was not just a viewer of art. He had painted representational landscapes in oils and watercolors from the time of his youth, well into his adult years, and before his visit to the Armory Show. He made a point of exploring art traditions in most every culture.

Jung's aesthetics ran along traditional and representational lines, much like Roosevelt's. But in his youth, the works of the Swiss artist Arnold Böcklin attracted Jung—Freud, too, as well as Hitler, who acquired 11 of Böcklin's paintings. Böcklin's paintings tend to be dreamy and darkly Romantic in spirit. His series, titled *The Isle of the Dead,* was of special interest to Jung. In 1900 in Munich, Jung saw the work of Franz von Stuck, who was inspired by Böcklin. Stuck's symbolist and highly erotic paintings and sculptures were at the center of the Munich Secession. Jung was impressed with Stuck's work.[11] Like many northern Europeans, Jung was already influenced by nontraditional and "strange," though still representational, images well before he encountered modern art in New York in 1913.[12]

Jung's negativity concerning modern art is well known and documented, perhaps no more strongly expressed than in his 1947 letter to Esther Harding. She had sent him a book of T.S. Eliot's poetry. Jung wrote to her: "I don't know T.S. Eliot. If you think his book is worthwhile, then I don't mind even poetry. I am only prejudiced against all forms of modern art. It is mostly morbid and evil. ..."[13]

He expressed his vitriol against modern art in his essays on Joyce and Picasso, published in 1932, and in various seminars and letters before and since that time.[14]

What *triggered* this deep-seated, long-standing complex?

I believe Jung's rejection of modern art stems from his experiences at the Armory Show. There is nothing to document this, but I think the possibility is worth drawing out. From 1900 to 1909, during his tenure at Burghölzli Psychiatric Hospital, Jung was exposed to the expressive work in drawing, painting, and sculpture of patients in various stages of mental illness, disease, and decay. Fragmentation, dissolution of boundaries, loss of representation, incoherence, loss of perspective, and extreme distortion were some of the outstanding characteristics of "patient art."

Jung looked at "patient art" with a scientific eye, aimed at psychiatric understanding of the patient's mental disorder. In this sense, what he saw at the exhibit would have been "familiar." All the *characteristics* of schizophrenic expression were here on display. He could take it in as a doctor and as a scientist.

But *something* got under Jung's skin. I think it was the fact that what he was seeing was the work of *artists*, not patients—at a major, world-class exhibition, put on and arranged *by* artists. I can well imagine that Jung experienced something of the fear akin to what Roosevelt experienced—not as a concern for America's manifest destiny, nor as a concern for the fate of European culture, but more that modern art *itself* was pathological and modern artists were analogous to schizophrenics, if not outright schizophrenic.[15] This attitude became a fixation that did not change until shortly before Jung died. As I'll illustrate, this change was enantiodromic and led to what I consider Jung's most important ideas relating to the future and, more precisely, in what sense his *Red Book* can be considered a guide. But back then, in 1913, aware of projection, as well as Freud's recent allusion to Jung's instability, there are reasons to suspect that Jung was troubled by his emotional volatility and that it heralded a breakdown.

In January 1913, three months before Jung went to New York, Freud suggested they break off their personal relationship, and Jung had acceded to this. Jung had written to Freud just before, claiming that "I am not in the least neurotic—touch wood! I have submitted … to analysis and am much the better for it."[16] This exchange of letters also reveals the degree of *emotional* swirl the two men were in with each other. Jung was still suffering Freud's rejection of *Wandlungen und Symbole der Libido,* published in 1912, and later translated as *Symbols of Transformation.* Recall that the subtitle of this work was "An Analysis of the Prelude to a Case of Schizophrenia." Jung most certainly would have been in a heightened emotional state over the collapse of their relationship when he was face to face with the images of modern art for the first time, not as *patient* material, but as the expression of *artists*.

When he returned to Europe, he began to express serious concern about his mental stability, and this increased through the end of 1913 and beyond. He resigned positions, temporarily broke off the connection with his confidant Toni Wolff, began to play daily at lakeside building little structures, and broke off serious reading.[17] Late in the year, Jung began to experience spontaneous and autonomous visions and voices and felt that he might be "doing a schizophrenia."[18] Jung wrote everything out in detail, but had difficulty understanding and interpreting what he was experiencing.[19] In some frustration, he began to paint. In October 1913, he had a vision of the flooding of Europe, and this repeated a second time. Taking these images personally, he felt threatened with breakdown. He wrote that he thought his mind had gone crazy. Likely, in November, he asked an inner female figure what it was that he was doing. She unambiguously said: "It is art." In a second conversation, she once again told Jung: "That is art." He was riled and announced, like Roosevelt: "No, it is not art!" Jung says, "she came through with a long statement" following this second declaration.[20] This statement is unreported.

On December 12, 1913, he had the vision that initiated his full "descent" into the imaginal world that would become the raw material for his *Red Book*.[21] Jung says he recognized the inner woman as "a patient, a talented psychopath who had a strong transference to me."[22] According to Shamdasani, the woman in question was Maria Moltzer.[23] Jung says, "She had become a living figure in my mind."[24] What Jung leaves unsaid is that Maria Moltzer moved to Zurich in 1910 to be trained by Jung as a psychiatrist. She became a nurse at Burghölzli and was Jung's assistant there working on child analysis. There are indications that Jung had an affair with her, and he had been in analysis with her.[25] She became an analyst, became Jung's assistant and a most important and influential colleague.[26] She played major roles in the Jungian community. She was a talented artist. She developed what she called her "Bible" and kept writings and images of her psychic experiences in it and encouraged her patients to do so as well.[27] She was a primary influence on analyst Franz Riklin in turning him away from being an analyst and pushing him to become an abstract painter.[28] Jung was aware of this in 1913 when Riklin became a student of impressionist painter Augusto Giacometti. Later, Jung said he wanted to avoid Riklin's fate at all costs.[29]

After seeing the Armory Show and observing Riklin's decline, Jung saw art as a pathway to ruin and why he must avoid Riklin's fate. And he must deny any push from Maria Moltzer—inner and outer— in this direction. So, he must deny that what he was doing was art.

Anyone who encounters Jung's *Red Book* experiences it *as* art, no matter what else it may be. If what Jung was doing was *not* art, as he held for most of his life, what, then, *was* he doing? Or was it art after all? And if so, in what sense? And does it make any difference in discerning the nature of *The Red Book* as a guide in the coming time?

What Did Jung Do?

The Munich Secession of young artists in 1892 is considered the first major break with the tradition of outer world representational and figurative art that had always dominated the culture of art. These artists rebelled against not only cherished traditions but also against the authority of the industrial, mechanistic, and economic forces that held art prisoner. They reveled in art forms of more primitive cultures, of art from the East, art from the medieval period, and art from folk and mythic traditions. Munich was the center of these "experiments" in breaking down the hegemony of "the academy" and focusing the origin of art on *the inner world as resource*. It was this scene in 1900 that Jung took in just before taking up his work with patients at Burghölzli at the age of 25.

Developments in the European art world during the first decade of the new century were fast and furious and led to many new "movements" and rapid "secessions." One of the most influential figures to emerge during this period was Stuck's student Wassily

Kandinsky. It was not only because of his art—he is recognized as the "father" of abstract painting—but because of his writing on his conception of the "new" art.[30] He wrote: "I value only those artists who really are artists, that is, who consciously or unconsciously, in an entirely original form, embody the expression of their inner life, who work only for this end and cannot work otherwise."[31] The group that formed around Kandinsky's aim was called "The Blue Rider," after a 1903 painting by Kandinsky. By "inner life," Kandinsky meant the artist's *spiritual* life. In 1911, the year of his first abstract painting, he published, *Concerning the Spiritual in Art.* This influential and seminal work became the manifesto of modern art, and it remains today the foundational text. He worked to separate art from its dependence on the "real" world, to focus art on a "new" world, the *inner* world. Kandinsky called this the artist's "inner need" to work from the promptings of the human soul. By 1912, *Concerning the Spiritual in Art* was widely known in Europe and the United States.

Kandinsky wrote that genuine art expressing the human soul was "prophetic." Indeed, his soul was expressing apocalyptic images before the First World War that pointed to the coming catastrophe. Beginning in 1911, he worked these "inner necessities" into a series of paintings called "Compositions." The allusion to music was deliberate, as Kandinsky yearned to create art that was as "abstract" as music was, that is, free of any dependence on representing the external world, free as it were to more fully express the realities of the inner world, reaching into the depths of the human soul.

Shamdasani, in his detailed introduction to *The Red Book,* describes how apocalyptic imagery was widespread and "in the air" at the turn of the century. He refers to Kandinsky's 1912 description of the "coming universal catastrophe." Jung does not refer to Kandinsky in any of his writings, letters, seminars, or in his *Red Book.*

While Kandinsky related to his apocalyptic images by painting them and creating a new art form (abstract art), Jung related to his apocalyptic visions as pointing toward possible madness and breakdown. Still, for both men, the outbreak of World War I in August 1914, served to confirm the "validity" of these dark experiences, but in quite different ways. For Kandinsky, this confirmation of his inner apocalyptic experiences led to the deepening of his *already* developed theory of the prophetic nature of modern art arising from the artist's inner need, his soul. For Jung, the confirmation of his apocalyptic experiences led to the realization that he was *not* mad, and he was not going mad, but that his experiences were giving birth to the development of a whole new psychology of the human soul and spirit, a psychology quite distinct from Freud's psychoanalysis.[32]

Jung may have seen Kandinsky's painting at the Armory Show ("Improvisation No. 27: Garden of Love II."). He may even have taken it as evidence of the madness that he saw while he took in the paintings and sculptures. What Jung saw set him against modern art for a long time and caused him to reject *as* art what he would do in relation to his inner experiences. It is clear, from the examples of Kandinsky and Hilma af Klint (among *many* others), that artists having inner experiences similar to Jung's did *not* think of these experiences as portending madness. Instead, as artists, they related to these experiences through *expression,* giving birth to new art forms, essential contributions to the making of modern art.

What can be said, I believe, is that the experience of the deep psyche can be the basis for many forms of expression, discovery, development, and creativity. The modernist impulse was illustrating this in *all* aspects of human culture, art, literature, and music as well as the sciences.

From the perspective of Jung's breaking away from the *dogma* of Freud, from his privileging inner experience over outer experience as a root "source," from his developing "new" means, modes, and methods of discovery, Jung was every bit a "modern" despite his self-proclaimed rejection of modern art.

When Jung "fell" into the unconscious with his consciousness intact, though shaken to the core, he took what he experienced as *real,* as real as the outer world we call reality. This is the singular key to exploring one's psyche in the way that Jung records in *The Red Book.* It is the essence of what artists and writers and many others discovered in the same period. Jung experienced the *autonomy* of the figures he met, the geographies he explored, the time scales in which he found himself immersed. He quickly gave up any "agenda" from the outer world and learned that *he* was to be subject to the agenda of the inner world, the agenda of the Other. He realized early on that it was the immersive experience *itself* that was necessary, the crucial step that could not be avoided. Still, the scientist and psychologist in him believed that it all needed understanding, explanation, interpretation, and its potentials drawn out. He realized as well that such work was a *separate* thing, but *not* the primary thing.

What he went through, what he recorded in dialogues, reflections, writings, and images in *The Red Book*, is, I believe, the single best psychological example of what the great poet Wallace Stevens understood: "Not ideas about the thing, but the thing itself."[33] *This is Jung's great gift to the world.*

But how does one take the inner world as real, as Jung and others have done, without its being or becoming madness? There is no simple or single answer to this. When Harvard mathematics Professor George Mackey asked the patient, "How could you, how could you, a mathematician, a man devoted to reason and logical proof ... how could you believe that extraterrestrials were sending you messages? How could you believe you are being recruited by aliens from outer space to save the world?" John Nash, one of the greatest mathematical minds of the 20th century, responsible for fundamental changes in many fields, replied, "Because the ideas I had about supernatural beings came to me the same way that my mathematical ideas did. So, I took them seriously."[34]

The Nobel Prize-winning Nash is proclaiming that his schizophrenic hallucinations and delusions come from the same place as his mathematical ideas. He describes his ideas as coming to him as if fully seeded, and that it was his labor to extract the growth potentials that would then become his fully flowered contributions. This is what Jung did. He took his inner voices and visions seriously. But Nash ended up in the psychiatric ward, and Jung did not. There are few people who can, like Jung and on their own, work their way out of a breakdown when madness threatens. And in today's world, any breakthrough of the autonomous psyche meets with immediate "treatment" in the form of medication to stop it. John Nash, following his recovery (after stopping psychotropic medications), felt that medication was highly overrated and interfered with his recovery. But in today's world, it is unethical and unprofessional to treat such experiences any other way, according to consensus opinion, a basis that John Nash found intolerable in relation to reality as well as the mind.[35]

How then, and in what way, can *The Red Book*, be a guide?

Jung's Imaginal Bounty

Looking back on his experiences recounted in his *Red Book,* Jung concluded: "All my works, all my creative activity, has come from those initial fantasies and dreams which began in 1912. ... Everything I accomplished in later life was already contained in them, although at first only in the form of emotions and images."[36]

It will take many years for scholars to trace the lines of development from the *Red Book* experiences to the completed major works. As Hillman and Shamdasani argue in *The Lament of the Dead,* most everything of consequence for a true understanding of Jung's work will need to be worked through again. This work is well underway, but no matter how rich the bounty of Jung's major works, I do not think this is the way to appreciate *The Red Book* as a guide for the coming time. We need to realize that what Jung was saying and doing—that the source of his great ideas, and his creativity in relation to them—was generated within his imaginal experiences of the Other. *That* was what provided the material for his greatest works, *that* was the source and origin of his ideas.

If the experiences of the Other hold the seeds of future development, as Jung says, then the crucial thing would be for *each* person to enter the *imaginal* ground and develop a relationship with the Other. What these experiences will be, what will be required to host them and to engage what the Other presents, cannot be predicted because it will be *unique* to each person. *The Red Book* tells the incredible story of what happened when Jung undertook *his* "experiment." Its *contents,* as well as the fruit of those experiences, must not become an object of imitation. One must seek one's own.

Jung says: "My science was the only way I had of extricating myself from that chaos. Otherwise, the material would have trapped me in its thicket, strangled me like the jungle creepers."[37] Few would have the science that Jung had to deal with experiences of the Other. But my reading of *The Red Book* leads me to discount Jung's notion that it was his *science* that enabled him to deal with the experiences. Rather, I believe it was Jung's readiness and persistent entering the imaginal space where the Other presented itself, inviting Jung to participate in the *reality* of the Other, to host, day after day, what manifested. Jung's eros *acts* of engagement in dialogue and expressive works of imagery I call the "Eros of Alterity," the literal *doing* it. That to me is the critical factor. When consciousness takes this form in relation to the Other, the Other will bring forth what cannot be predicted but will invariably, like dreams, bring forth the seeds of the future.

The Red Book, more than any other psychological document, lays bare the *story* quality of encounters with the Other, whether in dreams, visions, fantasies or active imaginations, including the expression of images (which are stories stopped in time). The importance of this is ignored, as most everyone wants to turn these experiences into "other" stories, stories called explanations, interpretations, understandings. These are stories, too, though clothing them in scientific garb disguises their nature. When this happens, we drop out of engaging psyche's unique stories. This can only be done through continuing the story, by becoming participants (characters) in the stories, by following what is *next*. This ongoingness and the immersion in stories are clear in *The Red Book*, and are a major aspect of the "power" and "dramatic draw" of *The Red Book*. This is the art not only of *The Red Book* itself, but the art that Jung engaged in with the living presence of the Other. As Robert Olen Butler says, "Art does not come from ideas. Art does not come from the mind. Art comes from the place where you dream."[38]

Jung's *Enantiodromia* and the Coming Guest

In 1982, I suggested that one of the major keys to understanding the meaning and purpose of Jung's work lies in his September 2, 1960, letter to Sir Herbert Read.[39] Now that *The Red Book* is available, I suggest that this letter is also an essential key to understanding the implications of *The Red Book,* as well as to how it may serve as a guide to navigating the future.

The occasion of Jung's writing to Read was Jung's appreciation for Read's essay "The Art of Art Criticism," published along with others' tributes celebrating Jung's 85th birthday.[40] The letter is long and complex—complex because Jung seemed to write in different voices in the letter. The first four paragraphs are a reprise of Jung's familiar scold against modern art with an emphasis on Joyce and Picasso. In the fifth paragraph, Jung becomes more reflective, ending the paragraph with a crucial question.

> The great problem of our time is that we don't understand what is happening to the world. We are confronted with the darkness of the soul, the unconscious. It sends up its dark and unrecognizable urges. It hollows out and hacks up the shapes of our culture and its historical dominants. We have no dominants anymore, they are in the future. Our values are shifting, everything loses its certainty, even *sanctissima causalitas* has descended from the throne of the axioma and has become a mere field of probability. Who is the awe-inspiring guest who knocks at our door so portentously?[41]

Jung returns to his antagonism against modern art by saying that the "creative artist will not trust it," that is, what the awe-inspiring guest presents. I do not think this is true but is an example of Jung's complex continuing to speak. The rest of the paragraph continues in this vein. The next paragraph brings Jung to express what I consider to be the central key to Jung's published work, including *The Red Book*:

> We have simply got to listen to what the psyche spontaneously says to us. What the dream, which is not manufactured by us, says is *just so.* ... It is the great dream which has always spoken through the artist as a mouthpiece. All his love and passion (his 'values') flow towards the coming guest to proclaim his arrival.[42]

Here we have an extraordinary conception of the artist as a mouthpiece of the great dream, as welcoming the "coming guest." It is clear that Jung here uses the "coming guest" as a metaphor for the essential nature of what visited him all those years ago beginning in 1912. And here, Jung says it is the *artist* who welcomes the coming guest. To me, this points to the unfolding *enantiodromia* of Jung's complex against modern art. It is implicit that Jung declares himself an artist and his art as welcoming the arrival of the coming guest.

The next paragraph shows perhaps the last vestige of Jung's railing against the negative aspects of modern art as showing "the intensity of our prejudice against the future." This mischaracterizes the very nature of modern art—particularly its prophetic aspects described by Kandinsky and others.[43]

The following paragraph articulates Jung's "new" voice about what is at issue:

> What is the great Dream? It consists of the many small dreams and the many acts of humility and submission to their hints. It is the future and the picture of the new world, which we do not understand yet. We cannot know better than the unconscious and its intimations. There is a fair chance of finding what we seek in vain in our conscious world. Where else could it be?[44]

To me, this is Jung's best description not only of the major purpose of his work but also of the nature of what he was doing in those early years that became the origin of his later and most profound work. This also indicates what *each* person can do to welcome the coming guest. It is an *individual* task. This individual task of welcoming the coming guest is the key to how *The Red Book* can be considered a guide in the coming time. It shows how Jung welcomed the coming guest and serves as a reminder to all of what is possible. Each person, in welcoming the coming guest, will have a different and unique experience. This is as it needs to be and as it should be. Jung's crucial point is made unmistakable by Harold Rosenberg:

Art consists of one-person creeds, one-psyche cultures. Its direction is toward a society in which the experiences of each will be the ground of a unique, inimitable form—in short, a society in which everyone will be an artist. Art in our time can have no other social aim—an aim dreamed of by modern poets, from Lautréamont to Whitman, Joyce, and the Surrealists, and which is embodied in the essence of the continuing revolt against domination by tradition.[45]

Yes, the artist in *each* of us.

A few months before Jung died, he received a gift from a young artist as an expression of gratitude for Jung's work. It was an *abstract* painting. Jung wrote back to the artist and said, "… the religious view of the world, thrown out at the front door, creeps in again by the back, albeit in strangely altered form—so altered that nobody has yet noticed it. Thus does modern art celebrate the great carnival of God."[46] Jung's inner battle with modern art was done, its *enantio-dromia* complete.

Do what you can, *now*, to welcome the coming guest.

Endnotes

[1] Psychiatrists at one time were called "alienists" because they worked with psychic experiences "alien" to normal consciousness. The more modern, and postmodern term, "other," has had a long and varied history in psychoanalysis, as well as the arts, literature, and criticism. I use the term here not so much in the technical sense of Lacan or Bion, or others, but in the simplest sense of *not constructed or constituted by ego consciousness.* I capitalize it to emphasize the *feeling* sense of "presence" and its myriad "personifications." This use of Other also lessens the proprietary claims of the ego.

[2] These ways of seeing the dream (as well as other manifestations of experience originating outside of consciousness) are described more fully in my book, *Psyche Speaks* (1987; reissued 2015). The gravity I refer to, pulls the ego to engage the offerings of the Other *imaginally.* This contrasts to the ego pulling these offerings into interpretation, explanation, understanding, and other more familiar, favored, and proprietary narratives. For most, the former is weak and the latter is all consuming.

[3] It was my privilege to experience some of the text and images of the *Red Book* during my early analysis with James and Hilde Kirsch in the 1960s. So, the impact of the material has been working on me for a long time. As Shamdasani notes in his *Introduction* to *The Red Book*: "Jung let the following individuals read and/or look at *Liber Novus*: Richard Hull, Tina Keller, James Kirsch, Ximena Roelli de Angulo (as a child), and Kurt Wolff." He further comments that, "It appears that he allowed those people to read *Liber Novus* whom he fully trusted and whom he felt had a full grasp of his ideas. Quite a number of his students did not fit into this category" (C.G. Jung, *The Red Book: Liber Novus*, ed. Sonu Shamdasani, tr. John Peck, Mark Kyburz, and Sonu Shamdasani (New York, NY: W. W. Norton, 2009), 215). I appreciated the trust the Kirsches expressed in me in letting me have access. After seeing the full published text and seeing all the images, it surely was a small part, but it made all the difference nonetheless.

[4] In *Beethoven's Hair,* Russell Martin tells the dramatic story of Beethoven's "use" of his illnesses as a way of stimulating the depths of his

imagination. See Russell Martin, *Beethoven's Hair* (New York, NY: Random House, 2002).

5 The most important and enlightening work on Beethoven's unique-ness and his spiritual development is found in J. W. N. Sullivan's *Beethoven: His Spiritual Development* (New York, NY: Alfred A. Knoff, 1954).

6 For an excellent review of the scene and a valuable perspective on the importance of the Armory show, see Rosenberg's 1963 review on the 50th anniversary in Harold Rosenberg, "The Armory Show: Revolution Reenacted." *New Yorker* (1963) April 6: 99-115.

7 The kind of art Roosevelt championed can best be seen in John Gast's "American Progress" (1872). A good reference with commentary and image is available from the Archive for Research in Archetypal Symbolism at https://aras.org/sites/default/files/docs/00043AmericanProgress_0.pdf

8 The term "manifest destiny" has undergone many changes in meaning since its first appearance in 1845. Underlying all is the root idea that America is "special," not only among nations but in the "eyes of God." This view is now in another upswing that affects everything. The best review of the oscillations and strength of "manifest destiny" is Ronald Schenk's *American Soul: A Cultural Narrative* (New Orleans: Spring Journal, 2012). For a review of this important book, see Russell Lock-hart, "Review of *American Soul: A Cultural Narrative* by Ronald Schenk," *Psychological Perspectives* (2014) 57 (4): 454-459.

9 Leila Mechlin, "Lawless Art," *Art and Progress* 4, 1913: 840-841.

10 There is no absolute documentation that Jung attended the Armory Show. Shamdasani has examined what evidence there is and conclu-ded that "he likely attended the Armory Show," (C.G. Jung, *The Red Book*, 203) adding that Jung discusses the art of Duchamp and Picasso together in the 1925 seminar. Jung would have seen the art of Du-champ and Picasso together at the Armory and this *direct* experience is the likely source because of so little in the way of reference material on modern art in Jung's library.

11 Jung commented on Stuck's painting in *Wandlungen und Symbole der Libido,* published in 1912. Listing the many variations of dream con-tent that is sexual in nature, he refers to the "variations of Franz Stuck, whose snake-pictures bear significant titles like 'Vice,' 'Sin,' or 'Lust.'

The mixture of anxiety and lust is perfectly expressed in the sultry atmosphere of these pictures. ..." See C.G. Jung, *Symbols of Transformation*, in *CW*, vol. 5 (Princeton, NJ: Princeton University Press, 1967), 8-9. Stuck's most famous painting, entitled "Sin," is shown in plate 10 of the book.

[12] From the standpoint of art, Jung's daytime personality was at home with the general representational and figurative contents of art. But from early on, it is arguable that his nighttime personality was drawn to something "darker," something "behind" and "underneath," at the very least, something "different." Thus, his attraction to the work of Böcklin and Stuck as well as his attraction to the occult. The same sense of difference applies to Hitler, whose daylight personality was attracted most of all to Vermeer, but whose nighttime personality was drawn to Böcklin and Stuck. Stuck was Hitler's favorite artist even in childhood, see https://en.wikipedia.org/wiki/Franz_Stuck.

[13] July 8, 1947. Gerhard Adler, *C.G. Jung Letters*. Trans. by R. F. C. Hull. Vol. 1, 1906-1950 (Princeton, NJ: Princeton University Press, 1973), 469.

[14] Late in life his assessment profoundly changed under the influence of Sir Herbert Read. I explore the significance of this further on.

[15] Jung initially called Joyce and Picasso's art "schizophrenic," (David Cohen, "Herbert Read and Psychoanalysis", in *Art Criticism since 1900*. Ed. Malcolm Gee (Manchester: Manchester University Press, 1993), 174) but in revised versions used the expression "analogous to."

[16] Jung was making the point that analysis by someone else was more crucial than having only a self-analysis, as was the case with Freud. Freud scoffed at the notion that his own self-analysis would be inferior to Jung's being in analysis with Maria Moltzer (see endnote 23 for detail).

[17] See Deirdre Bair, *Jung: A Biography*. (Boston: Little, Brown and Company, 2003), especially her detailed account of this period in Chapter 7, "My *Self*/Myself."

[18] This characterization of the late 1913 period is from an interview with Jung by Mircea Eliade at the 1952 Eranos Conference. The interview, entitled "Recontre avec Jung," was published in *Combat: de la Résistance à la Révolution*, in Paris, October 9, 1952. An abridged version of this interview is available in *C.G. Jung Speaking: Interviews and*

Encounters. Edited by William McGuire and R. F. C. Hull (Princeton, NJ: Princeton University Press, 1977). In this interview, Jung recalls his troubled state in 1914, and remembers his lecture on schizophrenia to be delivered in Scotland, and says, "I'll be speaking of myself! I'll go mad after reading out this paper." (p. 233). After this lecture Jung learned that war had broken out, and he realized his dreams and visions were referring to the state of the world and not his mind. Jung says that deepening and validating and working out this relation between the collective unconscious and manifest reality occupied him from then on.

[19] The difficulty with interpretation and understanding was essential in leading Jung to the decisive step of developing an entirely *different* basis of dealing with the interior flow of dreams, visions, voices, and other such manifestations. Jung's capacity to hold the tension and stay with the doubts and uncertainties of "not knowing" is an extraordinary example of Keats's "negative capability." For one of the best treatments of this essential idea, see Andrés Rodríguez, *Book of the Heart: The Poetics, Letters, and Life of John Keats* (Hudson: Lindisfarne Press, 1993), especially the chapter entitled, "The Penetralium of Mystery."

[20] See C.G. Jung, *Memories, Dreams, Reflections* (New York, NY: Vintage Books, 1963), 186.

[21] For the vision and the painting, see "Descent into Hell in the Future" in C.G. Jung, *The Red Book*, Chapter 5.

[22] Jung, *Memories, Dreams, Reflections*, 185. Why Jung calls her a psychopath is not documented.

[23] For Shamdasani's identification of Maria Moltzer as the voice, see his *Introduction* to *The Red Book*, 199, and his 1995 article, "Memories, Dreams, Omissions," also *Jung in Context: A Reader*, (ed.) Paul Bishop (London: Routledge, 1999), 129. He says Jung knew her from 1912-1918. But Jung knew her as well at Burghölzli. Moltzer, a Dutch woman from a wealthy brewing family, became a nurse in order to combat the destructive effects of alcohol. In 1910, Jung wrote to Freud telling him that "between the two ladies there is naturally a loving jealousy over me" (Sigmund Freud, C.G. Jung, *The Freud/Jung Letters*, (ed.) William McGuire and Tr. by Ralph Manheim and R. F. C. Hull (Princeton, NJ: Princeton University Press, 1974), 351-52). Jung was referring to Maria Moltzer and Fraulein Boeddinghaus (see 351 n2,

and 352 n3). A few months earlier, Jung wrote to Freud: "The pre-requisite for a good marriage, it seems to me, is the license to be unfaithful" (ibid., 289).

24 It was from this experience with her, that Jung developed the concept of anima, and the idea that it was through the anima that a man experiences his soul. Moltzer also originated the idea of the intuitive function, which Jung acknowledged (see C.G. Jung, *Psychological Types*, in *CW*, vol. 6 (Princeton, NJ: Princeton University Press, 1971), par. 773, note 68).

25 Freud wrote in a December 26, 1912 letter to Ernest Jones that Jung "is behaving like the florid fellow that he is. The master that analyzed him could only have been Fräulein Moltzer, and he is so foolish as to be proud of this work of a woman with whom he is having an affair." See Sonu Shamdasani, *Jung and the Making of Modern Psychology: The Dream of A Science* (Cambridge: Cambridge University Press, 2003), 52). Jolande Jacobi, in her interview with Gene Nameche (interviewer for the Jung Oral Archives), said this about the affair: "I heard from others, about the time before he [Jung] met Toni Wolff, that he had a love affair there in the Burghölzli with a girl—what was her name? Moltzer." For more complete discussion, see Sonu Sham-dasani, *Cult Fictions: C.G. Jung and the Founding of Analytical Psychology* (London: Routledge, 1998), 57.

26 Moltzer was considered one of the "feminine element … from Zurich" (Sigmund Freud, C.G. Jung, *The Freud/Jung Letters*, 440). She can be seen with the others in the photograph of those attending the 1911 Weimar Congress (Sigmund Freud, C.G. Jung, *The Freud/Jung Letters*, insert between 444-445).

27 C.G. Jung, *The Red Book*, 204 n111. Shamdasani cites from the Fannie Bowditch Katz diaries, which have detailed records of her analysis with Moltzer as well as observations on many aspects of the analytical scene.

28 Riklin worked with Jung on the word association experiments at Burg-hözli and married Jung's cousin, Sophie Fiechter (See Deirdre Bair, *Jung: A Biography*, 222). Shamdasani notes that Moltzer had argued that the unconscious was art and had convinced Riklin that he was a misunderstood artist and led him away from being an analyst (see Shamdasani, "Introduction," *The Red Book*, 199). Mary Foote was one

of the American modernists who exhibited at the Armory show. Years later, Jung was impressed by her paintings of American Indians and how she captured their inner spirit. He took on the "drab little painter" (Deirdre Bair, *Jung: A Biography,* 361) for analysis in 1927, and soon she became the transcriber of Jung's seminars. For a generous appreciation of Mary Foote, see Deirdre Bair, *Jung: A Biography*, 360-363.

29 In a section omitted in the English edition of Jung's *Memories, Dreams, Reflections*, Jung speaks of the woman whose voice had told him his own work was art, and how this *same* woman "exercised a disastrous influence in men. She succeeded in talking a colleague of mine into believing that he was a misunderstood artist. He believed it and was shattered" (Sonu Shamdasani, *Cult Fictions: C.G. Jung and the Founding of Analytical Psychology*, 16). The colleague is most certainly Riklin, and the woman in question, Moltzer. It is this feature of hers that I believe forms Jung's basis for calling her a psychopath, in the sense of over determining the life of another. Jung referred to Sabina Spielrein as a hysteric, never as a psychopath. This is a further evidence that the anima voice was not Spielrein, as commonly assumed, but Maria Moltzer.

30 If Kandinsky was the "father" of abstract painting, then it was Hilma af Klint who was the "mother" and who antedated Kandinsky by five years. Klint heard voices that announced, "You are to proclaim a new philosophy of life and you yourself are to be a part of the new kingdom. Your labours will bear fruit." (see https://en.wikipedia.org/wiki/Hilma_af_Klint). This sort of inner prompting led to her first series of abstract paintings in 1906, entitled, "Primordial Chaos." She kept careful notes of her experiences which came to fill more than 150 notebooks and yielded more than 1200 paintings. She trained at the Swedish Academy of Fine Arts, but her real teachers were the figures she experienced in her inner world which she described as painting "through" her.

31 See Richard Stratton, "Preface to the Dover Edition" in Wassily Kandinsky, *Concerning the Spiritual in Art* (New York, NY: Dover Publications, 1977), vii.

32 While most characterizations of the differences between Freud's psychoanalysis and Jung's Analytical Psychology focus on their theories and concepts, what needs more attention is the crucial

difference between how experiences of the deep psyche are *related to*. This is made clear with the publication of *The Red Book*.

[33] Wallace Stevens, *The Collected Poems of Wallace Stevens* (New York, NY: Alfred A. Knoff, 1954), 534.

[34] Sylvia Nasar, *A Beautiful Mind* (New York, NY: Simon & Schuster, 1998), 11.

[35] Children come with a rich inner life, much of which becomes imaginal. This tends to be ever more neglected and suppressed as the child grows and the hegemony of the outer life nearly extinguishes the inner world. Central to a child's early life is *story*. This is also the case when the inner life erupts into overwhelming experiences such as occur in psychosis. For a "story" approach to psychosis and other major manifestations of the disturbed mind, see George Mecouch, *While Psychiatry Slept* (Santa Fe: Belly Song Press, 2017).

[36] Jung, *Memories, Dreams, Reflections*, 192.

[37] Ibid.

[38] Robert Olen Butler, *From Where You Dream: The Process of Writing Fiction* (New York, NY: Grove Press, 2005), 13.

[39] Jung's letter to Read (Gerhard Adler, *C.G. Jung Letters*. Trans. by R. F. C. Hull. Vol. 2, 1951-1960 (Princeton, NJ: Princeton University Press, 1975, 586-92) is one of only two illustrated letters in the two volumes of Jung's letters. It is not clear why Jung's letter to Karl Abraham in 1908 was chosen (Gerhard Adler, *C.G. Jung Letters*. Vol. 1, insert between 4-5). But the Read letter is of major historical importance and I believe the editors (Adler and Jaffé) recognized this. There is also a photograph of Read's visit to Kusnacht in 1949 (Plate III). At Eranos, in 1952, Read gave a lecture entitled, "The Dynamics of Art," in which he defended modern art and took Jung to task for his mistaken views on modern art. Jung walked out of the lecture, and this nearly ended their friendship. The rift healed. Read, knighted in 1953, became the chief editor of Jung's *Collected Works* along with Gerhard Adler, Michael Fordham, and William McGuire, with R. F. C. Hull as translator. It is intriguing, to say the least, that someone who was not an analyst was in this position. Sir Herbert Read was a poet, novelist, literary critic and art historian and an avid proponent of symbolist and modernist art movements and their importance in education.

[40] Adler, *C.G. Jung Letters*. Vol. 2, 586 n1.

41 Ibid., 590. Adler cites Jung's earliest childhood dream (the phallus as man-eater dream) and a "parallel" figure ("the pilgrim of eternity") described by the Irish poet George Russell (known also as Æ) in his *The Candle of Vision*. Adler says this book had a profound effect on Jung, though Jung does not reference Æ in any of his writings or letters. Æ is important because he discovered active imagination in 1884 and worked his conversations with dream and imaginal experiences into his poetry and his paintings. For a detailed look at Æ's contributions, see Russell Lockhart, *Psyche Speaks: A Jungian Approach to Self and World* (Wilmette: Chiron Publications, 1987; reissued Everett: The Lockhart Press, 2015), especially the chapter entitled, "Æ's Augury."

42 Adler, *C.G. Jung Letters*. Vol. 2, 591.

43 Ibid. Read replied to Jung's letter on October 19, 1960: "The whole process of fragmentation, as you rightly call it, is not, in my opinion, willfully destructive: the motive has always been (since the beginning of the century) to destroy the conscious image of perfection (the classical ideal of objectivity) in order to release new forces from the unconscious. This 'turning inwards'...is precisely a longing to be put in touch with the Dream, that is to say (as you say), the future. But in the attempt the artist has his 'dark and unrecognizable urges,' and they have overwhelmed him. He struggles like a man overwhelmed by a flood. He clutches at fragments, at driftwood and floating rubbish of all kinds. But he has to release the flood in order to get nearer to the Dream. My defense of modern art has always been based on this realization: that art must die in order to live, that a new source of life must be tapped under the crust of tradition" (Adler, *C.G. Jung Letters*. Vol. 2, 591 n8). Read makes clear that modern art cannot be only based on the "spirit of the time," as Jung claimed, but in its various ways was expressing the "spirit of the depths."

44 Adler, *C.G. Jung Letters*. Vol. 2, 591-592.

45 Harold Rosenberg, "Metaphysical Feelings in Modern Art," *Critical Inquiry* 2 (1975) 217-232.

46 Adler, *C.G. Jung Letters*. Vol. 2, 604.

"This Incandescent Matter":
Shudder, Shimmer, Stammer, Solitude

Josephine Evetts-Secker

This paper attempts to be as attentive as it can be to Jung's language; to explore its impact as a way of feeling into the integrity of the "content"; to let it register, for this will affect my reception of the images as well as the argument. Such attunement to text establishes essential reader-author trust.

Liber Novus, claimed by Jung to be the "nucleus" of his later work, was known to informed Jungians only through "a few tantalizing glimpses" until it was made available to the public in 2009.[1] With little knowledge of its existence and no knowledge of its imminent publication, in the September of that same year, I dreamed:

> We are in an upstairs room, above a big, ancient church. On a large lectern, there is a very large book, lying open. I assume it must be a Bible, but it was more like the Duc de Berry's *Grande Heures*. As we gather around it and I go toward the lectern, the volume bursts into flames. The dream words were: "it self-immolates!" I am stunned, amazed.

The next night:

> I have a sense of moving through huge buildings, on ground floors. I come to the end. I reach a door. I open it and stand looking out on a vast landscape. I have a sense of reaching the end of "something" and experiencing wholly new vistas.

The room I recognised as the library of a London church where we held choir practices and where I first sang polyphonic music. In the following spring, 2010, when I first saw Jung's newly published tome, it felt familiar. A strange, synchronistic introduction to the "beautiful and riddlesome totality" that was to challenge me.[2] The residual energy of those dreams helped shape my response to Jung's major opus.

Ulrich Hoerni rightly assumed that "competent interpretations will be given in forthcoming secondary literature."[3] Papers in this volume attest to that. But this is not an interpretive paper. My aim is simply to record personal responses to Jung's "incandescent matter."[4] This incandescence shook and still stirs me. Written in volatile times of cultural crisis, Jung's goal was to evolve a "new world view and god-image" in the throes of such crisis.[5] Whereas Nietzsche preached the death of God, Jung yearned for God to be reconceived, renewed, reimagined. He "wanted to go on living with a new god."[6] His imagination labours at this task. His ignited mine, for this is also my task.

As always in the background to my response to psyche lies Adam Phillips' dictum that we should not make psychoanalytical work into a "science of the sensible passions, as though the aim of psychoanalysis was to make people more intelligible to themselves rather than to realize how strange they are."[7] The uncanny strangeness of his own interior world Jung reveals throughout this monumental work that he chose not to publish in his lifetime. Uncanny is Jung's word as well as Freud's.

In the literature Hoerni predicted would follow publication, *The Red Book* has provoked intense reactions. It is a "poetic meditation";[8] a "daunting hermeneutical challenge";[9] a "work of conscience";[10] a "Gnosis for modernity";[11] a "Monstrosity, magnificent and grotesque";[12] "existential and postmodern."[13] Though experienced as alarmingly impressive, few have so far agreed with Giegerich that *The Red Book* fails, being "absolutely esoteric."[14]

Such diverse responses might remind us of a truth articulated in relation to Dostoyevsky's *Underground Man*, that "it is the fate of all great texts to be both mutable and many-faceted enough that every generation of readers can seek their own image within them."[15]

As an undergraduate I was set an essay topic about a poet I liked, instructed to justify the objection that his poetry "rings no bells," being linguistically and contextually local and idiosyncratic, ignoring The Tradition. I considered this fallible as chief criterion of value;

ringing allusive bells, which might be richly fueled by personal complexes in the service of art. With this critical approach still hovering, decades later I entered Jung's epic search for his "Way of What is to Come." Page by page, I experienced a veritable allusive tinnitus! Standard critical language proves inadequate to describe the density of reference; Jung goes so far beyond typical forms of intercultural, intertextual echo. If Hermes is the god of the pre-position, "between," his foot-and-finger-prints are everywhere, pointing in every conceivable direction, sometimes simultaneously! As Paul Bishop says, he goes far "beyond mere allusiveness."[16] Nevertheless, these resonances are peculiarly satisfying, embedding us culturally while pushing us beyond creedal comfort.

The central organizing convention of the *nekyia* is already well documented. So many reverberating tales of underworld descending: Orpheus, Odysseus, Inanna and so on. In our daily praxis, we encounter such personal, perhaps humbler, *katabases* in dreams. Typically, there are guides ... Anubis and Charon, even dogs and dolphins, angel escorts of various kinds. Clearly familiar with Dante's Virgil, Jung evolved Philemon from archaic sources. He was already a familiar soul-companion. Many Jungian writers have amplified this.

For me, numberless bells rang. Anglophone readers might also feel from time to time the energy of Bunyan's Evangelist leading his dreaming Pilgrim to the Celestial city. On arrival, the Pilgrim "saw that there was a way to Hell, even from the Gates of Heaven as well as from the City of Destruction." Pilgrim sets out on his fantasy progress: "As I walked through the wilderness of this world, I lighted on a certain place, where was a den, and I laid me down in that place to sleep; and as I slept I dreamed a dream. I dreamed, and behold I saw a man clothed in rags ..." This coloured my setting out into Jung's "eerie wasteland."[17] Bunyan's ragged wretch seeks the very salvation that Jung is compelled to challenge.

A reader such as I am, exposed to an English literature probably unknown to Jung, might also recognize figures like Alice's soul-guide, her White Rabbit, seducing her underground. Like Christian, Alice also finally woke from her dream's underworld. A recent, innovative verse-novel offers Sigmund Freud himself as psychopomp for 21st-

century man in an all-too current predicament, ringing the changes
on Dante's dark forest.

> When I was about halfway through life
> (always a cheery moment) I lost my wife
> to another man, and as is the natural way
> when a woman leaves her man of yesterday,
> she kept our child;
> 　　　　　　　　 … so at a stroke
> I found I was a lonely single bloke …
> Losing family and home, he takes his son on holiday to some
> engineered amusement park, not Dante's great forest!
> The theme park entrance is a lofty gate
> festooned with flags, and made to imitate
> a crude portal of rusticated stone,
> although it's actually made with blown
> concrete. Above the massive lintel rise
> three words in silhouette against the skies:
> 'Live the Dream.'[18]

They enter a fake world of "animatronic figures", "holograms,"
waxworks, every kind of simulation and tableaux, AstroTurf, plastic
headstones, neon moons. Freud invites him to "walk with me" and
shows him artificially contrived mythological haunts such as Circe's
island. *Homo denarius* is advertised at every turn. It is a wittily
serious, troublingly funny, whimsically satirical narrative of what the
author calls "Imagineering." This illuminates compellingly the
integrity of Jung's imagining beside this Disneyfied underworld, such
as we might fear we inhabit, the fake world of Trump, where sensible
categories of truth and authenticity break down. How prefabricated
this spirit of the times! The distinction between authentic Imagination and artificial Imagineering is helpfully provocative.

　　Jung's driving need was to validate inner experience, announcing
in his opening of "The Way of What Is to Come:" "If I speak in the
spirit of this time, I must say: no one and nothing can justify what I
must proclaim to you. Justification is superfluous to me, since I have
no choice, but I must."[19] John Milton's sense of his solemn task came to

mind. Leaving sublime heights and depths, the poet approaches earth again, changing key to introduce his epic of the human Fall:

> No more of talk where God or Angel guest
> With Man, as with his friend, familiar used
> To sit indulgent, and with him partake
> Rural repast ... I now must change
> Those notes to tragic —
> What in me is dark
> Illumine, what is low, raise and support
> That to the highth of this great Argument
> I may assert Eternal providence
> And justify the ways of God to men.[20]

Jung's own solemn tone and mission sometimes sounds like this, and one might also hear it in Nietzsche, speaking of his grandiose task, "to prepare a moment of supreme coming-to-oneself on the part of mankind ..."[21]

Paul Bishop notes the omnipresence of Nietzsche in Jung's experience and writing. In so many passages, not only in conjuring up Zarathustra but implicit everywhere, this background presence throughout is what might be experienced as Jung's own personal *ecce homo*. Occasionally, the lingering shadow of Dostoyevsky's *Underground Man* (a book Jung must have known) tempers Jung's apologia. The Russian's vivid self-abnegation is compensated by grandiosity. Like that of Nietzsche, it throws Jung's psychological self-assessments into relief. Their almost Messianic grandiosity was clearly understood by Jung.

It would be tedious to pursue such wide-ranging allusiveness further. What is striking is that no doubt in each culture or language context in which *The Red Book* is read, allusions specific to that culture will erupt, colouring and intensifying individual experience. All might be tracked archetypally.

Related to these global undercurrents, we might consider the experimental mixing of styles and genres, technical innovations compelled by other contemporary explorations of inner reality in the wake of the "discovery of the unconscious," even outside strictly psychoanalytic work. Kierkegaard developed his "dialectical lyric" under the same pressure in *Fear and Trembling*.[22] Hillman speaks of *The Red Book* in terms of "psychodramatics rather than psycho-dynamics."[23] Mixing of styles, mixing of genres, mixing of categories. Constantly ringing the changes: picaresque, autobiography, poetic memoir, allegory, poetic prose and pure lyric poetry, autobiography, soliloquy, Ignatian examination of conscience, confession, classical dialogue between soul and body, explicit passages of philosophical, theological and psychological exegesis, dithyrambic energies recalling Nietzsche.[24]

The writing moves far beyond most conventions of allusiveness, so that we might invoke New Testament Greek's *amphiballein*, positing an amphilectical technique alongside the dialectical. *Symballein* unites two parts; *diaballein* divides them; *amphiballein* casts all around, drawing all into the surrounding net of voices, dialects, and images. This multiplicity illustrates the "Pandemonium of Images" that Hillman locates in Jung's own self-analytical work.[25] This is how Jung coped with his own process, turning inward and letting the storms "transpose themselves into images," in advocacy of the reality of the psyche, giving fact and fiction equal validity. Shamdasani reports Jung's realization that "I went about with these fantastic figures as though they were patients and I was analysing them."[26] This aliveness is compelling, creating relationship between the characters and reader as though in a novel. I felt myself as participant on location, often resisting what I saw, heard and overheard, while also registering deep satisfactions and disturbing epiphanies; witnessing and undergoing inner experiences episo-dically. Chapters are deemed Adventures, and, like Don Quixote, I was compelled by each thing that happens next with the same ineluctable openness.

Such mixing of genres strict classicists would deplore. But by the 20th century, artists had gone far beyond initial condemnations of compounding in such modes as "tragi-comedy," "tragical historical," etc., that Shakespeare, profound psychologist that he was, recognised as psychically valid.[27] Contemporary critical theorists now advocate "Conceptual Blending Theory," perhaps enforced by Joyce studies. *The Red Book*'s morphing and mixing of styles and stylistic registers speaks to me of the "riddlesome multifariousness of the world"[28] in which Jung seeks reconciliation and union, with no injury to the integrity of contradiction and paradox. In all this I hear a polyphony of voices, a contrapuntal, contrary music.

All of the above acted as background music to my reading, sometimes muted, sometimes assertive, resounding on my particular wavelengths. What follows is more significant and pressing. The matter of incandescence. From the very beginning of the *Liber Novus*, we are challenged by experiences of ultimacy, trajectories into depth and height. We are introduced to the Overwhelming in Jung's statement of 1957 reflecting on the years during which he dared faithfully to elaborate to the limit the "inner images"; what had "burst forth from the unconscious, and flooded me like an enigmatic stream and threatened to break me." He was "swamped" with excess and, with some trepidation, even questioned his own sanity, admitting to Mircea Eliade that as a psychiatrist, he was worried that he was risking a "schizophrenia" as he attended to dreams and visions that "came to me from the subsoil of the collective unconscious."[29] He described having been "hit" by a "stream of lava."[30] Nevertheless, he chose to persist, to "deepen and validate" his discoveries.

This brought to his mind Nietzsche's problem, who, he felt, finally escaped the anguish of inner tension and oppositions by surrendering to madness. Jung disparaged Nietzsche's panegyric on inspiration,[31] in his early paper on cryptomnesia as a "description of the impotence of consciousness in face of the tremendous automatism driving up from the unconscious. Only this elemental force can wrench from oblivion the oldest and most delicate traces in a man's memory while he retains his full senses."[32] Such an evaluation of the mood, of being in a state of inspiration, "completely beside yourself" as Nietzsche extolled it, "inundated with alien ideas," a "consuming fire," was vital for Jung to adjudicate, since he would also experience the indomitable force of his own fantastic imagination during those years of composing and illustrating his black and red books. He concludes that "the work of genius is very different; it fetches up these distant fragments in order to build them into a new and meaningful structure." As Jung dealt with his own incandescence, he needed the balanced formulations of the late 1950s when he saw Zarathustra from a psychological perspective, supposing him to be caught between counteracting forces, unable to benefit from their tension, suppressing psyche's regulating function. He asserts the importance of

> coming to terms with the unconscious. The position of the ego must be maintained as being of equal value to the counter position of the unconscious and vice versa. ... the rediscovered unconscious often has a really dangerous effect on the ego ... a liberated unconscious can thrust the ego aside and overwhelm it. There is a danger of the ego losing its head, so to speak, that it will not be able to defend itself against the pressure of affective factors ... a situation often encountered at the beginning of schizophrenia. This danger would not exist, or would not be so acute, if the process of having it out with the unconscious could somehow divest the affects of their dynamism. And this is what does in fact happen when the counter-position is aestheticized or intellectualized. But the confrontation with the unconscious must be a many-sided one, for the transcendent function is not a partial process running a conditioned course; it is a total and integral event in which all aspects are, or should be, included.[33]

This caution he himself needed during those intensely creative and disturbing years of composition, subjecting himself to his own counsel to "have it out with the unconscious." Speaking with Salome about his "tears and laughter," being "rigid with tension," he concludes that "excessive tension seems to indicate the ultimate and highest possibility of feeling."[34] Salome brings him back to earth, responding that he has simply "fallen in love." So, Jung constantly interrogates his own excess.

In reading this visionary apologia, in "the service of the inexplicable," readers also can feel overwhelmed by the language of extremity, often theatrical and spectacular.[35] The verb "seize" is played as fugue with innumerable variations. Soul and will are "seized" and "grasped" by intense emotion, longing, or fear. At the same time, words strain to stretch beyond common feeling; we encounter the unbearable, unfathomable, unspeakable, immeasurable, endless, boundless, infinity. Horizons are unending, encounters are tremendous. There is often a sense of the sublime.

The vocabulary of light and fire burns everywhere; images are charged with radiance. Objects like garments shine and glow. This is most potent in the lyrical interludes where "streams of fire broke from [his] radiating body" as he "surges through blazing flames."[36] He is exposed to the "sun's active light and singeing power."[37] He "staggers drunk with fire," where imagery of intoxication, heat, and light coalesce. The "terrible" is always close by. Such intensity graduates to ultimate inflation: "I was completely sun ... as if I were the sun,"[38] reminiscent of his experience on the Rigi:

> I no longer knew which was bigger, I or the mountain ... dizzy heights where ever-new abysses and panoramas opened out before my gaze, until at last I stood on the peak in the strange thin air, looking into unimaginable distances. 'Yes,' I thought, 'this is it, my world, the real world, the secret where there are no teachers, no schools, no unanswerable questions, where one can *be* without having to ask anything.' I kept carefully to the paths, for there were tremendous precipices all around. It was all very solemn and I felt one had to be polite and silent up here, for one was in God's world. Here it was physically present.[39]

In his youth, as in his more mature fantasy, his excitement expressed awe, its overload psychically unmanageable without recourse to hyperbole. In describing his daily quests, metaphor is stretched to the limit, reaching back to Renaissance *concetti* and metaphysical conceit. "I ate the earth and drank the sun."[40] In the end all of this serves the psychological necessity that "Your darkness should grasp the light."[41] A daring Promethean challenge. But in the midst of the exaltation, there are very many balancing "buts." Despite the radiance, there is a "working light":

For he who comprehends the darkness in himself, to him the light is near. He who climbs down into his darkness reaches the staircase of the working light, fire-maned Helios.[42]

He begs for support in his staggering, pleading,

Give me your hand, a human hand, so that you can hold me to the earth with it, for whirling veins of fire swoop me up, and exultant longing tears me toward the zenith.

As human beggar, he then begs, forgetting that he has drunk the sun. He does what he thought Nietzsche unable to do.

Most prominent is the language of intoxication, yearning, longing, astonishment, exaltation. Jung's fallible "I" is repeatedly enraptured and bewitched. One adjusts to the scale, even in its most manifest overkill! Jung's surrender to his visionary experiences is qualitatively different from his diagnosis of Nietzsche's account of his state of inspiration. Jung lets the "musts" and "shoulds" of psychic necessity lead him. He is "led to images." "I found myself" becomes formulaic opening to many episodes, an introduction to action as it happens. "The following night ... I was led to a second image."[43] "The following night ... I found myself wandering once more ..."[44] At every point, he justifies superflux: "I say this ... because I have experienced it, it seized me beyond all measure."[45] Well might Jung the prophet in him ask, "Who has believed our report?"

Such positive heights are, of course, balanced by darkness and depth. Though soul experiences pleromatic measure, "Full of light, full of love, full of eternity,"[46] negative experience is equally absolute, encounters with "uttermost depths," haunted by the "unre-plenishable," the "cruelly repulsive," and, importantly, the banal and the ugly. He meets and knows extreme despair. "Horror paralyzes me," and he finds that the "power of abysmal evil ... the raw power comes after you."[47] He does not plan his itinerary; he comes across what he must meet. "On the following night I wandered to the northern land and found myself under a gray sky ..." where he meets "the Dark one" "at the last corner of the world." Here soul is challenged: "Why did you want to comprehend the darkness! But you had to or else it would have seized you. Happy the man who anticipates this grasp." This same Jeremiahn soul laments, "I perish on a dung heap," and "a dog mindlessly lifts his leg over me" and he "curses the hour of [his] birth," "knowing the horrors," born between faeces and urine, an Augustinian and Yeatsian admission. Yet he draws on the Hebraic understanding of the happy man, the Psalmist's *beatus vir,* who knows he is "entirely unable to live without evil,"[48] and yet recognizes that "happy is he who can be a hermit in his own desert,"[49] a final destination for his questing soul.

Like many contemporaries, after the moderating rationality of the enlightenment enterprise had supposedly calmed fevered souls, Jung was left hungry and cold. He repeatedly affirms his discontent with the merely scientific, the exclusively intellectual, being slave to explanation, usefulness, and meaning. He says he had become "a victim of my thinking ... I choke on my own knowledge."[50] Faith in "Logos ... the saving word ... reason and feeling" for him was shattered.[51] Yet he was profoundly discomforted by the demand to "do without meaning"[52] and "have my joy of explaining taken away."[53] More than most, he recognized the longing that made humans "cry out for the word which has only one meaning and no other, so that you escape boundless ambiguity,"[54] who have to find satisfaction in "the words that oscillate between nonsense and supreme meaning,"[55] to "entrust myself to confusion."[56] And yet he must also obey an irresistible "urge toward forbidden knowledge."[57] In this disorientating epistemological condition, he is called to waiting, yet "I wait without knowing what for,"[58] fated, paradoxically to be "on the lookout for things unseen"[59] and to be faithful to "un-openable and unsayable symbols."[60] In the final *Scrutinies,* after the perils he has endured, Jung acknowledges that "it is not too difficult to cite a theory to explain my experience and join it to the already known."[61] But being satisfied on intellectual terms alone does not satisfy "or remove even the smallest part of the knowledge that I have experienced the God. I recognize the God by the unalterableness of the experience. I cannot help but recognize him but by the experience." But still he resists: "I do not want to believe it ..." It is a sickness "from which we must heal ourselves." The culmination of all his inner trials is the realization that "God is our heaviest wound."[62]

This takes us to the condition of soul that evokes the "shudder," a word and an experience with which several of Jung's contemporaries, like Nietzsche and Kierkegaard, also struggled. I preface this reflection with Jung's admission: "I no longer wanted to seek myself outside of myself, but within. Then I wanted to grasp myself, and then I wanted to go on again, without knowing what I wanted, and thus I fell into the mystery."[63] He had already allowed the energy of a spirit, other than the spirit of the times, to be at work in his soul, the spirit "that rules the depths of everything contemporary."[64] In surrendering to the depths, "I had no choice." This is the source of the final inadequacy of the knowledge Jung had found so precious. What the "spirit of the depths" was to give him, "you cannot learn … it can only develop in you."[65] In this vulnerable state, he "fell into the mystery." He had no choice, because one immutable certainty for Jung was that "I wanted my god at any cost."[66] The cost was high, as the *Liber Novus* attests.

Jung was profoundly affected by Rudolph Otto's formulation of the holy, introducing the term that Jung took to heart, soul, and mind—numinosity. Otto's elaboration of the numinous, the *ganz Andere*, as the *mysterium tremendum et fascinans* haunts Jung's *Liber Novus*. This is the shudder of ecstasy and/or terror that accompanies the incandescence: "a horror crept over me. … Thus I stood and was terrified." But then, a gentler modality, "my soul whispered."[67]

Trembling and shuddering leaves one in no doubt of the reality of psychic happening. Greek *phrike*, the shiver of excitement, awe, dread. Jung valued this as necessary human response to a true religious encounter, relating to its actuality. Even fairy tale lads had to go out into the world to discover what fear was, to learn how to shudder.[68] In biblical records, fear and trembling is the essential reaction to the infinite or divine presence, Luther's *Furcht und Zittern*. Jung's immersion in the book of Job familiarized him with Job's exclamation, "I am afraid and trembling seizes my flesh."[69] Kierkegaard was also compelled by his *Frygt og Bæven*. Like the psalmist, all plead the fact that this is an involuntary physical reaction, "Fear and trembling came upon me ..."[70] Nietzsche constantly lays claim to the sensation of being shaken and overturned to his depths.[71] As wonder after wonder came toward Jung's courageous "I," he "saw and shuddered," not able to "grasp the monstrous,"[72] and though he desires "solace," he must endure the "shudder before ... the greatest."[73] Trembling in ecstasy is often the response to the "shimmer" that lights so many experiences of the depths, though human desire for the shimmering can mislead and belie soul-truth.[74] Significantly, Philemon retires "into the shimmering cloud of uncertainty,"[75] inevitably calling up the mystic's *Cloud of Unknowing*. Such unknowing has as much validity for the soul as transfiguration's clarity.

Paul Bishop reflects on Nietzsche's experiences of "unprecedented shudders" expressing inner intensities, but he accepts the need for silence about them.[76] This seems to be Jung's experience, too. Acting as psyche's mouthpiece, advocate, and dramatist with astounding faithfulness, yet Jung ends up rather like Milton's chorus registering Samson's ending, "Calm of mind, all passion spent."[77]

After so much eloquence and rhetorical power, as we enter *Scrutinies*, we encounter a different speech, a new "stutter" and "stammer." Jung perhaps comes to a similar place to that of T.S. Eliot, in his wartime metaphor capturing his "intolerable wrestle/With words and meanings," by means of a "raid on the inarticulate" when he is trying to be still, to let the darkness come upon him, "which shall be the darkness of God."[78] Not muteness. The trying to find words continues.

The sheer effort and imaginative stamina required for the writing of the *Liber Novus* is remarkable. One hears repeatedly such comments as "I am weary of hanging, weary of struggling after the immeasurable,"[79] constantly "seized beyond all measure."[80] But he persists even as he recognizes that "this is beyond words. ... I refuse to understand such things. I can't speak about them without becoming enraged."[81] Such experience takes him to the biblical place of the *tremens et stupens*, essentially, speechlessness, trembling, and astonished.[82]

Accusations about Jung's messianic complex might find fuel in *The Red Book*, but they would be mistaken. There is certainly a sense of calling, a sense of election, having felt quite "alone before God" from his youth."[83] But the responsibility he felt to be his inescapable fate was far more that of prophet than messiah. His regression into stammering and stuttering communicates a sense of the numinosity beyond words to articulate, perhaps also supposing the state of Moses, the stutterer, who needed his brother, Aaron, to speak for him. George Steiner suggests that the great critic will "feel ahead," he will "lean over the horizon and prepare the context of future re-cognition."[84] He comments perceptively that "the ineffable lies beyond the frontiers of the word." It was necessary for Jung to "break through the walls of language" to do justice to his visionary experience.[85] The task before Jung was exacting, to translate immediate inner reality. Poetry is tempted by silence, Steiner avers; and to speak is sometimes to say less. Jung perceived that like Moses he was leading his followers into wholly new soul-territory. *The Red Book* is a valiant attempt to create a language for the enterprise.

Stammering in the field of incandescence, his own burning bush one might say, took him into profoundest solitude. The solitary became a key figure in his drama, being alone with oneself. At the outset, he had announced: "I prepare you for solitude,"[86] for his soul had predicted the need for "dark solitude."[87] Being alone had to be borne before he could be the man happy "to be a hermit in his own desert."[88] He must "practise solitude assiduously without grumbling" for his "way leads to the depths."[89] "Practise" here is an active verb. Solitude at this depth does not come unsought; it is soul-labour. The truth that is revealed in *Scrutinies* is that though he might "stammer like a minor,"[90] it is part of learning to be a soul, which must happen in the world of men.

However, being alone also makes any form of discipleship problematical. In this Jung follows Nietzsche's protest: "I now go away alone, my disciples! You too now go away and be alone! ... You had not yet sought yourselves when you found me. Thus do all believers; therefore all belief is of so little account. Now I bid you lose me and find yourselves ..."[91] Jung also urges, "Your work would be completed if men managed their own lives without imitation."[92] His prohibition of imitation is a particularly vital, but problematic, precept from the founder of a "school" of psychology. Nevertheless, he insists to those who would adopt his ideas to discover "your own path. ... I warn you away from my own."[93] He even invokes the metaphor of virginity:

"My secret remains virginal and my mysteries are inviolable, they belong to me and cannot belong to you. You have your own."[94] This is an exacting charge that many Jungians often disregard. The injunction that we must work out our own salvation with fear and trembling is laid down here as a guiding reflection associated with his wisdom figure, Elijah: "He who enters into his own must grope through what lies at hand, he must sense his way from stone to stone."[95] But in this there is also ambiguity, for at the same time that he insists that there is no way but your own,[96] he must also accept that he must live "as if you were the whole of mankind."[97]

Solitude and silence. So Jung, typically, profusely, vocal and vociferous, posits the end of speech in solitude and silence, claiming throughout that what he says is beyond words and beyond understanding. With or without understanding, his task is to be an extraordinary pioneering advocate of the reality of the psyche. Alice and Bunyan's Pilgrim can wake up from their underground adventures and images: "And behold, it was a dream." When Alice is threatened by the Queen of Heart's menace, she fights back with an assertion of the instability of unconscious action: "You're nothing but a pack of cards!" Jung does not have this option. Jung must go on taking his many selves seriously, continuing to listen to them in full consciousness. His inner figures do the fighting back, Elijah and Salome retaliating, "We are real and not symbols."[98]

In defense of his "method" in *Memories, Dreams, Reflections*, he speaks of Philemon as psychic phenomenon and as real personality: There are things in the psyche which I do not produce, but which produce themselves and have their own life. ... it was he who spoke, not I. It was he who taught me psychic objectivity, the reality of the psyche."[99] *The Red Book* gives all figures the imaginative freedom to be and become as, and what, they must. If Soul lives through imagination, then we must "take seriously every unknown wanderer who personally inhabits the inner world."[100] "When I ask, 'where is my soul, how do I meet it, what does it want now?' The answer is: 'Turn to your images.' ... "Every psychic process is an image and an 'imagining.'"[101] This is the legacy of the Serpent: "I give you payment in images," followed by the vision ... "Behold ..."[102]

In a moving exchange among Jung's "I," Salome and Elijah, he realizes his longing for "the joy of men, for their fullness and freedom." He has now gained from the Serpent "hardness, wisdom and magical power,"[103] and feeling that "everything is completed in me," he also speaks of giving and gift. He urges a too-submissive Salome, "Give to me out of your fullness, not your longing."[104] She is urged not to forget to dance. Through the struggling after the immeasurable, after the solitude of the desert, the Serpent tells him that he (Serpent) can now "return to eternal glitter and shimmer," while Jung must return to his self, a "giddy and pitiful figure,"[105] subject to ruthless scrutiny. In all that is experienced through his erring, Jung realizes the astounding truth that it is in the land of men he has "learned to be a soul."

The term personification has been much used to describe the multitude of figures who invade and inhabit Jung's unconscious. The Greek rhetorical trope, *prosopopoeia*, goes deeper and further. For my purposes, Sonnino's rhetorical guide quotes Quintilian aptly:

> Effects of extraordinary sublimity are produced when the theme is exalted by a bold and hazardous metaphor and inanimate objects are given life and action...
> we display the inner thoughts of our adversaries as though they were talking with ourselves ... or ... we may introduce conversations between ourselves and others ... we are even allowed this manner of speaking to bring down the gods from heaven and raise the dead, while cities and peoples may also find a voice ... we cannot imagine a speech without imagination also a person to utter it ...[106]

This paper is a personal response to a textual reading-experience, not an attempt at interpretation. Only after attending to Jung's multivalent mythopoeic language could I begin to digest its illuminating of individuation *in extremis*, in all its transforming, sometimes banal, beauty, and wholeness. For me *The Red Book* offers soul some respite in a global culture where fake fantasies confront us in the imagineering shallows of the times and soul longs for imagination's true depths.

In our present culture, there is not a little suspicion of what Jung would call "numinosity," where it is often allied with the dubious category of the "romantic." Quantum physicists typically know better, often endorsing what one quantum scientist describes as "particularly transparent moments of encounter" with the divine.[107] Polkinghorne speaks of metaphor as "a strategy of desperation, not a decoration," carrying us into "regimes of thought which would otherwise be inaccessible."[108] Torrance further suggests that "whether we speak of the metaphorical character of metaphysics or the metaphysical character of metaphor, what must be grasped is the single movement that carries things beyond *meta.*"[109] This is the energy with which Jung's *Red Book* grasps us and the territory into which *The Red Book* takes us.

My time spent wandering with Jung in these "eerie ways" that prepare us for the what that is to come leaves me pondering what it is to be serious about the search for one's soul in the interacting fields of psychology, theology, art, and poetry. In all these realms, I now recognise not rigid atheism, but a valuable hermeneutic suspicion at the disposal of psyche. I end with such a feeling, such a drive, confessed by one poet, finding himself in sacred places: "It pleases me to stand in silence here; ... A serious house on serious earth" where he surprises "A hunger in himself to be more serious, /And gravitating with it to this ground ..."

After the compelling but searing intensities and hyperboles of Jung's inner incandescence, I resonate with a new valuing, a refreighting, of the adjective "serious." Such a mood also prevails at the end for Jung, who returns to a humbler self, a "giddy and pitiful figure,"[110] who makes a solemn declaration: "I decided to do what was required of me."[111] This touches a sensitive chord in the contemporary psyche, in estranged souls of those who also "want to go on living with a new god."

Endnotes

1. Sonu Shamdasani, "Introduction," in C.G. Jung, *The Red Book, A Reader's Edition* (New York, NY: W. W. Norton, 2012), 2.

2. C.G. Jung, *The Red Book: Liber Novus*, ed. Sonu Shamdasani, tr. John Peck, Mark Kyburz, and Sonu Shamdasani (New York, NY: W. W. Norton, 2009), 249.

3. Ulrich Hoerni, "The genesis of *The Red Book* and its publication," in eds. Thomas Kirsch and George Hogenson, *The Red Book: Reflections on C.G. Jung's "Liber Novus"* (London and New York: Routledge, 2014), 8.

4. C.G. Jung, *Memories, Dreams, Reflections* (New York, NY: Vintage Books, 1963), 199.

5. Murray Stein and Thomas Arzt; Note to contributors on the stated goal of this series, see Introduction.

6. Jung, *The Red Book*, 163.

7. Adam Phillips, *Terrors and Experts* (London: Faber, 1995), 87.

8. Christine Maillard, "Jung's 'Seven Sermons to the Dead': A gnosis for modernity—a multicultural vison of spirituality," in eds. Thomas Kirsch and George Hogenson, *The Red Book: Reflections on C.G. Jung's "Liber Novus"* (London and New York: Routledge, 2014), 86.

9. George Hogenson, "'The wealth of the soul exists in images': from medieval icons to modern science," in eds. Thomas Kirsch and George Hogenson, *The Red Book: Reflections on C.G. Jung's "Liber Novus"* (London and New York: Routledge, 2014), 94.

10. John Beebe, "The Red Book as a work of Literature," in eds. Thomas Kirsch and George Hogenson, *The Red Book: Reflections on C.G. Jung's "Liber Novus"* (London and New York: Routledge, 2014), 114.

11. Maillard, "Jung's 'Seven Sermons to the Dead'," 84.

12. Sanford Drob, *Reading the Red Book: An Interpretive Guide to Jung's Liber Novus* (New Orleans, LA: Spring Journal, 2012), xvii.

13. Ibid., 6.

14. Wolfgang Giegerich, quoted by Drob, 11.

15. Will Self, "Foreword," in Fyodor Dostoyevsky, *Notes from the Underground*, trans. Hugh Aplin (London: Hesperos Classics, 2016), vii.

16 Paul Bishop, "Jung and the Quest for Beauty", in eds. Thomas Kirsch and George Hogenson, *The Red Book: Reflections on C.G. Jung's "Liber Novus"* (London and New York: Routledge, 2014), 12.

17 Jung, *The Red Book*, 141.

18 Constantine Phipps, *What You Want: The Pursuit of Happiness* (London: Quercus Books, 2014), 2.

19 Jung, *The Red Book*, 119.

20 John Milton, *Paradise Lost.* Bk. 9. Lines 1-6 and Bk. 1. Lines 22-26.

21 Friedrich Nietzsche, *Ecce Homo*, trans. R. J. Hollingdale (Harmondsworth: Penguin Classics, 1979), 96.

22 Søren Kierkegaard, *Fear and Trembling*, trans. A. Hannay (London: Penguin Classics, 1985).

23 James Hillman, Sonu Shamdasani, *Lament of the Dead: Psychology After Jung's "Red Book"* (New York, NY: W. W. Norton, 2009), 33.

24 Nietzsche, *Ecce Homo*, 49.

25 James Hillman, *Healing Fiction: On Jung, Freud, and Adler* (Dallas, TX: Spring Publications, 1983/2004), 53.

26 Shamdasani, "Introduction," 12.

27 See for example, *Hamlet*, Act 2, Sc. 2.

28 Jung, *The Red Book*, 249.

29 Jung, quoted in Shamdasani, "Introduction," 28.

30 Jung, *Memories, Dreams, Reflections*, 199.

31 Nietzsche, *Ecce Homo*, 102.

32 C.G. Jung, "Cryptomnesia" (1905), in *CW*, vol. 1 (Princeton, NJ: Princeton University Press, 1970), par. 184.

33 C.G. Jung, "The Transcendent Function" (1916), in *CW*, vol. 8 (Princeton, NJ: Princeton University Press, 1969), par. 183.

34 Jung, *The Red Book*, 415.

35 Ibid., 120.

36 Ibid., 307.

37 Ibid., 259.

38 Ibid., 307.

39 Jung, *Memories, Dreams, Reflections*, 77-78.

40 Jung, *The Red Book*, 262.

41 Ibid., 251.

42 Ibid., 259.

43 Ibid., 184.

44 Ibid., 233.

[45] Ibid., 480.

[46] Ibid., 307.

[47] Ibid., 315.

[48] Ibid., 311.

[49] Ibid., 447.

[50] Ibid., 148.

[51] Ibid., 278.

[52] Ibid., 133.

[53] Ibid., 119.

[54] Ibid., 250.

[55] Ibid., 143.

[56] Ibid., 147.

[57] Ibid., 185.

[58] Ibid., 212.

[59] Ibid., 213.

[60] Ibid., 475 n24.

[61] Ibid., 480.

[62] Ibid., 481.

[63] Ibid., 202.

[64] Ibid., 119.

[65] Ibid., 204.

[66] Ibid., 316.

[67] Ibid., 378.

[68] Grimm, "Story of a Boy Who Went Forth to Learn Fear."

[69] Job 2:6, "Wenn ich daran denke, so erschrecke ich, und Zittern kommt meinen Leib an."

[70] Psalm 55:5.

[71] Nietzsche, *Ecce Homo*, 102.

[72] Jung, *The Red Book*, 376.

[73] Ibid., 383.

[74] Ibid., 478.

[75] Ibid., 477.

[76] Paul Bishop, *On the Blissful Islands with Nietzsche and Jung* (London: Routledge, 2017), 198.

[77] John Milton, "Samson Agonistes," line 1758.

[78] T. S. Eliot, "East Coker, V," in *Four Quartets* (London: Faber & Faber, 1964), 31.

[79] Jung, *The Red Book*, 444.

80 Ibid., 480.
81 Ibid., 320.
82 Acts 9:6.
83 Shamdasani, "Introduction," 5.
84 George Steiner, *Language and Silence* (London: Faber & Faber, 1968), 26.
85 Ibid., 30.
86 Jung, *The Red Book*, 123.
87 Ibid., 472.
88 Ibid., 447.
89 Ibid., 473.
90 Ibid., 506.
91 Nietzsche, *Ecce Homo*, 36
92 Jung, *The Red Book*, 542.
93 Ibid., 125.
94 Ibid., 178.
95 Ibid.
96 Ibid., 384.
97 Ibid., 200.
98 Ibid., 176.
99 Jung, *Memories, Dreams, Reflections,* 183.
100 Jung, *The Red Book*, 217.
101 C.G. Jung, "Foreword to Suzuki's 'Introduction to Zen Buddhism'" (1939), in *CW*, vol. 11 (Princeton, NJ: Princeton University Press, 1969), par. 889.
102 Jung, *The Red Book*, 435.
103 Ibid., 439.
104 Ibid., 438.
105 Ibid., 457.
106 Lee Sonnino, *Handbook to Sixteenth Century Rhetoric* (London: Routledge and Kegan Paul 1968), 54.
107 John Polkinghorne, *Reason and Reality* (London: SPCK, 1991), 2.
108 Ibid., 30.
109 A. J. Leggett, quoted in Polkinghourne, 10.
110 Jung, *The Red Book*, 457.
111 Ibid., 543.

"O tempora! O mores!"

Ann Casement

Preface

This essay owes its title to the *Catiline Orations* by Marcus Tullius Cicero, the Roman statesman, lawyer, philosopher, orator, historian, and linguist. Those words, which may be translated as "Oh for these times! Oh for our morals!" were an expression of Cicero's disgust at what he saw as the evil at work in the *Catiline Conspiracy* of first-century B.C.E. Rome.[1] An account of this incident along with further significant events from Cicero's time feature in this essay as they bear comparison with modernity. Like many others, I first came across Cicero while studying school Latin and have since continued to browse his writings as well as works relating to him. In addition, I had enjoyable conversations about Cicero and other prominent ancient Romans with a friend, the poet and classicist Robert Graves, and his wife, Beryl, at Canelluñ, their home in Mallorca.[2] With his Roman looks, military service during the First World War and knowledge of Latin, Graves could easily have passed for an ancient Roman, and Part Two of this essay is in memory of him. Both Graves and Jung were born under the astrological sign of Leo, making their domains in places of mountains and water ensconced in their Leonine *prides* of wife, family, muses, and followers, while Graves sported a lion's mane of hair into old age.

Part One – Cicero and Jung

In this (brief) inquiry into the overlap between first-century B.C.E. Rome and modernity, the focus is on similarities and differences between Cicero and Carl Gustav Jung. Indeed, they share several characteristics, and Jung references Cicero in *The Collected Works*. Their mutual censure of the times in which they lived is exemplified by the above quotation from Cicero and by Jung's critical appraisal of what he called the "spirit of this time."[3] He saw the latter as being negatively opposed to the "spirit of the depths."[4] Despite the fact they were not men of blood and iron, the latter being the ones who largely shaped the history of their times, Cicero and Jung attained many worldly achievements. Nonetheless, they were both essentially reflective principled thinkers. Cicero, through his philosophical writings, hoped to provide a moral code of living for ordinary Romans as the law was at the centre of his thinking. In somewhat similar vein, Jung's concerns were with a collective morality following the proclamation of the death of God in the second half of the 19th century. The *Red Book,* begun in 1914, depicts Jung's search for a new guiding spirit for the age in which he lived.

As they lived millennia apart, there are, of course, differences between Cicero and Jung, a principal one being the former's overvaluation of the properties of *reason*; while the latter stressed the urgent need to acknowledge the crucial role played by *irrationality* in human life. In his *Red Book,* Jung developed his notions of the self, shadow, trickster, persona, anima/animus, mana personality. Above all, the book represents an account of his *individuating process* and cosmology, both heavily reliant on mythology; it is nothing short of Jung's search for his *soul,* which he felt could only be done through discovering his own myth.[5] As there is a wealth of material in the book, this essay will focus on Jung's quest driven by "the intoxication of mythology"; an elaboration of Jung's and Cicero's myths will feature later. These will be related to the notion of the ambiguous *trickster,* a key figure in Jung's life and in Cicero's gravest crisis.

Cicero's writings give an insight into Roman *mores* and provide the bases from which to explore, retrospectively, ancient Rome at a pivotal point in its history as it links to modernity. Although over 2,000 years separate it from the early years of the 20th and 21st centuries, these three historical times represent periods of enormous turbulence and change in Western civilization. The guiding spirit of these epochs was seemingly based on rational forethought, though further inspection reveals they were largely motivated by underlying irrational forces. In myriad ways, Ancient Rome represents the foundation of Western civilization, as one need only think of Latin, revised by Cicero himself, that underpins many eponymous "Latin languages"; the revised calendar; Roman roads still in everyday use in many parts of Europe; democratic governance based on checks and balances; even Christianity, wherein the pope is a re-creation of the *Pontifex Maximus*, the head of the state religion.

Cyberspace

The development of superior technological and engineering expertise such as the deadly double-edged sword and other military and nonmilitary technology helped establish and maintain Rome as the superpower of the Western world for centuries. One can imagine the enthusiasm with which the Romans would have espoused the phenomenon that is colonizing and reshaping the world today—that of cyberspace. Social networks and social media are the offspring of Western culture's development of science and technology that are increasingly beyond any form of control. The presence of the ambiguous figure of the *trickster* is ubiquitous in cyberspace.

Facebook and Twitter were obviously not available to Cicero or Jung, though one may fantasize about Cicero tweeting "O tempora! O mores!" or Jung "The spirit of the depths." It is the pithy *message* that has, and always has had, an impact on the generality. Other memorable slogans from Western historicity are Caesar's "*Veni, vidi, vici,*" Jefferson's and Lincoln's "All men are created equal" from the Gettysburg Address, and, in recent times, Obama's "Yes we can," the Brexit campaign's "Take back control," and Trump's "Make America Great Again." These exemplify what the evolutionary biologist Richard Dawkins calls *meme-complexes,* processes of cultural evolution of copyable behaviour such as words that exert influence on the generality as they are disseminated through time. In Dawkins' vernacular, the *meme-complexes* of Caesar, Cicero, Lincoln and Jung are still going strong.

The tectonics reshaping the world in the past 10 years are the result of several factors that include increasing globalization; the major recession of 2008; the disintegration of weak states in Africa and the Middle East leading to the emergence of gangs like Islamic State, accompanied by the influx of refugees into Europe; terrorist attacks; piracy in the Indian Ocean; and the rapid expansion of social networking, the latter being both constructive and destructive. There are vintage years in history of which 2007 is an example, namely, the moment that Steve Jobs introduced the iPhone, "a pivotal junction in the history of technology—and of the world."[6] This, as well as the other technological innovations that exploded onto the world stage in the same year, are dramatically reshaping everything faster than "we have been able to reshape ourselves, our leadership, our institutions, our societies, and our ethical choices."[7] The monster, viz., science mentioned by the sick god, Izdubar, in *The Red Book* is exemplified by the uncontrollable spread of toxic misinformation (fake news) that is disseminated at high speed through rapidly developing new technology. As the exponential growth of the latter increases, the capacity of humankind to adapt to it, already superseded, is the Frankenstein monster that is endangering the well-being and very existence of humankind.

A related consequence of the above-named factors, along with the increasing speed of communication, has been the meteoric rise of populist movements headed by strong leaders that is changing the political and social landscape worldwide. From all quarters may be heard despairing cries at this reshaping of the world though this, apart from the current speed with which it is taking place, is not itself a new phenomenon. Jung's acute awareness of the way world history repeats itself is set out in the first few pages of *The Red Book* as follows:

> Filled with human pride and blinded by the presumptuous spirt of the times, I long sought to hold that other spirit away from me. But I did not consider that the spirit of the depths from time immemorial and for all the future possess a greater power than the spirit of this time, who changes with the generations. ... *But the supreme meaning is the path, the way and the bridge to what is to come. That is the God yet to come.*[8]

The Way of What Is to Come

In the era that Jung was compiling his *Red Book,* the dominant "spirit of this time" was the buildup to, and subsequent outbreak of, the First World War, followed by the horrors perpetrated throughout its duration.[9] Jung was a visionary, exemplified by his vision in 1913 of the flood in which float the bodies of countless thousands of the dead, and the subsequent one of the sea of blood.[10] Jung had these experiences in the year before the start of the Great War, along with the dream in which he slays the hero, Siegfried. Of the latter, Jung states the following: "I must say that the God could not come into being before the hero had been slain. The hero as we understand him has become an enemy of the God since the hero is perfection. ... The hero must fall for the sake of our redemption."[11] The hero that is referred to in this context represents reason and the idealized consciousness of the times. Siegfried (also the name of Richard Wagner's son) was the blond, blue-eyed Germanic hero who represented everything Jung treasured in himself—power, boldness, pride—that could not be killed in combat as Jung himself would have been overcome: "... so only assassination was left to me. If I wanted to go on living, it would only be through trickery and cunning."[12] Jung realized he had outgrown his former identification with the blond hero as follows: "If the God grows old, he becomes shadow ... and he goes down."[13] In Part Two of this essay, I will discuss the assassination of another godlike blond hero, Julius Caesar, which heralded the going down of the old gods represented by the worn-out ideals of the Roman Republic and the dawning of new consciousness, i.e., the *Pax Romana.* In similar fashion, the assassination of the Austrian Archduke Franz Ferdinand at Sarajevo in 1914 signaled the start of the World War I.

In *The Red Book,* Jung lays emphasis on the acknowledgement of the irrational, i.e., what is *beyond* reason, as being of vital importance for humankind. To illustrate this, the healing of the sick god, represented by Izdubar (an earlier name of the Sumerian Gilgamesh), is described in *The Red Book* in the following quotations: "Oh Izdubar, most powerful one, what you call poison is science...

we are nurtured on it from youth, and that may be one reason why we haven't properly flourished and remain so dwarfish."[14] Izdubar responds: "No stronger being has ever cut me down, no monster has ever resisted my strength. But your poison ... has lamed me to the marrow."[15]

In the late 17th and 18th centuries, the *Enlightenment* championed many causes, namely, reason, science, personal liberties, belief in God alongside the denouncement of organized religions (particularly Christianity), and opposition to the abusive governments found throughout Europe. In place of the latter, a system of checks and balances was advocated. Many *Enlightenment* thinkers, initially supportive of the French Revolution of 1789, turned against it because of its increasing barbarity. Following the revolution and the subduing of the 1848 revolutionary fervour that swept Europe, there was a suppression of irrationality such as in the ideas encapsulated in the movement known as *Romanticism*, the latter itself being, in large part, a reaction to the ideas embedded in *Enlightenment* rationality and to the Industrial Revolution. As *Romanticism* was deemed to have failed, the mid-19th century witnessed the twin processes of reason and science once more in the ascendant. *The Red Book* depicts Jung's turning away from the ideas embedded in reason and science in support of his claim that the major determinants of the savagery of the First World War coalesced around the fact that the "spirit of this time" arose from the repression of the irrational side of life and subsequent identification with rationality. As a result, there was an eruption into consciousness of the irrational and mythological contents in collective unconscious. "The spirit of the depths" was an expression of Jung's profound insight into the necessity of acknowledging the irrational as a *psychological* factor.

Part Two – The Myth of Romulus and Remus

Part Two focuses on a particularly turbulent epoch-making period of the late Roman Republic—one of the most star-studded eras in Western history. This includes such legendary names as Julius Caesar,

Cleopatra, Caesar Augustus, Mark Antony, Brutus, Cassius, Sparta-cus, Pompey, Crassus, and, of course, Cicero himself. It also represented a huge transition from the Republic, which came into being with the downfall of the ancient monarchy in 510 B.C.E., and lasted until the foundation of the Empire in 27 B.C.E. under Julius Caesar's grandnephew and adopted son, Octavius, later renamed Caesar Augustus. His famed *Pax Romana* heralded an emergence from the old myth of brother killing brother and the dawning of a new consciousness of relative peace and prosperity that lasted over 200 years. Prior to this, the last decades of the Republic were marked by civil wars, which were the result of huge power struggles that involved all the above-named protagonists.

In *The Red Book,* ego consciousness is identified with the "spirit of this time" that has to go down under into the mythological realm of the collective unconscious. This insight of Jung's has special relevance to the mythical origins of Rome prior to its foundation in 753 B.C.E., encapsulated in the story of the twin brothers, Romulus and Remus. This myth is associated with the astrological sign of Gemini, the natal sign of Presidents John Kennedy and Donald Trump, the current leader of the *Pax Americana*.[16] The myth itself revolves around the twins' decision to establish a city, giving rise to a power struggle between them over which part should represent its founding place. Remus, standing on the Aventine Hill, one of the seven hills of Rome, saw six vultures overhead and decided it was the place; Romulus, on the other hand, stood on the Palatine Hill and saw 12 vultures flying over it so he, in his turn, decided that should be the founding place. The fight between the two ended with Romulus killing Remus, thus becoming the first king of the city-state of Rome and giving it his name. The Palatine became the most desirable part of the city, with the wealthiest and most powerful, the *patricians,* having their luxurious homes there. The Aventine, lying across from the Palatine with the *Circus Maximus* between them, was the dwelling place of the poor. "Success and failure, prestige and shame—there, expressed in the very geography of the city, were the twin poles around which Roman life revolved."[17] The theme of polar opposites engaged Jung's creative thinking in *The Red Book,* wherein they are articulated as the "spirit of this time" as opposed to "the spirit of the depths."

The fratricide portrayed in this myth became imprinted in the Roman psyche throughout the long history of the Republic. In its dying days in the first century B.C.E., its founding myth resurfaced with a vengeance at the assassination of Julius Caesar. This, in turn, led to The Great Civil War of the Republic between the followers of Caesar, on one hand, and his assassins, led by Brutus and Cassius, on the other. These opposing forces finally erupted within the Caesar camp itself between Mark Antony and Octavius. In his work titled *On Duties,* Cicero critiqued Caesar's depraved ambition and cited him as one of the most vicious autocrats of history. In the turbulent months following Caesar's assassination, it was Cicero, through sheer force of character, who took charge of the state and "came to stand for future generations as a model of defiance against tyranny—an inspiration first to the American and then the French revolutionaries."[18] President John Adams, one of the architects of the Constitution of the United States, held Cicero in high regard and incorporated the latter's ideas on governance and the law into it.

The myth of Romulus and Remus also foreshadows the origin of the Romans' superstitious reliance on omens and augurs so that the perceived pragmatism, discipline, and rationality they were renowned for throughout their long history of dominance were underpinned by irrational beliefs. The ambiguity of living one's myth is in evidence here in obedience to Schopenhauer's *Will* blindly taking its course, both individually and collectively, to *the way of what is to come.*

The Republic of Rome

The supremacy of Rome was established in the second century B.C.E., when it finally crushed Carthage, its only major rival in the Mediterranean world. This was the fateful outcome of the two Punic Wars, which resulted in Rome becoming the superpower of the Western world. Although ample documentation exists about the Roman Republic in the first century B.C.E., it is largely written by and about powerful men such as Julius Caesar and Cicero, scions of aristocrats or of *equites,* knights who were mostly traders and businessmen. Another significant group was that of the *legionnaires* who fought Rome's wars of conquest, about whom there are written accounts, including Caesar's records of his victorious campaigns in Gaul and Helvetia. The comparatively sparse information that is available about the lives of ordinary people, the *plebians,* indicates that most of them inhabited the city-state itself, eking out their lives in narrow, treacherous streets with no public sanitation, street lighting, or police force to keep order. Even more miserable was the existence of the *slaves,* which led them to rebel from time to time, the most famous uprising being led by Spartacus, the Thracian slave and gladiator. He was a revolutionary, and, according to some accounts, a principled man, who briefly posed a challenge to the might of Rome. This rebellion was finally put down by Crassus in 71 B.C.E.

As conditions in the city-state were hazardous, even prosperous Romans did not travel about in it after dark for fear of attack. The only certainties for most of the population were death and taxes, the collection of the latter being sold by the Senate, Rome's governing body, to the highest bidder. The infamous Roman orgies that have attracted so much attention were, at that time, largely confined to the youth of wealthy aristocratic families, the latter of whom numbered around 20. It was those families who wielded the power in Rome and owned most of its wealth, as change was next to impossible in the Roman system of governance with too many checks and balances in place.

One result of this stasis was an acute shortage of land in Rome itself as well as its hinterland due to the accumulation of land in the hands of the same rich and powerful aristocratic families. This, along with serious difficulties arising from the outbreak of frequent hostilities between powerful strong men at the head of legions, problems associated with dire living conditions, the periodic influx of refugees, and gang violence, led to the Republic being constantly endangered by internal unrest. Externally, it was under threat from frequent uprisings by indigenous populations in its vast empire and to piracy on the high seas. The spirit of the times of first-century B.C.E. Rome reverberates tellingly with that of the modern world.

Cicero

Politically, men from the aforementioned patrician families held the power in Republican Rome by virtue of their membership in the Senate. From time to time, however, an unusually brilliant outsider rose to the ranks of the Senate, and one such outstanding figure was the son of an *equite,* Marcus Tullius Cicero, "the country boy," an origin he shares with Jung. While Cicero was still in his 20s, he had made his name as an exceptionally gifted lawyer and orator. From that vantage point, he went on to become a Senator, and, eventually, one of the two Consuls who held power for a year. The custom of having two Consuls elected annually was a key component of the checks and balances that kept any one individual from amassing too much power and aspiring to be king of Rome.

Throughout his life, Cicero was identified with the overarching priority of reason and with championing the ideals espoused by the Republic, namely, justice, good faith, harmony, discipline, prudence, and frugality among others. His book, *On Law,* inspired by Plato, states: "Law is the highest reason implanted in nature, which commands what ought to be done ... whose natural function is to command right conduct and forbid wrongdoing."[19] Its summary reads as follows: "Virtue is reason completely developed."[20] *The Law of the Father* is encapsulated in the myth associated with Cicero's natal sign of Capricorn, the sign ruled by the principle of the disciplinarian father. His shadow side was that he was vainglorious, leaving him vulnerable to the machinations of the *trickster,* which led to his downfall. Despite these human failings, Cicero's reputation has come down through history as a wise counselor and inspiration to such diverse luminaries as Augustine, Queen Elizabeth I, Hume, and Voltaire. Viewed in this light, Cicero bears a resemblance to the figure of Philemon in *The Red Book,* who features as an archetypal wise old man and guide to Jung.

The Catiline Conspiracy

Cicero's greatest crisis arose when he collided with what the eminent astrologer and Jungian analyst Liz Greene, in writing about Capricorn, describes as the "... avenging Lawgiver's strict and structured rules of life."[21] This occurred at the time of the Catiline Conspiracy led by "a louche patrician by the name of Lucius Sergius Catiline."[22]

At the height of Cicero's political power as Consul in 62 B.C.E., a populist uprising to bring down the Senate and take over Rome was attempted by Catiline, an arch *trickster*. He and his fellow young aristocratic conspirators had stirred up the populace, already dis-contented as the result of the recession occurring at that time, by spreading fake news that inflamed Rome with revolutionary fervour. Cicero managed, at great personal risk, to expose this revolution, at which point, some of the conspirators were arrested and brought to the Senate. Catiline escaped, though was later killed in battle, while the captive conspirators, with Cicero's consent, were condemned to death without trial. In this expeditious manner, he managed "to defeat the greatest of all conspiracies with so little disturbance, trouble, and commotion."[23] As a result, he was "publicly declared the Father of his Country."[24]

"Filled with human pride," Cicero endlessly boasted of this triumph in his writings and speeches, but the avenging Law of the Father, the central motif of his natal myth, was not to be escaped.[25] In 58 B.C.E., a bill was passed in the Senate by one of his enemies, the patrician *trickster* Clodius, covertly supported by the powerful Triumvirate of Caesar, Crassus, and Pompey. This stated that "any public official who executed or *had* executed a citizen without due process of law" should be exiled "with the denial of the traditional symbols of hospitality, fire, and water."[26] This was clearly aimed at Cicero, who, to save his life, had to shamefully take himself off to Thessalonica, where he came close to a complete breakdown before eventually being repatriated to Rome.

Cicero's heroic achievement in saving Rome turned against him, presaged in the sign of Capricorn as the opposing forces of the ambitious heroic son's clash with the stern lawgiver of the father. "Morality and shame, law and lawlessness, seem to comprise some of the polar opposites of Capricorn."[27] There is a telling example in the 1970s of another individual who transgressed The Law of the Father, namely, Richard Nixon. He, like Cicero, was a lawyer, statesman, and fellow Capricorn. In today's world, the beneficent law-giving father, personified by Cicero, has been corrupted into the image of the "strong leader," the *trickster/shadow* side of that archetypal figure. In the end, for all their brilliance in worldly matters, both Cicero and Nixon ended on the wrong side of history. In the case of the former, it was due to his conservative attachment to tradition—another characteristic of Capricorn. This may be seen in his undying loyalty to the *idea* of the Republic, but a Republic that was a corrupt version of its traditional ideals, while Caesar "with the pitiless insight of genius, understood that the constitution with its endless checks and balances prevented effective government."[28] The Roman Republic mirrors what is happening in the great power of today's world, echoing Jung's profound insight of the god growing old and becoming shadow.

Part Three – Jung's Quest for his Soul

Leo, the astrological sign depicted by the lion, "one of the Mother's accompanying beasts" stands for the fiery, instinctual side of anyone born under it.[29] Akin to Capricorn, "the symbolism of Leo circles around the theme ... of the hero and his father," but here it is "the hero's quest for his spiritual father."[30] At the time of another great crisis in Cicero's life, brought about by the death of his beloved only daughter, Tullia, in childbirth, he turned to the study of the nature of the gods, "the noblest of the studies for the human mind to grasp."[31] In typical Ciceronian mode, he explored this through an (imaginary) reasoned Socratic debate between the Greek philosophies of the Stoics, Epicureans, and Peripatetics. Jung, in his turn, at a time of great personal and collective crisis, turned to the same theme in *The Red Book,* though he did this through steeping himself in the irrational realm of the collective unconscious.

My interest in astrology was piqued through acquaintance with Liz Greene, from whom I gained some insight into its psychological acuity. As Jung states: "I do not hesitate to take the synchronistic phenomena that underlie astrology seriously. Just as there is an eminently psychological reason for the existence of alchemy so too in the case of astrology."[32] The dismissal of alchemy and astrology as irrational in today's world exists alongside a lack of awareness of its own irrationally driven by the blind *Will.*

The year 1914 was the ominous harbinger of a new conscious-ness in the West underwritten by increased reliance on science and technology. Jung, knowingly, chose this same year to transcribe his own odyssey into the *Red Book,* traveling in strange lands where he encountered myriad mythical figures. As alluded to in Part One, he resorted to being a *trickster* as the only possible way of freeing himself from identification with the blond hero. In view of this, it seems ironic that Jung is critical of the cunning Odysseus in the following statement: "He went astray when he played his trick at Troy."[33] As is well known, Odysseus's "trick" in creating the Trojan horse led to the end of the 10-year grim-visaged Trojan War, after which he embarked on his odyssey. Jung's inner voyage of discovery was likewise set against the backdrop of another epoch-changing war.

Homer's *Odyssey* is one of various myths that appear in *The Red Book,* though the leitmotif of the book is to be found in the myth that governs Jung's natal sign of Leo, namely, the Quest for the Grail. This features overtly in the text as a play wherein Jung is both audience and, at the same time, is identified with the characters. This telling depiction of the ambiguity inherent in mythology in being both personally relevant and, at the same time, impersonal in content is illustrated by the following quotations: "How closely Klingsor resembles me!"[34] "The audience is enraptured and recognizes itself in Parsifal. He is I."[35] "The lionskin of Hercules adorns his shoulders and he holds the club in his hand."[36] "I rise and become one with myself."[37] The Quest for the Grail, undertaken unwittingly by Parsifal, is there from the beginning of *The Red Book* and expressed as Jung's search for his soul.

Richard Wagner's opera *Parsifal* is the supreme depiction of Celtic legends that, in medieval times, melded with Christianity as the myth of The Quest for the Grail featured in Arthurian legend. Both Wagner and Jung were transformed through reading the philosophy of Schopenhauer, particularly the latter's assertion that the outer world of presentation is illusory or, in Jung's language, the "spirit of this time." Instead, it is the blind *Will* in the "spirit of the depths" that is the irrational prime mover in life. Wagner's debt to Schopenhauer lasted until his death and is expressed thus: "How can I thank him enough?"[38]

Parsifal was the last opera of Wagner's oeuvre, some of the principal themes of which are summarized here from an account in Bryan Magee's erudite book *Wagner and Philosophy*. The Order of the Knights of the Grail, swearing lifelong chastity, are guardians of the most numinous of objects, namely, the Chalice that Christ drank from at the Last Supper and the spear that pierced Christ's side on the Cross. The Knights regularly reenact the ritual of the Last Supper. Another knight, Klingsor, unable to control his sexuality, castrates himself and is not admitted to the Order. He transforms into a magician and gains possession of the spear, which he takes to his castle set in a magical garden. This loss results in the ritual becoming a jejune enactment. Amfortas, King of the Knights, sets forth to recover the spear but succumbs to the erotic temptress, Kundry, during which Amfortas is wounded with the spear by Klingsor. Kundry, the feminine figure in the story, is the lowly servitor of the Order, as well as the temptress in the power of Klingsor. Parsifal is the pure fool, killing birds with his bow and arrow, who stumbles into the Order and is permitted to stay by its wisest knight, Gurnemanz. But Parsifal never develops, remaining childishly unaware, so that he is banished from the Order. Thenceforth, he has many encounters with monsters and giants before bumbling into Klingsor's domain, slaying many of his knights and finally recovering the spear after resisting the seduction attempts of Kundry. Although Parsifal's sexuality is finally aroused, he manages to overcome its power (Schopenhauer's *Will*) through acceding to the competing power of compassion for the suffering of Amfortas. On Good Friday, when the world is renewed through repentance and transformation, Parsifal baptizes Kundry, releasing her from Klingsor's curse, and heals Amfortas's wound with the recovered spear.

Conclusion

Parsifal and *The Red Book* overlap each other, with the overarching theme of The Quest for the Grail resonating with Jung's quest for his soul. The figures represented in *Parsifal* recur many times in *The Red Book*, for example, the innocence of the pure fool/divine child,[39] the ambiguity of the anima figure, Kundry/Salome, as both seducer/destroyer and loving/nurturing mother,[40] the fear that Salome is after his head, a severed head standing also for castration, linking it to Klingsor's castration,[41] some complementarity between the dyad Elijah/Salome and the dyad Klingsor/ Kundry,[42] the *trickster* magician, Klingsor's magic garden with its links to the Garden of Eden, the setting of humankind's downfall that includes the serpent and with the Garden of Gethsemane, the setting of humanity's redemption,[43] Philemon, as the mana personality and Jung's inner guide, combines characteristics from both Gurnemanz and the wise magician, a transformation of the evil Klingsor,[44] Good Friday, the time of redemption of all souls,[45] The Last Supper,[46] Jung's Christ-like hanging from the Cross,[47] and the key notions of fulfilment and redemption, expressed in Jung's term individuation, that comes about through feeling not by intellectual means, which mirrors Parsifal's compassion for Amfortas, the latter bearing some resemblance to the wounded Izdubar referenced in Part One.

Toward the later part of *The Red Book,* the following words from Jung seem a fitting conclusion to this piece: "A living God ... fills us with reeling chaos ... that sweeps away the self into the boundless, into dissolution."[48] With extraordinary prescience, *The Red Book* depicts the blind *Will* in the depths of the collective unconscious that is now unleashed in cyberspace. In linking this to Jung's quotation, it seems apposite to suggest that *The Red Book* represents a key text from which to explore the mysteries of God's existence in cyberspace.

Endnotes

1 Marcus Tullius Cicero, *Cicero's Orations Against Catiline* (Oxford: Oxford City Press, 2010), 2.

2 Robert Graves produced two books on the Emperor Claudius, a descendant of Augustus Caesar, entitled *I, Claudius* (1934), and *Claudius the God and his Wife Messalina* (1935), published by Harmondsworth: Penguin. They are disguised semi-autobiographical accounts of Graves' relationship with the poet, Laura Riding—hence the title *I, Claudius*. Graves talked about Claudius as if he knew him well personally once saying to me: "Claudius is my best friend." A superb trilogy of historical fiction about Cicero written by the author, Robert Harris, entitled: *Imperium* (2006), *Lustrum* (2009), and *Dictator* (2015), is published by London: Hutchinson.

3 C.G. Jung, *The Red Book: Liber Novus*, ed. Sonu Shamdasani, tr. John Peck, Mark Kyburz, and Sonu Shamdasani (New York, NY: W. W. Norton, 2009), 229.

4 Ibid., 197.

5 The Jungian psychoanalyst, Wolfgang Giegerich, has produced several well-argued works in which he critiques Jung's religious and mythical bases for his psychology. These appear under the general title of "Collected English Papers" published by Spring Journal Books, New Orleans. Although an adherent of Giegerich's approach, I am, nonetheless, staying with Jung's original thinking throughout as it is pertinent to the contents of this chapter.

6 Thomas L. Friedman, *Thank You for Being Late* (London: Allen Lane, 2016), 20.

7 Ibid., 28.

8 Jung, *The Red Book*, 229.

9 This is the title of the section in *Liber Secundus* that illustrates the way the philosopher, Schopenhauer, impacted Jung's thinking from his time at university. *The Way of What is to Come* is an echo of "*… that which is yet to come.* Thus the bird builds a nest for the young it does not yet know" (italics added, Arthur Schopenhauer, *The World as Will and Presentation.* Vol. 1 (London: Pearson Longman, 2008), par. 191.) Schopenhauer found inspiration in the East, in particular in the *Bha-*

gavad Gita and the *Upanishads* from Hinduism, and Mahayana Buddhist texts that also impacted Jung's thinking, for instance, his use of the Hindu term, *maya,* which translates as illusion. Both thinkers acknowledge the misery and suffering of worldly existence, while Schopenhauer equates the *Will* with *thing in itself* (ibid., par. 131), akin to Jung's *collective unconscious,* namely, that which blindly motivates life. A portrait of the philosopher stood on Jung's desk. See: Sonu Shamdasani. *C.G. Jung: A Biography in Books* (New York, NY: W. W. Norton, 2012), 49. In association with The Martin Bodmer Foundation.

[10] Jung, *The Red Book*, 231.

[11] Ibid., 244-45.

[12] Ibid., 242.

[13] Ibid.

[14] Ibid., 278.

[15] Ibid.

[16] The *Lexington* column in the United States Section of *The Economist,* June 3rd-9th 2017, carried the following on the *Pax Americana*: "To internationalists, America enjoys special privileges as the designer of many multilateral organizations. No country has the same veto rights as America at the International Monetary Fund and the World Bank. No country has such power over which generals run NATO ... It is hard to convey how strongly that expansive worldview is rejected in Mr. Trump's White House."

[17] Tom Holland, *Rubicon: The Triumph and Tragedy of the Roman Republic* (London: Little, Brown, 2003), 19.

[18] Anthony Everitt, *The Life and Times of Rome's Greatest Politician: Cicero* (New York, NY: Random House, 2003), viii.

[19] Holland, *Rubicon*, 182.

[20] Ibid., 183.

[21] Liz Greene, *The Astrology of Fate* (London: George Allen & Unwin, 1984), 245.

[22] Holland, *Rubicon*, 196.

[23] Lucius Metrius Plutarchus, *Plutarch's Lives: The Life of Cicero* (New York, NY: Palatine Press, 2015), pages unnumbered.

[24] Ibid.

[25] Jung, *The Red Book*, 229.

26 Everitt, *The Life and Times of Rome's Greatest Politician: Cicero*, 142.

27 Greene, *The Astrology of Fate,* 284.

28 Everitt, *The Life and Times of Rome's Greatest Politician: Cicero*, 322.

29 Greene, *The Astrology of Fate*, 204.

30 Ibid.

31 Marcus Tullius Cicero, *The Nature of the Gods* (Oxford: Oxford University Press, 1998), 3.

32 C.G. Jung, "A Study in the Process of Individuation" (1939), in *CW*, vol. 9/I (London: Routledge & Kegan Paul, 1968), par. 608, n168.

33 Jung, *The Red Book*, 247.

34 Ibid., 302.

35 Ibid., 303.

36 Ibid.

37 Ibid.

38 Cosima Wagner, *Diaries*, Vol. 1, 618.

39 Jung, *The Red Book*, 254.

40 Ibid., 248.

41 Ibid.

42 Ibid., 324.

43 Ibid., 359.

44 Ibid., 312.

45 Ibid., 304.

46 Ibid., 317.

47 Ibid., 325.

48 Ibid., 338.

Jung's Red Book – A Compensatory Image for Our Contemporary Culture: A Hindu Perspective

Ashok Bedi

Whenever the consciousness of an individual is out of balance, the self incarnates in a compensatory dream to restore the balance. When the consciousness of a culture or an era is out of balance, artists, writers, and shamans carry the self of the collective to incarnate in word or image a compensatory perspective. Goethe's *Faust* and Jung's *Red Book* are two recent examples of a *magnum opus* where the self of the collective has incarnated, via the active imaginations of these creative individuals, to guide the telos of our matrix. The prescription of *The Red Book* as a GPS for our times will be amplified from a Hindu perspective. This essay is a hermeneutic reflection on Jung's *Red Book*.

Jung's *Red Book* – A Personal Odyssey or a Collective Vision?

To truly grasp the gifts of Jung's *Red Book*, the reader needs to get the ego out of the way to engage it.

> The first demand any work of art makes upon us is surrender. Look. Listen. Receive. Get yourself out of the way. There is no good asking first whether the work before you deserves such a surrender, for until you have surrendered you cannot possibly find out.[1]

Jung comments that there are two types of works of art—psychological and visionary:

> The psychological mode works with materials drawn from man's conscious life-with crucial experiences, powerful emotions, suffering, passion, the stuff of human fate in

general. All this is assimilated by the psyche of the poet, raised from commonplace to the level of poetic experience. ... That is why I call this mode of creation "psychological"; it remains within the limits of the psychologically intelligible...

The gulf that separates the first from the second part of *Faust* marks the difference between the psychological and the visionary modes of artistic creation. Here everything is reversed. The experience that furnished the material for artistic expression is no longer familiar. It is something strange that derives from the hinterland of man's mind, as if it had emerged from the abyss of pre-human ages, or from a superhuman world which surpasses man's understanding and to which in his weakness he may easily succumb. The very enormity of experience gives it its value and its shattering impact. Sublime, pregnant with meaning, yet chilling the blood with its strangeness, it arises from timeless depths: glamorous, daemonic, and grotesque, it burst asunder out of human standards of value and aesthetic form, a tarrying tangle of eternal chaos. On the other hand, it can be a revelation of beauty which we can never put into words. ... but the primordial experiences rend from top to bottom the curtain upon which is painting the picture of an ordered world, and allow a glimpse into the unfathomable abyss at this of the unborn and of things yet to be. ... The creator of this kind of art is not the only one who is in touch with the night-side of life; prophets and seers are nourished by it too.[2]

Both the Part 2 of Goethe's *Faust* and Jung's *Red Book* fall into this category of visionary art. These are archetypal compensations for the lopsided attitudes of their times—and our times. Goethe's *Faust* and Jung's *Red Book* are compensatory to the heroic and warriorlike attitudes of our times, particularly the contemporary West. Let us explore the visionary dimension of Jung's *Red Book* and its compensatory prescriptions for the ills of our times.

"Spirit of this Time" and the "Spirit of the Depths"

Jung's Odyssey begins with balancing engagement with the duality between the contemporary and the timeless dimensions of the human condition. In *The Red Book*, he attends to this split:

> I have learned that in addition to the spirit of this time there is still another spirit at work, namely that the depths of everything contemporary.[3]

This reflection is one of the central tenets of the Hindu philosophy. We live in the Ahamkara (Ego), which is guided by the Atman (Self). The Atman is a fractal of the Brahman (the collective) and its timeless flow. Chapters 10 and 11 of *Bhagavad Gita* are the most lucid descriptions of the Brahman consciousness. Here are a few excerpts:

> Lord Krishna said: O Arjuna, listen once again to My supreme word … I am the origin of celestial controllers and great sages also. One who knows Me as the unborn, the beginningless, and the Supreme Lord of the universe, is considered wise among mortals and becomes liberated from the bondage of Karma.
> …behold My hundreds and thousands of multifarious divine forms of different colors and shapes. Behold all the celestial beings and many wonders never seen before. Also behold the entire creation—animate, inanimate, and whatever else you would like to see—all at one place in My body.[4]

The core prescription of the Hindu individuation process is to align one's life with the awareness of the Brahman consciousness while discharging one's responsibilities in the present. This would be akin to Jung's *opus* engaging the "spirit of the depths" while staying engaged with the "spirit of this time." This prescription of Gita to balance the existence in the "spirit of this time" informed by the "spirit of the depths" is a major teleological instruction for modern humans caught in the Maya of here and now, without the context of the timeless wisdom of cumulative human consciousness, its cautions, and blessings.

The method of engaging the "spirit of the depths" is depicted as a dialogue between Jung and his Guru, the wise old man Philemon, in the *Scrutinies* section as well as with other inner incarnations of the emergent self in *The Red Book*. Goethe's *Faust* is also the German prototype of this process of active imagination between the protagonist Faust and his inner figures, including the Shadow—Mephistopheles. These works recapitulate the wondrous dialogue between the warrior Arjuna and his Charioteer and guide Lord Krishna in *Bhagavad Gita,* which is the Hindu prototype of the process of active imagination.

Philemonis Sacrum – Fausti Poenitentia

"Philemon's Shine—Faust's Penitence" is the inscription carved by Jung over the entrance to his Bollingen Tower.

> In the days when I first read *Faust* I could not remotely guess the extent to which Goethe's strange heroic myth was a collective experience and that it prophetically anticipated the fate of the Germans. Therefore, I felt personally implicated, and when Faust, in his hubris and self-inflation, caused the murder of Philemon and Baucis, I felt guilty, quite as if I myself in the past that helped commit the murder of the two-old people. The strange idea was alarming, and I regarded it as my responsibility to atone for this crime, or to prevent its repetition.[5]

Here, Jung captures the spirit and the dilemma of his times. It was a split between the hubris and the humility, materialism versus altruism, hero versus the wise old man. This dilemma and split played out in the German psyche leading to scourge of the Nazi movement. It is an unfinished business of the Western psyche and continues to plague the contemporary West and United States in its aggressive, isolationist, nationalistic, and narcissistic leanings. In *The Red Book,*

Jung struggles with this split. He must murder the heroic attitude—his ego position and, via his transcendent function, find a way to his inner wise old man, Philemon, and work through the split between the Red One and the Anchorite.

It Is About Service

What defines the archetype of the wise old man, Philemon? The anchorite is the archetype of service. Jung reflects on this issue with useful guidance:

> I conceive it to be the duty of every one who isolates himself by taking his own path (of individuation), to tell others what he has found or discovered whether it be a refreshing spring for the thirsty, or a sandy desert of sterile error. The one helps, the other warns.[6]

The teleologic instruction here is for contemporary society to move from the culture of narcissism to the ethos of altruism and service. This is exemplified in the lives of individuals like Bill Gates and Warren Buffet, who have mastered the realm of material success and then devoted their lives and riches to service of humanity.

While analytical and Western thought sees service as expiation of guilt for diverting personal and collective resources for the individuation process, the Hindu perspective on service is one of Dharma, or a divine offering. Once we have a sense of our telos or destiny via our individuation GPS, it is not out of guilt but devotion to the divine and to the collective that we become a willing and useful spoke in the cosmic wheel—the *unus mundus*. The nature of such service is outlined by Krishna in *Bhadavad Gita*:

> Do your duty dedicating all works to God in a spiritual frame of mind free from desire, attachment, and mental grief.

Those who always practice this teaching of Mine with faith and are free from cavil become free from the bondage of Karma.[7]

The Hindu Path to Individuation – From Hero to Anchorite

In the Hindu philosophy, the transition between different life stages is mediated via archetypal activations. These are ushered in via the archetype of the avatars of Vishnu. These avatars may be considered as archetypal activations that reset our emergent personal myth during nodes of crisis, trauma, developmental transitions to a new life stage, new initiations, and during synchronistic possibilities for creative enterprise.

Whenever there is a decline of Dharma (Righteousness) and a predominance of Adharma (Unrighteousness), O Arjuna, I manifest Myself. I appear from time to time for protecting the good, for transforming the wicked, and for establishing world order (Dharma).[8]

Thus, the transition from the hero to the anchorite in the Hindu tradition would be mediated by the archetype of incarnations of Vishnu. It helps the Hindu to make a transition between the four stages of his life. The human life is divided into four Āshramas (stages). They are Brahmacharya, G ihastha, Vānaprastha and Sanyāsa.

The first quarter of one's life, Brahmacharya ("meditation, or study of the Brahman") is spent in celibate, controlled, sober, and pure contemplation under a Guru, building up the mind for the realization of truth. Grihastha is the householder's stage, alternatively known as samsara, in which one marries and satisfies Kama (Eros) and Artha (possessions) within one's married and professional life. Vānaprastha is gradual detachment from the material world, ostensibly giving over duties to one's children, spending more time in contemplation of the Divine, and making holy pilgrimages. Finally, in Sanyāsa, the individual goes into seclusion, often envisioned as

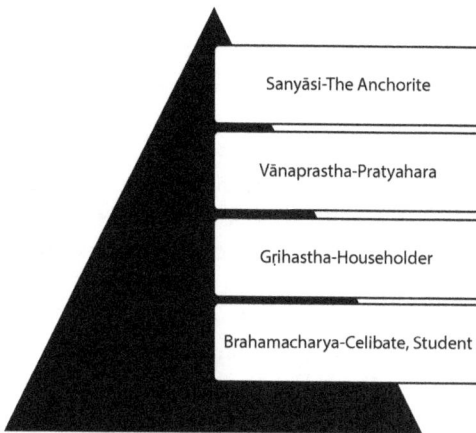

The Hindu Developmental Schema – the Stages of Life

renunciation, to find the Divine through detachment from worldly
life, and peacefully shed the body for the next life (or for liberation).

The West does not have a paradigm to stand down from the
hero archetype and to step into the anchorite. The West needed to
compensate for this void. Goethe's *Faust* and Jung's *Red Book* offer
this paradigm. The East has a long-established tradition of the four
stages of life to accomplish this crucial culmination of the
individuation process, the Sanyāsa. This helps the Hindu to stand
down from the ego's hero position and to step into the soul via
transcendence into the anchorite mode. On behalf of the collective,
Jung needed a myth to compensate for the West's embeddedness in
its hero position's temptations for power, prestige, and pelf, the three
temptations of Christ. The West made a Faustian bargain to sustain
this position. The shamans of the West, such as Jung, Dante and
Goethe, dreamed a way out of this sludge of its Faustian bargain to
step into the anchorite mode.

Edward Edinger's discussion of *Faust* is about how to maintain
our soul position in the face of these temptations, citing the Christian
prescription of the three temptations of Christ.[9] The Hindu

perspective has its four stages of life to deal with the tension of the opposites between "the Red One" and "the Anchorite" in the Hindu psyche. The Hindu paradigm is Pratyahara, or the withdrawal of consciousness from the mundane to the sacred, from outer to inner, from Maya and Karma to Dharma or Spiritual purposefulness. It is about standing down from the ego's heroic position in its embeddedness in Samsara, as shown in the character of "The Red One" in Jung's *Red Book*, into the Sunyata, the sacred void leading via transcendence into the Anchorite position.

Jung's "Commentary on *The Tibetan Book of the Dead*"[10] features this same struggle, showing the same tension between the *Chika Bardo* (Nirvana) and the *Sidpa Bardo* (Rebirth) and culminating in the third position, the *Chonyid Bardo*. This requires the subject to work through the tension between the hero and the anchorite modes of being and doing. In his *Red Book*, Jung struggles with this tension of the opposites in the Western psyche between the hero and the anchorite. In the process, he offers a compensatory myth for our times to retire the Faustian bargain. *The Red Book* offers a path to retire the sins of Faust and the restoration of Philemon, the anchorite, the Sanyāsa, to its rightful place in our emerging consciousness via Dharma, Service informed by Spiritual purpose.

Liber Quintus – the Fifth Book

Sonu Shamdasani depicts the layers of Jung's work in *The Red Book* as follows:[11]

Liber Primus: The Way of What Is to Come
Liber Secundus: The Images of the Erring
Liber Tertius: Scrutinies
Liber Quartus: "Philemon's Shrine – Faust's Penitence" at Jung's tower in Bollingen engraved in stone. (Sonu Shamdasani postulated: "The Tower may be regarded as a three-dimensional continuation of *Liber Novus*: its '*Liber Quartus*.'")[12]

This lays out the components of Jung's process. The essence of this process includes a dialogue between the ego and the unconscious, gradually moving toward a dialogue with the self, and the transformation of the self into the image of Philemon. This dialogue is further amplified via images and mandalas. Finally, there is a dialogue between Philemon and the dead ancestors to compensate and complement the missing pieces of the jigsaw puzzle in our ancestral paradigm and then to embody these core insights into stone at his tower—a repentance for the sins of their warrior culture and its deal with the devil and to honor the emergent wise old man, the guru Philemon, as an emergent myth for our collective. In his inner work, the myth of Philemon, particularly his murder by Mephistopheles on instructions of Faust, and repentance for this murder became the task for our collective. This was represented in the stone carving at Jung's tower in Bollingen: *Philemonis Sacrum – Fausti Poententia* ("Philemon's Shrine – Faust's Penitence").[13]

However, there is a fifth step in this process. This includes living out our personal myth. This may be considered as the fifth layer of Jung's process, which would insist on embodiment of these insights in life's work, the *Liber Quintus*. To make room for our individuation, we borrow time and resources from the collective. However, this debt must be repaid via service to the collective in the form and manner that the collective demands. Jung elaborated on this issue in his reflections about service as the culmination of the individuation process.

> Only to the extent that a man creates objective values can he and may he individuate. Every further step individuation (sobriety) creates new guilt and necessitates expiation. Hence individuation is possible only as long as substitute values are produced. Individuation is exclusive adaptation to inner reality (being oneself) and hence an allegedly 'mystical' process. The expiation is adaptation to the outer world. It has to be offered to the outer world, with the petition that the outer world accepts it.[14]

Jung's emergent personal myth was Philemon, who is the very embodiment of service. The story of Philemon and his wife, Baucis, is instructive at this point in our journey.[15] Baucis and Philemon showed hospitality toward the gods and were rewarded. According to the Greek myth, the gods Zeus and Hermes assumed human form and visited the earth disguised as poor travelers. When they reached Phrygia, they looked for shelter but were turned away by everyone except Philemon and Baucis. The old couple gladly shared their small amount of food and wine with the strangers. Baucis and Philemon realized that their guests were gods after noticing that the wine jug never ran out and that their poor wine was replaced by wine of the finest quality. Zeus and Hermes led the couple to a hill above Phrygia and sent a flood to destroy the land to punish the people who had turned them away. This is the tale of selfless service, even to strangers. In most traditions, including the Hindu, a guest is considered the incarnation of the Gods (*Atithi Devo Bhava*—Guest is God). When we honor a guest, even when they are strangers, we honor the divine. The traditional greeting in Hindus is "*Namaste*," which translates as "I honor the divine in you."

Living your personal myth, your Dharma, constitutes the central tenet of Karma yoga in Hindu philosophy. A life lived in accord with one's soul code is the seminal recommendation of *Bhagavad Gita*.

> One who does all work as an offering to God—abandoning attachment to results—remains untouched by Karmic reaction or sin, just as a lotus leaf never gets wet by water.[16]

Hindus recognize that Dharma is life lived when the soul is aligned with the intentions of the primal Spirit.[17] Here, the Atman-Self is aligned with the Brahman, the collective. Dharma is the spiritual purposefulness. There are four plateaus of Dharma. The Sva Dharma, or Self Dharma, is cultivating our personal potentials in accord with the Atman and Brahman. This prepares us for Ashram Dharma, where we put our personal gifts in service of our family. Having retired our family Dharma, we graduate to Varana Dharma, where we put our gifts and potentials in service of our community. When we attend to these three Dharmas, we are given a glimpse into the mysteries of the transcendent, the divine, the Brahman consciousness at the dusk of life in Reta Dharma, the path that leads to awareness of our higher *coniunctio* with the collective, what Jung might call the *unus mundus*. One teleological prescription of Jung's *Red Book* is for our collective to move from consumerism to altruism, from a focus on self to devotion to service. Our very survival as a human community may depend upon it.

Engagement of the Feminine in *The Red Book*

In *The Red Book*, Jung's engagement with the feminine is mediated by the imaginal figure of Salome. Salome fosters ambivalence in the Christian lexicon as the one righteous, the other unrighteous. The righteous Salome was the wife of Zebedee (*Matthew* 27:56), the mother of the disciples *James and John,* and a female follower of Jesus. This Salome was the one who came to Jesus with the request that her sons sit in places of honor in the kingdom (*Matthew* 20:20–21). She was also one of the women "looking on from a distance" when Jesus was being crucified, along with Mary Magdalene and Mary the mother of Joseph and James (*Mark* 15:40). These same women were together on the third day after the crucifixion, bringing spices to Jesus's tomb to anoint Him. When they encountered the angel, who told them that Jesus was risen, they ran to tell the disciples the good news (*Mark* 16:1–8). Mark's Gospel is the only one that mentions Salome by name.

The other, unrighteous Salome is not mentioned by name in the Bible, but we read about what she did in *Mark* 6. John the Baptist's fate was decided when Herodias's daughter (Salome) danced for Herod at his birthday banquet. Pleased with the girl's performance, Herod offered her a rash boon. Salome went to Herodias to ask her advice on what the gift should be, and Herodias told her to ask for the head of John the Baptist on a platter. Salome obediently asked Herod for this grisly gift, and, though the Bible says Herod was grieved, he honored his promise. John was beheaded in prison and his head given to Herodias's daughter, who took it to her mother (*Mark* 6:21–28).

It is interesting that Salome becomes the embodiment of the anima in Jung's active imaginations. What might be the teleological import of this choice? We may understand this better in the context of the dark Hindu goddess, Kali. Kali is the destroyer of the shadow in our personality and the community.[18] She then assimilates this darkness in her own being so that the world may live in the light of the Spirit. Kali is the fierce dark goddess who amputates the darkness of our soul and makes room for the light. Whenever a life is out of balance, the shadow aspects of the individual or culture get in the driver's seat. Then the archetype of the dark goddess Kali incarnates in our life to destroy the darkness of the personality and culture to make room for a new consciousness to emerge. It seems Jung had accurately intuited the emergence of the Kali archetype in our collective via her Western prototype in Salome. She will manifest in the contemporary culture to restore the balance of our embeddedness in our shadow globally. It is my speculation the Kali archetype may manifest in our environmental catastrophes, street wars between marauding gangs roaming our cities, skirmishes between racial groups, nuclear Armageddon, the collapse of our health care system, and gun violence going amok in schools and streets. In a post-apocalyptic world, a new and just world order will emerge. This teleology has been indicated in the Bible in the Apocalypse of John.

> And I saw a new heaven and a new earth: for the first heaven and the first earth were passed away; and there was no more sea.
> And I John saw the holy city, new Jerusalem, coming down from God out of heaven, prepared as a bride adorned for her husband.[19]

Perhaps this is also the key to the Jung's dialogue with the dead in the *Scrutinies*—the dead who have returned from Jerusalem, still seeking answers. Perhaps the transition through Salome's Kali phase is a necessary detour before our civilization can emerge as the holy city of the New Jerusalem. The New Jerusalem will honor the feminine political empowerment and the subjugation of the negative static-masculine world order.[20] This subjugation of Shiva by Kali may already have begun. This groundwork was laid by leaders like Golda

Kali (The Walters Art Museum, Baltimore)

Meir of Israel, Indira Gandhi of India, Margaret Thatcher of Great Britain, Angela Merkel in Germany, Theresa May in Great Britain, the near presidency of Hillary Clinton in United States, who won the popular vote and perhaps led the emerging feminine leadership in U.S.A. in promising candidates like Michelle Obama, Elizabeth Warren, and others. This incarnation of the Kali archetype was manifest on January 21, 2017, Donald Trump's first day in office as the U.S. president when millions of women across the globe and men who supported them stood in solidarity of this sisterhood to protest against the oppressive patriarchy.

The global feminist movement is in the process of its initiation into her own authority. The myth that best embodies this process is masterfully rendered by Sylvia Perera in her work on the *Descent to the Goddess*.[21] She postulates that Inanna, the innocent goddess of the upper world, must descend into the realm of her dark sister, Erizkegal. This entails surrender to her suffering and sacrifice but return to the upper world tempered by the experience of the dark side and empowered to claim her wholeness and equality with the men. Thus, Erizkegal and her Hindu analogues, Kali and Durga, are the guiding myths for our collective currently. This is the crossroad Jung reached in his *Red Book* in his dealing with Salome versus Philemon, his competing emerging myths, but it is left for us to make our own choice at this point in the history of our civilization. It is my postulate that the Philemon is the transitional archetype that will set the stage to welcome Kali (the destroyer) and Durga (the protector warrior) at the center stage in the emerging global consciousness. The feminine authority will ride the masculine order as Kali rides Shiva, who surrenders to her authority in this image.[22]

Jung further amplifies this emergence of the wise woman:

> … we are dealing with the heterosexual Eros or anima-figure in four stages, and consequently with four stages of the Eros cult. The first stage—Hawwah, Eve, earth—is purely biological; woman is equated with the mother and only represents something to be fertilized. The second stage [Helen of Troy] is still dominated by the sexual Eros, but on an aesthetic and romantic level where woman has

already acquired some value as an individual. The third
stage raises Eros to the heights of religious devotion and
thus spiritualizes him: Hawwah has been replaced by
spiritual motherhood. Finally, the fourth stage illustrates
something which unexpectedly goes beyond the almost
unsurpassable third stage: *Sapientia.* How can wisdom
transcend the most holy and the most pure? Presumably
only by the virtue of the truth that the less sometimes
means the more. This stage represents a spiritualization of
Helen and consequently of the Eros as such.[23]

This formulation of the engagement with the feminine is a derivative
of Jung's amplification of Goethe's *Faust.* However, there is a different
trajectory of engagement with the feminine in the Eastern Hindu
framework. This is amplified in the Kundalini yoga system, which is
a paradigm for the mysterious union, the *hieros gamos,* between the
masculine and the feminine, the Shiva and the Shakti energies of the
psyche. In Kundalini yoga, there are seven stages of engagement with
the feminine, starting from the first, or the root chakra, and going up
to the seventh, the highest chakra. These include engagement with
the feminine as mother embodied in the images of Durga. This is
followed by mother as a place of respite from the father's world as
Parvati. In the third chakra, she is represented as a muse inspiring
the warrior who is manifest in the archetype of Radha, who inspired
Krishna. This process culminates with the feminine as a lover, Uma,
the consort of Shiva in the fourth—the heart-chakra. Beyond this is
the stage of spiritualization of the anima as she becomes an
inspiration to Brahma for his voice and his music in the fifth, or the
throat, chakra as the goddess Sarasvati. In the sixth, or the eye,
chakra, Laxmi becomes ego guide giving Vishnu a third eye for "insight," and finally at the highest level of integration between the
masculine and the feminine in the seventh chakra she becomes the
soul guide to Shiva as Bhagwati, the Universal great mother and Aditi,
the great grandmother goddess of void and new creations. Some of
these goddess archetypes are discussed in my earlier publication.[24]

The role of the mother as Durga and Parvati as the respite would
be akin to the stage of Hawwah or Eve. In the third chakra, the feminine

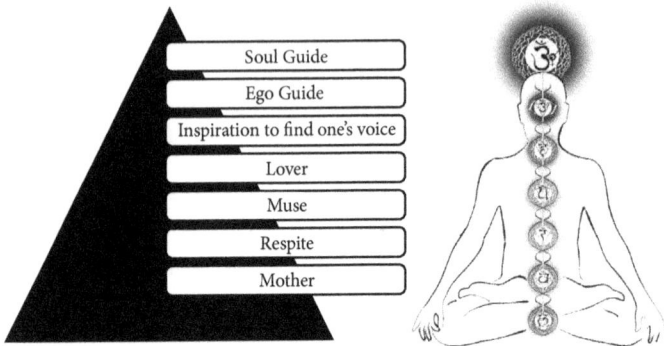

The Feminine Developmental Schema – A Kundalini Yoga Perspective

is perceived as a muse, Radha, and in the fourth chakra as a lover Uma, a more aesthetic figure and a romantic engagement with the feminine as Helen. In the fifth and the sixth chakras, she is perceived as a spiritual figure, Sarasvati and Laxmi, an inspiration and an ego guide as the Virgin Mary. However, in the seventh chakra of the highest level of engagement she is seen as a soul guide, the Universal great mother Bhagwati and Aditi, akin to Jung's formulation of *sapientia*.

In *The Red Book*, Jung's engagement with the feminine starts with mother as darkness that leads to the light. This is akin to Goethe's prescription to descent into the realms of the mothers to find a way to reclaim connection with the lost Helen anima. Jung states:

> The darkness is your mother; she behooves reverence, since the mother is dangerous. She has power over you, since she gave birth to you. Honor the Darkness as the light, and you will illuminate your darkness.[25]

This may correspond to the Mother as a dark place of origins, the Durga/Parvati of the lower chakras in the Kundalini Yoga. Then Jung goes on to relate to the mother as a place of respite akin to the Parvati as a place of respite for the weary Ganesha in the second chakra of Kundalini Yoga.

Fearless Girl (Photo by Mitali Kamdar)

O mother stone, I love you, I lie snuggled up against your
warm body, your late child. Blessed be you, ancient mother.
Yours is my heart and all glory and power—Amen.[26]

The emergence of the Kali and Durga feminine archetypes is
embodied in the fearless girl bronze statue facing down the Wall
Street Bull in Manhattan in the New York City. "Fearless Girl" is a
bronze sculpture by Uruguayan-born American artist Kristen Visbal,
depicting a defiant girl staring down the well-known Charging Bull,
a symbol of static, negative, masculine order. This statue was installed
on March 7, 2017, on the eve of the International Women's Day.[27]

The Red Book – The Teleological Perspective

The timing of the publication of *The Red Book* has interesting
implications. Why was this account of Jung's inner encounter not
published for about 100 years? It is my speculation that the "spirit of
his time" was not quite primed to attend to the "spirit of its depths."
Perhaps there is Hermes at work in this timing of the introduction of
the "spirit of the depths" implicit in Jung's *opus*. It took about 100
years to gradually prepare the culture to receive the gifts of the depths
and its timeless wisdom. The timing of the publication is also
synchronistic in that the technology has now matured for the material
to be reproduced in its original aesthetic form.

In India, it is said that the old souls have shamanic tendencies.
They readily connect with the flow of the collective and they dream
for their clans and their cultures. Jesus, Moses, Muhammad, Buddha
had such capacities. It is my postulate that Goethe and Carl Jung had
shamanic proclivity. Jung had prophetic dreams foreshadowing the
breakout of the World War I. His inner work in his own individuation
opus also pointed in this direction. His writings have both a
psychological and a visionary dimension. His *Red Book* in particular
is an archetypal, visionary piece of literature that channels the
collective psyche's compensatory activation—the necessity of the
death of the hero culture, the integration of its shadow, aligned with
the anima and the feminine functions, and the emergence of the

archetype of the Rishi—the anchorite, the wise old man—the guru; who serves, sacrifices and guides others through the example of his lived life of service and sacrifice embodied in the image of Philemon. Philemon is not just the embodiment of Jung's number two personality, his self, but the guiding myth of our times—a gift from the "spirit of the depths" that offers us a GPS to navigate the spirit of our times. This entails an *enantiodromia* from a culture of self to an ethos of service, from consumerism to altruism.

It is my postulate that Philemon is a transitional archetype that may make way for the activation of the Kali archetype that will do the necessary cleanup of the shadow dimensions of our present culture to make room for the new beginnings, the New Jerusalem that the Dead sought in the *Scrutinies* of Jung's *Liber Novus*. In its democratic, liberal persona, the West has repressed its Wotan longings, which have resurged in the current political climate. These repressed cultural complexes have returned with a vengeance and must be acknowledged and transmuted under the agency of the Philemon and Kali-*Sophia* archetypes so that we may be redeemed as a culture. Like Faust, our heroic culture must return to the realm of the mothers. This is exemplified in the goddess Inanna of the upper world, who must descend into the underworld of her twin sister Erizkegal—the dark Kali, to be murdered and kept rotting onto the meat hook before being revived and restored to her potential for wholeness.[28] Thus empowered, the feminine will take its rightful leadership in the global order. Once we retire this Faustian bargain with Wotan, we stand ready to be salvaged by the grace of the divine feminine oft quoted by Jung from Goethe's *Faust*,

> Gaze to meet the saving gaze,
> Contrite all and tender,
> For a blissful fate your ways
> Thankfully surrender.
> May each noble mind be seen
> Eager for Thy service;
> Holy Virgin, Mother, Queen,
> Goddess, pour Thy mercies![29]

Endnotes

[1] C. S. Lewis, *An Experiment in Criticism* (Cambridge: Cambridge University Press, 1961), 19.

[2] C.G. Jung, "Psychology and Literature" (1930), in *CW*, vol. 15 (Princeton, NJ: Princeton University Press, 1966), pars. 139-162.

[3] C.G. Jung, *The Red Book: Liber Novus*, ed. Sonu Shamdasani, tr. John Peck, Mark Kyburz, and Sonu Shamdasani (New York, NY: W. W. Norton, 2009), 229.

[4] "American/International Gita Society Bhagavad Gita," http://www.sacred-texts.com/hin/gita/agsgita.htm, Chap. 3, pars. 5-7.

[5] C.G. Jung, *Memories, Dreams, Reflections*, ed. Aniela Jaffé (New York, NY: Vintage Books, 1963), 234.

[6] C.G. Jung, *Collected Papers on Analytical Psychology*, ed. Constance E. Long, 2nd ed. (Kessinger Publishing, 2007), 443-444.

[7] "American/International Gita Society Bhagavad Gita," Chap. 3, pars. 3: 30-32.

[8] Ibid., chap. 4, pars. 7-8.

[9] Edward F. Edinger, *Goethe's Faust* (Toronto, Canada: Inner City Books, 1990), 77-78.

[10] Walter Evans-Wentz, *The Tibetan Book of the Dead (with a Psychological Commentary by C.G. Jung)* (Oxford: Oxford University Press, 1960).

[11] C.G. Jung, *The Red Book: A Reader's Edition* (New York, NY: W. W. Norton, 2012), 45.

[12] Sonu Shamdasani, ed., *Introduction to Jungian Psychology. Notes of the Seminar on Analytical Psychology given in 1925* (Princeton, NJ: Princeton University Press, 2012), Introduction, XIII.

[13] C.G. Jung and Aniela Jaffé, *C.G. Jung: Word and Image* (Princeton, NJ: Princeton University Press, 1983), 188.

[14] C.G. Jung, "Two Essays on Analytical Psychology" (1916), in *CW*, vol. 7 (Princeton, NJ: Princeton University Press, 1966), par. 1095.

[15] Baucis and Philemon: http://www.Mythencyclopedia.com/Ar-Be/Baucis-and-Philemon.Html.

[16] "American/International Gita Society Bhagavad Gita," Chap. 5, pars. 10-12.

17 Ashok Bedi, *Path to the Soul* (York Beach, ME: S. Weiser, 2000), 257.

18 Ashok Bedi, *Awaken the Slumbering Goddess - the Latent Code of the Hindu Goddess Archetypes* (BookSurge, 2007), 115.

19 *The Holy Bible*, The Book of Revelation, 21:23.

20 Gareth S. Hill, *Masculine and Feminine: The Natural Flow of Opposites in the Psyche.* (Boston, MA: Shambala Publications, 1992), 45-46.

21 Sylvia B. Perera, *Descent to the Goddess: A Way of Initiation for Women* (Toronto, Canada: Inner City Books, 1989).

22 Many thanks to the Walter Museum for the use of the Kali image reprinted with the kind permission of The Walters Art Museum, Baltimore.

23 C.G. Jung, "The Psychology of Transference" (1946), in *CW*, vol. 16 (Princeton, NJ: Princeton University Press, 1966), par. 361.

24 Ashok Bedi, *Awaken the Slumbering Goddess - the Latent Code of the Hindu Goddess Archetypes.*

25 Jung, *The Red Book,* 270.

26 Ibid., 271.

27 My gratitude to Ms. Mitali Kamdar for permission to use her "Fearless Girl" photograph.

28 Sylvia B. Perera, *Descent to the Goddess: A Way of Initiation for Women,* 9.

29 Johann Wolfgang von Goethe, *Faust: A Tragedy* (New York, NY: W. W. Norton, 1998), 344.

Why Is *The Red Book* "Red"?:
A Chinese Reader's Reflections

Heyong Shen

Jung's *Liber Novus* is red, and for me as a Chinese person, this color is so touching and moving. When I first held *The Red Book* in my hands in 2009, my immediate thought was: Why is it red? Also inside the book, when you open it and look at the first page of *Liber Primus*, you find a bold drawing of the letter "D" in a special shade of red to introduce the chapter, "The Way of What Is to Come." After that, almost every letter at the start of sentences or paragraphs is similarly colored in a shade of red. Then we find the mythical figure, Izdubar, clothed in red (with blue armor, image 36); the Red One is red, of course; and the image of Philemon, along with his clothing and his wings (image 154) and the atmosphere surrounding him, are almost totally colored in red. So red is not only the color of the book's cover; it is also the color of important contents within the book. What does this signify?

In Sonu Shamdasani's "Introduction," we discover a hint to the meaning of this omnipresent color, red. Cary Baynes, who was asked by Jung to make a fresh transcription of the *Red Book*'s text in the early 1920s, kept a notebook in the form of (unsent) letters to Jung. In one of them she writes:

> In another book of Meyrink's the 'White Dominican,' [sic] you said he made use of exactly the same symbolism that had come to you in the first vision that revealed to your unconscious. Furthermore you said, he had spoken of a 'Red Book' which contained certain mysteries and the book that you are writing about the unconscious, you have called the 'Red Book.'[1]

Jung was familiar with Meyrink's works, such as *The Golem*, *The Green Face*, and *The White Dominican*. In Shamdasani's footnote to

Cary Baynes's unsent letter, we find the following important information about Meyrink's mystical novel:

> The 'founding father' informs the hero of the novel, Christopher, that 'whoever possesses the Cinnabar-red Book, the plant of immortality, the awakening of the spiritual breath, and the secret of bringing the right hand to life, will dissolve with the corps ... It is called the Cinnabar book because, according to ancient belief in China, that red is the colour of the garments of those who have reached the highest stage of perfection and stayed behind on earth for the salvation of mankind.'[2]

The White Dominican is Meyrink's most esoteric novel, and it draws on the wisdom of a number of mystical traditions, the most important of which is Chinese Taoism. Following the Way, the Tao, Christopher, the hero of the novel, joins "the living chain" that stretches to infinity. For the Chinese Taoists, cinnabar-red is regarded as the color of life and eternity.

Cinnabar-red, or vermilion, is also called "Chinese Red." In China, the first documented use of the mineral cinnabar for a color pigment occurred in the Yangshao culture, around 5000 to 4000 B.C.E.: It was used to paint ceramic bowls for ritual ceremonies. From ancient times, cinnabar was regarded as the color of blood and thus the color of life, of the heart and soul. When Chinese objects colored with cinnabar were exported to Europe in the 17th century, it was one of most expensive pigments, almost as precious as gold leaf. At the time, it was used only for the most important decorations in illuminated manuscripts.

Jung wrote in the Epilogue to the *Red Book*: "I always knew that these experiences contained something precious, and therefore I knew of nothing better than to write them down in a 'precious,' that is to say, costly book and to paint the images that emerged through reliving it all—as well as I could."[3]

The Chinese characters for cinnabar-red (vermillion) are "Zhu-Hong." The first character is "Zhu," referencing a special tree with a red heart. This is its original form in the ancient oracles: 朮. The

Human faced fish decoration pottery bowl with Cinnabar-red color.
Yangshao Culture, Banpo style (4800-4300 B.C.E.) (Public Domain)

"point" at the center indicates "the red heart" of the tree. In ancient times, the pens used by emperors and the great Daoists were made of this wood. The second character, which means "red," is "*Hong*": 紅. This character is a combination of "fine silk" (*mi*: 糸) and "skill" (*gong*: 工). The image of "fine silk" is associated with the silkworm and the mulberry tree. The ancient Chinese people worshipped the mulberry tree because it was valued as the tree of life, or the mother tree, symbolizing the archetypal feminine. The Chinese character for "skill" is the original symbol for "shaman" (工). In the meaning of the original symbol and attested by the classical Chinese dictionary, the shaman is one who can communicate between heaven and earth, who can service the invisible (unconscious) realm and can dance to invite the spiritual (god), or the soul, to be present.

Another name for cinnabar in Chinese is "*Dan*," whose original character in the oracles was: 丹. The meaning of Dan in Chinese is related to alchemy and to Daoist practice. It is called "the cinnabar field," where essence and spirit are stored. As some translations expressed it, it is "the elixir field" or "the energy center." For Daoist Yoga, this is the focal point for the transmutation of the three treasures: *Jing* (essence), *Qi* (energy) and *Shen* (spirit). *Dan* is also a symbol, or word, for "the heart." Also, *Dan*, as cinnabar red, is a name for Dragon's blood and is a special ingredient in traditional medicine. In fact, it is a toxic mineral (mercury sulfide, HgS), but it possesses a healing function when combined with other herbs, as the five elements theory shows. According to the Herbal Classic of Shennong, cinnabar is taken as jade in the world of goods and has the function of keeping and nurturing the spirit and of making content and secure the Hun-Po, the soul.

So, the characters and symbols related to the Chinese name for cinnabar red, or vermilion, convey important symbolic meanings of great significance. C.G. Jung, who studied the *I Ching* and Chinese characters, once expressed his special feeling for Chinese characters as "readable archetypes."[4]

Translated into Chinese literally, *The Red Book* is "Red Book" ("*Hong Shu*"), and *Liber Novus* is "New Book." The original symbol for "New" in Chinese, is (斉), which means "getting wood" (maybe the wood of the special tree with a red heart, the first character for the cinnabar red mineral in Chinese). Synchronistically, "new" in Chinese (*Xin*) has the same pronunciation as the word for "heart" (*Xin*). So, the *Liber Novus*, the New Book, in the Chinese cultural context, also has the meaning of the "Book of the Heart." The image and meaning of the heart occupies a central meaning in Chinese culture and language, as well as in Chinese philosophy such as is found in the *I Ching*, Confucianism, Daoism and Buddhism. Based on them, we have inaugurated the "psychology of the heart" for our Jungian practice in China.[5]

Red is the color of the heart and blood, and it is also the color of the liver as well. In the 13th chapter of *Liber Secundus*, titled "Sacrificial Murder," the protagonist describes his encounter with the "liver." A shrouded woman tells him: "You know what the liver means, and you ought to perform the healing act with it."[6] After he eats the liver, Jung meets his soul.[7] On January 2, 1927, Jung had his "Liverpool" dream. In the center was a pool, and on it "stood a single tree, a magnolia, in a shower of reddish blossoms. It was as though the tree stood in the sunlight and was at the same time the source of light."[8] When Jung spoke of this dream, he said: "I had a vision of unearthly beauty, and that is why I was able to live at all. Liverpool is the 'pool of life.' The 'liver,' according to an old view, is the seat of life, that which makes to live."[9]

The liver is the seat of life! —just as in Chinese traditional medicine, the Yin-Yang and the Five Elements theory. The liver, whose nature is wood, feeds the heart, whose nature is fire, and so it makes it possible for a person to live. At the same time, according to Chinese tradition, the liver is the place of the "*hun*" ("cloud-ghost"), the soul, or anima in Jung's terminology. (Liverpool, the real city, contains the first, the oldest and largest Chinese population in Europe—another synchronicity.)

For Jung, this Liverpool dream is so important for his understanding of the self, for the individuation process, and for his life. He writes in *Memories, Dreams, Reflections*: "This dream brought with it a sense of finality. I saw that here the goal had been revealed. One could not go beyond the center. The center is the goal and everything is directed towards that center. Through this dream I understood that the self is a principle and archetype of orientation and meaning. Therein lies its healing function." Then he continues: "For me, this insight signified an approach to the center and therefore to the goal. Out of it emerged a first inkling of my personal myth. After this dream I gave up drawing or painting mandalas. The dream depicted the climax of the whole process of development."[10]

In *The Secret of the Golden Flower*, one finds the "the town plan" that depicts the scene of the "Liverpool" dream. As Sonu Shamdasani notes: "The sketch is the basis of image 159, linking the dream with the mandala."[11] This image is titled "Window on Eternity": In his "Commentary on 'The Secret of Golden Flower,'" Jung offers a written description of this picture: "A luminous flower in the center, with stars rotating about it. Around the flower, walls with eight gates. The whole conceived as a transparent window."[12] Jung mentions the mandala image and the Liverpool dream in many places of his writings and seminars, as for instance in *The Psychology of Kundalini Yoga*, where

"Window on Eternity" (From *The Red Book* by C.G. Jung, edited by Sonu Shamdasani, translated by Mark Kyburz, John Peck, and Sonu Shamdasani. Copyright © 2009 by the Foundation of the Works of C.G. Jung Translation 2009 by Mark Kyburz, John Peck, and Sonu Shamdasani. Used by permission of W. W. Norton & Company, Inc.)

he says: "I thought very well of myself that I was able to express myself like that: my marvelous center here and I am right in my heart. ... Now Liverpool is the center of life—liver is the center of life—and I am not the center ..."[13] In *Memories, Dreams and Reflections*, Jung recalls that after his Liverpool dream, he "painted a second picture, likewise a mandala, with a golden castle in the center."[14]

Of this mandala, Jung recalls: "When it was finished, I asked myself, 'Why is this so Chinese?' I was impressed by the form and choice of colors, which seemed to me Chinese, although there was nothing outwardly Chinese about it. Yet that was how it affected me.

"Golden, well-fortified castle" (From *The Red Book* by C.G. Jung, edited by Sonu Shamdasani, translated by Mark Kyburz, John Peck, and Sonu Shamdasani. Copyright © 2009 by the Foundation of the Works of C.G. Jung Translation 2009 by Mark Kyburz, John Peck, and Sonu Shamdasani. Used by permission of W. W. Norton & Company, Inc.)

It was a strange coincidence that shortly afterward I received a letter from Richard Wilhelm enclosing the manuscript of a Taoist-alchemical treatise entitled The Secret of the Golden Flower, with a request that I write a commentary on it."[15] We know that, as with the Liverpool dream, the *Secret of the Golden Flower* was very important to him. Jung says: "I devoured the manuscript at once, for the text gave me undreamed-of confirmation of my ideas about the mandala and the circumambulation of the center. That was the first event which broke through my isolation. I became aware of an affinity; I could establish ties with something and someone."[16] Jung took his meeting with Wilhelm to be one of the most significant events of his life. For Jung, Wilhelm through his translations of classic Chinese texts had inoculated the West with the living germ of the Chinese spirit. In the *Memories, Dreams, Reflections,* Jung says: "In remembrance of this coincidence, this 'synchronicity,' I wrote underneath the picture which had made so Chinese an impression upon me: 'In 1928, when I was painting this picture, showing the golden, well-fortified castle, Richard Wilhelm in Frankfurt sent me the thousand-year-old Chinese text on the yellow castle, the germ of the immortal body.'"[17] In *The Red Book*, we can see the detail of the picture with Jung's note: "Why is this so Chinese?"[18] We can still ask the same question about the color red of *The Red Book*.

"Chinese" is not just a name for some people or a country, just as "Chinese medicine" cannot be just understood as the "medicine of China." The core, or the secret, of the meaning of "Chinese" lies in the character "*Zhong*" (equilibrium).

The original form of the character of "*Zhong*" for the name of Chinese or China is Φ. The basic meaning of *Zhong* is "core," the center, the heart, the right time, the state of equilibrium and harmony. It is also the symbol for high noon. The name of the red color of *The Red Book* in Chinese is "*Zhu-hong*," which besides cinnabar-red or vermilion and the tree with a red heart, is also associated with the color of the sun at the moment of the high noon.

Zhong (equilibrium) is the main principle of the *I Ching*. As the second line and the fifth line of each hexagram, it is the center or mean for the inner and the outer trigrams. So *Zhong* conveys the meaning of the third, the balance of Yin and Yang, and the transcendent function. That is the exactly the meaning of *Zhong-Yi*, Chinese medicine, which uses the equilibrium principle for treatment. The image of the character for the Great Commentary of the *I Ching* (*Xici*) is closely related to the right side of the image for the color red (*Hong*): 絲. This image conveys the symbolic meaning of "knotted point," the core and the middle numbers of the trigrams.

Chinese culture is a culture of *Zhong*, equilibrium, and the word *Shou-Zhong* is a term for the basic Taoist principle. As Lao-tzu says, "All things carry Yin and have Yang, being harmony by equilibrium of vacancy."[19] *Zhong* (equilibrium) is the foundation of the Confucius tradition, just as is *Zhong-yong*, the Doctrine of the Mean: "When joy, anger, sorrow and happiness are not revealed, they are *Zhong*, in the mean. When they are revealed, they are *He*, in harmony. *Zhong* is the base of everything and *He* is the right way to reveal everything. If *Zhong* and *He* are achieved, the world would run smoothly."[20] For Buddhism, the Middle Way (*madhyamā-mārga*), as Buddha describes the Noble Eightfold Path that leads to liberation, also uses *Zhong* and *Tao* in Chinese.

The Red Book shows Jung searching diligently for the heart and soul, the middle Way and the Tao, the self and individuation. For instance, on 24 June 1914 Jung writes: "In the night my soul spoke to me: 'The greatest comes to the smallest.'"[21] Following one year of silence after this, Jung saw an osprey seize a big fish and rise into the skies, and he heard the voice again: "That is a sign that what is below is borne upward."[22] The image and meaning of the Chinese character *Zhong* (equilibrium) and the right part of the character *Hong* (red) imply precisely the union of below and above. As one reads "The Seven Sermons to the Dead" delivered by Philemon, one feels the meaning of the Tao or Buddhism, as in the teaching: "I begin with nothingness. Nothingness is the same as fullness. In infinity full is as good as empty. Nothingness is empty and full ..."[23]

In *Two Essays in Analytical Psychology*, Jung says: "... I might invoke Lao-tzu and appropriate his concept of Tao, the Middle Way and creative centre of all things."[24] In *Psychological Types*, Jung quotes several passages from Lao-tzu to explain the "the uniting symbol," as for example:

> There was something formless yet complete,
> That existed before heaven and earth;
> Without sound, without substance,
> Dependent on nothing, unchanging,
> All pervading, unfailing,
> One may think of it as the mother of all things under heaven.
> Its true name we do not know;
> 'Way' is the name that we give it.[25]

Jung says of this: "Unfortunately our Western mind, lacking all culture in this respect, has never yet devised a concept, nor even a name, for the *union of opposites through the middle path*, that most fundamental item of inward experience, which could respectably be set against the Chinese concept of Tao. It is at once the most individual fact and the most universal, the most legitimate fulfilment of the meaning of the individual's life."[26] For Jung, "*Tao* is the right way, the reign of law, the middle road between the opposites, freed from them and yet uniting them in itself. The purpose of life is to travel this middle road and never to deviate towards the opposites."[27] The aim of Taoist ethics is to find deliverance from the cosmic tension of opposites by a return to Tao.

On the last page of *The Red Book*, in the *Epilogue* Jung wrote in 1959, he mentions Richard Wilhelm and the *Golden Flower*. Jung writes: "I worked on this book for 16 years. My acquaintance with alchemy in 1930 took me away from it. The beginning of the end came in 1928, when Wilhelm sent me the text of the 'Golden Flower,' an alchemical treatise. There the contents of this book found their way into actuality and I could no longer continue working on it."[28] In his "Richard Wilhelm in Memoriam" address, Jung says: "Wilhelm accomplished his mission in every sense of the word. Not only did he make accessible to us the cultural treasure of ancient China, but, as I have said, he brought us its spiritual root, the root that has remained alive all these thousands of years, and planted it in the soil of Europe. … According to the law of *enantiodromia*, so well understood by the Chinese, the end of one phase is the beginning of its opposite."[29] Even though *The Red Book* is closed, the spirit of it continued, as people believe that Bollingen is the continuation of the *Red Book*, the *Liber Quartus*. Jung's acquaintance with alchemy and the confrontation with the world also represent the continuation. All of these are representations of the individuation process, which convey a revelation to us and to the world today.

"The Tao Is the Way." Richard Wilhelm translated the Chinese character of Tao into European language as "meaning," which Jung appreciated very much. Jung said: "We must continue Wilhelm's work of translation in a wider sense if we wish to show ourselves worthy pupils of the master. The central concept of Chinese philosophy is *tao*, which Wilhelm translated as 'meaning.' Just as Wilhelm gave the spiritual treasure of the East a European meaning, so we should translate this meaning into life. To do this—that is, to realize *tao*—would be the true task of the pupil."[30]

In Delphi, there is the *omphalos*. This symbol conveys the meaning of searching for the centre of all things, including the union of opposites. According to legend, Delphi, as the temenos for the *omphalos*, contains the means for communicating with God, or the spirit of the depths. If we still have the chance to communicate with the depths, as Jung did, perhaps we should remember the image and meaning of the color red, the principle of *Zhong* and "equilibrium." Or as Meyrink described it, the plant of immortality, the awakening of the spiritual breath, and the secret of bringing the right hand to life and of those who have reached the highest stage of perfection and stayed behind on earth for the salvation of mankind. As Jung's last sentence in *The Red Book* puts it so modestly: "I knew how frightfully inadequate this undertaking was, but despite much work and many distractions I remained true to it, even if another / possibility never ..."[31] So *The Red Book*, the *Liber Novus*, with the cinnabar-red cover and a book of the heart in Chinese, may serve as a guide for our world today.

Endnotes

1 C.G. Jung, *The Red Book: Liber Novus*, ed. Sonu Shamdasani, tr. John Peck, Mark Kyburz, and Sonu Shamdasani (New York, NY: W. W. Norton, 2009), 212.

2 Ibid., n180.

3 Ibid., 360.

4 In a letter to W. P. Witcutt, Jung wrote: "As you have found out for yourself, the *I Ching* consists of readable archetypes, and it very often presents not only a picture of the actual situation by also of the future, exactly like dreams." See Gerhard Adler, *C.G. Jung Letters*. Trans. by R. F. C. Hull. Vol. 2, 1951-1961 (Princeton, NJ: Princeton University Press, 1975), 584. In his foreword to Richard Wilhelm's translation of the *I Ching*, Jung also spoke of the Chinese symbols as "readable" archetypes.

5 See Heyong Shen, "Psychology of the Heart and Jungian Practice in China," based on the Fulbright scholar lectures (1996-1997), and the two lectures at the Eranos Roundtable Conference, "Psychology of the Heart, the Chinese Cultural Psychology" (Eranos Yearbook 66, 1997) and "Psychology of the Heart, Oriental Perspective of Modernity of East and West" (Eranos Yearbook 69, 2007). Also, Heyong Shen, *Psychology of the Heart* (Beijing, People's Publishing House, 2001).

6 Jung, *The Red Book,* 290.

7 Ibid., 290. "I kneel down on the stone, cut off a piece of the liver and put it in my mouth." The woman throws her veil back, and she is a beautiful maiden with ginger hair. She says to him: "I am your soul."

8 C.G. Jung, *Memories, Dreams, Reflections* (New York, NY: Vintage Books, 1963), 198.

9 Ibid.

10 Ibid.

11 Jung, *The Red Book,* 362.

12 C.G. Jung, "Commentary on 'The Secret of the Golden Flower'" (1938), in *CW*, vol. 13 (Princeton, NJ: Princeton University Press, 1967), par. 84.

13 C.G. Jung, *The Psychology of Kundalini Yoga: Notes of the Seminar Given in 1932* (Princeton, NJ: Princeton University Press, 1996), 100.

14 Jung, *Memories, Dreams, Reflections*, 197.

15 Ibid.

16 Ibid.

17 Ibid.

18 Jung, *The Red Book*, 163.

19 Lao-tzu, *Tao te Ching*, chapter 42 (Chuansha: Hunan People's Publishing House, 1999), 86-87.

20 *The Doctrine of the Mean* (Beijing: Sinolingua, 2006), 4-5.

21 Jung, *The Red Book,* 336.

22 Ibid.

23 Ibid., 346.

24 C.G. Jung, "The Relations between the Ego and the Unconscious" (1938), in *CW*, vol. 7 (Princeton, NJ: Princeton University Press, 1966), par. 365.

25 C.G. Jung, *Psychological Types*, in *CW*, vol. 6 (Princeton, NJ: Princeton University Press, 1971), par. 359.

26 Jung, "The Relations between the Ego and the Unconscious", *CW* 7, par. 327.

27 Jung, *Psychological Types*, *CW* 6, par. 192.

28 Jung, *The Red Book,* 360.

29 C.G. Jung, "Richard Wilhelm: In Memoriam" (1931), in *CW*, vol. 15 (Princeton, NJ: Princeton University Press, 1966), par. 94.

30 Ibid., par. 89.

31 Jung, *The Red Book*, 360.

The Red Book and the Posthuman

John C. Woodcock

I want to set to work. But you must build the furnace.
Throw the old, the broken, the worn-out, the unused, and
the ruined into the melting pot, so that it will be renewed
for fresh use.[1]

C.G. Jung

Jung and Nietzsche each made the great discovery of a reality that
"overcomes" the opposites. Nietzsche, the linguistic scholar and
philosopher, referred to this reality as self-presentational language
while Jung, the psychologist, names it as the objective psyche. Both
agree that this reality is "alive," with its own intentionality. For the
purposes of this essay I will call it *living language*. The discoveries of
both pioneers inaugurated a blossoming of cultural practices,
founded on incomplete interpretations of the *telos* of this living
language, which articulate the emergence of a variety of possible
worlds, among them the worlds of artificial intelligence, virtual
reality, biotechnology, nanotechnology, etc. This essay attempts to
describe a cultural practice that could emerge from a more complete
understanding of the *telos* of the psyche, or living language, a practice
that can articulate and manifest the possible world of the *posthuman*.

The Emergence of the Posthuman

Slavoj Žižek takes us on a startling tour of a city garbage dump while
talking about the psychology of our ecological crisis today:

> Part of our daily perception of reality is that this [garbage—
> my insert] disappears from our world ... you *know* it's
> there ... but at a certain level of your most elementary
> experience it disappears from your world. ... I think about
> a certain obvious paradox. ... This is I think a nice example
> of what in psychoanalysis we call disavowal. I *know* very
> well but I act as if I don't know. ... I know very well that
> there may be global warming etc. ... but after reading a
> treatise on it what do I do? I step out. I see, not the
> mountains of garbage that I see now behind me, I see nice
> birds singing and so on and even if I *know* rationally that
> catastrophe is a danger I simply do not believe that this
> world can be destroyed.[2]

Žižek is pointing us to the dominant style of dissociated consciousness as which we exist today! We have fabricated a technological
world founded on the logic of abstract language, which "thinks" in
totalities, "wholes," "systems," etc. Žižek uses such global, totalizing
concepts to draw us into this world of global warming, world
catastrophe, ecological disasters, environmental crises, climate
change, overpopulation, world famine, etc. This abstract language has
brought forth its corresponding appearances, or "things"—representations arising from measurements and calculations of a
mathematical or physical world. Abstract language of "wholes" or
totalities, along with its corresponding appearances, constitutes a
world which reflects a particular style of consciousness that can be
aptly described as "alien"—a world that, according to Žižek, is "a
terrifying new abstract materialism; a kind of a mathematical
universe where there is nothing; there are just formulas, technical
forms and so on."

This form of "alien" consciousness apperceives earthly affairs as
from "outer space," and we participate in this style of consciousness
and its appearances when we *think* its language of abstract totalities.

At the same time, Žižek points out, we inhabit another world
altogether, a *personal* empirical world, i.e., the world we encounter

when we turn off the TV and walk out the door—a world of the senses, our normal, embodied world.

Žižek is telling us that the abstract knowledge gained from the fabricated world, in which the style of consciousness that I call "alien" reigns, simply does not reach down to touch our down-to-earth, empirical consciousness. We just go about our ordinary lives, while at the same time we may be horrified with the latest media news about dire warnings of catastrophe couched, as they have to be, in global, abstract concepts, or mediated images. The one form of consciousness is dissociated from the other.

And yet, Žižek's analysis now seems out of date. Hints of further changes in the appearances are beginning to draw our attention, as much of our contemporary art is now showing us. For example, the *Sydney Biennale Art Exhibition* (2016) was conceived to address the question:

> If each era has a different view of reality, what is ours? With our growing dependence on the virtual world of the Internet, the distinction between that world and the physical one is becoming ever less defined. Many artists are attempting to access the 'in-between'—the place where the virtual and the physical fold into one another.[3]

I found my way to a particular work of artist Grayson Perry, "The Annunciation of the Virgin Deal."[4] This artwork is showing us an emerging new reality. Two worlds, virtual and physical, are chaotically colliding, conflating, interpenetrating, uniting, or fusing. In Perry's work of art, we can see all the ordinary or personal items that we use intelligently to move about in the customary style of our modern culture: cups, coffee maker, magazines, cushions, tea towels, technological devices, etc. If we look more closely at these items, another feature that we normally take completely for granted begins to stand out—the ubiquitous presence of labels: "bourgeois and proud," "organic," "local," "plastic," "Penguin Books" (on the mugs); "make tea, not war" (on the towel), etc. The angel's body is portrayed as a cardboard cutout figure. She is pointing to portraits of Bill Gates and Steve Jobs that are hung on the wall. The iPad on the table is showing a news item, "Bakewell sells to Virgin for $270M."

What is the mode of being of such equipment? Ordinary personal items are now fused with messages that are utterly alien to anything personal or individual. Perry shows a chaotic concatenation of the virtual and the physical throughout his painting and, in so doing, is disclosing a world to us—one normally concealed from us. This structure of an "alien" consciousness, now conflated with a traditional and personal consciousness, constitutes a new kind of being and world that we may well call the posthuman. And as I said, contemporary art is showing us this world.

Shortly after my visit to see the work of Grayson Perry, I visited an art show here in Sydney (July 2016) presenting a display of modern art explicitly on the theme of the posthuman. The curators' introduction describes those artists whose works encouraged us to ask what it means to be human today and what it might mean in the future. Drawing inspiration from science fiction, robotics, bio-technology, consumer products, and social media, they offered experiences that raised questions around the idea of the posthuman, a concept that signals new understandings of humanity and a breakdown of boundaries between what we think of as natural and artificial.[5]

Some of these works combine real human body parts and machines in order to "speak" this new way of being.[6] This art is in effect announcing a further step in cultural development taking place in response to a background psychic transformation that has always-already happened. Žižek is drawing our attention to a cultural dissociation between a personal earthbound consciousness and an alien "out in space" style of consciousness, the world of one having nothing to do with the world of the other. Contemporary art, on the other hand, is hinting at the possibility that the "alien" form of consciousness is no longer to be thought of metaphysically as spatially "outside" or beyond earthly existence but rather as "incarnated within" the earthly, personal style, interpenetrating or enfolded with it, while remaining as alien. This new understanding is bringing into being an entirely new world of appearances and an explosion of corresponding cultural practices, i.e., the world of the posthuman!

In order to explore the essence of posthuman *being*, we must turn to the "meaning-giving" background that informs all appearances, cultural practices, and their corresponding beliefs. This meaning-giving background is, of course, the objective psyche. We may therefore approach the essence of the posthuman by appeal to those dreams and visions that hint at transformations in the psychic background. Consider, for example, the following dream:

> A man is among us; he looks quite normal, but he is in fact alien. He is friendly, wants to, needs to, live amongst us, and is warmly welcomed. Many therapists are excited and thrilled with the glamour of his gifts, which include space ships that could fly at dizzying speeds. I join in with this madness for a bit but lose interest and instead grow increasingly alarmed. I try to warn others. I decide to act. I want to burn him and race around looking for a flamethrower. Instead I kept grabbing fire extinguishers and spray him with those. They are useless. He tries to stop me and we seem to realize that there was nothing personal in this. He wants simply to live here and I could sense incredible danger to us. I say, 'It's just that our species can't survive if you stay. We need to survive too!' Then I go back to my frantic search. He says, responding to my alarm, 'Do you mean, what if I spit on the carpet or people?' And he does so, thus at last revealing the danger. A terrible poison was in his spittle; it dissolves flesh leaving horrible forms, like a fly dissolves its meal. ...[7]

This dream, along with many others at the time (1990s), had an inceptive character, opening me up to new thinking and exposure to fresh appearances. It shows an "alien" who is at the same time human, whose spittle melts discrete concrete, earthly forms. The logic of this image informs Žižek's analysis as he tours through the city garbage dump, demonstrating how the "alien" language of globalisation, totalisation, systems thinking, etc.—all abstractions—*works* on individual, empirical things or forms. Our modern technological culture privileges abstract wholes over empirical things so that, within the technological world, individual, empirical objects, including each of us, are logically downgraded. Individual empirical things collectively become garbage ("worthless or nonsensical matter"), obsolete before they leave the factory—everything replaceable, dispensable.

Under conditions of cultural stability, reified pairs of opposites such as inner/outer, spirit/matter, mind/body, subject/object, truth/falsity, etc., are preserved in the many cultural practices and institutions founded on them. The present upheavals and instability of cultural forms founded on the reification of these pairs of opposites are a reflection of a self-transformation in the psychic background having always-already occurred, as my dream suggests.

The modern genius giving eloquent expression to this enormous and profound reconfiguration of the psyche was, of course, Nietzsche.

Nietzsche's Discovery of the "Alien"

I interpreted my dream in terms of it being (a memory of) a self-presentation of the psyche (as reflected in living language) in the throes of a transformational process. From this perspective, the "alien" is a form of language that is the logical foundation of our entire technological world, "speaking" as it does in abstract totalities and "dissolving" the individuality of linguistic entities, which then become merely parts of a whole that "stands outside" earthly existence (hence "alien"). Prior to this "alien" language becoming reified as an entirely new set of (technological) appearances and practices, beliefs, etc., it had emerged or broken free from within the chaos of a breakdown of habituated and ossified habits of thought—those logical structures (pairs of opposites) that constitute the linguistic foundation of an entire cultural way of being, philosophically known as the Metaphysical world.

Nietzsche was the great pioneer of language who discovered this "alien," living language! He tells us explicitly, for example, of his experience with its power and numinosity as he wrote the dithyrambic *Thus Spake Zarathustra*:

> [O]ne is the mere incarnation, *mouthpiece* [my italics] or medium of an almighty power. … One hears—one does not seek; one takes—one does not ask who gives: a thought suddenly flashes up like lightning, it comes with necessity, unhesitatingly—I have never had any choice in the matter. … Everything happens quite involuntarily, as if in a tempestuous outburst of freedom, of absoluteness, of power and divinity. *The involuntariness of the figures and similes is the most remarkable thing; one loses all perception of what constitutes the figure and what constitutes the simile; everything seems to present itself as the readiest, the correctest and the simplest means of expression* [my italics].[8]

Nietzsche's participation with the fires of living language opened his eyes to a momentous event as having always-already occurred in the psychic background of appearances:

> Already, early in his career, he had understood and articulated the essential nature of language as rhetorical rather than re-presentational or expressive of a referential, proper meaning. … It marks a full reversal of the established priorities which traditionally root the authority of language in its adequation to an extralinguistic referent or meaning. …[9]

De Man's understanding here of Nietzsche's works gives us a hint of the transformation in the psychic background at the time of Nietzsche's (and later, Jung's, as we will see) discoveries. Nietzsche discovered that the essence of language is rhetorical! Another way of saying this enormous claim is that language essentially comprises self-presentational, *living* figures of speech, having no external referents![10]

The essence of language thus lies beyond the subject/object polarity, as Nietzsche knew. Owen Barfield calls this essential character of language, after Coleridge, "transformed inspiration." When realized or intuited as such, it yields "new meanings for old and [gives] birth to a future that has originated in present creativity instead of being a helpless copy of the outwardly observed forms of the past."[11]

Nietzsche's astounding discovery announces the close of a stable reality (the Metaphysical world), as founded on habituated pairs of opposites such as inner/outer, spirit/matter, truth/falsity, etc. If tropes are the truest nature of language, then, from a psychological point of view, Nietzsche, in encountering living language, also discovered the objective psyche as living, self-presentational figures of speech. As Nietzsche noted, he is thus our first psychologist!

Jung's Discovery of the "Alien"

During Jung's ordeal, as recorded in *The Red Book*, he also became a "mouthpiece of an almighty power," like Nietzsche before him—the almighty power of living language:

> [A]t the outset of *Liber Novus*, Jung experiences a crisis in language. The spirit of the depths, who immediately challenges Jung's use of language along with the spirit of the time, informs Jung that on the terrain of his soul his achieved language will no longer serve. His own powers of knowing and speaking can no longer account for why he utters what he says or under what compulsion he speaks.[12]

Jung describes his ordeal in terms of fire and storms, explicitly comparing his experiences with those of Nietzsche and Hölderlin:

> One thunderstorm followed another. My enduring these storms was a question of brute strength. Others have been shattered by them—Nietzsche, and Hölderlin, and many others. ... I was so frequently wrought up ... it was as if I were hearing [language—my insert] with my ears, sometimes feeling it with my mouth ... below ... everything was seething with life. ... A message had come to me with overwhelming force. ... I hit upon this stream of lava, and the heat of its fires reshaped my life. ... The primal stuff ... this incandescent matter ... material that burst forth ... and at first swamped me.[13]

This small sample of Jung's ordeal, along with the translators' understanding as quoted above, shows that, from start to finish, Jung's ordeal comprised a breakdown in "achieved" language, i.e., traditional or habituated forms of language that stabilize the real appearances of the world, as also happened to Nietzsche.

From the ordinary human perspective, "achieved" or "dead" language is used as a pragmatic tool for our purposes. Achieved language is collectively interpreted as having reliable external references, constituting what we normally call "reality." Such interpretations stabilize culture. We generally know what to do or how to respond when we speak in such pragmatic ways. But, when the psyche undergoes a transformation, interpretations of language as referential or as having external meaning simply collapse and living language, i.e., inceptive language that "speaks" in self-presentational figures of speech, breaks free and through.

This living language has an "alien" character, at times frighteningly so, as a fury of destructive spiritual power is released, bringing to an end all reified or habituated forms of achieved language. Jung, like Nietzsche before him, participated in the collapse of traditional linguistic structures (achieved language) and plunged into the fiery chaos that follows. In so doing, he made the momentous discovery of living language—inceptive language that can renew and transform the "wasteland."

Jung's destiny was to discover the reality of the objective psyche, which lies *"beyond"* the inner/outer disjunction. The reality of living language can only be reached when "achieved" or traditional language and its stable, logical forms, such as inner/outer, spirit/matter, subject/object, are destroyed. Jung's immense difficulty in bringing this emerging reality to language is shared by other investigators of living or inceptive language.

For example, Owen Barfield, in speaking about imagination advancing to transformed inspiration (living language), suggests that "it will be accompanied by something like a transition from metaphor to transformed personification and from myth and symbol to transformed allegory."[14] Barfield made a literary attempt to portray the inceptive character of transformed inspiration in his unusual book, *Unancestral Voice*—the genre of which remains uncertain. It comprises a series of "dialogues" with a spiritual being called the Meggid. Barfield, like Jung before him, subsequently struggles to describe his participation with transformed inspiration in the prosaic terms of achieved language, i.e., language that participation leaves behind:

> For what, after all, was the 'it' that happened? Since he had never told anyone about it, he had not yet made any attempt to clothe it in words. It was, however, something like this. He did *not* hear any voice. And yet a train of thought began presenting itself to him in the same mode in which thoughts present themselves when we hear them from the lips of another. They included thoughts which he himself was not aware of having ever previously entertained. For the most part the thoughts which were 'given' in this way were naked of words. He himself had to find the words before he forgot the thoughts.[15]

We may also turn to Heidegger and his enigmatic book, *Contributions to Philosophy*, of which it is said:

> There is less consensus about this book than about nearly any other twentieth-century philosophical text. Is it 'Heidegger's major work' or 'metaphysical dadaism'? An earthshaking achievement or laughable gibberish. ... As an account of the 'essential happening of be-ing,' the text resembles a treatise; as an investigation of the roots of concepts, it resembles history of philosophy; as an analysis of a crisis, it resembles cultural critique; as an invocation of a moment of decision, it resembles prophecy; as a self-conscious deployment of language, it resembles poetry. ... This new thinking is marked by its attention to the hidden and possible *as such*, by its distrust of all efforts to *represent* [my italics] the inceptive event, and by its ambition to *participate* in the event, not simply to observe it.[16]

The Red Book, Contributions to Philosophy, Thus Spake Zarathustra, and *Unancestral Voice* have the literary power to draw us into at least a vicarious experience of the *reality* of living language—an inceptive language that is "alien" to achieved or traditional language forms.

Jung says that, at the time of the *Red Book*, he felt "the gulf between the external world and the interior world of images in its most painful form." He could not find a way of *bringing to language* what he had in fact experienced. He could not *say* the coming into being of an entirely new world of appearances which "go beyond" the traditional pairs of opposites and yet remain *as* empirical.[17]

Nor could Heidegger, according to Polt.[18] Nor could Barfield. It's a task that lay in the future, maybe now, in *our* posthuman time!

The "Descent of the Alien" and the Posthuman

At this point we are ready to explore the inestimable relevance of *The Red Book* to our present times (2017).

I began my essay with Slavoj Žižek, who shows how the stability of our culture is strained to breaking point as we strive, through our outmoded cultural practices and beliefs, to maintain a dissociation between an alien technological world, grounded in abstract global language, and a down-to-earth personal or empirical world of local concerns. This structure of dissociation is grounded in a metaphysical interpretation of the *telos* of the psyche as discovered by Nietzsche and Jung.[19]

I then introduced some examples of contemporary art, along with one of my dreams, suggesting a new interpretation of the *telos* of the psyche, pictured now as the "alien" incarnating into, or conflated with, the earthly, giving rise to an entirely new set of appearances and cultural practices.

Jung (and Nietzsche before him) discovered "alien" living language, i.e., inceptive language as it "released" from reified achieved language. In its nature, this living language lies "beyond" all reified opposites (inner/outer; spirit/matter; mind/body, etc.), as well as the law of contradiction and linear notions of past, present, and future—

all those linguistic structures that "ground" a stable reality (the Metaphysical world) and corresponding cultural practices and beliefs.

As a result of this discovery, as we saw, Jung felt a painful dichotomy between the autonomous reality of the psyche and the reality of external or empirical life, based as it is on stable, traditional pairs of opposites. Through a metaphysical interpretation of living language or the objective psyche, he privileged the former and logically downgraded the latter.[20] Those cultural (technological) practices founded *only* on this "alien" language, as privileged by the modern mind, come into existence at the expense of ordinary empirical life, which must therefore be logically downgraded in favor of the emerging technological world and its appearances.

Jung's discovery of the autonomous psyche *as such* nonetheless points the way for us to begin to "speak" the *telos* of the psyche—a task that Jung could not complete—in our time of the posthuman.

I'd like to begin this exploration with a dream:

> I am way above the Earth, near the edge of space and I am attempting to come down to Earth in a new way, no parachute. I start to descend; whispers of air pass me by as I gather speed. I am trying to put on a warm jacket, but my thumb gets caught in the sleeve, and I am now rushing toward Earth. The perspective changes to ground level where I am watching a transparent man land safely, like a cat. He is nearly invisible, but I can see him. Apparently, I am to participate in the descent of this marvelous being and at the same time witness his earthly incarnation.

As in my previously reported dream, this dream seems to speak of the "alien" descending to Earth, now with my participation in that descent. Simultaneously, I am witnessing the new *transparent being* on earth.

Jung was troubled to the end by the "[t]horny problem of the relationship between eternal man, the self and earthly man in time and space." He tells us a frequently cited dream that, for him, illuminates this problem. The dream shows a UFO ("alien") looking down from the sky at him. Jung's dream and following discussion shows his clear *theoretical* understanding of the need for the empirical human to relate to the eternal in accord with the *telos* of the psyche, i.e., to "experience ourselves *concurrently* [my emphasis] as limited and eternal."[21]

At the same time, the "thorny problem" of *saying* this "concurrence" in language (thereby bringing it into existence) remained for the future. Jung's theoretical formulations of this "concurrence" are all linguistically grounded in the metaphysical disjunction between achieved and living language. In other words, Jung was able to *theorize* the necessity of a concurrence or interpenetration of the human and the eternal, in accord with the *telos* of the psyche, but he could not *say the posthuman world into existence* through inceptive language.

My dream shows a "moment" in cultural development as we further synchronize with the *telos* of the psyche, in our time—the time of the posthuman—as indeed my earlier dream also suggests (namely a "descent to earth" and an appearance of "transparency").[22] How are we now to understand this further movement?[23]

Living language, well understood by Jung to be "eternal," i.e. "alien," to our achieved (earthly) or traditional language, is now to be interpreted or thought as "amongst us," "on Earth," i.e., as *empirical* while at the same time remaining as *alien* and *beyond*. This "descent" is also intuited by contemporary art, as I have described above. In our posthuman world, this "alien" living language is no longer to be thought as a reality *separate* from the ordinary external or empirical world, as Jung's formulations presuppose.[24] Instead, it is to be thought *as* the language of ordinary things appearing in the real world while remaining, at the same time, *as* "alien" and *beyond*. The image of transparency is crucial to this new thinking.

A transformation in our understanding of language (and therefore of all future cultural forms founded on this language) is taking place, one which simultaneously "speaks" the things of this earthly world as ordinary things, while at the same time offering the possibility of each linguistic thing becoming transparent to a living world of infinite depths of meaning—an "alien" world that may once again speak to us from the "beyond," make its claims on us, and teach us a new way of (posthuman) being that is more in accord with the claims of Life—an "alien" world that is, at the same time, always-already *us*!

In Owen Barfield's book, *Rediscovery of Meaning*, he addresses this possibility of "transformed inspiration," which will be "spoken" into existence by words that would

> convey reasonably identifiable and repeatable meanings ... 'soft-focus' meanings ... a whole new way of using language. ... the true utterance of 'double vision', simultaneous ... awareness of both the opposite sides of the threshold.[25]

The Red Book, as a literary form, represents Jung's struggle with bringing to language (and therefore into existence) the simultaneity of "transformed inspiration" *and* ordinary empirical perception. Barfield describes interiorized or transformed inspiration as involving "the notion of some communication with individual entities, individual beings beyond the threshold."[26] Jung's *Red Book* experiences are exemplary of such transformed inspiration while at the same time he invokes ordinary language with its "identifiable and repeatable meanings," as Barfield says. The various styles within *Liber Novus* together demonstrate Jung's struggle to find that polysemous language:

> The language in *Liber Novus* pursues three main stylistic registers. ... One of them faithfully reports the fantasies and inner dialogues of Jung's imaginal encounters, while a second remains firmly and discerningly conceptual. Still a third writes in a mantic and prophetic, or Romantic and dithyrambic, mode.[27]

Jung's struggles have laid down a path to the future. He showed the way to the reality of living language—what he calls the objective psyche. He showed us that there *is* such a reality! We can even venture that he called it forth in inceptive fashion! He further demonstrated that this reality, alien as it is to traditional forms of language, *wants* something of us. As Jung has said, "'the woman within me' did not have the speech centres that I had. And so I suggested that she use mine. She did so and came though with a long statement."[28]

Jung's initiation into the reality of living language shows that it has its own intelligence and consciousness and that it wants to "speak." To do so requires an act of service from the posthuman mouthpiece, as Nietzsche also understood. We each must consent to surrendering our "speech centres" (or artist's hand, etc.) for that purpose. The way to such surrender lies within the definition of the posthuman—that "human-alien" being who has the capacity, as Barfield says, to participate with transformed inspiration.

The Alien "Speaks"

To conclude I want to offer a dream that may show us how the speech of the *other*, now in its logical status as human-alien, may be now received and "spoken," i.e., when achieved language becomes *transparent* to living language:

> I am wandering the streets, alone. I find myself in a hall where some ritual is going on, conducted by an older man. The participants are each undergoing a perfunctory ritual, i.e., they are just going through the motions. It has a Masonic-Christian feel to it. We are all sitting on our knees on carpet. When he sees me, he suddenly becomes interested, more alive, and asks me to go through the ritual, which now comes alive. There is a line on the floor. I am to touch my head on that line, i.e., submit. I do so as he intones the ritual of confessions. As I touch the floor with my head, he smiles and says warmly you are forgiven, everything. Then he comes over to me and crouches, whispering in my right ear for some time. As I listen I hear the voice of the *other*, a higher pitch, unearthly, i.e., the angel is speaking to me though him. I have trouble understanding most of it but the angel talks for some time. When finished I get up but have trouble speaking. My right hand begins to write autonomously. I scribble 'interlocutor'.[29]

This dream suggests that now, in our posthuman era, ordinary, achieved language can become transparent to living language, or the speech of the alien *other*, i.e., at least to "he who hath ears." According to the logic of the posthuman, as shown in my dream, a gesture of total submission is required in order to "hear" the speech of this "alien."[30]

This dream, along with many others over the years, has steered me toward the development of a cultural practice that is founded on this new, posthuman interpretation of the *telos* of the psyche. In the dream, "I get up but have trouble speaking. My right hand begins to write autonomously. I scribble 'interlocutor.'" I have been writing for decades—author of 15 books and many essays. During this entire time, I have been unable to name the genre of my writing. This possibly new form of literature is generated when I surrender my willful strivings, recording psychic self-presentations as they emerge, moving from memories, to dreams, reflections, an etymological study of a word, recalling the words of another author, until the usual separation of inner and outer dissolves. I have written several books that are expressive of this style and I am now beginning to suspect that my task is to find a literary genre as one possible cultural practice that is founded on the interpretation of our new essence as posthuman beings.

The configuration of the posthuman is the foundation of a new mode of being, if resonant cultural practices can be produced to articulate it and maintain it. In my view, our survival depends on this effort. Our obsessive, mad zeal to discover alien life on planets out in space, with whom we cannot possibly communicate, is a pitiable attempt to end our modern, nihilistic isolation with its correlative practices of environmental destruction. We have forgotten that the "alien" is the lost voice of Being, or reflected Life (i.e., the psyche), that our ancestors knew so well and for whom it "spoke" as *other*, from "out there," as the *living* world, inspiring us, offering guidance, and announcing our fate. *The Red Book* is a record of Jung's sustained encounters with this "lost" or forgotten voice of Being, which also inspired and guided him, and laid out *his* fate. As he later said, "it has cost me 45 years so to speak, to bring the things that I once experienced and wrote down into the vessel of my scientific work."[31]

The crucial difference between Jung's encounter and that of our ancestors lies in Jung's momentous discovery of the reality of the psyche (or living language) *as such*, i.e., no longer only as reflected in the natural world. We can begin to understand the different logic (i.e., from that of our ancestors) underpinning Jung's experiences with phenomenological hints contained in such passages as the following:

> He recalled that beneath the threshold of consciousness, everything was animated. At times, it was as if he heard something. At other times, he realized he was whispering to himself.[32]

Jung thus encountered the voice of Being as "within" and yet "objective" ("I" and yet "not I"), the same logic underlying Barfield's *transformed* inspiration. Jung's great discovery inaugurated a lifelong effort to think the "concurrence" of the objective psyche *as such* and empirical reality—a "thorny problem" that remained with him his entire life, as I discussed earlier.[33] This "thorny problem" lies at the heart of Jung's and all subsequent attempts to reanimate nature, since the animating factor or meaning giver, according to its *telos*, has "departed" nature and has always-already emerged as *psychic reality*, discoverable *as such*! The question of *thinking* the "concurrence" of psychic and empirical reality depends utterly on how we interpret the *telos* of the psyche in its achieved status of "the departed."[34] I hope to have shown here that, since Jung's momentous discovery of psychic reality *as such*, Western culture has continued its interpretive gestures, mainly through its art, until reaching our present-day understanding of the *telos* of the psyche in terms of the posthuman.

The posthuman *way of being* understands our world as linguistically configured yet objective. This understanding gives us the potential capacity to perceive the world normally as configured by achieved language (empirical reality) while offering the possibility of that "surface" linguistic world becoming transparent, opening up to its own psychic depths of meaning. We need to develop an entirely new set of cultural practices that can articulate and maintain this new posthuman reality.

Endnotes

1 C.G. Jung, *The Red Book: Liber Novus,* ed. Sonu Shamdasani, tr. John Peck, Mark Kyburz, and Sonu Shamdasani (New York, NY: W. W. Norton, 2009), 345.

2 Slavoj Žižek, "Slavoj Zizek Speaking on Love and Search for Meaning When None Exists," in *Examined Life,* https://www.youtube.com/watch?v=iGCfiv1xtoU.

3 Stephanie Rosenthal, artistic director for the 20th Biennale, Sydney. Quote taken from a display at the art show.

4 Grayson Perry, "The Annunciation of the Virgin Deal," http://www.mca.com.au/exhibition/grayson-perry/.

5 Anna Davis and Houngcheol Choi, http://www.mca.com.au/exhibition/new-romance/.

6 For example, the body fat of the artist used to fuel an engine. See Stelarc and Nina Sellars, *Blender* (2005/2016), http://www.mca.com.au/exhibition/new-romance/.

7 This passage is an excerpt. The dream in its entirety may be found in my book. See John Woodcock, *Mouthpiece* (CreateSpace, 2015), 8-9.

8 Friedrich Nietzsche, "Introduction," in *Thus Spake Zarathustra* (London: T.N. Foulis, 1909).

9 Paul de Man, "Rhetoric of Tropes (Nietzsche)," in *Allegories of Reading* (New Haven: Yale University Press, 1979), 106.

10 This of course is what Jung means by "objective psyche." Also for Heidegger the essence of language is *saying as showing*! See Martin Heidegger, "The Nature of Language," in *On the Way to Language* (New York, NY: Harper & Row, 1971), 37ff.

11 Owen Barfield, "Imagination and Inspiration," in *The Rediscovery of Meaning* (San Rafael: Barfield Press, 1977), 127.

12 Jung, *The Red Book,* 222.

13 C.G. Jung, *Memories, Dreams, Reflections* (New York, NY: Vintage Books, 1963). All quotes are from Chapter VI: "Confrontation with the Unconscious." Also see Mark Kyburz, John Peck and Sonu Shamdasani, "Translators' Note" in Jung, *The Red Book,* 223 for further examples.

14 Barfield, "Imagination and Inspiration," in *The Rediscovery of Meaning,* 128-9.

[15] Owen Barfield, *Unancestral Voice* (Middletown: Wesleyan University Press, 1965), 16. See n31 for a comparison with Jung's experiences in *The Red Book.*

[16] Richard Polt, *The Emergency of Being: On Heidegger's Contributions to Philosophy* (Ithaca: Cornell University Press, 2006), 1-2 and 104.

[17] For a fuller discussion of Jung's efforts to *say* the new reality see my essay, "The Hidden Legacy of The Red Book," in Thomas Arzt, ed., *Das Rote Buch: C.G. Jungs Reise zum "anderen Pol der Welt." Studienreihe zur Analytischen Psychologie, Bd. 5* (Würzburg: Königshausen & Neumann, 2015), 161-194.

[18] "Plato might suggest … that what is lacking in Contributions is a descent from the ultimate to the quotidian … we need to … [find] connections between primordial time-space and ordinary, linear time." See Polt, "Afterthoughts," in *The Emergency of Being,* 214. Note that this connection remained a "thorny problem" for Jung to the end. See Jung, *Memories, Dreams, Reflections,* 322.

[19] The dissociation is maintained through a habit of thought that metaphysically interprets living language as located spatially in the beyond, i.e., "up there."

[20] For example, see C.G. Jung, *The Symbolic Life,* in *CW,* vol. 18 (Princeton, NJ: Princeton University Press, 1980), par. 630 and Jung, *Memories, Dreams, Reflections,* 225.

[21] Jung, *Memories, Dreams, Reflections,* 323ff.

[22] My previous dream also presents an image of transparency as being "redemptive." See n7.

[23] James Hillman understands transparency in terms of empirical humanistic attributes, as was Jung's understanding when he suggested that the human embody the *essential.* My interpretation of the *telos* of the psyche understands transparency as an attribute of *language!* See James Hillman, *The Myth of Analysis* (New York, NY: Harper TorchBooks, 1972), 92.

[24] I.e., "out in space" or metaphysically transcendent.

[25] Barfield, "Imagination and Inspiration," in *The Rediscovery of Meaning,* 129.

[26] Barfield, "Imagination and Inspiration," in *The Rediscovery of Meaning,* 128.

27 John Peck, Mark Kyburz, and Sonu Shamdasani, "Translators' Note," in Jung, *The Red Book*, 222.

28 Jung, *Memories, Dreams, Reflections*, 186. Also see par. 1, 178.

29 This dream and my discussion appear in John Woodcock, "An Example of the New Art Form" in *The Coming Guest and the New Art Form*, (Bloomington: iUniverse, 2014), 48.

30 Jung demonstrates this "submission" when he surrenders his speech centres to the *other* "within."

31 Quoted by Sonu Shamdasani, "Introduction," in Jung, *The Red Book*, 219b.

32 Sonu Shamdasani, "Introduction," in Jung, *The Red Book*, 200b. Also see note 15.

33 See note 18.

34 *Thinking* the concurrence of psychic and empirical reality is the *a priori* to perceiving the "things" of the posthuman world.

Bibliography

A

Adler, Gerhard. *C.G. Jung Letters*. Trans. by R.F.C. Hull. Vol. 1, 1906-1950. Princeton, NJ: Princeton University Press, 1973.

Adler, Gerhard. *C.G. Jung Letters*. Trans. by R.F.C. Hull. Vol. 2, 1951-1961. Princeton, NJ: Princeton University Press, 1975.

Adorno, Theodor W. and Max Horkheimer. *Dialectic of Enlightenment: Philosophical Fragments*, ed. Gunzelin Schmid Noerr. Stanford, CA: Stanford University Press, 2002.

Aeschylus. *The Seven Against Thebes*, ed. and trans. David Grene, Richmond Lattimore, Mark Griffith, and Glenn W. Most. Chicago, IL: University of Chicago Press, 2013.

"American/International Gita Society Bhagavad Gita": http://www.sacred-texts.com/hin/gita/agsgita htm. Accessed 4/7/2013, 2013.

Arendt, Hannah. *The Origins of Totalitarianism*. New York, NY: Harcourt, 1976.

Aristotle. *Complete Works*, ed. Jonathan Barnes. Princeton, NJ: Princeton University Press, 1984.

Arzt, Thomas, ed. *Das Rote Buch: C.G. Jungs Reise zum "anderen Pol der Welt"*. *Studienreihe zur Analytischen Psychologie*, Bd. 5. Würzburg: Königshausen & Neumann, 2015.

B

Bair, Deirdre. *Jung: A Biography*. Boston, MA: Little, Brown and Company, 2003.

Barfield, Owen. *The Rediscovery of Meaning and Other Essays*. San Rafael, CA: Barfield Press, 1977.

Barfield, Owen. *Unancestral Voice*. Middletown, CT: Wesleyan University Press, 1965.

Barker, Margaret. *The Great Angel: A Study of Israel's Second God*. Louisville, Kentucky: Westminster/ John Knox, 1992.

Baucis and Philemon: http://www.mythencyclopedia.com/Ar-Be/Baucis-and-Philemon.html.

Bailly, Jean Sylvain. *Histoire de l'astronomie ancienne, depuis son origine jusqu'à l'établissement de l'école d'Alexandrie.* Paris: Debure, 1775.

Bailly, Jean Sylvain. *Traite de l'astronomie indienne et orientale.* Paris: Debure, 1787.

Beck, Roger. *Planetary Gods and Planetary Orders in the Mysteries of Mithras.* Leiden: Brill, 1988.

Beck, Roger. *The Religion of the Mithras Cult in the Roman Empire.* Oxford, UK: Oxford University Press, 2006.

Bedi, Ashok. *Awaken the Slumbering Goddess—the Latent Code of the Hindu Goddess Archetypes.* BookSurge, 2007.

Bedi, Ashok. *Path to the Soul.* York Beach, ME: S. Weiser, 2000.

Beebe, John. "*The Red Book* as a Work of Conscience; Notes from a seminar given for the 35th Annual Jungian Conference, C.G. Jung Club of Orange County, April 10th 2010," *Quadrant*, XXXX:2 (Summer 2010): 41-58.

Beebe, John and Ernst Falzeder, eds. *The Question of Psychological Types: The Correspondence of C.G. Jung and Hans Schmid-Guisan. 1915-1916.* Princeton and Oxford: Princeton University Press, Philemon Series, 2013.

Benjamin, Walter. "Central Park," trans. Lloyd Spencer and Mark Harrington. *New German Critique* 34 (Winter 1985): 32-58.

Benjamin, Walter. "The Work of Art in the Age of Mechanical Reproduction." In *Illuminations*, trans. Harry Zorn, London: Cape, 1970.

Betz, Hans Dieter (ed. and trans.). *The "Mithras Liturgy": Text, Translation and Commentary.* Tübingen: Mohr Siebeck, 2003.

Biegel, Rebekka Aleida. *Zur Astrognosie der alten Ägypter.* Göttingen: Dieterichsche Universitäts-Buchdruckerei, 1921.

Bishop, Paul. "Jung and the Quest for Beauty." In (eds.) Thomas Kirsch and George Hogenson, *The Red Book: Reflections on C.G. Jung's Liber Novus.* London: Routledge, 2013.

Bishop, Paul. *On the Blissful Islands with Nietzsche and Jung.* London/New York: Routledge, 2017.

Blavatsky, H. P. *Isis Unveiled: A Master-Key to the Mysteries of Ancient and Modern Science and Theology*, 2 volumes. London: Theosophical Publishing Co., 1877.

Blavatsky, H. P. *The Secret Doctrine: The Synthesis of Science, Religion, and Philosophy*, 2 volumes. London: Theosophical Publishing Co., 1888.

Blom, Philipp. *The Vertigo Years: Change and Culture in the West 1900-1914*. London: Orion Publishing Co., 2009.

Boechat, Walter. *The Red Book of C.G. Jung: a Journey into Unknown Depths*. London: Karnac Books, 2016.

Bousset, Wilhelm. *Hauptprobleme der Gnosis*. Göttingen: Vandenhoeck & Ruprecht, 1907.

Brude-Firnau, Gisela. "From *Faust* to Harry Potter: Discourses of the Centaurs." In Hans Schulte, John Noyes, and Pia Kleber (eds.), *Goethe's "Faust": Theatre of Modernity*. New York, NY: Cambridge University Press, 2011.

Bude, Heinz. *Gesellschaft der Angst*. Hamburg: Verlag des Hamburger Instituts für Sozialforschung, 2014.

Bunyan, John. *The Pilgrim's Progress*. London: Penguin Classics, 1987.

Burwick, Frederick. *Poetic Madness and the Romantic Imagination*. University Park, PA: Pennsylvania State University Press, 1996.

Butler, Robert Olen. *From Where You Dream: The Process of Writing Fiction*. New York, NY: Grove Press, 2005.

C

Campion, Nicholas. *What Do Astrologers Believe?* London: Granta Publications, 2006.

Campion, Nicholas. *Astrology and Cosmology in the World's Religions*. New York, NY: NYU Press, 2012.

Campion, Nicholas. *Astrology and Popular Religion in the Modern West*. Farnham: Ashgate, 2012.

Carroll, Lewis. *Alice in Wonderland*. Any Edition.

Cicero, Marcus Tullius. *The Nature of the Gods*. Translated by P.G. Walsh. Oxford, UK: Oxford University Press, 1998.

Cicero, Marcus Tullius. *Cicero's Orations Against Catiline*. Literal Translation by Rev. Dr. Fraser Giles. Oxford City Press, 2010.

Coleman, William Emmette. "The Sources of Madame Blavatsky's Writings." In Vsevolod Sergyeevich Solovyoff, *A Modern Priestess of Isis*. London: Longmans, Green, and Co., 1895.

Copenhaver, Brian P. (ed. and trans.). *Hermetica: The Greek Corpus Hermeticum and the Latin Asclepius in a New English Translation*. Cambridge, UK: Cambridge University Press, 1992.

Cumont, Franz. *Textes et monuments figurés relatifs aux mystères de Mythra*. Brussels: Lamertin, 1896.

Cumont, Franz. *The Mysteries of Mithra*, trans. Thomas J. McCormack. Chicago, IL: Open Court, 1903.

Cutner, Herbert. *Jesus*. New York, NY: The Truth Seeker Co., 1950.

D

D'Ailly, Pierre. *Tractatus de imagine mundi Petri de Aliaco*. Louvain: Johannes Paderborn de Westfalia, 1483.

De l'Aulnaye, François-Henri-Stanislas. *L'histoire générale et particulière des religions et du cultes*. Paris: J.B. Fournier, 1791.

De Man, Paul. *Allegories of Reading: Figural Language in Rousseau, Nietzsche, and Proust*. New Haven, CT: Yale University Press, 1979.

Demosthenes. *On the Crown*, trans. A.W. Pickard-Cambridge. In A.W. Pickard-Cambridge (ed. and trans.), *Public Orations of Demosthenes*, 2 volumes. Oxford, UK: Clarendon Press, 1912.

Dieterich, Albrecht. *Eine Mithrasliturgie*. Leipzig: Teubner, 1903.

Dilthey, Wilhelm. "Dichterische Einbildungskraft und Wahnsinn." In *Die geistige Welt: Einleitung in die Philosophie des Lebens*, vol. 2 [*Gesammelte Werke*, vol. 6]. Stuttgart; Göttingen: Teubner; Vandenhoeck & Ruprecht, 1994. 90-102.

Dostoyevsky, Fyodor. Trans. Hugh Aplin. *Notes from the Underground*. London: Hesperus Classics. 2006.

Dourley, John. "Recalling the Gods: A Millennial Process." In Spiegelman, J. M. (ed.), *Psychology and Religion at the Millennium and Beyond*. Tempe, Arizona: New Falcon Publications, 1998.

Drob, Sanford. *Reading the Red Book. An Interpretive Guide to C.G. Jung's Liber Novus*. New Orleans, LA: Spring Journal Books, 2012.

Dupuis, Charles. *Origine de tous les cultes, ou religion universelle*. Paris: H. Agasse, 1795.

Dupuis, Charles. *Planches de l'origine de tous les cultes*. Paris: H. Agasse, 1795.

E

Eagleton, Terry. *Literary Theory: An Introduction* (Great Britain: Blackwell, 1983).

Edinger, Edward. *The Creation of Consciousness. Jung's Myth for Modern Man*. Toronto: Inner City Books, 1984.

Edinger, Edward. *The Aion Lectures. Exploring the Self in C.G. Jung's Aion*. Toronto: Inner City Books, 1996.

Edinger, Edward. *The New God-Image*. Wilmette, IL: Chiron Publications, 1996.

Edinger, Edward. *Goethe's Faust: Notes for a Jungian Commentary (Studies in Jungian Psychology by Jungian Analysts)*. Toronto: Inner City Books, 1990.

Edwards, M. J. "Gnostic Eros and Orphic Themes." In *Zeitschrift für Papyrologie und Epigraphik* 88, 1991.

Enzensberger, Hans Magnus. *Mittelmaß und Wahn: Gesammelte Zerstreuungen*. Frankfurt/Main: Suhrkamp, 1991.

Euripides. *Heracleidae*, trans. Ralph Gladstone. Chicago, IL: University of Chicago Press, 1955.

Everitt, Anthony. *The Life and Times of Rome's Greatest Politician: Cicero*. New York, NY: Random House, 2003.

Evans-Wentz, Walter, ed. *The Tibetan Book of the Dead* (with a psychological commentary by C.G. Jung). Oxford, UK: Oxford University Press, 1960.

F

Faracovi, Ornella Pompeo. *Gli oroscopi di Cristo*. Venice: Marsilio Editori, 1999.

Fideler, David. *Jesus Christ, Sun of God: Ancient Cosmology and Early Christian Symbolism*. Wheaton, IL: Quest Books/Theosophical Publishing House, 1993.

Forshaw, Peter. "Curious Knowledge and Wonder-Working Wisdom in the Occult Works of Heinrich Khunrath", in R. J. W. Evans and Alexander Marr (eds.), *Curiosity and Wonder from the Renaissance to the Enlightenment*. Farnham: Ashgate, 2006.

Freud, Sigmund. "Group Psychology and the Analysis of the Ego" [1922]. SE 18. Strachey, James et al. (eds.) *The Standard Edition of the Complete*

Works of Sigmund Freud. London: The Hogarth Press and the Institute of Psychoanalysis, 1953-74.

Freud, Sigmund. *Civilization and its Discontents*, trans. and ed. James Strachey. New York, NY: W.W. Norton, 1961.

Freud, Sigmund and C.G. Jung. *The Freud/Jung Letters*. Ed. William McGuire and trans. by Ralph Manheim and R. F. C. Hull. Princeton, NJ: Princeton University Press, 1974.

Friedman, Thomas L. *Thank You for Being Late: An Optimist's Guide to Thriving in the Age of Accelerations*. London: Allen Lane, 2016.

G

Gerhardt, Oswald. *Der Stern des Messias*. Leipzig: Deichert, 1922.

Giegerich, Wolfgang. "*Liber Novus*, That is, The New Bible: A First Analysis of C.G. Jung's *The Red Book*". In *Spring: A Journal of Archetype and Culture* 83 (Spring 2010).

Gieser, Suzanne. *The Innermost Kernel: Depth Psychology and Quantum Physics—Wolfgang Pauli's Dialogue with C.G. Jung*. Berlin: Springer, 2005.

Godwin, Joscelyn. *The Theosophical Enlightenment*. Albany, NY: SUNY Press, 1994.

Goethe, Johann Wolfgang. *Faust: A Tragedy* (Norton Critical Editions). Trans. by Walter Arndt, ed. by Hamlin, Cyrus. Second Edition. New York, NY: W.W. Norton, 1998.

Graf Dürckheim, Karlfried. *Alltag als Übung*. Bern: Huber, 2012.

Greene, Liz. *The Astrology of Fate*. London: George Allen & Unwin, 1984.

Greene, Liz. *Jung's Studies in Astrology: Prophecy, Magic, and the Qualities of Time*. Abingdon: Routledge, 2018.

Greene, Liz. *The Astrological World of Jung's Liber Novus: Daimons, Gods, and the Planetary Journey*. Abingdon: Routledge, 2018.

Greisman, Harvey C. and George Ritzer. "Max Weber, Critical Theory, and the Administered World." In *Qualitative Sociology* 4, no. 1 (Spring 1981): 34-55.

Guggenbühl-Craig, Adolf. *Eros on Crutches. Reflections on Amorality and Psychopathy*. Dallas, TX: Spring, 1980.

Gurdjieff, G. I. *Meetings With Remarkable Men*. London: E. P. Dutton, 1964.

H

Haggard, H. Rider. *She: A History of Adventure*. London: Longmans, 1887.

Hammer, Olav. *Claiming Knowledge: Strategies of Epistemology from Theosophy to the New Age*. Leiden: Brill, 2004.

Hanegraaff, Wouter J. *New Age Religion and Western Culture: Esotericism in the Mirror of Secular Thought*. Leiden: Brill, 1996.

Hanegraaff, Wouter J. "Reconstructing 'Religion' from the Bottom Up." In *Numen: International Review for the History of Religions*, 63 (2016), 577–606.

Heelas, Paul. *The New Age Movement*. Oxford: Blackwell, 1996.

Heidegger, Martin. *Einführung in die Metaphysik*. Gesamtausgabe, Bd. 40. Frankfurt/Main: Vittorio Klostermann, 1983.

Heidegger, Martin. "The Question Concerning Technology." In *Basic Writings*, ed. David Farrell Krell. London: Routledge & Kegan and Paul, 1978.

Heidegger, Martin. *Off the Beaten Track*. Cambridge, UK: Cambridge University Press, 2002.

Heidegger, Martin. *On the Way to Language*. New York, NY: Harper and Row, 1971.

Heindel, Max. *The Rosicrucian Cosmo-Conception, or Mystic Christianity*. Oceanside, CA: Rosicrucian Fellowship, 1909.

Heindel, Max. *The Rosicrucian Mysteries*. Oceanside, CA: Rosicrucian Fellowship, 1911.

Heindel, Max. *The Message of the Stars: An Esoteric Exposition of Medical and Natal Astrology Explaining the Arts of Prediction and Diagnosis of Disease*. Oceanside, CA: Rosicrucian Fellowship, 1918.

Hill, Gareth S. *Masculine and Feminine: The Natural Flow of Opposites in the Psyche*. Boston, MA: Shambala Publications, 1992.

Hillman, James. *Anima*. Dallas, TX: Spring Publications, 1985.

Hillman, James. *Healing Fiction. On Jung, Freud and Adler*. Dallas, TX: Spring Publications, 1983 & 2004.

Hillman, James. *The Dream and the Underworld*. New York, NY: Harper and Row, 1979.

Hillman, James. *The Myth of Analysis*. New York, NY: Harper Torch-Books, 1978.

Hillman, James. "Dionysus in Jung's Writings." In *Mythic Figures: Uniform Edition of the Writings of James Hillman,* vol. 6.1. Putnam, CT: Spring Publications, 2007.

Hillman, James and Shamdasani, Sonu. *Lament of the Dead: Psychology after Jung's Red Book.* New York, NY: W.W. Norton, 2013.

Higgins, Godfrey. *Anacalypsis*, 2 volumes. London: Longman, Rees, Orme, Brown, Green, and Longman, 1836.

Hodges, Horace Jeffery. "Gnostic Liberation from Astrological Determinism," *Vigiliae Christianae* 51:4, 1997.

Hoeller, Stephan A. *The Gnostic Jung and the Seven Sermons to the Dead.* Wheaton, IL: Quest, 1982.

Hoeller, Stephan A. *Jung and the Lost Gospels: Insights into the Dead Sea Scrolls and the Nag Hammadi Library*. Wheaton, IL: Quest, 1989.

Holden, James H. "Early Horoscopes of Jesus." In *American Federation of Astrologers Journal of Research* 12:1, 2001.

Holland, Tom. *Rubicon: The Triumph and Tragedy of the Roman Republic.* London: Little, Brown, 2003.

Huang, Taoist Master Alfred. *The Complete I Ching*. Rochester, VT: Inner Traditions, 1998.

I

Irenaeus. *Irenaei episcopi lugdunensis contra omnes haereses.* Oxford, UK: Thomas Bennett, 1702.

J

Jaffé, Aniela. *From the Life and Work of C.G. Jung.* Einsiedeln: Daimon Verlag, 1989.

Jaffé, Aniela. *Was C.G. Jung a Mystic?* Einsiedeln: Daimon Verlag, 1989.

Jaffé, Aniela. *C.G. Jung: Word and Image.* Princeton/Bollingen Paperbacks. Princeton, NJ: Princeton University Press, 1983.

Jenkins, Sylvia P. "The Depiction of Mental Disorder in *Die Leiden des jungen Werthers* and *Torquato Tasso* and its Place in the Thematic

Structure of the Works," *Publications of the English Goethe Society*, NS 62 (1991-1992): 96-118.

Jung, C.G. *Aion. Researches into the Phenomenology of the Self.* In *CW*, vol. 9/II. Princeton, NJ: Princeton University Press, 1968.

Jung, C.G. *Analytical Psychology: Its Theory and Practice.* London: Routledge & Kegan Paul, 1968.

Jung, C.G. *Answer to Job.* In *CW*, vol. 11. Princeton, NJ: Princeton University Press, 1969.

Jung, C.G. "A Psychological Approach to the Dogma of the Trinity." In *CW*, vol. 11. Princeton, NJ: Princeton University Press, 1969.

Jung, C.G. "A Study in the Process of Individuation." In *CW*, vol. 9/I. Princeton, NJ: Princeton University Press, 1968.

Jung, C.G. "Archetypes of the Collective Unconscious." In *CW*, vol. 9/I. Princeton, NJ: Princeton University Press, 1968.

Jung, C.G. "Concerning the Archetypes with Special Reference to the Anima Concept." In *CW*, vol. 9/I. Princeton, NJ: Princeton University Press, 1968.

Jung, C.G. "Commentary on 'The Secret of the Golden Flower.'" In *CW*, vol. 13. Princeton, NJ: Princeton University Press, 1967.

Jung, C.G. *Dictionary of Analytical Psychology.* London and New York, NY: Ark, 1987.

Jung, C.G. *Erinnerungen, Träume, Gedanken von C.G. Jung.* Zurich: Ex Libris, 1962.

Jung, C.G. "Flying Saucers. A Modern Myth of Things Seen in the Skies." In *CW*, vol. 10. Princeton, NJ: Princeton University Press, 1964.

Jung, C.G. "Foreword to Suzuki's 'Introduction to Zen Buddhism.'" In *CW*, vol. 11. Princeton, NJ: Princeton University Press, 1969.

Jung, C.G. "Good and Evil in Analytical Psychology." In *CW*, vol. 10. Princeton, NJ: Princeton University Press, 1964.

Jung, C.G. *Jung Speaking: Interviews and Encounters.* Ed. by William McGuire and R. F. C. Hull. Princeton, NJ: Princeton University Press, 1977.

Jung, C.G. *Jung on Astrology*, selected and introduced by Keiron le Grice and Safron Rossi. Abingdon: Routledge, 2017.

Jung, C.G. "Cryptomnesia." In *CW*, vol. 1. Princeton, NJ: Princeton University Press, 1970.

Jung, C.G., ed. *Man and His Symbols*. New York, NY: Dell, 1964.

Jung, C.G. *Memories, Dreams, Reflections*, ed. Aniela Jaffé. New York, NY: Vintage Books, 1963.

Jung, C.G. *Modern Psychology: Notes on Lectures Given at the Eidgenössische Technische Hochschule, Zürich by Prof. Dr. C.G. Jung, October 1933-July 1941*, 3 volumes, trans. and ed. Elizabeth Welsh and Barbara Hannah. Zürich: K. Schippert & Co., 1959-60.

Jung, C.G. *Mysterium Coniunctionis*. In *CW*, vol. 14. Princeton, NJ: Princeton University Press, 1963.

Jung, C.G. "New Paths in Psychology." In *CW*, vol. 7. Princeton, NJ: Princeton University Press, 1966.

Jung, C.G. "On the Psychology of the Unconscious." In *CW*, vol. 7. Princeton, NJ: Princeton University Press, 1966.

Jung, C.G. "On the Nature of the Psyche." In *CW*, vol. 8. Princeton, NJ: Princeton University Press, 1969.

Jung, C.G. *Psychology and Alchemy*. In *CW*, vol. 12. Princeton, NJ: Princeton University Press, 1968.

Jung, C.G. *Psychological Types*. In *CW*, vol. 6. Princeton, NJ: Princeton University Press, 1971.

Jung, C.G. *Psychology of the Unconscious*, trans. Beatrice M. Hinkle. New York, NY: Moffat, Yard & Co., 1916.

Jung, C.G. "Psychological Commentary on 'The Tibetan Book of the Great Liberation.'" In *CW*, vol. 11. Princeton, NJ: Princeton University Press, 1969.

Jung, C.G. "On the Relation of Analytical Psychology to Poetry." In *CW*, vol. 15. Princeton, NJ: Princeton University Press, 1966.

Jung, C.G. "On the Psychology and Pathology of So-Called Occult Phenomena." In *Psychology and the Occult*. London: Ark, 1987.

Jung, C.G. "Richard Wilhelm: In Memoriam." In *CW*, vol. 15. Princeton, NJ: Princeton University Press, 1966.

Jung, C.G. *Symbols of Transformation*. In *CW*, vol. 5. Princeton, NJ: Princeton University Press, 1967.

Jung, C.G. "The Development of Personality." In *CW*, vol. 17. Princeton, NJ: Princeton University Press, 1964.

Jung, C.G. *The Red Book: Liber Novus*, ed. Sonu Shamdasani, trans. John Peck, Mark Kyburz, and Sonu Shamdasani. New York, NY: W.W. Norton, 2009.

Jung, C.G. *The Red Book: Liber Novus. A Reader's Edition,* ed. Sonu Shamdasani, trans. John Peck, Mark Kyburz, and Sonu Shamdasani. New York, NY: W.W. Norton, 2012.

Jung, C.G. "The Philosophical Tree." In *CW*, vol. 13. Princeton, NJ: Princeton University Press, 1967.

Jung, C.G. "The Psychological Aspects of the Kore." In *CW*, vol. 9/I. Princeton, NJ: Princeton University Press, 1968.

Jung, C.G. *The Psychology of Kundalini Yoga: Notes of the Seminar Given in 1932*. Princeton, NJ: Princeton University Press, 1996.

Jung, C.G. "Psychology and Literature." In *CW*, vol. 15. Princeton, NJ: Princeton University Press, 1966.

Jung, C.G. "The Meaning of Psychology for Modern Man." In *CW*, vol. 10. Princeton, NJ: Princeton University Press, 1964.

Jung, C.G. "The Psychology of Transference." In *CW*, vol. 16. Princeton, NJ: Princeton University Press, 1966.

Jung, C.G. "The Relations between the Ego and the Unconscious." In *CW*, vol. 7. Princeton, NJ: Princeton University Press, 1966.

Jung, C.G. *The Spirit in Man, Art and Literature*. In *CW*, vol. 15. Princeton, NJ: Princeton University Press, 1966.

Jung, C.G. "The Spirit Mercurius." In *CW*, vol. 13. Princeton, NJ: Princeton University Press, 1967.

Jung, C.G. "The Structure of the Unconscious." In *CW*, vol. 7. Princeton, NJ: Princeton University Press, 1966.

Jung, C.G. "The Tavistock Lectures." In *CW*, vol. 18. Princeton, NJ: Princeton University Press, 1976.

Jung, C.G. "The Spiritual Problem of Modern Man." In *CW*, vol. 10. Princeton, NJ: Princeton University Press, 1964.

Jung, C.G. "The Transcendent Function." In *CW*, vol. 8. Princeton, NJ: Princeton University Press, 1969.

Jung, C.G. *Two Essays on Analytical Psychology*. In *CW*, vol. 7. Princeton, NJ: Princeton University Press, 1966.

Jung, C.G. "The Undiscovered Self (Present and Future)." In *CW*, vol. 10. Princeton, NJ: Princeton University Press, 1964.

Jung, Emma. *Animus and Anima*. Dallas, TX: Spring Publications, 1985.

Jünger, Ernst. *Typus, Name, Gestalt*, Sämtliche Werke, Bd. 13. Stuttgart: Klett-Cotta, 1981.

Jünger, Ernst. *An der Zeitmauer*. Sämtliche Werke, Bd. 18. Stuttgart: Klett-Cotta, 1981.

K

Kandinsky, Wassily. *Concerning the Spiritual in Art*. New York, NY: Dover Publications, 1977.

Kant, Immanuel. "An Answer to the Question: What is Enlightenment?" Source: Immanuel Kant. Practical Philosophy, Cambridge University Press, trans. and ed. by Mary J. Gregor, 1996.

Kerényi, Karl. "Prolegomena," in *C.G. Jung and Karl Kerényi, Essays on a Science of Mythology*, trans. R. F. C. Hull. Princeton, NJ: Princeton University Press, 1969.

Kierkegaard, Søren. *Fear and Trembling*. Trans. A. Hannay. London: Penguin Classics, 1985.

Kirsch, Thomas and George Hogenson, eds. *The Red Book: Reflections of C.G. Jung's Liber Novus*. London & New York: Routledge, 2013.

Khunrath, Heinrich. *Von hylealischen, das ist, pri-materialischen catholischen, oder allgemeinem natürlichen Chaos, der naturgemessen Alchymiae und Alchemisten*. Magdeburg, 1597.

L

Lammers, Ann Conrad and Adrian Cunningham, eds. *The Jung-White Letters*. London: Routledge, 2007.

Larkin, Phillip. *Collected Poems*. London: Faber and Faber, 2003.

Lao-tzu. *Tao te Ching*. Chuansha: Hunan People's Publishing House, 1999.

Leo, Alan. *Astrology for All*. London: Modern Astrology Office, 1910.

Leo, Alan. "The Age of Aquarius", *Modern Astrology* 8:7, 1911.

Leo, Alan. *Esoteric Astrology*. London: Modern Astrology Office, 1913.

Leo, Alan. *Dictionary of Astrology*, ed. Vivian Robson. London: Modern Astrology Offices/L.N. Fowler, 1929.

Levinas, Emmanuel. *Otherwise than Being or Beyond Essence*. Pittsburgh, PA: Duquesne University Press, 1998.

Lewis, Clive Staples. *An Experiment in Criticism*. Cambridge, UK: Cambridge University Press, 1961.

Lockhart, Russell. *Psyche Speaks: A Jungian Approach to Self and World*. C.G. Jung Lectures, Inaugural Series. C.G. Jung Foundation of New York, 1982.

Lockhart, Russell. *Psyche Speaks: A Jungian Approach to Self and World*. Wilmette, IL: Chiron Publications, 1987 (Reissued Everett: The Lockhart Press, 2015).

Lockhart, Russell. Review of *American Soul: A Cultural Narrative* by Ronald Schenk. *Psychological Perspectives* (2014) 57 (4): 454-459.

Long, A.A. *From Epicurus to Epictetus*. Oxford, UK: Oxford University Press, 2006.

Lyotard, J.F. *The Postmodern Condition: A Report on Knowledge*. Minneapolis, MN: University of Minnesota Press, 1984.

M

Magee, Bryan. *Wagner and Philosophy*. London: Penguin Books, 2000.

Main, Roderick. "New Age Thinking in the Light of C.G. Jung's Theory of Synchronicity," *Journal of Alternative Spiritualities and New Age Studies* 2, 2006.

Malinowski, Bronisław. "Myth in Primitive Psychology" [1926], in *Magic, Science and Religion and other Essays*. Garden City, NY: Doubleday, 1948. 72-123.

Martin, Russell. *Beethoven's Hair*. New York, NY: Random House, 2002.

Massey, Gerald. *The Natural Genesis*, 2 volumes. London: Williams & Norgate, 1883.

Massey, Gerald. "The Hebrew and Other Creations, Fundamentally Explained," in *Gerald Massey's Lectures*. London: private publication, 1887.

Massey, Gerald. "The Historical Jesus and Mythical Christ." In *Gerald Massey's Lectures*. London: private publication, 1887.

Mathiesen, Thomas J. *Apollo's Lyre: Greek Music and Music Theory in Antiquity and the Middle Ages*, Lincoln and London: University of Nebraska Press, 1999.

May, Rollo. *Power and Innocence. A Search for the Sources of Violence.* New York, NY: W.W. Norton, 1972.

McGuire, William and R.F.C. Hull (eds.). *C.G. Jung Speaking: Interviews and Encounters*. Princeton, NJ: Princeton University Press, 1977.

Mead, G.R.S. *Pistis Sophia: A Gnostic Miscellany: Being for the Most Part Extracts from the Book of the Saviour, to Which are Added Excerpts from a Cognate Literature*. London: Theosophical Publishing Society, 1896.

Mead, G.R.S. *Echoes from the Gnosis*. London: Theosophical Publishing Society, 1906-1908.

Mead, G.R.S. *The Mysteries of Mithra*, Volume 5 of *Echoes from the Gnosis*. London: Theosophical Publishing Society, 1907).

Mead, G.R.S. *A Mithraic Ritual*, Volume 6 of *Echoes from the Gnosis*. London: Theosophical Publishing Society, 1907.

Mechilin, Leila. "Lawless Art." *Art and Progress* (1913) 4: 840-841.

Mecklin, John. "2017 Doomsday Clock Statement," *Science and Security Board: Bulletin of the Atomic Scientists*, www.thebulletin.org (accessed March 7, 2017).

Mecouch, G. *While Psychiatry Slept*. Santa Fe, NM: Belly Song Press, 2017.

Meister Eckehart. *Schriften und Predigten*, ed. Herman Büttner. Jena: Diederichs, 1921.

Melville, Herman. *Billy Bud*. New York, NY: Tom Doherty Associates, 1988.

"Memories Protocols," Carl G. Jung Protocols, Library of Congress.

Meyer, Marvin, ed. *The Nag Hammadi Scriptures: The International Edition*. San Francisco, CA: Harper, 2007.

Milton, John. *Paradise Lost*. Book 9. Any Edition.

N

Nasar, Sylvia. *A Beautiful Mind*. New York, NY: Simon & Schuster. 1998.

Nicolescu, Basarab. *From Modernity to Cosmodernity: Science, Culture, and Spirituality*. New York, NY: SUNY, 2014.

Nietzsche, Friedrich, *Nachlaß 1880-1882* [*Kritische Studienausgabe*, vol. 9], ed. Giorgio Colli and Mazzino Montinari, Munich; Berlin and New York, NY: dtv; de Gruyter, 1999.

Nietzsche, Friedrich. *Basic Writings*, ed. Walter Kaufmann. New York, NY: Modern Library, 1968.

Nietzsche, Friedrich. *Daybreak*, trans. R.J. Hollingdale. Cambridge, UK: Cambridge University Press, 1982.

Nietzsche, Friedrich. *Nachlaß 1882-1884* [*Kritische Studienausgabe*, vol. 10], ed. Giorgio Colli and Mazzino Montinari, Munich; Berlin and New York, NY: dtv; de Gruyter, 1999.

Nietzsche, Friedrich. *The Portable Nietzsche*, ed. Walter Kaufmann. New York, NY: Viking Penguin, 1968.

Nietzsche, Friedrich. *Thus Spoke Zarathustra*. Harmondsworth, UK: Penguin, 1969.

Nietzsche, Friedrich. *Thus Spake Zarathusta: A Book for All and None*. Trans. by Thomas Common. London: T. N. Foulis, 1909.

Nietzsche, Friedrich. *Also sprach Zarathustra*. Chemnitz: Ernst Schmeitzner, 1883-84.

Nietzsche, Friedrich. *Ecce Homo*. Trans. R.J. Hollingdale. Harmondsworth, UK: Penguin Classics, 1979.

Nietzsche, Friedrich. *Human All Too Human*. Trans. Marion Faber. London: Penguin Classics. 1994.

Noll, Richard. *The Jung Cult: Origins of a Charismatic Movement*. Princeton, NJ: Princeton University Press, 1994.

Noll, Richard. "Jung the Leontocephalus." In Paul Bishop (ed.), *Jung in Contexts: A Reader*. London: Routledge, 1999.

North, J.D. *Stars, Mind, and Fate*. London: Continuum, 1989.

O

Origen. *Contra Celsum*, trans. Henry Chadwick. Cambridge, UK: Cambridge University Press, 1953.

Ouspensky, P.D. *In Search of the Miraculous*. New York, NY: Harcourt, Brace, 1949.

Owen, Alex. "Occultism and the 'Modern Self' in Fin-de-Siècle Britain." In Martin Daunton and Bernhard Rieger (eds.), *Meanings of Modernity*. Oxford, UK: Berg, 2001.

Owens, Lance S. "Foreword." In Alfred Ribi, *The Search for Roots: C.G. Jung and the Tradition of Gnosis*. Los Angeles, CA: Gnosis Archive Books, 2013.

Owens, Lance S. "The Hermeneutics of Vision: C.G. Jung and Liber Novus." In *The Gnostic: A Journal of Gnosticism, Western Esotericism and Spirituality*, Issue 3 (July 2010), 23–46.

Owens, Lance S. *Jung in Love: The Mysterium in Liber Novus*. Gnosis Archive Books, 2015.

Owens, Lance S. "Jung and *Aion*: Time, Vision and a Wayfaring Man." In *Psychological Perspectives*, 2011, 54:253-89.

P

Perera, Sylvia Britton. *Descent to the Goddess: A Way of Initiation for Women*. Toronto: Inner City Books, 1989.

Phillips, Adam. *Terrors and Experts*. London: Faber & Faber, 1995.

Phipps, Constantine. *What You Want: The Pursuit of Happiness*. London: Quercus Books, 2014.

Plato. *Collected Dialogues*, ed. Edith Hamilton and Huntington Cairns. Princeton, NJ: Princeton University Press, 1989.

Plato. *Timaeus*, in *The Collected Dialogues of Plato*, ed. Edith Hamilton and Huntington Cairns. Princeton, NJ: Princeton University Press, 1961.

Plotinus. *The Enneads*, trans. Stephen MacKenna, 6 volumes. London: Medici Society, 1917-30; repr. London: Faber & Faber, 1956.

Plutarch, *Lives*, vol. 1, trans. Bernadotte Perrin. London; New York, NY: Heinemann; Macmillan, 1914.

Plutarchus, Lucius Metrius. *Plutarch's Lives: Life of Cicero*. New York, NY: Palatine Press, 2015.

Polkinghorne, John. *Reason and Reality: The Relationship Between Science and Theology*. London: SPCK, 1991.

Polt, Richard. *The Emergency of Being: On Heidegger's "Contributions to Philosophy."* Ithaca, NY: Cornell University Press, 2006.

Porphyry. *De antro nympharum*, in Thomas Taylor (ed. and trans.), Select Works of Porphyry. London: Thomas Rodd, 1823.

R

Radkau, Joachim. *Das Zeitalter der Nervosität. Deutschland zwischen Bismarck und Hitler.* München: Propyläen, 1998.

Reitzenstein, Richard. *Poimandres: ein paganisiertes Evangelium: Studien zur griechisch-ägyptischen und frühchristlichen Literatur.* Leipzig: Teubner, 1904.

Reitzenstein, Richard. *Die hellenistiche Mysterienreligionen.* Leipzig: Teubner, 1910.

Reitzenstein, Richard. *Mysterienreligionen nach ihren Grundgedanken und Wirkungen.* Leipzig: Teubner, 1910.

Rilke, Rainer Maria. "The Ninth Elegy." In *Selected Poems*, trans. J.B. Leishman. London: Penguin, 1988.

Rodríguez, Andrés. *Book of the Heart: The Poetics, Letters, and Life of John Keats.* Hudson: Lindisfarne Press, 1993.

Rolfe, Eugene. *Encounter with Jung.* Boston, MA: Sigo Press, 1989.

Roosevelt, Theodore. "A Layman's Views of an Art Exhibition." In *Outlook* (1913) 103: 718-720.

Rosa, Hartmut. *Beschleunigung. Die Veränderung der Zeitstrukturen in der Moderne.* Frankfurt/Main: Suhrkamp, 2005.

Rosenberg, Harold. "The Armory Show: Revolution Reënacted." *New Yorker* (1963) April 6: 99-115.

Rosenberg, Harold. "Metaphysical Feelings in Modern Art." In *Critical Inquiry* (1975) 2: 217-232.

Rowland, Susan. *Jung as a Writer.* New York and London: Routledge, 2005.

Rowland, Susan. *Remembering Dionysus: Revisioning Psychology in C.G. Jung and James Hillman,* London and New York, NY: Routledge, 2017.

Rudhyar, Dane. *Astrological Timing.* New York, NY: Harper & Row, 1969.

Rümke, A.C. and Sarah de Rijcke. *Rebekka Aleida Biegel (1886-1943): Een Vrouw in de Psychologie.* Eelde: Barkhuism, 2006.

S

Samuels, Andrew. BBC Radio 4, *Today* (broadcast 28 October 2009).

Schelling, F.W.J. *Idealism and the Endgame of Theory: Three Essays,* ed. Thomas Pfau. Albany, NY: State University of New York Press, 1994.

Schelling, F.W.J. *The Ages of the World*, trans. Frederick de Wolfe Bolman, Jr. New York, NY: Columbia University Press, 1942.

Schenk, Ronald. *American Soul: A Cultural Narrative*. New Orleans, LA: Spring Journal, 2012.

Schmidt, Jochen and Sebastian Kaufmann. *Kommentar zu Nietzsches "Morgenröthe"*; *Kommentar zu Nietzsches "Idyllen aus Messina"* [*Nietzsche-Kommentar*, vol. 3/1]. Berlin and Boston, MA: de Gruyter, 2015.

Schopenhauer, Arthur. *The World as Will and Presentation*. Volume One. Trans. by Richard E. Aquila in Collaboration with David Carus. London: Pearson Longman, 2008.

Schultz, Wolfgang. *Dokumente der Gnosis*. Jena: Diederichs, 1910.

Schweizer, Andreas. "The Book of the Play of the Opposites." In Andreas Schweizer and Regine Schweizer-Vüllers (editors), *Stone by Stone*. Einsiedeln: Daimon, 2017.

Sellars, John. *Stoicism*. Berkeley, CA: University of California Press, 2006.

Shamdasani, Sonu. "Memories, Dreams, Omissions." In *Spring Journal of Archetype and Culture* 57, 1995.

Shamdasani, Sonu. *Cult Fictions: C.G. Jung and the Founding of Analytical Psychology*. London: Routledge, 1998.

Shamdasani, Sonu. *Jung and the Making of Modern Psychology: The Dream of A Science*. Cambridge, UK: Cambridge University Press, 2003.

Shamdasani, Sonu. *C.G. Jung: A Biography in Books*. New York, NY: W.W. Norton, 2012.

Shamdasani, Sonu. ed. *Introduction to Jungian Psychology. Notes of the Seminar on Analytical Psychology given in 1925*. Princeton, NJ: Princeton University Press, 2012.

Shen, Hyong. *Psychology of the Heart*. Beijing, People's Publishing House, 2001.

Siegel, Daniel. *The Developing Mind*. New York and London: The Guilford Press, 1999.

Silk, M.S. and J.P. Stern. *Nietzsche on Tragedy*. Cambridge, UK: Cambridge University Press, 1981.

Sloterdijk, Peter. *Die schrecklichen Kinder der Neuzeit*. Berlin: Suhrkamp, 2014.

Sloterdijk, Peter. *Eurotaoismus. Zur Kritik der politischen Kinetik.* Frankfurt/Main: Suhrkamp, 1989.

Smith, E.M. *The Zodia, or The Cherubim in the Bible and the Cherubim in the Sky.* London: Elliot Stock, 1906.

Sonnino, Lee A. *Handbook of Sixteenth Century Rhetoric.* London: Routledge & Kegan Paul, 1968.

Spano, M. V. "Modern(-ist) Man in Search of a Soul: Jung's Red Book as Modernist Visionary Literature" (2010), cgjungpage: http://www.cgjungpage.org/index.php?option=com_content&task =view&id=934 &Itemid=1, accessed 27 September 2012.

Spiegelman, J. Marvin. *The Tree: Tales in Psycho-mythology.* Phoenix, AZ: Falcon Press, 1982.

Spiegelman, J. Marvin. *The Quest: Further Tales in Psycho-Mythology.* Phoenix, AZ: Falcon Press, 1984.

Spiegelman, J. Marvin. *Jungian Psychology and the Passions of the Soul.* Las Vegas, NV: Falcon Press, 1989.

Spiegelman, J. Marvin. *Reich, Jung, Regardie and Me: The Unhealed Healer.* Las Vegas, NV: New Falcon Publications, 1992.

Spiegelman, J. Marvin. *Rider Haggard, Henry Miller and I: The Unpublished Writer.* Las Vegas, NV: New Falcon Publications, 1997

Spiegelman, J. Marvin. "C.G. Jung's Answer to Job: A Half Century Later." In *Journal of Jungian Theory and Practice* 8/1, 1999.

Spiegelman, J. Marvin. *The Divine WABA (Within, Among, Between, Around): A Jungian Exploration of Spiritual Paths.* Portland, Maine: Nicolas Hays, 2003.

Stein, Murray. "Introduction." In (ed.) Murray Stein, *Jung on Evil.* Princeton, NJ: Princeton University Press, 1995.

Steiner, George. *Language and Silence.* London: Faber & Faber, 1967.

Steiner, Rudolf. *Friedrich Nietzsche. Ein Kämpfer gegen seine Zeit.* Weimar: E. Felber, 1895.

Steiner, Rudolf. *The Reappearance of Christ in the Etheric.* Spring Valley, NY: Anthroposophic Press, 1983.

Steiner, Rudolf. *Evil*, ed. Michael Kalisch. Forest Row: Rudolf Steiner Press, 1997.

Stevens, Wallace. *The Collected Poems of Wallace Stevens*. New York, NY: Alfred A. Knopf, 1954.

Sullivan, J.W.N. *Beethoven: His Spiritual Development*. New York, NY: Random House, 1960.

T

Tacey, David. *The Darkening Spirit. Jung, Spirituality, Religion*. London/ New York, NY: Routledge, 2013.

Tacey, David. *Jung and the New Age*. Hove: Brunner-Routledge, 2001.

Tarnas, Richard. *The Passion of the Western Mind: Understanding the Ideas that Have Shaped Our World View*. New York, NY: Random House, 1991.

Taylor, Thomas, (trans.). *Ocellus Lucanus, On the Nature of the Universe; Taurus, the Platonic Philosopher, On the Eternity of the World; Julius Firmicus Maternus, Of the Thema Mundi; Select Theorems on the Perpetuity of Time, by Proclus*. London: John Bohn, 1831.

The Economist. June 3rd-9th, 2017. "Lexington: Like a wrecking ball", United States Section.

Theierl, Herbert. *Nietzsche—Mystik als Selbstversuch*. Würzburg: Königshausen & Neumann, 2000.

The I Ching or Book of Changes, The Richard Wilhelm Translation rendered into English by Cary F. Baynes, 3rd ed. Princeton, NJ: Princeton University Press, 1967.

The Doctrine of the Mean. Beijing: Sinolingua, 2006.

The Zohar. Translated by Sperling, H. and Simon, M. London: Soncino Press, 1933.

U

Ulansey, David. *The Origins of the Mithraic Mysteries*. Oxford, UK: Oxford University Press, 1991.

Urs Sommer, Andreas. *Kommentar zu Nietzsches "Jenseits von Gut und Böse"* [*Nietzsche-Kommentar*, vol. 5/1]. Berlin and Boston, MA: de Gruyter, 2016.

V

von der Heydt, Vera. *The Psychology and Care of Souls*. London: Guild of Pastoral Psychology, 1954.

von Franz, Marie-Louise. "The Unknown Visitor." In *Archetypal Dimension of the Psyche*. London: Shambhala, 1999.

W

Wagner, Cosima. *Diaries, Vol. 1. 1869-1877*. Trans. by Geoffrey Skelton. New York, NY: Harcourt. 1978.

Wimsatt, W.K. and M.C. Beardsley. *The Verbal Icon: Studies in the Meaning of Poetry*. Lexington, KT: University of Kentucky Press, 1954.

Wuest, Patricia Viale. *Precession of the Equinoxes*. Atlanta, GA: Georgia Southern University, 1998.

Woodcock, John. *The Coming Guest and the New Art Form*. Bloomington, IN: iUniverse, 2014.

Woodcock, John. *Mouthpiece*. CreateSpace, 2015.

Y

Yeats, William Butler. *The Second Coming* (1919). In *Collected Poems of William Butler Yeats*. London: Macmillan, 1933.

Z

Zambelli, Paola. *The Speculum astronomiae and its Enigma*. Dordrecht: Kluwer Academic, 1992.

Žižek, Slavoj. *The Abyss of Freedom; Ages of the World*. Ann Arbor, MI: University of Michigan Press, 1997.

About the Contributors

Thomas Arzt, Ph.D., was educated in Physics and Mathematics at Giessen University (Germany). Research Assistant at Princeton University (USA) with the special focus on atomic, nuclear and plasma physics. 1988 Training and Certification in Initiatic Therapy at the "Schule für Initiatische Therapie" of Karlfried Graf Dürckheim and Maria Hippius-Gräfin Dürckheim in Todtmoos-Rütte (Black Forest, Germany). 2016 Training Program Continuing Education in Analytical Psychology at ISAP Zurich. Since 1999, President and Managing Director of *Strategic Advisors for Transformation GmbH*, an international consulting company for simulation technology, complexity management, and "Strategic Foresight under Deep Uncertainty" in Freiburg, Germany. He resides in Lenzkirch (Black Forest, Germany). Major publications: Various publications on Naturphilosophie in the context of Wolfgang Pauli und C.G. Jung: *Unus Mundus: Kosmos und Sympathie* (ed., 1992), *Philosophia Naturalis* (ed., 1996), *Wolfgang Pauli und der Geist der Materie* (ed., 2002). Editor of the German series *Studienreihe zur Analytischen Psychologie*. Web page: www.thomasarzt.de; contact email: thomasdrarzt @gmail.com

Ashok Bedi, M.D., is a Jungian psychoanalyst and a board-certified psychiatrist. He is a member of the Royal College of psychiatrists of Great Britain, a diplomate in Psychological Medicine at the Royal College of Physicians and Surgeons of England, a Distinguished Life Fellow of the American Psychiatric Association. He is a Clinical Professor in Psychiatry at the Medical College of Wisconsin in Milwaukee and a training analyst at the C.G. Jung Institute of Chicago. His publications include *Crossing the Healing Zone* (2013), *Awaken the Slumbering Goddess: The Latent Code of the Hindu Goddess Archetypes* (2007), *Retire Your Family Karma: Decode Your Family Pattern* (2003) and *Path to the Soul* (2000). He is the liaison for the IAAP for developing Jungian training programs in India and leads the annual "A Jungian Encounter with the Soul of India" study group to several centers in India under the auspices of the New York

Jung Foundation. Web page: www.pathtothesoul.com; contact e-mail: ashokbedi@sbcglobal.net.

Paul Bishop, D.Phil., studied at Magdalen College, Oxford (1985-1989, 1990-1994), and spent a year as Lady Julia Henry Fellow at Harvard (1992-1993). He has published widely on Analytical Psychology and its relation to German culture, including *On the Blissful Islands: With Nietzsche & Jung in the Shadow of the Superman* (2017), *Carl Jung* (2014), *Reading Goethe at Midlife: Ancient Wisdom, German Classicism, and Jung* (2011), and *Analytical Psychology and German Classical Aesthetics: Goethe, Schiller, and Jung* (2 vols., 2007-2008). He holds the William Jacks Chair in Modern Languages at the University of Glasgow. Contact email: Paul.Bishop@glasgow.ac.uk.

Ann Casement, LP, is a senior member of the British Jungian Analytic Association, associate member of the Jungian Psycho-analytic Association, member of the British Psychoanalytic Council, New York State Licensed Psychoanalyst, who worked for several years in psychiatry from the late 1970s. She chaired the UK Council for Psychotherapy (1998-2001), served on the Executive Committee of the IAAP (2001-2007), and on the Ethics Committee (2007-2016), becoming its chair in 2010. She has lectured worldwide, published several books and contributes articles and reviews to *The Economist*, as well as to international psychoanalytic journals. Major public-ations: *Carl Gustav Jung* (2001), *Who Owns Psychoanalysis?* (2004, nominated for the 2005 Gradiva Award), *Who Owns Jung?* (2007), and *The Blazing Sublime* (in press). She served on the Gradiva Awards Committee in New York (2013), and is a Fellow of The Royal Anthro-pological Institute and The Royal Society of Medicine. Her private practice is in London. Contact email: adecasement@gmail.com.

Josephine Evetts-Secker, M.Phil., graduated from University of London 1963 and 1966 and the C.G. Jung Institute, Zurich (1989). She taught at the University of Calgary (Department of English) and retired with Emeritus status to return to England in 1997. She is currently Co-Chair of AGAP (Zurich) and is active in the London training group, IGAP. She lectures for ISAP Zurich, IGAP, and London's Guild of Pastoral Psychology and Jung Club, as well as in the USA. She was a founding source of the Calgary Jung Society, where she still lectures. She has edited volumes of fairy tales and published various articles on literature and psychology and poetry. Major publications: *Tales of Mothers and Sons* (1998), *Tales of Fathers and Sons* (1998), *Tales of Fathers and Daughters* (1997), *Tales of Mothers and Daughters* (1996). In conjunction with Spring Journal Books, she gave the 2011 Zürich Jung Lectures, accompanying the book: *At Home in the Language of the Soul: Exploring Jungian Discourse and Psyche's Grammar of Transformation* (2012). She is also an active-retired Anglican priest in the Mulgrave parishes near York. She has Jungian practice in Whitby, Yorkshire. Contact email: revj@evetts-secker.co.uk.

Nancy Swift Furlotti, Ph.D., Jungian Analyst, did her analytical training at the C.G. Jung Institute of Los Angeles, where she served as a past president, and at the M.-L. von Franz Zentrum in Switzerland. She was a founding member and a past president of the Philemon Foundation. She is currently on the board of Pacifica Graduate Institute, founding member of the recently established Kairos Film Foundation that oversees the movies, *A Matter of Heart* and *The World Within*, the Remembering Jung Video Series, and current projects, and is co-chair of the C.G. Jung Professorial Endowment at UCLA. She has published numerous articles and book chapters on various topics including Mesoamerican mythology and the environment, narcissism, and *The Red Book*. She co-edited *The Dream and its Amplification* with Erel Shalit. Through her publishing company, Recollections, LLC, she brings into print unpublished works by first generation Jungians, such as Erich Neumann. Web page: www.nancyfurlotti.weebly.com; contact email: nfurlotti@mac.com.

Liz Greene, Ph.D. in Psychology and Hypnotherapy, Los Angeles University/Hypnosis Motivation Institute (1971), Diploma in Transpersonal Psychotherapy, Centre for Transpersonal Psychology, London (1978), Diploma in Analytical Psychology, Association of Jungian Analysts, London (1983), Ph.D. in History, University of Bristol (2010). Professional astrologer 1967-today; Director of Centre for Psychological Astrology, London, 1982-today; Analytical psychologist 1983-2013 (now retired); M.A. in Cultural Astronomy and Astrology, Bath Spa University and University of Wales, 2007-2014; Tutor on the training course for ISAP (International School of Analytical Psychology, Zurich), 2014; Tutor on the training course for the Jung Institute, Zurich, 1996; Tutor on the M.A. in Humanistic Psychology, Antioch College, Yellow Springs, Ohio/London, 1985-1987; Tutor on the training program for the Association of Jungian Analysts, London, 1983-2014. Major publications: *The Horoscope in Manifestation: Psychology and Prediction* (2001*), The Dark of the Soul: Psychopathology in the Horoscope* (2003), *Jung's Studies in Astrology: Magic, Prophecy, and the Qualities of Time* (2018). Web page: www.cpalondon.com; Contact email: juliet@cpalondon.com.

John Hill, M.A., was born in Dublin, Ireland. He received his degrees in philosophy at the University of Dublin and the Catholic University of America, Washington, D.C. He trained at the C.G. Jung Institute, Zurich, and has practiced as a Jungian analyst since 1973. He became a training analyst of the C.G. Jung Institute in 1981 and was a member of the selection committee for twenty years. In 2003, he became a member of Zurich's International School for Analytical Psychology (ISAP). For seven years he was academic director of ISAP's annual conference, *The Jungian Odyssey*. He is IAAP Liaison to Georgia and has recently taken up acting, playing leading roles in performances on *The Jung/White Letters, The Jung/Neumann Letters* and *The Red Book*. Major publications deal with The Association Experiment, Celtic Myth, James Joyce, Dreams, Fair Tale Drama, and Christian Mysticism. In 2010, he published his first book: *At Home in the World: Sounds and Symmetries of Belonging*. Web page: www.johnhill.ch; contact email: johnrayhill@mac.com.

Stephan A. Hoeller was educated in seminary in Hungary and at the University of Innsbruck in Austria. Having come to reside in the United States, he was associate professor of religious studies at the College of Oriental Studies in Los Angeles, California. He is a bishop in the Gnostic Church, and the author of five books, two of which concern C.G. Jung: *The Gnostic Jung and the Seven Sermons to the Dead* (1982) and *Jung and the Lost Gospels* (1989).

Russell Lockhart, Ph.D., is a Jungian Analyst in private practice in Everett, Washington. He is the author of *Words as Eggs* (1983/2012), *Psyche Speaks* (2014), *Dreams, Bones, and the Future* (with Paco Mitchell), *The Final Interlude: Advancing Age and Life's End* (with Lee Roloff, 2016)) and many articles in the field of depth psychology. He is a graduate of the C.G. Jung Institute of Los Angeles (1974), where he served as Director of Training (1978-1980). He was educated at the University of Southern California (B.A. 1960, M.A. 1962, Ph.D. 1965). He has held faculty and research positions at University of California, Santa Barbara, Los Angeles Berkeley, and the UCLA Neuropsychiatric Institute, as well mentoring advanced students at International College, Union Graduate Institute, and Pacifica Graduate Institute. He is coeditor of Owl & Heron Press (with Paco Mitchell), Editor and Publisher at The Lockhart Press, and President of RAL Consulting, Inc., which operates an international trading room for education in the psychology of the financial markets and global economies. His current work focuses on the fictive purpose of dreams, the commodification of desire, and a novel entitled, "*Dreams: The Final Heresy*." Contact email: ral@ralockhart.com.

Lance S. Owens, M.D., is a physician in clinical practice and a historian with focused interest in C.G. Jung and Gnostic traditions. Since release of *The Red Book: Liber Novus* in 2009, Dr. Owens has published several historical studies focused on the intimate relationship between Jung's collected writings and the visionary experiences recorded in the *Red Book* and the *Black Book* journals. Major publications: "The Hermeneutics of Vision: C.G. Jung and Liber Novus" (*The Gnostic: A Journal of Gnosticism, Western Esotericism and Spirituality* (2010)), "Jung and Aion: Time, Vision and a Wayfaring Man" (*Psychological Perspectives* (2011)) and *Jung in Love: The Mysterium in Liber Novus* (2015). He is the creator and managing editor of The Gnosis Archive, gnosis.org, the primary internet archive of classical Gnostic sources, including the Nag Hammadi texts. Contact email: lance.owens@comcast.net.

Dariane Pictet, M.A., is originally from Geneva, Switzerland. She has a degree in Comparative Religion from Columbia University and trained in Analytical Psychology at the C.G. Jung Institute, Zurich. She has also trained in Existential Psychotherapy at Regents College, London. She is a Training Analyst at the International School of Analytical Psychology in Zurich and the Guild of Analytical Psychology in London. She enjoys Poetry and Yoga, and lectures in the UK and abroad. Major publications: "Rumi: Poet of the Heart" (Jungian Odyssey Series Vol. I), "Kali - The Protective Mother and the Destroyer" (Jungian Odyssey Series Vol. II), "Compassion in Buddhism" (Jungian Odyssey Series Vol. V) and "An Exploration of Silence in Christian Mysticism" (Jungian Odyssey Series Vol. VI). Web page: www.dariane.info; contact email: darianep@btinternet.com.

Susan Rowland, Ph.D., studied at Oxford University, University of London and University of Newcastle (Ph.D.). She is Chair of M.A. Engaged Humanities and the Creative Life at Pacifica Graduate Institute, and teaches on the doctoral program in Jungian psychology and Archetypal Studies. Author of *The Sleuth and the Goddess in Women's Detective Fiction* (2015), she has also written books on literary theory, gender and Jung including *Jung as a Writer* (2005), *Jung: A Feminist Revision* (2002), *C.G. Jung in the Humanities* (2010), and *The Ecocritical Psyche: Literature, Evolutionary Complexity and Jung* (2012). Her new book is *Remembering Dionysus: Revisioning Psychology and Literature in C.G. Jung and James Hillman* (2017). Web page: www.susanarowland.com; contact email: srowland@pacifica.edu.

Andreas Schweizer, Dr. theol., studied theology and comparative religion in Zurich as well as Egyptology with Professor Erik Hornung in Basel. He has been training analyst since 1986, first at the C.G. Jung Institute in Küsnacht and currently with ISAP Zurich. He is president of the Psychology Club, founded in 1916 by C.G. Jung, and was for 14 years president of the Eranos Conference in Ascona. Major publications: *The Sungod's Journey through the Netherworld* (2010) and *Bausteine: Reflexionen zur Psychologie von C.G. Jung* (ed., 2016). Contact email: an-schweizer@bluewin.ch.

Heyong Shen, Ph.D., professor of psychology at South China Normal University and the City University of Macao; Jungian analyst/IAAP, and Sandplay Therapist/ISST, founding president of the Chinese Federation for Analytical Psychology and Sandplay Therapy, the main organizer of the International Conference of Analytical Psychology and Chinese Culture (1998-2015), speaker of Eranos Conferences (1997/2007) for the Psychology of the Heart, and Fulbright scholar in Residence (1996-1997). Heyong Shen has published 60 papers and 12 books. He is the chief editor for the Chinese translation of the *Collected Works* of C.G. Jung, and chief editor of the Chinese Journal of Analytical Psychology. He and his group set up 70 work stations at orphans (and earthquake zones) in the mainland of China for psychological aids, with the project named the Garden of the Heart & Soul. Contact email: shenheyong@hotmail.com.

J. Marvin Spiegelman, Ph.D., earned his doctorate in psychology at the University of California, Los Angeles in 1952 and the Analyst's Diploma at the C.G. Jung Institute, Zurich in 1959. He has been in practice in Los Angeles ever since, serving in the Society as the first Director of Training and is now senior analyst. He has taught at UCLA for seven years, USC for 10 years, Pacifica for five years and Hebrew University. He is the author of 10 books, co-author of four and editor of six along with more than 100 journal articles. He was awarded an Archive in his name at UCLA in 2014. Dr. Spiegelman passed away on Sept. 22, 2017 at the age of 92.

Murray Stein, Ph.D., studied as an undergraduate at Yale University (B.A. in English) and attended graduate school at Yale Divinity School (M.Div.) and the University of Chicago (Ph.D. in Religion and Psychological Studies). He trained as a Jungian psychoanalyst at the C.G. Jung Institute of Zurich. From 1976 to 2003 he was a training analyst at the C.G. Jung Institute of Chicago, of which he was a founding member and President from 1980 to 1985. In 1989, he joined the Executive Committee of IAAP as Honorary Secretary for Dr. Thomas Kirsch as President (1989-1995) and served as President of the IAAP from 2001 to 2004. He was president of ISAP Zurich 2008-2012 and is currently a training and supervising analyst there. He resides in Goldiwil (Thun), Switzerland. His special interests are psychotherapy and spirituality, methods of Jungian psychoanalytic treatment, and the individuation process. Major publications: *In Midlife, Jung's Map of the Soul, Minding the Self, Soul: Retrieval and Treatment, Transformation: Emergence of the Self,* and *Outside, Inside and All Around.* Web page: www.murraystein.com; contact email: murraywstein@gmail.com.

Liliana Liviano Wahba, Ph.D., Clinical Psychology and Post doctorate at the University of São Paulo Medical School. She is a psychologist, professor doctor at the Universidad Católica de São Paulo Centre of Jungian Studies, and co-ordinator of the Post-Graduate Program in Clinical Psychology. She is a Jungian analyst and former president of the Brazilian Society for Analytical Psychology (SBrPA). Her main focus of research is creativity, culture, and psychological development. She published the book *Camille Claudel: Criação e Loucura* (*Camille Claudel: Creation and Madness*) and has contributed with many articles and chapters to journals and books. She is also the Director of Psychology of the OSCIP – Civil Society Organization for Public Interest – "Ser em Cena: Theatre for Aphasics". Web page: http://www.pucsp.br/pos-graduacao/mestrado-e-doutorado/psicologia-psicologia-clinica; contact email: lilwah@uol.com.br.

John Woodcock, Ph.D. Education: 1999 Ph. D. in Consciousness Studies, Union Institute & University, Cincinnati, OH; 1983 M.A., Major: Counselling Psychology, CSUN, Northridge, CA. John is author of 15 books, written in a variety of styles, as he attempts to describe and more importantly, show, a kind of art form to "speak" into existence a new structure of consciousness that appears to be arising as a response by the psyche to our present "chaos." John traveled to the U.S.A. in 1979 where he lived for the next 24 years. He now lives with his wife in Sydney, after returning to Australia in 2003. He continues to work as a Jungian psychotherapist and focuses on his research into the question (variously formulated) that has guided his life and work for over 20 years: How can the unknown future be spoken into actuality from within the chaos of our times? Major publications: *The Peril in Thinking* (2015), *Oblivion of Being* (2015), *The Coming Guest and the New Art Form* (2014). Web page: www.johnwoodcock.com.au; contact email: jcw@johnwoodcock.com.au.

www.ingramcontent.com/pod-product-compliance
Lightning Source LLC
Chambersburg PA
CBHW030634270326
41929CB00007B/74